T0355538

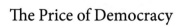

The Price of Democracy

The Price of Democracy

HOW MONEY SHAPES POLITICS
AND WHAT TO DO ABOUT IT

JULIA CAGÉ

Translated by Patrick Camiller

Harvard University Press

Cambridge, Massachusetts, and London, England   2020

First printing

First published in French as *Le prix de la démocratie,* Fayard, Paris
© *Librairie Arthème Fayard,* 2018

Preface first published in the paperback edition of
Le prix de la démocratie, Gallimard, Paris
© Julia Cagé, 2020

Cataloging-in-Publication Data available from the Library of Congress
ISBN: 978-0-674-98728-9 (alk. paper)

Contents

Acknowledgments

Why is it a problem that some financially contribute much more than others to the workings of democracy—for example, by buying media outlets, funding think tanks, or making donations to political parties? The idea for this book began to grow four years ago, when I was putting the finishing touches to its predecessor, *Saving the Media*. It then went through various stages alongside the writing of academic articles on which I have drawn here. My paper "The Price of a Vote: Evidence from France, 1993–2014" played a particularly important role: its striking results concerning the effects of campaign spending in a country like France only strengthened my belief in the need for a comparative long-term study of different models of public and private funding of democracy. My thanks therefore go first of all to my co-author in that investigation, Yasmine Bekkouche, as well as to Thomas Ferguson and the Institute for New Economic Thinking (INET) for the confidence they showed in funding this research agenda and the major data collection work that it involved.

This book also owes a great deal to all the other researchers with whom I studied the private funding of democracy—and with whom I continue to navigate the long, never-ending stream of research. At present I am working with Malka Guillot on French tax data, in order to gain a better understanding of how economic inequalities reinforce political inequalities, and above all of what motivates donations to political parties and campaign spending. Her familiarity with the FELIN (Sampled Income Tax) files has proved invaluable, and I am grateful to the Committee on Statistical Confidentiality and the Secure Data Access Center for the permission it gave to work on these files.

Together with Edgard Dewitte, I have tackled 150 years of British history in an attempt to grasp how campaign spending has affected the results scored by political parties. I would like to thank him for the faith he had in the project, especially as it was far from obvious that we should be going back to an age when candidates offered to drive voters to the booths in a horse-drawn carriage. In fact, I owe Edgard a double debt of gratitude, since he helped me throughout the writing of this book to collect archival material and to understand the nuances of legislation in different countries. Special thanks also to Elisa Mougin, a truly outstanding research assistant, ever ready to add her skills in exploring the sometimes mine-strewn terrain of the transparency of political parties; to Benedetta Ruffini for her invaluable research on Italy; to Alexandre Diene for help with my study of Germany; and to Clara Martínez-Tolenado for research in the case of Spain. The law can sometimes be hard to fathom for those unfamiliar with all its subtleties, and I should like to thank Bastien Cueff for the light he shed on a number of legal matters.

At Sciences Po Paris, where I have been an Assistant Professor in Economics since 2014, I had the good fortune to benefit from a multidisciplinary research environment, especially as co-leader of the "evaluating democracy" axis at the Laboratory for the Interdisciplinary Evaluation of Public Policies (LIEPP). Sciences Po students from around the world— from Venezuela through China and Australia to Benin—are a tremendous source of inspiration, and my daily interaction with them, particularly in my classes on the future of the media, constantly fuels my reflections and research.

My research in recent years has also been enriched by my work with Nicolas Hervé and Marie-Luce Viaud at the National Audiovisual Institute (INA), and by our lively discussions of the crisis of the media and democracy and the use of random selection of representatives. Marie-Luce, who taught and gave me so much, departed from our midst far too early, before she had a chance to read this book. I hope she would have liked it, even if I can do no more than imagine all the discussions to which it will not lead. Marie-Luce, we miss you terribly.

Thanks to the whole team at Wedodata, and especially Karen Bastien, Brice Terdiman, and Nicolas Boeuf, who agreed to work with me on this book and brought some rather over-academic figures to life! Thanks also for their work on the leprixdelademocratie.com website, an indispensable tool for the further continuation of debate.

My editor at Fayard, Sophie Kucoyanis, gave me a free hand and showed complete trust in me. I should like to thank her for this. Thanks also to Agathe Cagé, who opened my eyes to certain weaknesses in my writing (through her attentive reading of the text) and to the need for "cross-breeding" among intellectuals.

Thanks, finally, to Thomas, who lived through every line of this book. Thanks for your unfailing support, your tireless patience, your precious intellectual contribution, and above all your love, which gave me the energy to see the project through to the end.

Preface

I began to write this book in 2015—which feels like a century ago. In France, Emmanuel Macron had not yet become president, nor had Donald Trump in the United States. Italy was still governed by Matteo Renzi, and David Cameron had not yet come up with the brilliant idea of holding a referendum on Brexit to strengthen his position in the Tory Party.

When I delivered the manuscript to my French publisher, in May 2018, some still thought that Lula might stand as a candidate in the Brazilian presidential election, and no one could imagine the wave of yellow vests that was about to break over France. Optimists still believed that a second referendum would be held in the United Kingdom (which is not out of the question, though things are not moving in that direction), while Trump was preparing to nominate Brett Kavanaugh for the Supreme Court, burying all hope that it might become a progressive force again in the coming decades.

Time has speeded up, as it were, and the crisis of representative democracy seems to have reached a paroxysm in the last few years. Brazil is today ruled by a former army officer with an authoritarian bent, Jair Bolsonaro, who ill-treats culture as well as the environment. In France, no one raises the roof any longer when the Far Right comes first in the European elections. But the *gilets jaunes* crisis has dramatically highlighted the representation deficit affecting a large part of the population, as well as the need for a radical reshaping of democracy. In Spain, the far right Vox party entered Parliament in April 2019, less than two years after Alternative für Deutschland in Germany. And in the United States, Donald Trump—still obsessed with his wall on the Mexican border—spends his time launching extensive operations to expel migrants. The European Union is not far behind in this respect, writing new pages unworthy of its history when it closes its ports to NGO vessels packed with migrants who have narrowly escaped death.

The term "illiberal democracy" has entered common parlance, as if the very existence of democracy did not rest upon a number of unalterable principles. The first of these principles, in the name of which I decided to write this book, is "one person, one vote"—not "one euro, one vote," "one diploma, one vote," or "one media outlet, one vote." It seemed to me imperative to place an often ignored issue at the center of debate: the capture of the democratic process and public debate by the most advantaged sections of society. They have achieved this through the power of their wallets—whether by donating to political parties and election campaigns, by financing think tanks and other foundations, or by acquiring an equity stake in influential news media.

The Price of Democracy traces more than fifty years of attempts to regulate Western democracies, which, despite the growing weight of private interests, once involved innovative systems for the public funding of parties and elections. There has been a refusal, however, to think this question through to the end, to learn from previous imperfect but instructive efforts, and to take full advantage of them in a new and better system. In light of the first two parts of the book, the latest events may be seen as vagaries of history: some may find a place in textbooks in the years ahead, while others will doubtless sink into oblivion—only time will tell. The essential point remains that today those who win are those who pay. And in many countries, the system now in place encourages donations in such a way that the poor pay to satisfy the political preferences of the superrich.

Recent political developments, on both sides of the Atlantic, have only increased the urgency of the proposals presented in Part Three. They all indicate that, if we are to haul ourselves out of the present crisis of representative democracies, we need to begin by drastically curtailing the weight of private funding and private interests, with a ban on corporate political donations where they are presently permitted and a low ceiling on individual donations (I propose 200 euros per year per citizen). Next, innovative strategies will be needed for public funding of the democratic process (I support the idea of Democratic Equality Vouchers), and finally, the instruments of the law-based state must be used to ensure better representation of the working classes in the legislature (through the creation of what I call a "mixed assembly"). These solutions draw on the numerous historical experiences described throughout the book, whether they eventually proved fruitful or ended in failure. In any event, the election of Bolsonaro and the *gilets jaunes* crisis do not call these proposals into question—on the contrary, they further demonstrate their necessity.

Let us dwell a little longer on the recent past: the *gilets jaunes* movement in France, the emergence of a new generation of Democrats in the United States, and the return of the Socialists to power in Spain. Though national events, each of these has had echoes far beyond the country's borders, and the analysis in this book allows us to see them in a new light.

The *Gilets Jaunes:* A Full-Scale Explosion of the Crisis of Representation

The *gilets jaunes* are a multifaceted movement that has proven difficult to analyze over time. There are few similarities between the early demonstrations of October and November 2018 and the spiraling violence in 2019 when the movement has been on the decline. But two key dimensions are the purchasing-power crisis that has affected the least well-off sections of society and the profound sense of injustice, bound up with Emmanuel Macron's economic and fiscal policies, which fueled the explosion of popular anger.

Although the *gilets jaunes* movement erupted in response to an increase in carbon tax, the first point to make is that this followed a whole series of measures that had been eroding the purchasing power of the popular classes, from cuts in housing benefits through a postponement of local tax exemptions to a rise in social security contributions for retired people. These decisions were made not because the state coffers were empty but because they had just been emptied. By whom? From the very first weeks of his five-year term, Emmanuel Macron fast-tracked tax breaks to the rich by abolishing the Impôt de Solidarité sur la Fortune (ISF) wealth tax and introducing a flat rate levy on capital—all for the benefit of the "top rope climbers" endlessly extoled by the young president.

You may be asking what this has to do with the funding of democracy. Well, *The Price of Democracy* establishes the important finding that donations to political parties are a class phenomenon, including in a country like France where they are capped. The phenomenon did not begin with the funding of Macron's La République en Marche. But it did take on a new dimension with the emergence of this new party, whose funding supposedly comes only from private donations, though tax relief for donors means that much of it is provided indirectly from the public purse. In May 2018, when I put the finishing touches to this book, the available data on Macron's campaign spending did not allow me to do more than calculate on the back of an envelope the relative weight of the largest donations; so, in Chapter 2 I note that 2 percent of donors made 40–60 percent of the contributions to Macron's presidential campaign. Since then, however, a number of news media—*Le Journal du Dimanche,* Radio France, *Le Monde,* and so on—have been able to examine the structure of these donations, particularly their geographic origin, and to bring out their extraordinary degree of concentration.[1] Between its creation in March 2016 and December 2017, the En Marche! party raised nearly 16 million euros, of which 48 percent came from a total of 1,212 donations of 4,500 euros or more, from a maximum of 800 donors. An unhoped-for electoral success—from just 800 donors! Which parts of the country did these donations come from? More than a half from Paris (2.1 million inhabitants), nearly 100 times more than from Marseille (870,000 inhabitants) and over 200 times more than from Lille (232,000 inhabitants). The Sixteenth Arrondissement alone, with more than one million euros in donations, contributed more than Lille, Strasbourg, Nice, Marseille, Montpellier, Toulouse, Bordeaux, and Nantes together. Yes, that's right, one million! And the residents of the Seventh Arrondissement were no less generous. Probably they were afraid of falling behind rich French expatriates: more than a million of the 16 million euros raised between March 2016 and December 2017 came from the United Kingdom, and more than 370,000 euros from the United States. In fact, Macron projected fundraising dinners in New York and London as one of the symbols of his "modernity."

But let us return to the essentials. Beyond all these figures, what really counts is that 800 donors alone funded a half of Emmanuel Macron's presidential campaign; 800 donors made a candidate and a party—and therefore an election. How many trade-offs did this involve? That is the whole question, which the *gilets jaunes* echoed in their way. Those who donated virtually nothing to fund the campaign not only received nothing in return but soon realized that the reality of Macron's economic policy was an upward transfer of purchasing power—a transfer from those who have next to nothing to those who, we are asked to believe, always have a packed suitcase at hand, ready to decamp because their lives are not worth living under a tax system so oppressive that it allowed them to accumulate their wealth in the first place.

What was the mechanism leading from 800 donations to a bonanza of tax breaks? Forgive me if in this preface I do not go into the twists and turns of the relationship between money and politics. I would just like to stress one point: a reader used to news reports about the hundreds of millions of dollars spent in American political life might think that the corresponding sums in France, though running into seven figures, are too low to play a significant role. But in a system where electoral spending is capped—as it is in France, but not the United States—what you need to watch is not the string of digits but the concentration of donations. For if 800 donors are enough for victory, then the "real" value of each contribution is out of all proportion to its face value.

Of course, there was not "corruption" in the narrow sense of quid pro quos, something given for something in return. We know nothing of what was said (though we may have our suspicions), and the tax breaks were given to a whole group rather than a few individuals; one can always think of some who gave but did not receive, just as some received without having to put their hands in their pockets. Of course, there was nothing legally culpable. But we need to look beyond what is and is not legal—for it is the law itself that must be changed. The reader has to ask herself what kind of democracy she wants to live in. The researcher's task is to produce facts that make things clear. In this respect, it is interesting to compare the structure of donations—which I present in Chapter 3—and the evolution of purchasing power according to one's position in the distribution of income. In France, as in other Western democracies, it is not "the rich" but the richest of the very rich who contribute financially to political life. Whereas fewer than 0.8 percent of fiscal households contribute each year financially to a political party, they represent 2.7 percent of the richest 10 percent, 3.8 percent of the richest 1 percent, 5 percent of the richest 0.1 percent, and—most striking of all—more than 10 percent of the 0.01 percent of French people with the highest incomes.

So, who has gained fiscally over the past two years? The very rich among the richest. If we take into account the few *gilets jaunes* "reforms" that Macron conceded to those on the lowest incomes in order to escape from the crisis of early 2019, the gain in the average French person's purchasing power since the beginning of his five-year term is all of 1 percent. But the gain is 6.4 percent for the most affluent 1 percent, and 17.5 percent for the 0.1 percent of French people with the highest incomes.[2] If the *gilets jaunes* crisis was so sharp, sometimes resulting in scenes of violence, it was because these figures point to a crisis of representation. The popular classes, with good reason, do not feel represented by the political regime in place, which for several months has been conducting a class-oriented economic policy.

One final point on the *gilets jaunes*. When I began to write this book in 2015, independently of the French political context, I was following on from my previous work on the dangers to journalistic independence and the health of our democracies that stemmed from the rise of media billionaires whose capital lay mainly in other sectors. It was an academic work, based on systematic data gathering and historical analysis of the public and private funding of Western democracies over the past fifty years. During the four years that it took me to complete the book, the French political landscape was turned upside down, with the election of Emmanuel Macron and the collapse of the two main parties, the

Socialist Party and the Républicains, which had embodied political alternation throughout the Fifth Republic.

The election of Macron occupies only a minor place in this book. But as an academic—and irrespective of my political convictions—I could not pass over what seemed like a textbook case of the dangers that the dependence of political movements on private finance poses to the very idea of *representative* democracy. To be sure, Macron's En Marche! was not entitled to any direct public funding when it first appeared. But it is the forms of direct public funding that have to be entirely reformed— which is what I propose with the idea of Democratic Equality Vouchers. It is true that the donations received by En Marche! did not exceed the legally defined ceiling. But it is that ceiling that needs to be brought much lower, because today it allows a small number of individuals to have much greater political weight than the overwhelming majority of citizens. The emergence of the *gilets jaunes* movement has been a powerful reminder of this.

What If the United States Awakened?

Fortunately, not all is gloom and doom. Although the crisis of representative democracies seems to have speeded up in the past few years, the events of the past few months have not always been negative, especially as some of them have been a response to aberrations in our institutional systems. Perhaps the most alarming is the election of a racist and misogynist US president who is evidently opposed to press freedom and who conducts international politics in a haphazard manner, his eyes fixed on his Twitter account and his finger never far from the nuclear button. This is posing questions to Republicans, too, but let us start with the Democrats.

In Chapter 6, I underline the responsibility that Barack Obama and other Democrats have had for the collapse of public funding in presidential elections (a system that goes back more than forty years) and the capture of American democracy by megarich donors. Hillary Clinton, in her campaign, both raised and spent more than her rival Donald Trump—and I am not thinking here of the lavish remuneration she received for her speeches at Goldman Sachs or Citibank. The hold of a handful of rich contributors (and corporations) over the Democrats is not unrelated to their election defeats, for Democratic billionaires are just as conservative as their Republican counterparts on economic matters, and in election campaigns, as well as in power, their party has far too often skated over the central issue of the explosion of inequalities. The good news, however, is that some Democrats have finally woken up to the reality and begun to oppose it. Since February 2019, Alexandria Ocasio-Cortez's remorseless five-minute attack on the corruption of American political life by "dark money" has become the most watched political video ever.[3]

In a sense, Bernie Sanders opened the way in the presidential primaries of 2016 by funding his campaign mostly with small donations. It was not enough for him to win, but it did show doubters that "the rank and file" could be an important source of funding and that popular mobilizations could make it possible to raise millions from ordinary donors. Besides, the Democrats are well equipped to raise small sums, especially since their ActBlue platform (a nonprofit organization founded in 2004) really took off in 2018. Between 2014 and the midterm elections in 2018, this organization apparently netted more than $2.9 billion for Democratic candidates.[4] And between January 2017 and September 2018 alone, it raised nearly $564 million, or approximately 55 percent of all individual contributions to Democratic candidates for the House of Representatives and the Senate. Is this a new way of doing politics?

Two lessons may be drawn from the success of ActBlue. First, thanks to the mobilization of small donors (those donating less than $200), a number of Democratic candidates have become able to "compete" financially (in terms of campaign spending) with their Republican opponents, who are spoon-fed donations by Sheldon Adelson and other billionaires. This was particularly visible during the 2018 midterms, and it was a source of concern for Republicans who had not seen the blue wave coming. Who would have thought a few months earlier that Democratic candidates would end up raising much more than their Republican rivals ($1.4 billion against $880 million), thanks largely to donations less than $200? A popular financial mobilization can thus enable "left" parties to offset at least part of the structural disadvantage I describe in Chapter 3:

that is, the fact that donations to political parties and election campaigns are a class phenomenon that by and large benefits the most conservative parties; a much larger proportion of the superrich make contributions, and, when they do, these are much larger than those of citizens on low incomes. Of course, ActBlue is a long way from ensuring political participation on a genuinely equal basis—that would require initiatives such as the Democratic Equality Vouchers—but it still marks an important step forward.

The second lesson—which is more interesting so long as it is not overlooked—is that the Democrats can do without "their" billionaires. They can campaign and win by relying on the mobilization of working-class supporters, without first having to bend a knee to moneyed interests, to organize fundraising dinners, and to make inevitable promises there that subsequently become binding. The Democrats do not have to act like Joe Biden, promising rich donors that they will not "demonize" the rich. (Biden knows all about this: he was one of the Democrats who supported Reagan's proposal to cut the higher tax rate to 28 percent in 1986.) Nor do they have to drive this home by asserting that they will not change anyone's standard of living (by which Biden means that of the rich, although the poor can also draw the appropriate conclusions), that nothing will change fundamentally in the event of a Democratic victory at the polls.[5] Good heavens, inequalities won't know what hit them!

The Democrats can do without their billionaires. So, if they decide not to, they can no longer hide behind formulas such as "There is no alternative." How many candidates claim to prefer a different system where they are no longer funded by the rich, fundraising dinners are a distant memory, and super PACs look like something out of an ancient photograph! And how many candidates conclude with a sigh: "As things stand, we have no choice!" But the truth is that even today there are other options. And if they do not accept this, it is because they will not change "how things stand" if they are elected. It is imperative to change the present state of things, for the Democrats as well as the Republicans. The health of democracy itself is at stake.

Besides, everything suggests that if the Democrats do without mega-donations, they will perform better at the polls. For their base not only donates; it also knows how to mobilize. Time spent with ordinary citizens does not translate into a string of zeros, but it is measured by the spread of ideas and the power of convictions. Whereas Democratic platforms in the last few years testify to the remoteness of party elites from the central issue of rising inequalities, a greater reliance on members' activism will help to restore a bond of trust with the American working classes. The Democratic National Committee (DNC) seems finally to have understood this point, now that it has decided to encourage small donations for the 2020 presidential campaign by offering a place at one of the two primary debates to candidates with at least 65,000 donors behind them and a minimum of 200 donors in each of twenty US states.[6]

It is not really known how the Republicans will react; things can change quickly, and history unravel as soon as it is written. Faced with the flow of small donations into the Democratic campaign, the Republican billionaires will probably dig deeper. But if that is the consequence of the Democratic renewal—and the Koch brothers, Peter Thiel, and Sheldon Adelson, unlike nearly all their fellow citizens, have bottomless pockets—it will wreck all the efforts to "democratize" American political life at the level of funding. Hence the need for legislation rather than a reliance on good will. I discuss in the book all the limitations of recent Supreme Court decisions that have gradually undone the regulation of campaign funding; the battle can and must continue to reverse those handed down in the case of Citizens United or *McCutcheon v. Federal Election Committee*.

If I was being optimistic, I would say that the Republicans themselves may draw the lessons of ActBlue's success. They have just launched a similar platform of their own: WinRed (the name itself being a brainchild of Donald Trump, who recently declared that "while Democrats act, Republicans win"[7]). But I am optimistic about our collective capacity to change things at the level of the law and the institutions—not about the individual will to self-regulation. I am optimistic about our collective capacity to press governments to ban donations above a limit of, say, $200—not about the willingness of candidates to refuse anything greater. Even Elizabeth Warren, who, at the beginning of the Democratic primaries, undertook to abstain from fundraising galas and recourse to large donors, has given ground in the end.[8] True, this was only to pay for access to a DNC-managed database on millions of voters (which she did with great caution and for "very good reasons"); she did not make the application herself, there was no fundraising dinner, and so on. But she did give ground, like others before her—Beto O'Rourke, for instance, turned to wealthy donors in June despite his early campaign promises[9]— and, unless the game rules change, like others after her.

I cannot write anything here about the results of the 2020 elections. There is little doubt that Donald Trump will be the Republican candidate, and most probably he will exacerbate the divisions in America by making further racist statements. On the Democratic side, the primaries are much more open—with strong showings by Elizabeth Warren, Joe Biden, Bernie Sanders, Beto O'Rourke, Kamala Harris, and the surprise candidate Pete Buttigieg, who has been particularly successful in raising funds. What is certain, unfortunately, is that the candidates' popularity will continue to be measured each quarter by the amounts of money they collect. And in this respect, there is no reason to be glad about the other surprise candidacy, that of the billionaire and Democratic megadonor of recent years Tom Steyer.

The Return of the European Left?

Being limited to the present, I can say nothing about what will happen in Spain in the next few months; nor does anyone know, after Pedro Sánchez's failure to form a government. But I can speak of the past, which will cast some light on the present. And since we must know how to welcome good news, we should note that the Left does well at the polls when it conducts a "left" economic policy (in favor of the popular classes and a narrowing of inequalities). The Spanish case is striking from this point of view, and it is interesting to recall—even if there is no causal link—that in the past ten years Spain has bucked the trend in many Western democracies, by increasing the public funding of parties and the reimbursement of campaign expenses, as well as by prohibiting corporate donations to parties. Let us look at this a little more closely.

In Spain, the first Institutional Act governing elections took effect in 1985, and an Organic Law on the Funding of Political Parties was adopted in 1987. This law pointed in the right direction, but it also contained many inadequacies. Fast forward: the Socialist José Luis Zapatero unexpectedly won the general elections in 2004, but then from 2010 he conducted a policy of austerity and reforms that even the ultraconservative Spanish Right would not have dared to implement, including, among other delights, a salary cut for public servants, a pension freeze followed by the raising of the retirement age, an increase in value-added tax, measures to "flexibilize" the labor market (a "social-democratic" constant for the trendy twenty-first-century Left, from Tony Blair through Gerhard Schröder to Matteo Renzi), and so on. It was hardly surprising, then, that Mariano Rajoy's right-wing Popular Party romped home in the elections of 2011. Fast forward another seven years—during which an important reform in 2014 prohibited corporate donations to political parties—to Pedro Sánchez's takeover as prime minister in June 2018, following a motion of no confidence in the Rajoy government. Sánchez's Socialist Party (PSOE) then came first in the legislative elections of April 2019—a victory largely explicable by the ambitious reforms he had initiated on assuming office. These included a 22 percent increase in the minimum wage, the indexing of pensions to inflation, the reopening of public healthcare to undocumented workers, the creation of 30,000 civil service jobs together with a pay raise, and, last but not least, the welcoming of the *Aquarius* migrant rescue ship that Italy and France had shamefully turned away.

A link may be made between the funding of political parties—particularly the trend in corporate donations—and Socialist policies in government. Other forces have also been at work, of course, and many of Sánchez's reforms have done no more than reverse the previous backsliding under Zapatero. Nevertheless, PSOE's left turn has occurred in one of the few Western democracies to have clamped down on private funding of the democratic process and considerably increased its public funding (now 5.6 euros a year per adult), at the very time when past gains were unraveling elsewhere and many governments of the Left were pursuing conservative economic policies.

The Price of Democracy, a Year On

The publication of my book in French, and the many exchanges it prompted, gave me a clearer vision of the reforms needed to address the grave crisis of representation facing Western democracies. The ending of tax relief associated with political donations, a strict ceiling on donations, Democratic Equality Vouchers (DEVs), and a mixed assembly: these remain my four central proposals, now enriched by discussions with political representatives and, above all, citizens aiming for greater participatory democracy.

If I were to rewrite the book today, I would lay greater emphasis on the anonymity of Democratic Equality Vouchers. Each voucher represents 7 euros of public money that each citizen can allocate on her annual tax return to the political movement or movements of her choice. Naturally, the tax authorities will keep no trace of the preferences expressed by their citizens: that seemed to me an obvious prerequisite for such a system of public funding—which is probably why I did not highlight it more. But here I would like to mention the technological solutions that can ensure anonymity and that are already in use in electronic voting systems. In practical terms, once a citizen has declared his income under his unique taxpayer number, he will receive a new personal code (or DEV code) permitting him to "vote"—that is, to allocate his Democratic Equality Voucher anonymously. If necessary, proof of this vote can be securely registered on a blockchain,[10] so that the voter can check that it has been taken into account. But the tax authorities have no way of associating the unique taxpayer number with the unique DEV code; the only information at their disposal concerns the general allocation of all DEVs, which they use to distribute the respective amounts among various political movements. In other words, the DEVs do not in any way threaten the confidentiality of political preferences.

Recent events, particularly the *gilets jaunes* movement in France with its demand for a "referendum democracy" applicable to new legislation and the recall of political representatives, have also led me to think of DEVs more in terms of participatory democracy. For I firmly believe that representative democracy and its intermediate bodies (especially political movements) can mesh with the growing legitimate demand for an extension of the tools of participatory democracy. I see my proposal for Democratic Equality Vouchers as a constructive variant of the recall referendum and a real alternative to referendum democracy; the latter is anyway largely illusory, because the complex social and economic issues facing us cannot be decided with a "yes or no" vote but require in-depth consideration in a parliamentary context. Whereas "recall" procedures weaken the functioning of institutions by making elected representatives vulnerable during their term of office, Democratic Equality Vouchers enable them to see reforms through to the end, while giving citizens an annual opportunity to express their dissatisfaction—or satisfaction. This can take the form of a financial sanction, not only for the party in government but also for opposition parties whose counterproposals are seen as too feeble. Such a system will permit the renewal of democracy and the regular emergence of new political forces, while also introducing a genuinely permanent democracy.

Another important point that I may not have sufficiently stressed in this book is that permanent democracy must begin inside political parties themselves. In most democracies, there is too little regulation of how parties function; we therefore find ourselves with political forces whose statutes do not exactly gleam with transparency (if they are public at all) and whose leaderships consist of a few individuals, or even just one. It is imperative to set rules that force parties into some degree of internal democracy. For example, to benefit from DEVs or to run candidates in elections, a political movement might be required to publish its statutes and to have a democratic internal regime, such that the whole membership regularly (e.g., once every four or five years) elected the chairperson / first secretary / national secretary, or even the whole executive bureau, in an open and transparent process. These minimum conditions would already be a major step toward greater democracy in existing political movements. But it might be possible to establish a more ambitious system, in which any citizen helping to fund a movement through DEVs—and wishing to let this be known—could vote for the election of its leaders. To develop a fully fledged democracy, it is high time that our thinking gave a place to collective organizations capable of breathing new life into democracy.

This is not the place to discuss the advisability of open primary elections. Let me just note that it is doubly wrong to use the French presidential election of 2017—which saw the unprecedented defeat of the two traditional parties of the Right and the Left—as final proof of the ineffectiveness of such primaries. Those who argue in this way draw conclusions that do not take into account the specificities of one historical moment—particularly the fact that, despite the decision by the Républicains to hold an open primary, François Fillon would almost certainly have won if it had not been for the revelations in *Le Canard Enchaîné* about his wife's fake employment. More important, however, is the misperception of open primaries as the reason why the traditional parties are in crisis. The fact is that the crisis has been smoldering for decades, since long before the first primaries were introduced in France. And primaries should be seen more as an attempted solution to the crisis, an (admittedly imperfect) way of restoring a bond of trust between citizens and their representatives. Those who blame the open primary system for the crisis propose no genuinely democratic alternative and act as if there were no danger in reversing what many consider to be important democratic gains. It may well be true that the autocratic running of a movement guarantees stability of its political line, but is that really what we want? Believing as I do in representative democracy, I think it is important to stress the need to democratize its institutions— otherwise, citizens will eventually sweep away representative democracy as a whole. In short, we should say yes to the renewal of political movements and the replacement of old parties with new forces (which is sometimes necessary), and no to the delusion that autocracy and supreme leaders can override collective deliberation and normal voting procedures within democratic organizations.

Too often, leaderships display tunnel vision in considering the reform of political life, focusing only on its consequences for their own party rather than for the system as a whole. Perhaps it is too harsh to blame them for this, but the resulting situation explains why it is so difficult to reform our institutions and the funding of political life. In any event, the discussions I have had around the idea of Democratic Equality Vouchers have led me today to propose "alternative" versions that take account of the fears of political leaders. Ideally, Democratic Equality

Vouchers would replace both tax relief associated with private donations to political parties or campaigns (a deeply inequitable system that means that citizens in general finance the political preferences of the superrich) and the direct public funding of parties (an inefficient system that freezes funding for the four or five years between elections and does not allow citizens to express themselves in the interval). In the spirit of private companies, some parties are scared that the elimination of direct public funding would cut across their need for stable finances to pay full-timers, most of whom are employed on permanent contracts; they therefore stick to the existing system in order to keep their organizations in business. However, this argument seems easy to demolish. Take the recent experience of the French Socialist Party: it received nearly 25 million euros per year in public funding between 2012 and 2017, employing a hundred or more people and seeing no reason to expect a collapse in resources. But today, with less than 8 million euros a year in direct public support, it has had to lay off around fifty employees overnight. If there had been an annualized system of DEVs, it might have allowed the party to foresee its electoral meltdown, and above all to cut its wage bill much more gradually as the negative signals kept coming in. Nevertheless, let us take seriously the fear that some parties feel with regard to DEVs and agree on a reform that could be quickly introduced at zero cost. In a first phase, while the existing direct subsidies were retained, DEVs could be used to replace the indefensible tax relief system (for which I have heard no one present the slightest argument during a year of discussions). We might then have DEVs with a value of 3 or 4 euros a year per citizen, introduced in parallel to direct public funding. This would make it possible to experiment with the new system for several years, drawing lessons from any failures (perhaps an initially low take-up) and successes (such as the emergence of new political forces that did not have to start by appealing for private finance). It would also help to give existing parties a better idea of how they can fund themselves with DEVs. Then, at the end of this experimental period, nothing would prevent us from imagining an extension of DEVs to the whole system for the public funding of democracy.

Rethinking Political Movements and Election Campaigns

The experience of the past year has also made me realize that this book probably focused too much on the funding of political parties and movements, and not enough on election campaigns, especially at the local level. Although I briefly mentioned a proposal to introduce a "democracy bank," it deserved more space. It is also interesting to note that in the United States, for example, all proposals for alternative funding of the political process center on campaigns rather than parties. But the existing two-party system, in which Democratic and Republican candidates (often as a result of primaries in their respective parties) alternate in power, is very different from the French, Spanish, and Italian systems. In France, many candidates in municipal elections run as independents and therefore cannot benefit from the financial support given to any party. They are still entitled to reimbursement of campaign spending up to 47.5 percent of the official ceiling, but this applies only to candidates who obtain more than 5 percent of the first-round vote. This type of funding sharply divides candidates into two categories: (1) those who have the means to pay their campaign expenses upfront or the necessary guarantees to obtain a bank loan, and (2) all the others who, like most French people, have low incomes and no accumulated wealth, and are often refused a bank loan to cover even the publicly refundable part of their expenses.

Lacking sufficient funds, working-class candidates mostly give up any idea of running for election. Those who go ahead often find themselves in a parody of democracy, since, unlike better-funded rivals, they cannot pay for the production of election statements for potential voters, the use of reserved space opposite voting stations, or the printing of ballot papers in their name on election day. Of course, it is always possible to vote for a party anyway—you need only print out a ballot paper at home in the right format—but how can candidates in this situation have the slightest chance of winning? Out of the thirty-four lists presented at the most recent European elections in France, twenty asked voters to print out their own ballot papers! Thus, even before the introduction of a Democracy Bank, it could be decided that the state rather than individual candidates should fund the printing of posters, election statements, and ballot papers. The establishment of a Democracy Bank would allow the state—through a special branch of the Public Investment Bank in France, for example—to advance to all candidates a sum equivalent to the ceiling for reimbursement. The financial risk to the state would be minimal, since it would affect only those candidates obtaining less than 5 percent of the vote.

A final question, which must also be addressed openly and transparently, is who can stand as a candidate. The answer usually given today is "anyone," but the system is hypocritical insofar as many "candidates" do not have the means to go through with it. A properly functioning democratic process requires there to be enough candidates, but one cannot imagine candidates by the hundreds (irrespective of the forms of public funding). There is no magical mathematical equation that would provide the "right" solution to this problem. It can emerge only through collective deliberation.

Some have suggested polling as an answer, but although that may make sense nationally, it is much more difficult to set up at a local level. In the United States, the Democratic National Committee decided to allow a place at TV debates to candidates who receive enough donations from a sufficient number of donors. In a system such as the one I advocate, which gives less weight to private funding than to public funding (proportionate to the preferences expressed by citizens), one can imagine the introduction of decentralized Democratic Equality Vouchers, along similar lines to the democratic vouchers in Seattle. While DEVs at the national level would permit the funding of political movements, each citizen would also be allocated a democratic voucher for each local election, with a value equivalent to that of today's campaign reimbursements (in proportion to the number of voters), which could then be assigned to the candidate of his or her choice. As for DEVs, and to avoid an endless multiplication of candidates, only those receiving a sufficient number of democracy vouchers (say, 5 percent if they are to remain in the spirit of the present system) would actually be entitled to benefit from them. The remaining vouchers would be assigned in accordance with the overall preferences expressed by citizens.

Although I freely admit that my proposals in *The Price of Democracy* are far from perfect—and I look forward to debates in coming years about possible improvements—I would like to take this opportunity to correct a deliberate misreading that some have used to impugn my proposed reforms (beginning with the ceiling on donations to parties and campaigns). To be brief: I have never said, written, or thought that at every election the candidate who spends the most is the one who wins. I have never said, written, or thought it for the simple reason that it is false. Indeed, I was at pains in the book to cite counterexamples, some of which concern me directly. And those who brush aside my assertion that private moneyed interests are increasingly capturing the democratic process and who argue that my whole starting point is therefore empirically unfounded, either have not read what I wrote (in which case I can hope for the best) or are guilty of an incredible bad faith (but nothing stops them from changing). What I wrote—and amply documented by constructing databases on campaign spending and local and national election results in France and the United Kingdom over several decades—is that statistically speaking, and with a focus only on the causal effect of election spending, the candidate who spends the most will on average, other things being equal, obtain the largest number of votes. On average and other things being equal: it is a question of a statistical regularity, valid also in its exceptions, which tells us that private money plays such a central role in politics today that "one euro, one vote" defines our democracies better than "one person, one vote." Hence the need for major reforms. Let us not refuse to face the facts.

The Need for Open, Pluralist Debate on Politics and the Economy

I would like to conclude this rapid survey by underlining the importance of political and electoral competition and the need to open a political and economic debate. Both are especially necessary in these troubled times, when full-scale attacks against representative democracy (whose present imperfections are undeniable) are bubbling up together with assertions of all-powerful expertise and a new one-dimensional thinking. In France, the Macron regime resulting from the 2017 elections is seeking to block off alternatives, so that the only choice is between the path of reason (the new "progressivism" installed in the Elysée Palace) and the madness of "populism." Ostensibly, there is no longer a left-right divide or, more generally, legitimate differences on politics and economics: everything is a matter of reason and expertise, in practice strongly skewed in favor of the superrich. However, nothing could be further from the truth than to say that differences no longer exist. On the contrary: to borrow Thomas Piketty's formulation in *Capital and Ideology*, the dimensions of political conflict have never been so numerous. What the proponents of convergence forget is that left-right differences have simply changed position. By closing off any reduction in social-economic inequality, in the name of shibboleths such as globalization, international division of labor, capital mobility, or budgetary orthodoxy, they risk exacerbating identity differences and, in effect, make ethnic and migratory issues play a growing role in electoral contests.[11] Contrary to such claims, however, globalization, division of labor, the impossibility of taxing capital, and so on are not leaden constraints that we are collectively unable to throw off. They are what they are because politics has made them so. It is too often overlooked that economics is not an exact science pointing implacably to the steps we need to follow. Economics is only politics; it exists at any moment only through the institutions that define it. The European Union is a striking case in point.

Despite their claim to modernity, today's self-styled "progressives" merely rehearse old arguments from a century ago when they fetishize expert knowledge and the "depoliticization" of public debate. In the 1920s Walter Lippmann, one of the thinkers of modern neoliberalism, was already calling for rule by experts and a depoliticization of government—an argument based on the idea that the global division of labor is an end in itself.[12] In his view, the field of politics had to be purged of all conflict:

> Although it is the custom of partisans to speak as if there were radical differences between the Ins and the Outs, . . . in stable and mature societies the differences are necessarily not profound. . . . If they were profound, the defeated minority would be constantly on the verge of rebellion. An election would be catastrophic, whereas the assumption in every election is that

the victors will do nothing to make life intolerable to the vanquished and that the vanquished will endure with good humor policies which they do not approve. . . . An election rarely means even a fraction of what the campaigners said it would mean. . . . In fact, one might say that a nation is politically stable when nothing of radical consequence is determined by its elections.[13]

You could think you were listening to Joe Biden: fear not, rich Democratic donors, nothing will change if I'm elected! Lippmann goes on to make another interesting point about election campaigns. What is so important about them, he asks, if in the end it matters so little who is victorious? For "the expenditure of money to overcome the inertia of the mass of voters" fuels the excitement of these campaigns.[14] In other words, election spending is part of the illusion of representative democracy in which Lippmann seems to place his hopes. Also of interest is his criterion for judging "good democratic government that is at once effective and pragmatic":[15] namely, the people's quality of life, its living standards, not its capacity to govern itself freely.

In the 1930s, Lippmann's arguments for a complete depoliticization of government were already taken apart by, among others, the American philosopher John Dewey, who pointed out that the global division of labor was not at all an end in itself or a necessity in the face of which the "masses" had to remain passive. On the contrary, through their constant participation, the masses can modify their environment. And it is their absence from decision-making that prevents the human species from freeing its potential and adapting to a changing environment. Today we are being reminded of this by teenagers such as Greta Thunberg and Youth for Climate activists, who refuse to sit idly by in the face of climate change and supposedly inescapable environmental realities. Although this mobilization seems less extensive in the United States than in Europe, it is interesting to note that the "Millennials" are also attempting to organize politically around such figures as Saikat Chakrabarti, the chief of staff to Alexandria Ocasio-Cortez and cofounder of Justice Democrats.

How could we better summarize the *gilets jaunes* movement than with this quotation from Dewey? "No government by experts in which the masses do not have the chance to inform the experts as to their needs can be anything but an oligarchy managed in the interests of the few."[16] "An oligarchy managed in the interests of the few": it is a fine definition of Macronism in power. And the *gilets jaunes* movement may be seen as an attempt by the masses to increase their visibility, to inform the experts as to their needs (not only to make ends meet toward the end of the month, but also the more "political" need to make their voices heard in public space). This helps us to grasp the full absurdity of talk about "Gallic resistance to change," trotted out by people for whom democracy means the top-down imposition of change on passive masses, rather than government interaction with active masses and collective deliberation to decide what needs to change. It is not resistant masses who are standing in the way of change, but rather the oligarchs who cling to old forms of rule and shelter behind an illusion of representation to reject legitimate demands for mass participation.

The Left, as embodied in the parties and organizations of the past few decades, has its own share of responsibility for this refusal of political representatives to meet the legitimate demand of the masses for greater representation. But it is not enough to note that Left governments—in the United States, the United Kingdom, Germany, Italy, and so on—have abandoned class struggle and lost any resolve to reduce social and economic inequalities. I amply document this trend in the book, not only by plotting the changed sources of funding for these parties and the social origin of their elected officials, but also on the basis of my reading of various authors, from Thomas Frank and Katherine Cramer to Arlie Hochschild, who have tried to understand the motives of yesterday's Tea Party voters and today's supporters of Donald Trump. However, these points have a meaning only in the context of a genuinely political (that is, ideological) alternative, whereas it has become fashionable to denounce, without proposing anything instead, the "ideology of diversity" (as Mark Lilla calls it) that the Left has purportedly embraced.[17] Lilla writes that the Left is in the grip of "a crisis of imagination and ambition," but he proposes nothing to solve it. Throughout his book, he wages war on "identity liberalism," attacking the academic world in an unreferenced and often misogynistic logorrhea (a word that some will see as a reprehensibly female expression), yet his only horizon is a return to a "republican left" that he does not even take the time to define with any precision. It is tempting to see in this a parallel to the work of another intellectual so prone to denunciation, Yascha Mounk, who lectures the masses for being seduced by the propaganda of "illiberal democracy."[18] But what does Mounk offer against the rise of what he calls "populisms"? Nothing less than a return to the Frontier and "inclusive patriotism," an ultimate retreat in the face of "illiberal democrats." Compare that with Mark Lilla: "We're all Americans and we owe that to each other. That's what liberalism means."[19] We have seen more ambitious and more clearly focused programs.

I will not venture here to define what a real politics of emancipation and social justice would look like; that can only be the fruit of long collective deliberation. But let me just say that we urgently need to go beyond the identity conflict and to tackle the great unanswered issue of borders and the collective regulation of human and economic flows. Another burning issue is the reduction of inequalities, which also requires addressing head on the organization of our educational systems.[20] And that cannot be done independently of political movements and the constant involvement of citizens in this task of deliberation and organization. From this point of view, Democratic Equality Vouchers and a mixed assembly are two building blocks for the articulation of representative democracy and participatory democracy. The questions we have to solve—from global warming to a reshaping of the health system, the challenges of an aging population, and the democratization of higher education—are radically new and immensely complex, and the answers can come only through the participation of each and every one of us. Whatever our wider convictions, we cannot resign ourselves to a democracy where only the rich and the experts know the path of reason, and where political and economic differences have been conjured away. I have a profound belief in democracy, and it is wrong to suggest that citizens are turning their backs on it. What they are turning their backs on is not democracy but its present forms, which, without money, leave them without voices. Let us get down to reforming it.

Paris, August 1, 2019

The Price of Democracy

Introduction: Democratic Exhaustion

THIRTY-TWO EUROS. The price of your vote.

"But my vote isn't for sale!" Yes, I know what you are thinking. It is a long time since elections were held in the open air, so that local potentates could keep an eye on the votes cast by hands they had greased. Yet facts are facts. The more that candidates spend during an election campaign, the more they can rent large halls, fill them with supporters, distribute leaflets and messages, flood the media and social networks, and the more they increase their prospects of victory—in the United States, of course, but also in Europe, and nowhere more than in France.[1] Money still occupies center stage in politics; democracy means who pays wins. This book, for which I built a novel database about the evolution of political funding and campaign spending around the world, dissects these mechanisms with a scalpel—and, above all, draws lessons from the present excesses and proposes innovative rules for tomorrow's rediscovery of democracy.

Thirty-two euros. That's the price of your vote.

Just think that each year the French state allocates less than one euro per capita to the *direct* public funding of democracy,[2] yet reimburses on average nearly 165 euros a year to the 290,000 taxpayers who help to fund the political party of their choice—and nearly 5,000 euros to each of the 2,900 households that donate the most![3] These figures explain the question marks surrounding the quality of our democracy. For why should public money allow some people to "buy" the equivalent of nearly five votes, or as many as 150 votes or more in the case of those with the greatest wealth? Does anyone really think that our democracy needs this extra bias in favor of the richest?

Nor does this take into account the tax spending associated with campaign donations.[4] While the state refunds an average of 52 million euros *per year* to candidates taking part in the electoral process— therefore much more during election years—the various campaigns receive 12 million euros in private donations, which give rise to tax reductions worth nearly 8 million euros. Only 8 million against 52 million, that's true, but those 8 million are divided among a few tens of thousands of individuals who have expressed their political preferences through *private* donations (that is, hundreds of euros in public money per donor, or thousands of euros for the richest), whereas the 52 million euros in *public* funding are divided among all French citizens (= less than one euro each).

The following statistic sums up the absurdity, and the injustice, of the French system. In 2016, the state spent 29 million euros just on tax allowances related to party donations for the richest 10 percent—twenty-one times more than it spent for the least well-off half of taxpayers.[5] And it spent as much for the richest 0.01 percent as it did for the least well-off 50 percent.

Not only does our democracy mean who pays wins; France, like many other Western countries, has institutionalized a system in which the state subsidizes the political preferences of the wealthiest citizens on top of the private money they donate. It is a public funding system that does not benefit all political movements in the same way: parties "on the right" receive average annual donations much greater than those flowing to parties "on the left" of the political spectrum. Such a system may potentially boost the capacity of the wealthiest social groups to win election battles and to "buy" public policies of their choosing.[6] More generally, it may serve to transform the conditions under which all political movements operate (on the "left" as well as the "right") and to blur some of the fine borderlines that have long ensured a degree of representation for the least well-off sections of society.

If, as a voter, you have long given up on the democratic game—why bother to play if my vote counts for so little, why bet on something else if the die is already cast?—you should at least be shocked as a citizen-taxpayer by this level of inequality and by the way in which public money is spent. Take one example. For someone with a taxable income of 100,000 euros, the real cost of a 6,000-euro donation to a political party is just 2,040 euros. The remaining 3,960 euros are a cost borne by the state—that is, by taxpayers as a whole. What would the same donation cost a student, a worker without job security, or a pensioner with taxable income below 9,000 euros? The answer: 6,000 euros.[7] More than half of households are exempt from income tax in France—which means that, although they have a heavy tax burden in other respects, they must pay any political contributions in full, whereas contributions from the wealthiest sections of society are offset by state subsidies to the tune of two-thirds. Those who can pay the most pay the least. That is how the tax system operates in the indirect public funding of democracy in France. It is a regressive and unjust system, in which the poor pay for the rich.

To simplify, we may say that there are today three categories of citizens: (1) "ordinary" men and women, constituting the great majority, who simply express their preferences through elections and benefit only marginally from the public funding of democracy; (2) "activists" or party members, who devote both time and money (membership dues) to the party of their choice but are often "forgotten" in the allocation of fiscal largesse; and (3) generous donors (or plutocrats, if you prefer) who take full advantage of tax reductions and are massively subsidized by other taxpayers, including the least well off, in the exercise of their political preferences. The balance of forces has never been very favorable to "ordinary citizens," and there was a time when "activists" could delude themselves that they were on an equal footing with the "megadonors." More and more, however, it is the latter who call the shots and make off with the winnings.

Not only is this system regressive and profoundly unequal; it threatens in the coming decades to fuel even greater inequalities, an even more massive rejection of politicians, institutions, and the democratic process, and a rise of far right movements that may get totally out of hand. In the twenty-first century, it is not so much diplomats who prevail over men of action, but businessmen who prevail over elected policymakers. Besides, in a country such as the United States, foreign embassies are there to be bought. Like "assholes" (*les cons*) in a popular French saying, rich people will try anything on—that's how you recognize them.

Rejecting Electoral Democracy and Its Public Funding: A Dangerous Response to a Real Crisis

This book will track the (often fruitless but always instructive) attempts to regulate the relations between money and democracy, and above all to draw lessons for the future. I shall start from the principle that it is possible to change things, so long as everyone gets to grips with the terms of this key debate. That involves going in some detail into the legislation and experiences of various countries.

The story is not entirely negative—especially on this side of the Atlantic, where there is still a strong attachment to a certain democratic and egalitarian ideal. In France and Belgium, for instance, donations to political parties and campaigns have been strictly regulated since the early 1990s—which has in effect limited the power of the wealthiest sections of society. Upper limits also exist in Italy and Spain, but they have been set at a higher level there. In other countries where such rules are not in force, such as Germany and the United Kingdom, efforts to achieve greater transparency have been made in the last few years, in order to lessen the danger that politicians will be taken captive by private interests. The public funding of democracy—a system that took such a long time to establish and whose philosophical-political foundations and practical functioning have never been sufficiently debated or theorized— is an excellent thing in itself, despite all its imperfections and the reforms that need to be made to it.

But what do we actually see? In a growing number of countries, there is a challenge to the very idea of a ceiling on private donations, in the name of a sacrosanct "freedom of speech" with which conservatives seek to preserve at all costs their financial trump cards. More troubling still, however, is the questioning of any system of public funding of political life. The widespread sense that electoral democracy has been captured by a small minority—a feeling that corresponds to tendencies in the real world—leads all too often to rejection of any form of such democracy. In the United States, where studies have clearly established that politicians cater to the wishes of the rich, voter turnout is in decline, and a large majority of citizens refuse to accept that their tax money should be used to fund elections.[8] The 2016 presidential election, which saw Donald Trump's disturbing victory, officially marks the end of the public funding of democracy in the United States, a system going back more than forty years. The growing abstention in France suggests that things are heading in the same direction there. In a way, what we are witnessing is the failure of representation (Figure 1).

In Italy, the Five Stars Movement has made an end to the public funding of political parties one of its main hobby horses. It did not take long to make progress: a law ending direct funding was adopted in 2014, and the last funding came to an end in 2017. The election of 2018, with

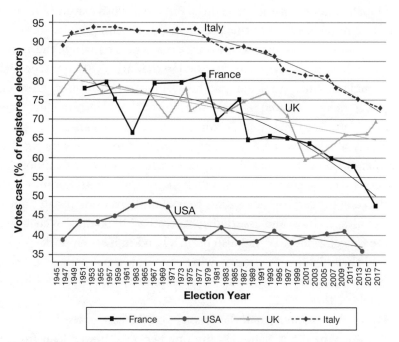

Figure 1. The failure of representation? A general decline in voter turnout at parliamentary elections since 1945: France, United States, United Kingdom, and Italy

its victory for the Five Stars Movement and the far-right Lega, was the first to take place there for forty years without the reimbursement of campaign spending. Meanwhile, the Italian government each year subsidizes the political preferences of the more affluent, and only the more affluent, sections of society.[9]

Of course, the rise of populist movements has to do with more than just the capture of electoral democracy by private moneyed interests. It cannot be reduced to that, but we can still ponder the connection. For example, we can wonder about the £32.7 million spent in the Brexit referendum, the costliest in the United Kingdom's history, or about the health of a democratic system that provides for almost no public funding of its political parties, yet allows a millionaire to spend more than £400,000 to splash bulldogs with Union Jack neckties all over the country's popular press.[10] That millionaire, doubtless too busy to walk his own dog (or to defend its interests), even forgot to declare this spending to the Electoral Commission, which later fined him a paltry £12,000.

Donald Trump is not keen on dogs. But money also played an important role in the election of this president tinged with populist authoritarian colors, in a country where only a few scraps remain of the ambitious public funding system established in the early 1970s. It is true that he spent less on his campaign than his Democrat rival, Hillary Clinton, who was richly endowed by large sections of the American elite. (The massive "free" coverage that Trump won with his various excesses was certainly a factor, because it meant that he had to pay less for his TV campaign.) Yet in the weeks before the vote he netted tens of millions of dollars in extra contributions, much more than Mitt Romney had achieved at the same stage in 2012. Tens of millions from private equity companies, casinos, and assorted conservative billionaires! Well aware of the role of money, Trump also put his hand in his own pocket as he neared the finishing line in key swing states.[11] Is it not perhaps money, rather than Russia, "fake news," or James Comey, that explains his improbable victory?

We might say money *and* the Russians in the case of the French Far Right, since the Front National's funding benefited from a loan from a Czech-Russian bank. Its clinching argument was: "French banks don't lend." Far though it is from my intention to give any credence to Marine

Le Pen, it is true that financial difficulties facing a party with repeated electoral success behind it can raise questions about the adequacy of the present system of public funding. François Bayrou—Macron's ephemeral justice minister, who resigned following suspicions of bogus employment before he could carry through his law on the moralization of political life—did propose the establishment of a "democracy bank," but the idea did not last much longer than his job.[12] Moreover, it left open an important question. Does not the refusal to allocate more public money to the funding of political democracy play into the hands of private interests?

The costs of democracy are not necessarily very high in absolute terms. In France, the spending of all eleven presidential candidates in 2017 came to a total of 74 million euros, or less than 1.50 euros per adult. There is no need to follow the American example by allowing candidates to spend a billion euros each. But if the lower (even reasonable) costs are very unevenly distributed, and above all if a handful of rich private donors contribute the most to campaign spending and the functioning of political parties, the entire system is in danger. What the data tell us is that in France or the United Kingdom the 10 percent of megadonors account for more than two-thirds of the total sum of donations. And what history teaches us is that there will never be an end to the excesses unless private funding is capped and a system of adequate public subsidies is introduced.

The End of Parties?

Another common response to the crisis of electoral democracy—and of the representative principle—is a rejection of parties. The Five Stars Movement, which has crippled the public funding of Italian democracy, defines itself first of all as an "anti-party"—neither right nor left; neither party nor labor union. This old idea of doing away with party divisions and ancient collective structures, in the name of a new efficiency serving the general interest, tends to be reheated and served again at regular intervals. And at the same time, obsessed with being "on the march," some politicians have perhaps not taken the trouble to enter deeply into the political thought of a General de Gaulle.[13]

Parties evidently lead to division: de Gaulle could hardly have claimed paternity rights over that idea. It is as old as political parties themselves. In the nineteenth century, the tendency to produce division was already being used as an argument against their emergence. The perception of parties as troublemakers led many authors of the time to write of them in the language of the market.[14] So, if parties betoken both democratization and marketization of the political system, why not allow money into them? A nihilistic attitude to parties fosters the distortions of private funding.

So it was that money entered politics and surged onto the terrain of elections. Today, private donations—by individuals, but also by companies where it is allowed—provide 70 percent of resources for the Conservative Party in the United Kingdom, 40 percent for Forza Italia, and nearly 20 percent for the Republicans in France. The direct result is the end of one form of division: class struggle. The interparty strife underlying the great battles for social gains gave way to "cultural" class conflict once the parties of the Left also started to canvass private donors. Take the case of the British Labour Party, founded by the trade unions and for a long time the party of the workers' movement. Until the middle of the 1980s, the working classes made up a third of Labour MPs. But then they gradually disappeared from Parliament, while private donations were becoming a larger source of party income than membership dues. By 2015, individual and corporate donations accounted for 38 percent of the Labour Party's resources, compared with 31 percent for members' contributions. Today, manual and office workers represent less than 5 percent of MPs in the United Kingdom, and less than 2 percent of members of Congress in the United States (against 54 percent of the active population). As for France, not a single member of the National Assembly is drawn from the working class.

The Liberal Critique of Electoral Democracy

Nevertheless, the challenge to electoral democracy does not come only from people such as Hugo Chávez, Jean-Luc Mélenchon, Beppe Grillo, and other "populists," any more than it can be identified only with abstentionists. One would like to hear the working classes protest more against the representation deficit of which they are the primary victims, for when the game is "one euro, one vote" they are the losers right from the start. But the fact that political parties have abandoned class struggle on the economic terrain means that the transmission belt for workers' grievances now lies broken. As in Antonioni's film *Il Grido,* "The Cry," the working class has fallen silent, condemned to give up what it has and repeat itself in a kind of purposeless drifting. When it is not simply evicted, it finds itself split up and segregated both geographically and educationally.

Who, then, do we hear raise the cry against democracy? Not the workers, no, but those with money and time to make themselves heard; those who think democracy is still *too* representative and above all too restrictive, because it does not leave them free to make the best use of their money. It is a more insidious, and much more dangerous, critique. I am thinking in particular of all those iconic Silicon Valley figures who have become figureheads of libertarian thought and whose cry is obviously not in defense of the workers' interests.

Libertarianism against democracy? The opposition takes shape primarily in the refusal of high-tech billionaires to pay their taxes. It is not that they do not wish to take part in the collective effort—to quote their own rhetoric—but simply that they are better placed than anyone else to decide how their money can be used most fruitfully—for the common good, of course. The state, by definition, is slow, inefficient, and most often corrupt. The state "captures," in every sense of the term, whereas freedom allows people to fulfill themselves. So, why tax the new-generation philanthropists when all they are asking is to give proof of their generosity? These heroes of the new modernity are constantly creating foundations and investing millions of dollars in them, be it for peace, the environment, or the war on want. So what is the good of taxing them? Shouldn't all these torchbearers be left in peace? The fact that such questions are being asked today is symptomatic of the contradiction inherent in the very idea of philanthropy in a democracy.

I shall investigate the whole panoply of think tanks, foundations, and media outlets on which the wealthiest citizens can draw to influence not only election results but the very terms of public debate. It is the foundations, often generously subsidized by the state through tax relief, that enable a handful of individuals to substitute themselves for the democratic choices of the majority—as if the superrich were better suited than democratically elected governments to decide which activities should or should not be funded in full or in part. It is important to realize how the public good is used as cover for the capture of democracy, since many get caught in the web of these Communicators 2.0 and end up applauding the "generosity" of global tax exiles.[15] In reality, what is taking shape are the first stages of a new electoral system based on an income threshold.

Take the media hype in 2016 when Mark Zuckerberg and his wife announced that they were creating a special foundation and endowing it—what generosity!—with 99 percent of their shares in Facebook.[16] The only glitch is that the so-called Chan Zuckerberg Initiative—modestly named after Mark and his spouse—is a limited liability company; it therefore enjoys major tax breaks in relation to profits and inheritance duty, while leaving Mark Zuckerberg with ultimate control of the organization. We should also add that whenever Zuckerberg sells Facebook shares to fund his foundation—at a rate never higher than $1 billion a year—he can claim it as a deduction from his taxable income, saving himself hundreds of millions in taxes. What was that about generosity? Ah yes, and I almost forgot the self-promotion angle. For Facebook, it is also a free publicity exercise on a vast scale, at a time when the social network badly needs to give its image a boost.

Of course, in today's globalized world the funding of social democracy poses a lot of new challenges, and it is true that national egotism is gaining strength. But that is no reason to shrink from these challenges—to give up on the state and rely on the supposed humanism of a handful of billionaires. We need to rethink how the state organizes and finances democracy; we need to do this at a European level and stop imagining that high-tech superstars will solve the problems in our place. What must be firmly rejected is the idea that large corporations should set the course for society as a whole.

The libertarians would certainly love that. The leading figure here is Peter Thiel, the originator of the Paypal online payment system, who—though he makes less noise about it—is also widely known as the man who contributed $2.6 million to Ron Paul's Super Political Action Committee, "Endorse Liberty," during the 2012 presidential campaign. Note that this critic of big government was not really contradicting himself: it is a characteristic of the libertarian movement to defend an idea of liberty that is immediately contradicted by real world practices. The core libertarian belief that the wishes of the individual take precedence over everything else simply "overlooks" that the conquering ambitions of a philanthropist—just think of Elon Musk's colonial designs on the planet Mars—can easily impinge on the liberty (and general interest) of the majority. For libertarians, there are those who succeed and those who fail—would Emmanuel Macron say anything different? Ayn Rand's novel *Atlas Shrugged* (1957), which has become the bible of these Silicon Valley "thinkers," opens with the image of a tramp to whom the main protagonist, Eddie Willers, does not even bother to listen. Why should he? Libertarians reject any notion that the wishes of the majority should be collectively represented.

"So what?" you may ask. Is it not their most basic right? Is everyone not free to argue for their own conception of the state? Sure they are. But I am also free to criticize them. And if I do that here, it is because I am aware that libertarians, though a long way from victory at the polls, have partly won the battle of ideas. It is a fact that only today's financial winners have their preferences represented. It is a fact that, even in a country such as France, where for a long time philanthropy was not a prominent part of the culture, public funding of the common good is being supplanted by private funding of what has effectively become a privatized public good. And philanthropy—the idea that bigtime winners are ultimately better suited than the majority to decide what is good for us all—poses a threat to the basic principles that should underpin any genuine democracy.

What If We Were to Dream of a Perfect System?

The perfect regime for libertarians is one in which the state no longer exists—or, as they would probably prefer to say, plays only a minimal role. Electoral democracy does not completely disappear, but all are free to use all means—especially money—to advance their interests. Once "elected," the government is there only to guarantee its own nonintervention; its sole aim is to preserve all the "liberties." The freedom to succeed, now reduced to a matter of individual will, is also the freedom to fail. It is also the freedom for a tobacco giant like Philip Morris to fund the Christian Democratic Union (CDU) and its allied Christian Social Union (CSU), the Free Democratic Party (FDP), and the Social Democratic Party (SPD) all at once—and too bad if Germany, along with Bulgaria, is the only EU country that is still only at the stage of discussing a ban on publicity for tobacco products.

From this point of view, the libertarian regime is perfectly oligarchic. Theoretically, of course, no one is in command, but in fact it can only be the minority of superrich who deserve to command because they know best. One is tempted to describe this as a "plutotechnocracy."[17] As for the majority, they have to be content with one or two euros a year in public funding for political parties. And even that is forthcoming only where repeated populist attacks on subsidies and conservative assaults on "big government" have not whittled the figure down to zero.

In his preface to the French edition of Max Weber's *Politics as a Vocation,* Raymond Aron wrote that "all democracy is oligarchy, all institutions are imperfectly representative." He did not mean this as a denunciation, but on the contrary as a congratulatory recognition that there never has been and never will be a "perfect regime." So, we are supposed to settle for democracy as it operates today, to close our eyes to its capture by a minority. Why? Because we can't have anything better, and any dream or illusion that we might can only end in disaster? According to the same logic, why should we not welcome the fact that in most democracies today the state funds political preferences out of its tax revenue—but only for the wealthiest minority? Bertolt Brecht was right: "Laws are made only to exploit those who do not understand them." In other words, we have a threepenny democracy, a theater of the absurd where the majority who vote—when they vote—end up doing so against their own interests.

None of these paths is agreeable to me. The reality does not satisfy me, and it is definitely possible to do better. I refuse to settle for being powerless, to accept that, faced with an unrepresentative oligarchy, all we can do is bow our heads and acquiesce—or abstain and let others get on with it.

In this book, I shall therefore try to chart a different course. I shall use a number of approaches, the first being that of history, economics, and political science, with special reference to archival material that allows us to trace the slow, faltering development of systems regulating the funding of political life. This requires a new kind of database on the historical evolution of private and public funding around the world. My attention will often focus on Western Europe and North America, where the historical data are most plentiful, but we shall see that important lessons may also be drawn from more distant lands such as Brazil and India. The reader will, I hope, forgive the plethora of tables and figures, for we have to pay the price of that effort—by measuring the annual public and private funding of political parties and by drawing international comparisons over time—if we are to understand the forces in play today and to propose the nitty-gritty of credible and effective alternatives.

Within this historical and comparative perspective, the book will look at the dangers of an oligarchic drift in politics in the early twenty-first century. In the United States, where the past few decades have swept away all regulation of political democracy, politicians now heed the preferences only of the richest sections of society, and money corrupts politics and democratic debate a little more with every day that passes. In France, fortunately, we are still a long way from that. But we should be aware that private donations by the wealthiest classes—with large state subsidies out of general taxation—have a not insignificant impact on election results. As we shall see, this causal effect on local elections in France is such that it may largely explain the "strange defeat" of the Right in the legislative elections of 1997, four years after the Socialist debacle in 1993 and just two years after Jacques Chirac's victory in the presidential election of 1995. How is that? Candidates of the Right, used to relying on corporate donations, did not manage to recover from the new ban on these in 1995; whereas candidates of the Left, who had mostly never benefited from such donations, did not suffer in the same way, and in fact spent relatively more than their opponents during the short campaign following the announcement of the earlier-than-scheduled election.

Beyond the strictly political realm, moreover, the rich contribute a proportionately higher share of their income to the funding of the common good, through donations to various associations and projects that they consider priorities. To get around the limits on the direct public funding of political life, they use their wealth to influence the electoral, legislative, and regulatory process by funding think tanks, research centers, and media outlets. In most democracies, there is a growing concentration of the news media in the hands of a few billionaires.

The central issue here is, of course, the confusion between the general interest and particular interests. The present work, based as it is mainly on historical, legislative, and statistical research, will demonstrate the growing role of money in our democracies and study the ways in which it influences political decisions. When state spending gives way to private foundations, there is a great danger that democracy will become no more than a façade. Is that inevitably in store for us? I do not think so, and that is why this book will propose a number of extensive reforms. It will set out the real conditions for the establishment of a permanent and participatory democracy in France and elsewhere.

Dynamically Equal Funding and a Mixed Assembly: The Dual Democratic Revolution

The aim of the three proposals in the last part of this book is that we should again be able to define democracy as "one person, one vote."

The first points to a completely new model for the funding of political parties and movements and election campaigns. A key component of this is the equal representation of private preferences through the issuing of Democratic Equality Vouchers (DEVs), so that each year, on filing their tax returns, all citizens choose the political party or movement to which they want "their" seven euros of public money to be allocated. It would be seven full euros, because the allocation would happen without any extra spending and replace the flawed and regressive system of public funding in place today (a system based on past electoral success, on fiscal expenditure linked only to party donations by the rich, and so on).

One advantage of Democratic Equality Vouchers over the present system is that they would shorten the time it takes to fund the relevant bodies of a functioning democracy. Today, the direct public funding of parties is frozen for a period of four to five years (depending on the country), because the funds are distributed in proportion to the number of votes received at the last elections. Democracy, however, is not frozen in time. New initiatives emerge every day in civil society. The purpose of political parties is not just to be election machines; they should be thought of as platforms enabling the advance of public debate, in periods between elections as well as during them. So, why wait five years each time to grant the funds they need for their survival? DEVs would allow some of the cards to be dealt again each year (only some, because the seven euros of those who decide not to make a choice would be distributed in accordance with the previous election results). Furthermore, with a system of DEVs, one person = the same public funding for each citizen = one vote. It would mean an end to the absurd system whereby the poor pay to satisfy the political preferences of the rich.

For DEVs to be really effective—for the positive effects of this modernized system of public funding not to be stymied by private money—my second proposal is to set much tighter limits on electoral spending and on private contributions to parties and campaigns. In countries where corporate donations to parties and campaigns still exist (Germany, United Kingdom, Italy, and elsewhere), I propose that they should be prohibited. As to individual donations, I propose a ceiling of 200 euros a year in order to equalize the potential weight of all citizens. If the political weight of private money is not limited, then politicians will continue to run around looking for funds, and only the preferences of the wealthiest will be represented, as they are today. I want to emphasize this point most strongly: yes, the existing democratic system is partly corrupt, but the correct response is not to say: "They're all rotten to the core; let our tax money be spent on schools and hospitals, not on maintaining politicians." The right response is: private money corrupts the political process, so let's keep private money out. And since politics costs a lot, let us adequately fund democracy with public money. Only with a sizable, egalitarian, and transparent system for the public funding of political democracy will money be available tomorrow for the schools and hospitals that the majority of people need. Those who flood the electoral process with private money rarely ask government to increase their own taxes to pay for basic public goods.

With these two reforms—the creation of Democratic Equality Vouchers and a drastic curbing, or prohibition, of private funding—the politicians who today pander to the preferences and priorities of their rich backers will tomorrow address the preferences of the majority (the citizens who elect them). But that will not be enough: the funding issue is important, but it cannot be the only answer to the crisis of democracy. The representation deficit that a majority of citizens endure today is much graver and deeper. It is necessary to go further and embrace the third proposal in this book: a mixed assembly. Why? Because, as things stand today, the popular classes are no longer politically represented.

Such an assembly might take the following form. Parliaments as they exist today in many countries claim to represent citizens regardless of their social origins, but in practice they virtually exclude the working classes from national representation. New rules for the funding of democracy will not be sufficient to reverse such a major trend, to solve such a profound crisis, although they may certainly help in that direction. It is also necessary to rethink the very rules of representation. Under the reform I propose, a third of seats in the national assembly will be reserved for "social representatives," elected proportionally on lists reflecting the socio-occupational reality of the population. For example, in the case of France, at least 50 percent of the men and women on these lists will have to be manual or office workers. More specifically, two elections will take place simultaneously to elect representatives to the national assembly. The voting rules for two-thirds of the seats (those held by deputies from local constituencies) will remain unchanged, while in the other third there will be a system of proportional representation based on national lists *with socio-occupational parity*. A minimum of one half of the candidates on each list will be required to exercise a (broadly defined) working-class occupation at the time of the election, including, of course, all the new precarious jobs and forms of micro-entrepreneurship. The popular classes will thus be significantly more represented on the parliamentary benches than they are today, with tangible consequences for policy directions, since, as we shall see, socio-occupational origin directly influences how parliamentary representatives vote.

A mixed assembly is certainly a major reform, but its radical character is an answer to today's radical exclusion of the working classes from the parliamentary process. We can no longer put up with the hypocritical workings of our debased democratic systems, which only represent the interests of money and provide fuel for toxic voting and nihilistic behavior. As in the case of gender parity, we must use all means available under the rule of law to tackle the issue of social parity at the roots.

Such is the direction I chart in this book. Thank you, dear reader, for following me in it. Let us begin with a world tour of the funding of electoral democracy: first, the twists and turns of private finance, then the often improvised and flawed attempts to introduce public funding, and finally the reasoned proposals for a way out of these contradictions. Some of the results I will present may shock you; as a citizen, I myself have often been scandalized to discover, for example, the level of inequality that today governs the funding of our political democracy. But do not lose all hope in electoral democracy: it needs to be rebuilt, not abandoned. History is filled with democratic resurgences and innovations. Let us not dwell only on the negative side, but also draw the lessons of all those positive experiences! This book has some surprises in store for you. And although it is a long road to the dual democratic revolution I outline, it is worthwhile taking it.

PART ONE

WHEN THE POOR
PAY FOR THE RICH

1

The Cost of Democracy: First Benchmarks

DEMOCRACY rests on a promise of equality, which too often shatters against the wall of money. We tend to forget that providing for democracy comes at a price. This is not necessarily very high in absolute terms—which shows, by the way, that a rational collective solution is within reach. But if the costs are very unevenly distributed, and if the weight of private money in the total funding is not severely restricted, then the whole system is in danger.

In this first chapter, we shall review the evolution of election spending in recent decades in a number of countries, beginning with France, the United Kingdom, Germany, and the United States. In some cases, this spending is mainly charged to the candidates themselves, who are then reimbursed by the state in full or in part; this happens especially in countries that use a first-past-the-post system, with one MP per constituency. In countries with a system of proportional representation, the parties support the bulk of campaign spending and serve as an intermediate body between the public coffers and the candidates. Campaign funding and party funding: the heads and tails of the ringing coinage of democracy, which, as in Perrault's fairy story of the donkey with golden dung, keeps multiplying.

As we shall see in later chapters, however, what really counts is who produces the coinage. Public funding or private donations: depending on which it is, the same level of campaign spending can reflect diametrically opposite realities. For in politics, donkey dung is rarely silent when it is made of gold. And the weight of private donations can prove heavy to bear.

The Price of Elections

Democracy is first of all elections. What gesture can be simpler or less onerous than to slip a ballot paper into a box? To go to a polling station one Sunday *en famille* seems an act uncontaminated by the logic of the market. Polling stations are the schools of the republic. The attendants are ordinary citizens, just like you or me, who have chosen to give a little of their time to democracy. The only condition is that they should be on the electoral register. There's no gain from it—except the satisfaction of taking part in a democratic high mass, scheduled to finish in time for evening mass at 8 o'clock, or of counting the votes in boxes that are often too empty. How long ago seem the days when you had to have some property to vote!

What, then, is the cost of elections? In 2016, a victorious candidate for the US Senate spent on average more than $10 million.[1] In France, the average parliamentary candidate reckons on much less: a little more than 18,000 euros in 2012,[2] although the figure rises to 41,000 euros for the lucky winners. In the United Kingdom—where, as in France, there is a legal ceiling on campaign expenditure—the average for the general elections in 2015 was 4,000 euros, rising to 10,000 euros for those who came out on top.

Such is the real cost of elections: campaign spending by the candidates plus spending by parties and interest groups.[3] The money that each of these puts on the table to convince voters of how they should vote is spent on a range of methods such as public meetings, leaflets, house-to-house canvassing, publicity campaigns, and—to an increasing extent—the direct purchase of space and visibility in the media and social networks. In the last few decades, such expenditure has been continually growing in a number of democracies, with the exception of those that regulate it.

The gap between election spending in the United States and in the United Kingdom or France is clearly not due to cultural differences. It is not the case that we have, on the one side, austere Brits worried over the money spent on leaflets with the parsimony familiar from Ben Jonson's *Volpone* and, on the other side, the Great Gatsby, willing to spend as if there were no tomorrow to win over his fellow Americans. Nor do the differences in question reflect a greater taste for electoral contests on the other side of the Atlantic. If the sums spent could be equated with the degree of popular interest in elections, then the highest spending ought to go together with the highest degree of commitment. But of all the Western countries, the United States has the lowest voter turnout. The differences in campaign costs are not cultural differences; they are the direct result of election laws that have lasting, and often neglected, effects on the structure of the democratic process.

High-Cost Democracy

How much is a parliamentary candidate willing to put on the table to have a chance of winning? To answer this question, we first need to ask another one: How much is an election candidate *permitted* to put on the table? The amount not only varies from country to country but also fluctuates sharply from period to period.

Is the Feast Over?

A first, seemingly evident fact is that, if no limits are set, candidates tend not to limit themselves and are capable of spending sums that beggar belief. To grasp this fully, it may be helpful to look back at the nineteenth century. In the United Kingdom, one of the first countries to limit election spending with the Corrupt Illegal Practices (Prevention) Act of 1883,[4] the total expenditure of parliamentary candidates (expressed in today's euros, adjusted for inflation) regularly exceeded 200 million euros: 191 million in 1868, 184 million in 1874, and 228 million in 1880. This was more than ten times the sums spent today—even though there was a smaller number of voters to "convince," and the real national income per adult was nearly five times lower. Before a ceiling was placed on election spending in 1883, it could sometimes rise above one hundred euros *per voter*. Today, by comparison, the total amount spent per voter registered for British parliamentary elections varies between 0.40 and 0.50 euros per election (Figure 2).[5]

This nosedive in election expenditure appears even more clearly if it is expressed as a proportion of national income per adult: in 1868, each candidate spent on average a little more than 185,000 euros, or thirty times the annual national income per adult head of the population! This suggests that—over and above the suffrage restrictions—only the richest citizens could aspire to stand for seats in Parliament. Today, however, the average spending of a candidate in parliamentary elections repre-

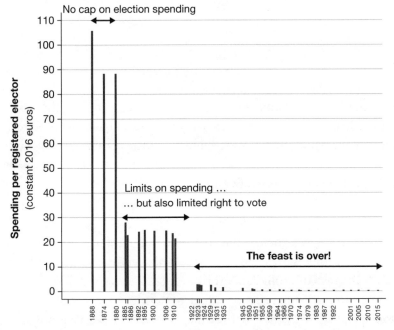

Figure 2. Total spending of candidates per registered elector, UK parliamentary elections, 1868–2015

If the total election spending of all candidates in UK parliamentary elections in 1868 is divided by the number of people on the electoral register, the spending per elector amounts to 105 euros (in constant 2016 euros). The spending per elector was 21.50 euros in the 1911 parliamentary elections, and 0.35 euros in those of 2015.

sents scarcely more than 10 percent of per capita national income.[6] In other words, expressed in terms of national income per adult head of the population, the average spending of candidates has been divided by 262 in the course of the past 150 years. Such a radical cut needs to be explained.

Are candidates perhaps more "honest" in their way, more determined to convince people through their ideas than through electoral propaganda? Or is the decline in spending linked to new campaign technology, especially the use of (less expensive) social networks? On the other hand, what could tens of thousands of euros per candidate have been used for in the nineteenth century, when radio and television did not exist, and when it is hard to imagine candidates having recourse to highly paid communication consultants? There is no lack of spicy examples in the history books, such as the fact that transport for voters was one of the main items of declared expenditure. (For a long time, moreover, candidates often directly reimbursed voters for their transport costs—though God forbid we should see this as a possible source of corruption![7]) Voters' transport might include not only first-class train tickets (often cheaper than carriage hire) but also overnight hotel accommodation and compensation for loss of pay due to turnout at the polls. It is interesting to pore over parliamentary debates of the time and listen to MPs argue that if voters had to pay for such things themselves, they would simply not bother to cast their ballot.

The truth is that if British parliamentary candidates spend little on elections today, it is because they are not authorized to spend more. The law has made its move—which is a good thing—and limits possible excesses. If candidates could flood the online media and social networks—as they were able, a century and a half ago, to win the support of voters installed in comfortable couchettes—there is every reason to think that they would do so. The US presidential campaign in 2016, with the suspicions of foreign interference that followed it, is a clear sign that this is the direction in which we are heading, as is the scale of campaign spending in a number of other countries.

But I saw you raise an eyebrow. Is a cap on expenditure really a good thing? Libertarians of every stripe will jump from their padded chairs and bang the table: "Why shouldn't I be allowed to do what I like with my money? Why should I spend just a few tens of thousands of dollars when I'm in a position to spend millions? Let the others do the same if they want!" Is it really necessary to discuss this argument? Citizens are not equal when it comes to the size of their pockets; they do not all have the same funds to spend on their campaign, or the same possibility to raise them from elsewhere. To allow all candidates to spend as much as they like is tantamount to introducing a new property qualification. For only those rich enough or with the right connections would be able to stand—or, more precisely, to stand with more than a zero chance of being elected. This immediately raises several questions about the representativeness of candidates selected in this way. We shall see in Chapter 11 that in a democracy like the United States, where each candidate's campaign spending literally runs into the millions, the ostensible people's representatives cannot be said—if we consider their socio-occupational origins—to represent any but the wealthiest sections of society. In other words, ordinary workers are the main groups missing from the parliamentary benches. The United Kingdom, though never close to parity, does a little better in this respect: 20 percent of MPs were of working-class origin in the period after the Second World War.

Excessive campaign spending also entails a major danger of corruption. A politician is all the more prone to accept kickbacks and other secret money if she has to spend several millions to have any chance of being elected.[8] The game changes if campaign spending is entirely covered by the public purse: candidates are then encouraged to spend roughly equal amounts, and above all they do not have to sacrifice their convictions or integrity in the chase after money. As a matter of fact, proposals for a cap on campaign spending have often been considered alongside the public funding of elections.

Cap Spending, but Fund Elections

In France, election spending has been limited by law only since 1988 in the case of national elections (and since 1990 for local elections).[9] Although the rules have been slightly modified since then and vary from election to election, the ceiling on expenditure essentially depends—as in the United Kingdom—on the number of people on the electoral register. Moreover, candidates are restricted in how they are able to use their funds. Candidates at an election in France may not—even if they have the means—buy publicity for themselves on television or radio.[10]

The other side of this is that the state bears a sizable share of campaign costs, since candidates receiving more than 5 percent of the votes in the first round may have their spending reimbursed up to nearly a half of the capped amount. This refunding of campaign expenditure was introduced at the same time as the ceiling on expenditure. Nor is this a peculiarity of France. In Canada, the Election Expenses Act of 1974 both introduced tight limits on the campaign spending of parties and candidates and provided for the reimbursement of expenditure.[11] The same was true in Spain, where the first constitutional election law was enacted in 1975.

Of course, the reimbursement of election spending does not necessarily go together with the existence of a ceiling, although anyone who advocates reimbursement out of the public purse automatically favors a cap on (at least refundable) expenditure. The state, unlike many private donors, does not have bottomless pockets. So those who support reimbursement from the public purse will logically support a cap on private contributions and therefore on campaign expenditure. Otherwise, what would be the point of publicly funded reimbursement of expenditure if this was in the end drowned beneath a flood of private money? (We shall see that one of the main weaknesses of the German model, despite its generous support for political parties, is precisely that it does not limit private donations, so that ultimately the economic policies of any government reflect the interests of the auto industry—which, taking its lead from BMW, funds all the parties each year—more than those of the majority of German citizens.) The public funding of election campaigns is a tool for fighting the corruption of electoral life; to be complete, the arsenal requires tight regulation of the size of expenditure.

Regulation of election spending does not necessarily imply its reimbursement. A low ceiling can be set on what candidates are allowed to spend, without the state's necessarily bearing the cost of some of that spending. This is the case in the United Kingdom, as we have just seen, and it is also the case in Belgium. In fact, Belgian election law does not provide for any system of public funding or reimbursement of election expenditure.[12] Yet such spending has been tightly capped ever since 1989, so that during an election period parties can spend no more than one million euros, and candidates no more than a few thousand euros.[13]

In the end, in relation to the number of registered voters, spending for legislative elections is higher in France (a system combining regulated expenditure with public funding) than it is in the United Kingdom (where spending is capped but borne entirely by candidates and parties). In 1993, for instance, 2.80 euros were spent in France per citizen on the electoral register, whereas the comparable figure for the United Kingdom was 0.46 euros (Figure 3). The difference is partly due to the fact that the number of candidates in each constituency tends to be higher in France

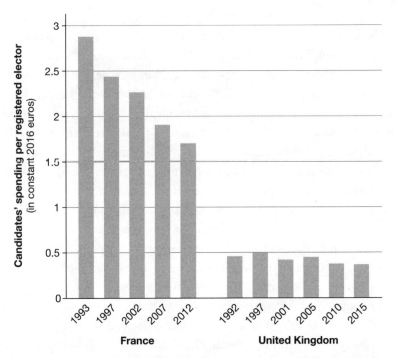

Figure 3. Aggregated spending of all candidates per registered elector, French and UK legislative elections, 1992–2015

If the aggregated spending of all candidates in French legislative elections (107 million euros) in 1993 is divided by the number of citizens on electoral registers (37.9 million), the spending per registered citizen comes to 2.80 euros. The corresponding figure for the 1992 parliamentary elections in the UK was 0.46 euros.

than in the United Kingdom, mainly because of the system of two-round voting.[14] But the main reason for the difference is the stricter regulation in the United Kingdom.[15]

Given that there is no limit to the donations that parties or candidates can receive in the United Kingdom—and, as we shall see, private enterprise does not hold back from great generosity—everything suggests that if there were no cap on election spending it would be much higher there than in France. In any case, because of its one-legged system of regulation, it would seem that British parties have the means to spend much more than they do at present. This also raises questions about the motivation of donors.

If we combine the lessons of these different experiences, what can we ultimately conclude about campaign spending in these "regulated" democracies? First, it does not exceed a few euros per registered voter. One might even be tempted to say that the level of spending is rather low—and that is the argument regularly used by all who refuse to accept that in a country like France, money in politics as it exists today could weaken the very foundation of the democratic process: one person, one vote. Anyway, as we shall see in Chapter 8, even these relatively low amounts are enough to swing a considerable number of votes. According to my estimates, during the 2017 legislative elections in France, 40 million euros (barely 0.002 percent of French GDP) would have been enough to swing 30 percent of votes and to redraw the electoral map.[16] In other words, without a spending cap, a few billionaires could easily "buy themselves" an election result. Another way of approaching the subject is to look at what happens in countries where such a cap does not exist.

But If Everything Is Permitted, Is Nothing Forbidden?

Political Parties Matter

To begin with, let me emphasize that if democracy is first of all about elections, it is also about political parties. This may sound obvious to some and yet it deserves emphasis. While trust in political parties tends to be even lower than trust in government,[17] it is important to remember that effective democratic deliberation and decision-making cannot take place without collective organizations like political parties. Of course, I do not mean here that political parties as they exist today are perfect institutions that do not deserve some of the mistrust they face. Parties need to be reformed, restructured—and most often democratized; they need to innovate so as to engage better with citizens, recruit young members, and nominate working-class candidates. They also need to rethink their funding.

We should not give up on political parties; they are essential to an effective democracy, as was already stressed by Maurice Duverger in his seminal work of 1951.[18] Or to put it another way, I strongly disagree with the opening sentence of Peter Mair's recent book: "the age of party democracy has passed."[19] Mair might be right in his perception of a crisis of Western democracy and in his insistence that parties are increasingly failing to engage ordinary citizens.[20] But there is no alternative. And, in fact, Mair fails to offer any.

It is hard to think of representation without political parties. I shall return in Chapter 9 to permanent and direct democracy and discuss popular referenda in particular. In principle, referenda can allow voters to participate in democratic decision-making without the intermediation of political parties, and this can sometimes play a very useful role. As we will see, however, direct democracy and referenda also raise serious issues about campaign funding and often require various forms of political organization to raise voters' awareness and to develop the public conversation. Above all, most laws, state budgets, and public policies and regulations require extensive parliamentary deliberation and amendment-making processes before final adoption. Political parties play an essential role in organizing parliamentary elections and deliberation.

Of course, some argue that "technocracy"—the reign of experts and technicians—could work better than a combination of political parties and democracy and that in general we should prefer "objective" nonpartisan experts to elected politicians. In an influential article, Alan Blinder, for example, argues that "the real source of the current estrangement between Americans and their politicians is . . . the feeling that the process of governing has become too political."[21] Drawing from the example of central bank independence, he proposes to extend the model to other arenas such as tax policy. However, contrary to what he claims, the optimal tax rate on capital gains is not a purely technical but a *highly political* issue. Representative government requires political parties to aggregate information and preferences from diverse electorates about the likely consequences of policy decisions.

It is also worth stressing that one-party or hegemonic-party political systems—where elections take place without alternation in power—cannot be considered as democratic. For those who doubt it, John H. Aldrich and John D. Griffin have provided a brilliant demonstration in their study of political change in the American South.[22] The South is of particular interest because there have been a few times when there has been a competitive party system, and many times when there has not, especially in the Jim Crow era, when the Democratic Party operated in effect as the hegemonic party.[23] Aldrich and Griffin show that democracy has failed there in periods without real electoral competition, and that the emergence of a competitive party system in the 1970s and 1980s was associated with better political and social outcomes for the general public. When the South was far from having a fully developed two-party system, central characteristics associated with a well-functioning democracy were missing in comparison with the North. In particular, Southern members of both the House of Representatives and the Senate were far less responsive, and often fully unresponsive, to their citizens' preferences. But almost as soon as a fully developed two-party system emerged in the South, the degree of elite responsiveness looked just like that found in the North.

Of course, the functioning of political parties varies from country to country, or between a US-style two-party system and a multiparty democracy such as those in France or Italy. In 1911, the political scientist Robert Michels described in his seminal work what he viewed as the iron law of political parties: oligarchic and bureaucratic elites tend to take control of them and to forget the social classes they are supposed to represent.[24] Michels's attitude to the Social Democratic Party in his native Germany also reminds us that a disillusionment with party politics is as old as electoral democracy itself.[25] In 1961, while praising Michels's theory of political parties as an imperfect form of collective organization, US political scientist Seymour Martin Lipset argued that different organizational forms (such as open primaries to select candidates in the US context) can make parties more responsive to popular demand.[26]

I shall later investigate campaign finance in European democracies and Canada, along with the United States. I start from the assumption that a properly functioning democracy requires careful consideration of the functioning and funding of political parties. One of my key proposals, for Democratic Equality Vouchers (DEV), would allow voters to exercise a degree of control and to contribute to the renewal of political parties, not only at election time but also on a year-by-year basis. But first we need to look more closely at the private funding of parties in all Western democracies.

No Limits, German Style

Let us begin with a perhaps unexpected case: Germany. France's neighbor across the Rhine offers an interesting and paradoxical example of a country that developed quite early an innovative and sophisticated system of public funding of political parties (and even of political foundations intended to inform public debate), but that has been unable, or unwilling, to limit private donations, especially from big business. In

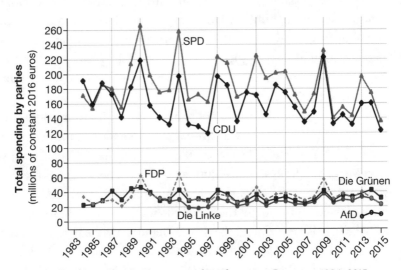

Figure 4. Total spending by the main political parties, Germany, 1984–2015
In 2015, the SPD spent 135.6 million euros. The vertical bars indicate the years of legislative elections in Germany, 1984–2015.

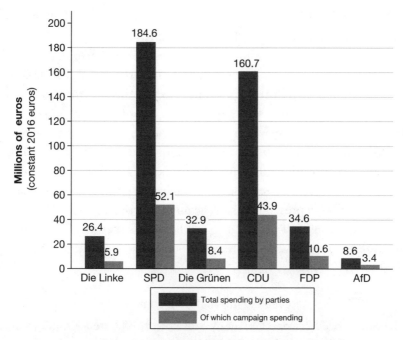

Figure 5. Total annual spending by the main political parties, including campaign spending for elections, Germany (annual averages calculated for the 1984–2015 period)

In the 1984–2015 period, the SPD spent an annual average of 184.6 million euros, of which 52.1 million euros went to election campaigns.

practice, this concerns donations mainly from the export sector, which may affect party policies on trade surpluses or on regulation of the auto industry through such measures as a ban on diesel.

In Germany, campaign spending by candidates and parties is not capped, any more than is the amount of donations that parties can receive. What is the effect of this on the costs of democracy? I shall concentrate here on the main German parties, from left to right: Die Linke (the post-Communist party), the Social Democratic Party (SPD), Die Grünen (the Greens), the Christian Democratic Union (CDU), the Free Democratic Party (FDP), and Alternative for Germany (AfD), the recently formed party of the German Far Right.[27] During the period from 1984 to 2015, each of these parties spent an average of more than 80 million euros a year, or 1.40 euros per adult German citizen (Figure 4).

We should distinguish the two main parties, the SPD and CDU, whose average annual spending for the period came very close to 173 million euros (or three euros per adult head of the population), from the "small" parties, which spent a little under 32 million euros a year. The AfD is a newcomer: its expenditure was low in 2015, but this will increase in the coming years because the party's high score in September 2017 (12.6 percent of the vote) will give it considerable access to public funding.

If we add up the spending of the five main parties, we find that an average of 476 million euros (or 7.87 euros per adult) was spent annually by the political parties in Germany over the past thirty years. Campaign spending represented a significant proportion of this—28 percent on average. Thus, out of the 184.6 million euros that the SPD spent in an average year, 51.2 million corresponded to campaign spending (Figure 5).

A Revealing International Comparison

The difference between Germany and both the United Kingdom and France—where spending is limited by law, especially in election periods—is striking on both the left and the right, particularly with regard to total annual spending. On average, the SPD spent 2.6 times more per annum than the French Socialist Party (PS) during the 2012–2016 period, and the difference was the same between the CDU and the French Républicains (Figure 6).[28] Nor is this pattern peculiar to the "large" parties, since the German Greens spent an annual average of 35.5 million euros during this period, or four times more than the French Greens (8.8 million euros).

Of course, Germany has a larger population than France, but this is by no means sufficient to explain the differences in spending. Per head of the adult population, the SPD's annual average spending during these years (2.40 euros) was twice as high as that of its French counterpart.

It should be noted that, relative to population size, the spending of Spanish parties is also very large, but that, as we shall see in Chapter 3, they receive comparatively little from private donations; the explanation for this is the generous public funding of political parties introduced in 1985. Thus, Spanish parties are among the biggest spenders per head of

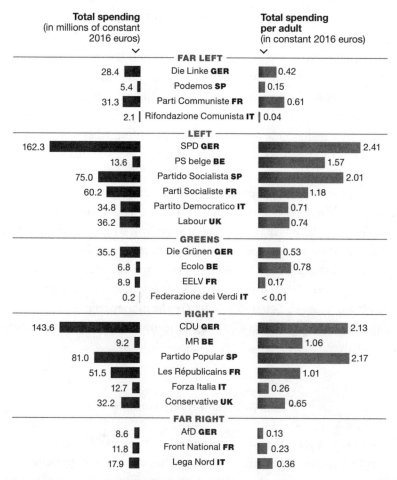

Total spending (in millions of constant 2016 euros)		Total spending per adult (in constant 2016 euros)
FAR LEFT		
28.4	Die Linke **GER**	0.42
5.4	Podemos **SP**	0.15
31.3	Parti Communiste **FR**	0.61
2.1	Rifondazione Comunista **IT**	0.04
LEFT		
162.3	SPD **GER**	2.41
13.6	PS belge **BE**	1.57
75.0	Partido Socialista **SP**	2.01
60.2	Parti Socialiste **FR**	1.18
34.8	Partito Democratico **IT**	0.71
36.2	Labour **UK**	0.74
GREENS		
35.5	Die Grünen **GER**	0.53
6.8	Ecolo **BE**	0.78
8.9	EELV **FR**	0.17
0.2	Federazione dei Verdi **IT**	< 0.01
RIGHT		
143.6	CDU **GER**	2.13
9.2	MR **BE**	1.06
81.0	Partido Popular **SP**	2.17
51.5	Les Républicains **FR**	1.01
12.7	Forza Italia **IT**	0.26
32.2	Conservative **UK**	0.65
FAR RIGHT		
8.6	AfD **GER**	0.13
11.8	Front National **FR**	0.23
17.9	Lega Nord **IT**	0.36

Figure 6. Annual spending by the main political parties (Germany, France, Italy, Spain, Belgium, and the United Kingdom), annual averages 2012–2016

the adult population (just after Germany), and this is true even on the right (the Partido Popular spends even more than the CDU). Of course, this includes election spending partly reimbursed by the state, which may distort the comparisons if we are not careful. In France, for instance, the fact that campaigns are candidate-led rather than party-led artificially reduces the spending costs borne by parties. What, then, is the picture in Spain if we separate out election spending? In 2015, the Spanish Socialist Party (Partido Socialista Obrero Español, PSOE) spent 87 million euros, of which roughly 30 percent (25 million) consisted of election expenses almost fully reimbursed by the state. All in all, apart from election expenditure, the average annual spending of the PSOE came to 61.8 million euros for the 2012–2016 period, or 1.66 euros per adult head of the population (much higher than the 1.20 euros of the French Socialist Party). Similarly, the nonelection spending of the Partido Popular averaged 60.8 million euros, or 1.80 euros per adult, whereas that of the Republicans in France did not average as much as 1.10 euros per annum during the period.

In sum, the rules governing relations between money and politics display a large difference between countries. What consequences does this have? To what extent are the divergent spending structures reflected in election campaigns, the election results of various parties, the renewal of political personnel, the emergence of new movements, and the public policies of governments? To answer these critically important questions, we first need to have a better idea of where the money comes from: public funding or private "generosity"? Clearly, the implications vary depending on the answer.

Public Funding, Private Funding

Elections cost a lot. Or rather, a number of Western democracies have chosen to allocate large, sometimes huge, sums of money to them. The differences among countries reflect their regulations governing the amount that candidates are permitted to spend; we have briefly indicated the situation in a selection of countries. But they also reflect different regulations governing what individuals and / or companies are permitted to donate. The next two chapters will focus on the private funding of democracy and examine in detail various national models. We shall see that the amounts and the players in question differ fundamentally from country to country. In Germany, the automaker Daimler gives each year with its left hand 100,000 euros to the SPD, and with its right hand the same sum to the CDU. Of course, this has nothing to do with Daimler's wish to avoid at all costs a legal ban on diesel in cities—heaven forbid! In France, companies are no longer permitted to donate to political parties; but when they were, a company such as Bouygues did not hesitate to show great liberality in its use of checkbooks, caring little about the political colors of recipients. Fifty shades of generosity.

National differences in the size of party spending ultimately reflect different ways of publicly funding democracy. We have seen, for example, that British political parties spend much less on average each year than their German counterparts. But this does not mean they are less captive to private interests—on the contrary. The Conservative Party receives annually more than 25 million euros in private donations, or 5 million more than the CDU in Germany (not in itself cause for complaint). But this simply indicates that the United Kingdom does not have a system for the public funding of political parties, whereas German parties receive, in addition to private donations, a generous public subsidy dependent on their past election successes.

In other words, a government that wishes to influence the direction of politics by means of private money and the injection of public funds has several weapons at its disposal. Let us now look at these in order, so that we can eventually give answers to the following questions. How much does the state spend each year to fund the political preferences of its citizens, and to what extent does the amount vary with their income? In countries where there is little regulation, does the massive injection of private money render public subsidies ineffectual? What are the actual consequences of the various models of funding? Do what we might call "market models" favor more conservative parties over movements more inclined to social protest? Do such models lead to unequal representation of people's political preferences and to skewed public policies? These questions urgently require answers, because in a number of countries today the public funding of democracy is under threat. In some cases it has already been abolished, with often dramatic consequences that include the development of self-perpetuating inequalities.

The aim of this book is to make readers more aware of current practices and to give them all the cards they need to choose the model most likely to restore the health of democratic systems. The key question is what reforms must be made without delay to curb the role of private money in our democracies—and to reestablish the fundamental principle of "one person, one vote." But please be patient: that will be addressed in Part Three.

2

The Private Funding of Democracy:
A System Designed for the Rich

Private Funding of Democracy: An Only Partly Regulated System—And for How Much Longer?

As long as there have been elections, there has been (often justified) fear of electoral fraud driven by corruption. Buying votes, buying politicians, manipulating the media: we did not have to wait for *House of Cards* and the delightful Frank Underwood to discover the possibilities open to ambitious people who embrace the morals of Shakespeare's Richard III. "Conscience is but a word that cowards use, / Devised at first to keep the strong in awe: / Our strong arms be our conscience, swords our law. / March on!" (or "En marche!" as Macron might say). So opines King Richard, a Machiavellian politician much given to elaborate thinking. It is a useful reminder from history.

And yet, in many countries it has taken a long, or even very long, time to regulate the private funding of democracy—that is, to limit the private contributions to the electoral process that are such a potent source of corruption. The United States was one of the earliest to regulate (partly to differentiate itself from the aristocratic, anti-democratic Old World) but also one of the earliest to undo what had been done. The first drive to curb corruption in federal elections goes back to 1867, when the Naval Appropriations Bill was introduced to prevent Navy officers and government employees from soliciting money from naval yard workers. Soon the regulation was extended: it became illegal for government employees to solicit or make donations for federal elections,[1] and in 1907 the Tillman Act prohibited corporate funding of national election campaigns.[2] But the limits also soon became apparent—particularly in the absence of a regulatory authority.[3]

The Semblance of Legislation in the United States

Still today, direct corporate contributions to election campaigns are illegal in the United States. Individual donations are permitted, however. In principle, individual donations to federal election campaigns—or, more precisely, to a candidate's local committee—are capped at $2,700 per election. But citizens may also contribute up to $5,000 a year to political action committees (PACs), private organizations that play an extremely important role in American political life, either by supporting a candidate or often, on the contrary, by "destroying" one.[4] In addition, they may donate as much as $10,000 a year to local party committees and $33,900 to national political parties. And finally, they are permitted to show their generosity by contributing up to $101,700 to other national party committees, particularly in the framework of national conventions or the construction of party offices.[5] All in all, therefore, an individual is authorized to spend tens of thousands of dollars a year promoting his or her ideas in the American electoral arena.

Not only are these high thresholds; the system does not even function anymore, since the limits have lost all meaning because of the existence of "super PACs" (pressure groups that escape any ceiling and can receive unlimited donations even from companies). As a result, election spending in the United States today runs into the billions. In 2016 and 2017, an annual average of 11.50 euros per adult American went to election spending. These "super PACs" are not unrelated to the recent distortions of American democracy, which has been captured by what one is tempted to describe as a "caste." These distortions affect both the Republicans and the Democrats, leaving the door wide open to populist candidates eager to denounce the subjection of elites to powerful moneyed interests. We shall return to this in Chapter 7. But before we examine these latest aberrations and the way in which "super PACs" have succeeded in almost totally destroying the US regulatory system, let us continue our overview of how various countries regulate (or fail to regulate) private political funding.

The United Kingdom and Germany: Deregulated Democracy

In the United Kingdom election spending has been regulated for decades, but the same is not true of donations. Thus, Patrick H. Gregory could freely donate the modest sum of £1 million to the Conservative Party in August 2017, eclipsing Michael Davis and the check for £508,000 he had signed a few weeks earlier. Let us hope that Davis's appointment as chief executive officer of the party (in June 2017) has given him sufficient comfort. Or perhaps he has received it from his fellow donor David E. D. Brownlow, a self-styled "entrepreneur and philanthropist," whose donation of £566,750 to the party coffers in June 2017 was surely unrelated to his appointment as "vice-chairman responsible for campaigning and incumbency."

"So what?" you may ask. So what if a company such as JCB, which makes agricultural and construction machinery, including for the government and defense, gave £1.5 million to the Conservative Party in May 2017? All individuals and all companies are free to express their political preferences, and who am I to see such donations as a backstairs way up the political ladder? They are transparent, after all.

So what if Philip Morris Gmbh, the German branch of the American tobacco giant, gives money nearly every year not only to the Christian Democratic Union (CDU) but also to the CSU (Christian Social Union) and Free Democratic Party (FDP), and (regularly enough) even to the Social Democratic Party (SPD)? Between 2001 and 2015, it allocated close to 900,000 euros to the funding of German political life.[6] Who could see the slightest link with the long-drawn-out debate on the kind of tobacco advertising ban that has been in place for many years in most other European countries? Did I hear the word "lobby"? Who could think there was the slightest connection with the Filtergate scandal? While the tobacco industry regularly sponsors party congresses in Germany, the world's largest cigarette corporations—including Philip Morris—have been sued for falsifying test results by means of tiny holes in filters that artificially lower tar or nicotine readings.

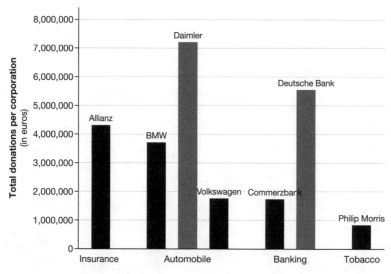

Figure 7. Sums donated by selected corporations by industrial sector, to the main German parties, 2000–2015

And what of the 1.8 million euros that Volkswagen paid to German political parties between 2000 and 2015, or BMW's 3.7 million, or Daimler's 7.2 million?[7] How could that have anything to do with Dieselgate, an example of fixing in the auto industry? We can be glad that such donations no longer (entirely) protect the industry from legal action, but they do mean that German automakers have privileged access to the corridors of power.

Figure 7 presents a few examples of the close relations between industry and politics that corporate party funding perpetuates in Germany. The size of the contributions is certainly striking. In Chapter 7 I shall examine these dangerous liaisons at much greater length.

France: Late Regulation

In France, where virtually nothing was done until the late 1980s, a number of laws have been passed since 1988 to cap the private funding of politics and, as a quid pro quo, to allow for forms of public funding.[8] In 1990, the newly formed National Commission on Campaign Accounts and Political Funding (CNCCFP) was assigned to check and approve the accounts of political parties and campaigns.[9] This is the body that regularly features in the media when journalists pore over the election expenses of candidates—from the private jets of the independent Pyrenean candidate Jean Lassalle to the communication expenditure of Sarkozy's former prime minister, François Fillon.

Until 1988, political parties were simple associations in the sense of the law of 1901 "relating to contracts of association."[10] They could receive membership dues but not donations or bequests (only associations of "public utility" were entitled to those).[11] Officially at least, although there was no legal ceiling on the election expenses of candidates, the relative "poverty" of parties meant that, on paper, they had to make do with the scant dues contributed by their members. The exception was the Communist Party (and to a lesser degree the Socialist Party): it was a comparatively well-off party thanks to its mass membership (who paid a fixed 1 percent of their income) and thanks to its members elected to public office, who handed over all their allowances to the party and received an income from it in return.

I said that this was how things happened "on paper," because under the Fifth Republic secret government allocations, employers' money, and many a slush fund have never ceased to oil the wheels of political life; I can only suggest that readers nostalgic for the Giscard years of the 1970s should dip into André Campana's book *L'Argent secret* (Secret Money).[12] To be sure, it tells us more about "money power" than disco glitter balls, but in those days, if you wanted to be number one, it was good if you could count on friends at the top. It's the same now. We may smile at the financial woes of Bouygues Construction in the Chanteloup-les-Vignes housing development project—the company paid kickbacks worth 5 million new francs in the 1970s to the ruling Union of Democrats for the Republic (UDR) party, without eventually winning the contract—but the Libyan financing of Sarkozy's presidential campaign in 2007 involved sums no less substantial. As for today, I will say nothing here about the suspicions of corruption hanging over the Bolloré Group, in relation to a little helping hand with elections (under-invoiced advisory and communication missions) in return for port concessions in Togo and Guinea-Conakry.

But I am getting ahead of myself. A lot of water has flowed under the bridges—including those on the Danube—since the old days when the

French employers' association went by the name of CNPF (Conseil National du Patronat Français).[13] In particular, political parties have finally acquired a real legal existence as far as financing arrangements are concerned. Since 1988, a party defined as an "association" under the law of 1901 has been subject to the law of March 11, 1988, governing the financial transparency of political life.[14] In France, only political parties coming under the law of March 11, 1988, are authorized to finance a candidate in an election.

Furthermore, not only do the laws of 1988 and January 15, 1990, provide for a system of (direct and indirect) public funding of democracy; they also lay down a structure for its private funding, authorizing individual and corporate donations to election candidates but also limiting their amount. Thus, by the end of the 1980s, an individual was permitted to donate up to 30,000 francs to a candidate in any given year (roughly 7,300 euros in today's money, adjusted for inflation), and a company up to 50,000 francs (or roughly 12,000 euros). As to political parties, the ceiling was 50,000 francs for an individual and 500,000 francs for a company. And it is certainly the case that companies contributed generously to the funding of political life between 1990 and 1995.

Today, corporate donations to election campaigns and political parties are forbidden by law, while individual donations to political parties and groups are capped at 7,500 euros a year.[15] Donations to election campaigns—whether presidential, legislative, or municipal—are limited to 4,600 euros per election. These sums may appear low, especially in international terms (my colleagues in North America, used to campaign funding in the millions, cannot help smiling when I mention them), but, as we shall see, they result in hugely unequal participation in our democratic system. Who can afford to spare a few thousand euros for the expression of their political preferences? Since the "price of a vote" is only a few dozen euros (as we shall see in Chapter 8), a campaign donation of 4,600 euros may end up having a significant impact on an election. Finally, let us note that in an election year such as 2017, a citizen in France was able to devote as much as 21,300 euros to the defense of his or her political interests. First, 7,500 euros could be given to a political party, then 4,600 euros to a candidate in the presidential election, another 4,600 to a candidate in the legislative elections, and yet another 4,600 to a candidate in the elections for the Senate.

Belgium: Waves of Reform to Stop the Waves?

In Belgium, donations by private individuals could not reach such heights. Although the regulation of private funding was introduced at roughly the same time as in France—through the Law of July 4, 1989, on the limitation and monitoring of election spending, and the funding and transparent accounting of political parties—the thresholds today are much more restrictive there.[16]

As in France, companies are not permitted to make donations to political parties. Individuals cannot donate more than 500 euros a year to a party, and the total of all their contributions must not exceed 2,000 euros. It is therefore one of the strictest systems in the world regulating the private funding of democracy. It is also consistent with the low ceiling on campaign spending by candidates and political parties, since there would not be much point in authorizing higher limits for donations if the recipients could not make full use of the extra money. It is the British system—a ceiling on expenditure but none at all on donations—that raises questions about its consistency. Clearly, the regulatory systems in various countries were never designed in a consistent and comparative manner. It is time for their citizens to take the matter in hand.

Unevenness in the Private Funding of Democracy

In Belgium, 2,000 euros, in France, 7,500: Is that a lot or very little? Many would be inclined to say they are small sums—either to applaud the healthiness of French-style democracy as opposed to American distortions or, on the contrary, to rail against the lack of funding for political organizations in the electoral contest. "An election is not cheap": such is the constant refrain of those who oppose any cap on the funding of political democracy in France. You cannot campaign without serious money, they say; the first task in informing citizens is to spend enough to convince their "available brain time" of the benefits of your program.

How can you convince people without spending millions? And if the most you have coming in is 7,500 euros at a time, it will take a while to get enough together. But is 7,500 euros really so little? It depends on your point of view, of course. For example, the net minimum wage for someone on a thirty-five-hour week in France comes to 1,142 euros a month or 13,704 euros a year; the spending limit of 7,500 euros would therefore represent more than half their total annual income. It is hard to see how they could ever make full use of the opportunity given to them to contribute to the democratic process.

The sum of 7,500 euros is also more than four times the monthly median wage in France.[17] It is no easier to imagine any citizen, even the most committed, spending more than a third of their annual income on the political process!

Yet it is very often the average voter whom our politicians address when they claim that their decisions maximize the public utility. Those who fulminate against the low ceiling on donations are therefore often the very first to claim they are thinking along the same lines as multiple small donors. For the political process looks nicer with the illusion of an equal mass of voters, each contributing to it according to their means. On the posters, Madame Michu, Mrs. Average, wins hands down against Liliane Bettencourt, the archetypal billionaire heiress—just as few would prefer Gaddafi to the clownish, good-natured Monsieur Hulot.

On the posters, okay, but in reality? If we look for a moment at Emmanuel Macron's presidential campaign, what do we find? While small donors appear on his posters (30,000 private individuals gave money), only a handful of generous (and wealthy) sponsors set the rules of the game. On the one hand, a third of contributions to his En Marche! movement were apparently below thirty euros and two-thirds below sixty euros, the median sum being fifty euros.[18] On the other hand, only 2 percent of the donations were above 5,000 euros—the only problem being that 2 percent of 30,000 donors translates into 600 rich donors, who gave between 3 and 4.5 million euros.[19] In other words, 2 percent of donors accounted for 40 to 60 percent of the 7.5 million euros in donations that the movement received. We would like to give more precise figures, but that is not possible; the parties in the new world blossoming before us do not shine with greater transparency than those in the old world. It is also tempting to say, through gritted teeth, that these 2 percent of generous donors got their money's worth; for a modest outlay of 2,500 euros (once allowance is made for tax write-offs), the hundred wealthiest French men and women gained an average tax reduction of 1.5 million euros a year under the Macron presidency, in just the first few months of his five-year term.[20] That represents a return of nearly 60,000 percent on their investment, for those who decided to contribute to his campaign.

In this respect, rich people in France have no reason to be envious of their American counterparts, who have also just pocketed one of the largest tax cuts in history, benefiting only large corporations and the wealthiest 1 percent of the population.[21]

A System for the Most Privileged

The Unjust French Tax Rules on Donations and Membership Fees

In France, donations to political campaigns and parties also give rise to "gift receipts" entitling the donors to a tax write-off, since they are considered as donations to public interest entities (the entity in question here being the "fiscal agent" or the "electoral finance association for the benefit of a political party or group with one or more candidates").[22] The tax reduction is equal to 66 percent of the donated sum, provided that this sum is no higher than 20 percent of the donor's taxable income. If it rises above that level, the excess is carried forward to the following five years and entitles the donor to a tax reduction on the same terms.

Of course, to benefit from a tax reduction, the donor must also be liable to income tax.[23] Let us be clear, then, about how the tax reduction is actually calculated. Take a person with a taxable income of 100,000 euros who has donated a total of 6,000 euros to political parties (where the ceiling is 7,500 euros). This donation is comfortably within the limit of 20 percent taxable income (in this case, 20,000 euros). Since the total donation is well below this dual ceiling, the tax reduction applies in full and comes to $6,000 \times 66$ percent = 3,960 euros. In other words, the real cost of the political donations for this individual with a gross income of

100,000 euros is only 6,000–3,960 = 2,040 euros. The rest is covered by the state—that is, by taxpayers as a whole.

What would be the cost for an individual with a gross income below 9,700 euros (the entry threshold for the first bracket of the tax scale applicable to a share of the family quotient) who decides to make a donation of 6,000 euros? The answer is 6,000 euros—because, being exempt from income tax, he or she cannot be entitled to any tax reduction (apart from the fact that the ceiling of 20 percent of taxable income would anyway mean that the individual cannot benefit in full from the reduction). If we then consider that low-income households make up more than a half of the total in France, the example is far from simply anecdotal.

Let us put this in another way. The present system is such that the rich actually pay out only a third of the donations they make to the parties or candidates of their choice; the rest is covered by the state—that is, by money from our taxes (particularly value-added tax [VAT] and other indirect taxes, which everyone has to pay). However, the least well-off citizens—and this is the ultimate paradox—pay every cent of their political contributions. The present French system of tax relief covers not only donations to candidates and political parties but also the dues paid by party members.[24] In other words, the poorest half of French people cannot have part of their dues offset through the tax system, whereas the other half, who are liable to income tax, have a right to be reimbursed. This nullifies—or even reverses—the effect of the sliding scale of subscriptions that many parties operate. In the Green party, Europe Écologie–Les Verts (EELV), for example, the monthly subscription is 36 euros for those without secure employment, whether students or others whose income is below 1,200 euros a month. The real cost for people in these groups is therefore 36 euros. For members who earn 1,500 euros a month, the subscription is 100 euros—but the real cost, once their 66 percent tax relief is taken into account, is 34 euros. As to parties that levy a uniform or almost uniform subscription, the effect is that it works out two-thirds cheaper for taxpayers than for members not liable to income tax. Public policy therefore completely counteracts the attempts of parties to democratize their membership profile. It is a cockeyed system if ever there was one.

Finally, we should note that tax relief applies not only to membership dues but also to the contributions of elected party members—or, in the language of the Finance Ministry, "contributions paid by the holders of national or local elective office." In fact, the reduction is much more flexible in their case, since their contributions are not subject to the ceiling of 7,500 euros. Individuals in elective office who declare their income as part of a couple can claim relief up to 66 percent of their contributions, with a ceiling of 15,000 euros *per taxable household*. A senator, for example, living mainly on allowances from the state, can claim a tax reduction of 10,000 euros by virtue of the contributions that she decides to make to her own party—under a law that conforms to very personal interests.

Thus, the public funding of political life is much less substantial for the millions of low earners than it is for the better-off sections of French society. With respect to donations to political parties, the state spends twenty-one times more in tax relief to the wealthiest 1 percent of the population than to the least well-off half of taxpayers. It is a scandalous state of affairs, especially as this profoundly unjust system applies not only to political funding but to all donations, including those to media interest groups such as Presse et Pluralisme or J'aime l'Info. This is why in 2015, in my book *Saving the Media*, I argued for a "British-style" system of matching contributions for donations to not-for-profit media outlets, whereby the state would pay the equivalent of tax benefits directly to political foundations.[25] I shall return to this idea in Chapter 10, with a wider application to the funding of political parties.

Interestingly, trade union membership dues are an exception insofar as those who pay them receive a tax credit. The tax credit associated with "trade union dues for wage-earners and pensioners" carries the same benefit for taxable and nontaxable households, since those who pay no income tax (and therefore receive no rebate) are nevertheless entitled to a check from the tax authorities. The tax credit linked to union dues is equivalent to 66 percent of the sum in question. However, the contributions taken into account cannot exceed 1 percent of the person's net taxable income, so that, once again, the least well-off cannot benefit as much as the rich from the credit. In fact, for a taxpayer earning 50,000 euros in net taxable income and paying 300 euros in membership subscriptions (less than 1 percent of his salary), the amount of the tax credit is 300×66 percent $= 198$ euros. His contribution therefore costs him only 102 euros. But for a taxpayer with net taxable earnings of 20,000 euros and paying 300 euros in membership subscriptions, the tax credit is only 200 euros $\times$ 66 percent $= 132$ euros (since his contribution qualifies for tax relief only up to 1 percent of his income $= 200$ euros). In the end, his contribution costs 168 euros, against 102 euros for the taxpayer with an income 2.5 times greater.

So in France, the poorer you are, the more you pay to participate in social and political democracy. Has the time not come for a change?

Widespread Inequality

Unfortunately, this inequality in the state funding of political preferences is by no means specific to France. In Canada, the Political Contribution Tax Credit, first introduced in 2004, is really a tax rebate rather than a tax credit, so that only households liable to income tax can benefit from it.[26] As a result, those in the highest income groups do not pay the full cost of their donations to political parties, whereas the least well-off do precisely that. And things are the same in Italy, Spain, and Germany.[27] The system is particularly startling in Italy, where party membership dues do not involve an entitlement to tax relief, but the political contributions of those holding elective office do.[28] (The only exception here is the United States, where donations to political parties and campaigns create no entitlement to tax relief.[29])

In some cases, however, measures have been taken in favor of small donations. In Spain, the first 150 euros of donations carry tax relief of 75 percent, whereas the reduction is only 30 percent for donations above 150 euros (with a ceiling of 10 percent of the net taxable base).[30] Similarly, in Germany tax relief applies only to small donations, and in addition there is a top-up system whereby political parties receive 0.45 euros for every euro donated per person per year, up to a limit of 3,300 euros. Thus, an individual who donates 3,300 euros to a party actually adds 4,785 euros to its coffers (once the state's automatic contribution is taken into account). For some parties, this system of top-ups accounts for more than half of their direct public funding, the other half depending on their share of the vote in the last elections. (We shall look in

Chapter 5 at different public funding models and at the amounts at stake.) Such incentives encourage small donations—which may be thought of as a good thing—but they still do not extend to the least well-off donors.

Of course, there are more extreme systems that favor the highest income groups more than the Canadian, Italian, French, Spanish, or German system does. But is that the direction in which we want to go? In Brazil, for example, at least until the year 2015, there was no fixed ceiling on the sums that citizens or companies were allowed to donate. No absolute figure. Companies could donate up to 2 percent of the gross value of their sales during the year preceding an election. Large corporations could therefore contribute a lot to the funding of elections—but not small firms. And the more money a corporation made, the more it could contribute. A strange approach to democracy! Corporate political donations have been prohibited since 2015 and the eruption of the Petrobras scandal.[31] But where does that leave individual donations?

In Brazil today, the richest sections of society are allowed by law to give more than the poorest. *By law.* Donations are capped at 10 percent of gross income during the year preceding the election—which means that a citizen earning 10 million euros can give as much as 1 million euros, while a citizen earning 13,000 euros (the country's median income) cannot give more than 1,300 euros. Why were the inequalities not reduced in Brazil, even under Lula?[32] Perhaps what has just been said provides a part of the explanation.

All the attention is now on Petrobras and the prison sentence handed down on Lula. No doubt the system of kickbacks operated by the oil giant in the 2000s, which played a large role in political funding, was nothing short of a scandal. However, the whole system of funding democracy in Brazil is a problem that needs root-and-branch reform; a ban on corporate donations was a first necessary step, but it is necessary to go further. The establishment in 2017 of a public fund to finance election campaigns is an excellent measure that should certainly be applauded in a global context in which, as we shall see, many democracies are doing away with the public funding of their political life. But much remains to be done, especially moves to set new rules for individual donations to election campaigns.

What If Everyone Were to Donate?

I hope the reader is now convinced that the fiscal measures applicable in many democracies to donations to political parties and election campaigns are unfair. One natural reaction might be to ask why tax rebates should not simply be converted into equal tax credits for all households, whether or not they are liable to pay income tax. This would seem to be a minimum reform, which would cancel the regressive character of the present system under which the poorer you are, the more you pay.

The problem is the following. If we take the case of France, the existing system has been devised with a limited number of political contributors in mind. If all French men and women chose to donate as much as the rich do today (and we shall see in the next chapter that the great majority do not make any donations, while those with the greatest wealth give enormous sums), or, more generally, if a new system allowed everyone in France to benefit from a public contribution in the way that rich people do today for their political activities, then the system would simply not be financially viable. Let us imagine for a moment that each of the 37 million households benefited from a public contribution of 5,000 euros (the amount of the tax rebate currently received by those who donate the permitted maximum of 7,500 euros per party). The total cost to the treasury would then be 165 billion euros, more than three times the national education budget. And even if spending per household was only 200 euros (the size of the tax rebate corresponding to the average donation of 300 euros in the present system), the total cost would still be 7.3 billion euros, or virtually the entire higher education budget.

If the system is to be made more equal, it needs to be modified as a whole. We might be tempted to call the current system hypocritical, because it claims to work for "everyone" but was in fact designed for the few. Only a deeper, egalitarian overhaul would get us out of this hypocrisy: such is the idea behind my proposal for Democratic Equality Vouchers (DEVs), which I shall present in detail in Chapter 10. For the moment, let us continue with our tour of the world.

The Hypocrisy of Italian-Style "Democracy out of Taxation"

Plutocracy through the Tax System

In Italy, this unjust system of tax reductions is combined with an even more unjust "two per thousand" system. Citizens can devote two-thousandths (0.2 percent) of their total tax liability to the political party of their choice; all they have to do, at the end of their tax return, is fill in the "sheet specifying the destination of the 8 per thousand, 5 per thousand, and 2 per thousand." There are three figures—8, 5, and 2—because in Italy the taxpayer has not one or two but three decisions to make with regard to the proper use of public funds. The first concerns religion (8 per thousand, or four times more than politics: who said the Church does not engage in politics in Italy?); the second concerns research, heritage funding, or sporting activities (5 per thousand); and the third (2 per thousand) concerns political parties.[33] Do you want two thousandths of your taxes to be distributed to a political party? Well, it is enough to place your chosen party's code (A20 for the Democratic Center, for example) in the correct box and to sign on the dotted line. The only condition, of course, is that your wish to do this is strong enough for you to take the trouble to find the list of codes (fewer than thirty, but findable only at the end [p. 123!] of the explanatory notes on your tax return published online by the tax authorities). Good luck to you. I wouldn't like to be in the shoes of an Italian Thomas Thévenoud, the French former Socialist Party minister convicted of "omissions" in his tax return and given a one-year suspended jail sentence.[34]

Two percent of your taxes: that's not just a trifling one or two euros. The amount depends on your tax bill, which means on your total income. The richer a citizen you are in Italy, the more the state offers you the possibility to fund *gratis* the political party of your choice. And there is no ceiling on the amount a single individual can donate with this mechanism; the only limit is the "2 per thousand," which means that a wealthy businessman who pays a million euros a year in taxes can, if he wishes, get the state to hand over 2,000 euros to the political party of his choice. Conversely, a low-grade employee who pays 1,000 euros in taxes can allocate a mere 2 euros of public money to his preferred party, and someone below the threshold for income tax can allocate nothing at all. Zero: that's really not much. In other words, if a committed citizen wants to dip into his pocket to support his political preferences, he can do so, generously, since the state will pay for him. All he has to do is be rich enough. And the richer he is, the more the state—that is, all other citizens—will pay for him.

I do not know why economists insist on teaching their first-year students that you never get anything for nothing—or, in their inimitable language, that there's no such thing as a free lunch. To begin with, it is factually untrue: there is such a thing as a free lunch, particularly for the most affluent citizens, and sometimes they receive the blessing of a good number of economists. Just read Tancrède Voituriez's *L'Invention de la pauvreté* (The Invention of Poverty, 2013), which provides a hilarious description of the profession. And there are the constantly perfected systems of tax deduction, relief, or credit, often established on the pretext of encouraging generosity, which enable the superrich to fund all their preferences for free on the backs of the least well off. It is as if by definition a rich man's preference—because his success indicates superior abilities—was worth more than a poor man's; as if the lead climber's rightful task was to set the direction, pulling the others up behind. Anyway, what is the point of reducing poverty?

So, Italy's "2 per thousand" system invented the dual vote. Each citizen gets to vote twice: once at the ballot box, where it's one person, one vote; and once on their tax form, where it's one euro, one vote. It's a pity this was not explained more clearly during the debates that preceded its introduction—a pity, above all, that none of its jubilant initiators thought of pointing out that it effectively deprives a quarter of Italians of their second "vote," since the amount they pay in taxes is zero. Two-thousandths of zero: that means you get no vote. Doubtless none of the lawmakers was in that situation.

Some speak of "tax democracy," a sort of freedom granted to citizens outside election periods to express their preferences on an annual basis, rather than every four or five years. I would be more inclined to call this a system of "tax plutocracy": an electoral farce. Writing in *Songs of Twilight* in the 1830s, Victor Hugo conjured up "Foul-breathed, black-nailed censorship / The low-browed hound that follows all power." The context has changed, but how can we not be struck by such trends? On the pretext of "fairness" and "tax democracy," they have led to a new kind of disfranchisement by skillfully muzzling the preferences of the "have-nothings," of the jobless, incomeless, paperless, and now voteless—a twilight of democracy that paves the way for right-wing populism.

This does not mean that I am against allowing taxpayers to choose each year the parties they wish to support, instead of linking public money to the results of past elections. Our contemporary democracies suffer from funding systems that skew the political contest in advance. Recent experiments (such as Italy's "2 per thousand") have a huge potential to go awry, but I am convinced that it is possible to draw some useful lessons from them, so long as citizens get involved in this key debate and do not let themselves be intimidated by its seemingly technical nature. The proposal I make at the end of this book is meant to point in this direction, by allowing all citizens to specify, on each year's tax return, the sum that they wish to allocate to the political party of their choice. The Italian example shows that this would be very easy for the tax authorities to implement. But the essential point is that this annual choice should be made on a footing of equality: one person, one euro, one vote. There is no reason why some citizens should have more "votes" than others because they are better off financially—indeed, it is extremely harmful; nor is there any reason why everyone else should pay out of their taxes for the rich to have those extra "votes."

The "2 per Thousand" in Figures

Let us return to the way in which the Italian system functions. How much money does it involve? Little. For very few citizens choose the "2 per thousand." On average, between 2015 and 2017, only 2.7 percent of taxpayers (slightly more than 1.1 million individuals) put a cross in the famous box that allowed them to fund the party of their choice (Figure 8).[35] All in all, the system cost only 15.3 million euros in 2017 (a little under twelve euros per taxpayer who used the system). It is hard to understand why the take-up was so low, when the act of checking the box did not cost the taxpayer anything! Not to check it meant forgoing the opportunity to fund a party free of charge, when others were doing this with money raised from all taxpayers, including those who left the

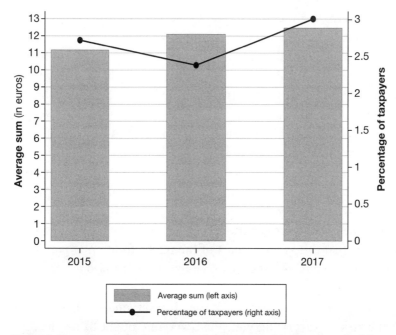

Figure 8. "2 per thousand": Percentage of taxpayers and average size of public subsidy, Italy, 2015–2017

In 2015, 2.72 percent of Italian taxpayers (1.1 million) checked the "2 per thousand" box on the tax return. The average public subsidy they thereby allocated to their chosen political parties was 11.20 euros.

box empty. This probably has to do with the general lack of trust in political parties, which is even stronger in Italy than elsewhere in Europe.[36] In fact, a referendum took place in 1993 to put an end to the public funding of parties in Italy. Not only did 90.3 percent vote to end it, but more than three-quarters of voters turned out on the day.[37] What should we conclude? It would probably be better to allocate less money per taxpayer to such systems of public funding, but to do so on a basis that is much more egalitarian, democratic, and participatory.

Surprising though it is that so few Italians take advantage of this system, the truth—and the hypocrisy—is that it is not actually designed for all Italians to use it. In fact, the intention is that only a tiny minority will take the opportunity it presents. When it was first implemented, the state set an upper limit to the amount it would allocate to parties each year.[38] Yet in 2015 the total amount paid out by Italian taxpayers (12.4 million euros) exceeded the legal limit of 9.6 million euros—a limit that now stands at 25.1 million euros. When divided among 40.7 million taxpayers, these 25.1 million euros are the equivalent of 0.62 euros per Italian! And that means not two-thousandths of the income tax total, but 0.136 of one-thousandth.

The truth is that this system was dreamed up by and for a minority. We can see this more clearly if we calculate what would be its cost if things were different. The total amount of income tax paid by all Italians is today 183,203 million euros. So, if everyone used the "2 per thousand," it would involve the state in spending roughly 370 million euros a year—nearly fifteen times more than the limit that the law allows. And we know that this is only a part of the public funding of political life, since tax expenditure linked to donations to parties also needs to be factored in.

This system is not meant to be used by everyone, but I would argue, at the risk of surprising you, that everyone ought to use it: that is, everyone should use today's system for want of anything better, but also make use tomorrow of the Democratic Equality Vouchers system outlined in Chapter 10, which will allow every citizen, regardless of income, to give the same sum to the political party of his or her choice. I understand the widespread lack of trust in political parties. But it is important to stress that failure to use the system, once it exists, is the worst of solutions. After all, those who put it in place do use it—to their own advantage. If, as a citizen, you think it is more urgent today to fund schools or hospitals than political parties in Italy, you may be right in principle, but you are on the wrong track in terms of method. You risk opening the way for the election of political parties that, partly thanks to this system, would prefer to cut public spending rather than promote social expenditure and progressive taxation. Similarly, an end to public funding would be the worst response to the downward spiral of our democracies, which are being drowned beneath a flood of private money. What is needed, on the contrary, is to break the hold of private money over the electoral process and to replace it with sizable, even-handed public funding.

Who Profits from the Crime?

The "2 per thousand" system is extremely unequal. Which parties has it benefited most? Or rather, which party? The answer is that the reform has benefited the party that introduced it, the Democratic Party; 51 percent of the taxpayers who used the "2 per thousand" between 2015 and 2017 chose it against other parties. Figure 9 shows the percentage of taxpayers who chose each of the thirty parties that benefited from the system. Far behind those supporting the Democratic Party, 13 percent of the taxpayers who used the "2 per thousand" system allocated their donation to the Northern League, followed by the Sinistra Ecologia Libertà (SEL, Left, Ecology, Liberty) party.

It is also interesting to note that the Democratic Party profited twice over from the "2 per thousand" system. As Figure 10 clearly shows, the taxpayers who chose it were better-off than the average, with the result that not 51 percent but 54 percent of the total sum allocated under the

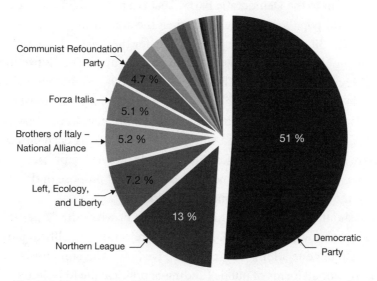

Figure 9. "2 per thousand": Percentage of taxpayers represented by each party, Italy, 2015–2017

Between 2015 and 2017, 51 percent of the taxpayers who checked the "2 per thousand" box on their tax returns chose the Democratic Party and 13 percent the Northern League.

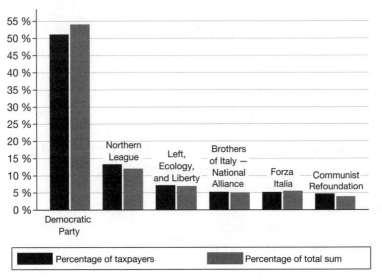

Figure 10. "2 per thousand": Percentage of taxpayers and percentage of total sum represented by each party, Italy, 2015–2017

system went to the Democratic Party. That is a much higher figure than its electoral popularity at the time when the system was introduced (a little under 30 percent of the popular vote for the 2008–2013 period).

But should we be blaming the Democratic Party? The "2 per thousand" is certainly imperfect, but it is an innovative system that makes it possible to annualize the public funding of parties, whereas most other models, including the French, freeze this at a moment in the past. And the tax return is a simple and efficient means of asking each citizen to declare his or her preferences, while naturally preserving privacy. As we shall see, the Democratic Equality Vouchers that I propose in this book take some of their technical inspiration from it.

We should also recall the historical moment when the "2 per thousand" system was introduced. In 2014, the rejection of political parties in Italy had gone a long way, and the Five Stars Movement was campaigning for all forms of public funding of political life to be jettisoned. In fact, as we can tell from its absence in Figures 9 and 10, Italian taxpayers are unable to allocate their "2 per thousand" to the Five Stars Movement. Opposed since its creation to the public funding of parties, this movement refuses to take advantage of the "2 per thousand," while encouraging all Italian taxpayers not to use this system. At the same time, its rejection of the "2 per thousand" means that the Five Stars Movement does not have to meet the requirements under Articles 3, 4, and 5 of Law No. 149/2013 that its statutes should be democratic and transparent. More generally, this strange "2 per thousand" system stems from the mood of discouragement and fatalism that gripped Italy after the collapse of the First Republic in 1992 (as we shall see in Chapter 6, when we examine the lost opportunities opened up by systems of direct public funding of parties).

The main defect of the "2 per thousand"—and it is not unimportant—is that it makes each person's contributions dependent on his or her income level. What should really take its place is a public funding system that equalizes the votes of all citizens: the Democratic Equality Vouchers. But it was better to establish the "2 per thousand" than to give in to popular pressure by excluding any public funding of Italian political life and leaving a little more of it captive to private money.

Let us recapitulate. On the one hand, in many countries today, the private funding of democracy is highly unregulated. In particular, there is no upper limit on private donations to political parties and campaigns, and often no limit on corporate contributions either. The result? As we shall see in the next chapter, the logical outcome in these deregulated democracies is extremely high levels of private funding (tens of millions of euros) and their unequal distribution among the various parties. Historically, the most conservative parties have benefited the most, while the more progressive parties that benefit from it today often do so at the cost of abandoning their struggle to defend the working classes. In some countries, moreover, large-scale private funding nullifies all efforts to use public funding to make the democratic system more equal and representative.

On the other hand, rather late in the day, a number of countries such as France have introduced much stricter controls on the private funding of political life and on levels of election expenditure. These systems are far from perfect, however, and they work more to the advantage of the richest sections of society. We shall now try to quantify these defects.

3

The Realities of Private Funding:
When the Taxes of the Many Pay for the
Conservative Preferences of the Few

The Private Funding of Democracy by Income Level, or the
Regressive Redistribution of Our Tax Money

We have seen that, all around the world, tax relief systems associated with private political donations have been designed with a minority in mind, and that they have an unfortunate tendency to favor the richest sections of society. But who actually contributes how much to the private funding of political parties? How does the size of donations to political parties vary with income level?

To answer these questions, I have used extremely detailed fiscal data. Since 2013, French tax returns allow us to differentiate "donations and membership dues paid to political parties" from other donations.[1] I am therefore in a position, for the 2013–2016 period, to study precisely the characteristics of taxpayers who participate in the private funding of democracy, and above all to calculate the fiscal expenditure associated with it. In other words, I am able to calculate how much public money the state spends each year to satisfy the political preferences of citizens in accordance with their income levels. And the results are edifying. I will explain them in some detail—perhaps more than readers outside France would need. But the French data are unique, and important lessons can be drawn from them as to how unequal the public as well as the private funding of parties and elections is in Western democracies.

A Handful of Donors Contribute Tens of Millions of Euros

On average, the total donations to political parties declared each year to the French tax authorities amount to 101 million euros—that is, 1.5 times more than the direct public funding of political parties.

The total amount of donations dipped from 128.8 million euros in 2013 to 79.9 million in 2016. But we should bear in mind that 2013 was a special year because of the so-called "Sarkothon," the major fundraising campaign waged by Nicolas Sarkozy's Union for a Popular Movement (UMP) party following the rejection of his accounts (discussed further below). The drop between then and 2016 reflects a decline both in the number of tax households declaring at least one donation and in the average size of donations (Figure 11). The number of donors fell from 414,000 in 2013 to 291,000 in 2016.[2] The latter figure represents barely 0.79 percent of tax households. Yet the money they give to political parties

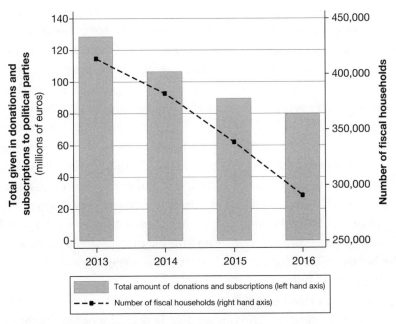

Figure 11. Donations and membership dues paid to political parties: Total sums given and total number of fiscal households, France, 2013–2016

In 2013, 413,757 taxpayers declared at least one donation or subscription to a political party. The total sum given in donations and subscriptions comes to 128.5 million euros.

is 1.5 times higher than the amount of public funding; or, scaled to the number of taxpayers, the private spending of the 291,000 donors is more than 160 times greater than the public investment in political parties. And the concentration in the hands of the richest donors has intensified in recent years, as we shall see in a moment.

Only a very small minority of French people—fewer than 300,000 today—contribute financially each year to political parties, or at least declare their contributions in their tax return.[3] Even if membership numbers remain a taboo subject in political movements, we know for sure that 300,000 contributors is far less—two to four times less, depending on the estimate—than the combined membership of political parties.[4] Above all, 300,000 donations to political parties is six times less than the number of taxpayers who declare trade union membership dues (1.7 million). We shall return to this below, because it is evidence that in France, as in many other countries, unions are ultimately faring much better than parties. They continue to fight for the most disadvantaged, whereas a number of ostensibly progressive parties have abandoned the terrain of social justice and representation of the "lower classes," precisely in order to obtain more in the way of private donations. Hence the need to rethink political democracy by the yardstick of social democracy and to bring an element of social representation into the National Assembly, as I shall propose in Chapter 11. For while labor unions are doing better than parties, achieving greater popularity because they are more representative, it is the parties that profit from the checkbooks of the rich. Not only is the distribution of union dues more equal than that of contributions to political parties; the average figure of union subscriptions is lower (around 164 euros). Hence the need for a much tighter structure to regulate private funding of the democratic process. But before we jump too far ahead, let us return to our few hundred thousand donors to political parties.

Among this small group, the average donation slipped from 311 euros in 2013 to 275 euros in 2016 (Figure 12).[5] Is that a lot or not much? For the donors themselves—with wealthy taxpayers to the fore—it represents an extremely small proportion of their income, only just above 0.007 percent in 2016. (This suggests that, if there were no upper limit, the richest donors would probably contribute much more than 7,500 a year;

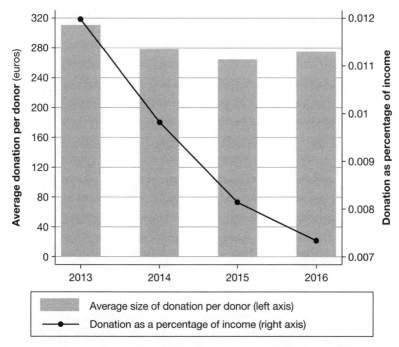

Figure 12. Average donation to political parties per donor, France, 2013–2016
In 2013, taxpayers who contributed to a political party gave an average of
311 euros. The donation size averaged 0.007 percent of the taxpayer's income.

as we shall see, they are on average approaching the legal maximum.)
And the proportion is even smaller if we consider the real cost of the
donations, since the great majority of these taxpayers benefit from tax
relief to the tune of 66 percent.

If we now consider for a moment the totality of tax households—
rather than just donors—what do we find? Owing to the combined fall
in the average size of donations and in the total number of donors, the
average donation by a French taxpayer fell from 3.5 to 2.2 euros between
2013 and 2016. One can argue over the reasons for this fall, but it seems
to me much more important to emphasize that 2.2 euros per taxpayer
(in 2016) remains higher than the public funding of parties in the same
year (1.7 euros per taxpayer). In other words, despite the ceiling that some
regard as low by international standards, French political parties depend
more on private donations than public subsidies for their operation.

Let us further note that the reduced "generosity" of French people is specific to the donations and membership dues paid over to political parties; although it partly reflects a wider disaffection with politicians, it by no means corresponds to a general decline in donations to charities. If we consider all donations—not only to parties—then we find that since 2006 (with the sole exception of 2016), the number of donors, the total amount of donations, and the average size of donations have not stopped growing in France (Figure 13). This is consistent with what we have seen in the case of Italy: while very few Italian taxpayers (fewer than 3 percent) choose the "2 per thousand" for the funding of political parties, more than a half use the "5 per thousand" for the funding of research, heritage, or sport.

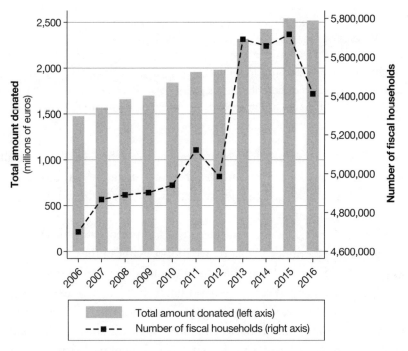

Figure 13. Total sum donated to all associations (including political parties) and total number of donating fiscal households, France, 2006–2016

In 2006, 4.7 million taxpayers declared at least one donation to a nonprofit association in France. The total sum of these donations was 1.5 billion euros.

Who are the few hundred thousand French people who contribute each year, through their donations or membership fees, to the private funding of political life?

Donations to Political Parties: A Class Phenomenon

I have calculated the number of contributors per income decile and the average size of their donations to political parties.[6] If we first take taxpayers *en bloc*, including those who contribute nothing, we find that the average amount of money they donate rises very sharply with their income. Whereas 10 percent of French people with very low incomes give on average less than 10 eurocents a year to political parties, the average donation rises to nearly 370 euros for the richest 0.01 percent (Figure 14). Moreover, although the average level of donations is in excess of one euro from the sixth income decile upward, it is really within the tenth decile that everything is decided. In other words, it is only the very rich among the rich who contribute financially to political life. Let us be perfectly

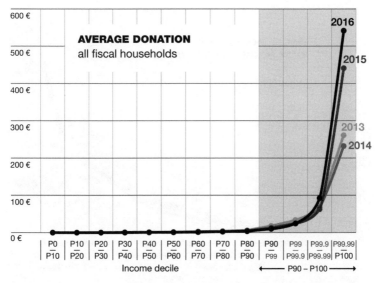

Figure 14. Donations and subscriptions to political parties by income level, France, 2013–2016

In 2016, considering all fiscal households, each taxpayer in the first decile of income distribution contributed an average of 0.074 euros to political parties.

clear what we are talking about here. In 2016, the entry point in terms of declared annual income to the 10 percent of French people with the highest income was 59,000 euros; the entry requirement for the top 1 percent was 147,000 euros, and for the top 0.1 percent it was 370,000 euros. Finally, those who belonged to the top 0.01 percent were taxpayers whose declared income was in excess of 993,000 euros.

To begin, let us note the greater probability that a very rich tax-payer will make a donation to a political party. Whereas in 2016, only 0.79 percent of tax households declared a donation, the figure was higher than 10 percent among the 0.01 percent of French people with the highest income (Figure 15). You're privileged, so you declare your donation—bravo!

Furthermore, the average size of donations in this income group was much greater than in others. If we focus just on the donors, the unequal allocation of donations to political parties and movements shows up even more strongly. At the lower end of the income scale, donors contribute

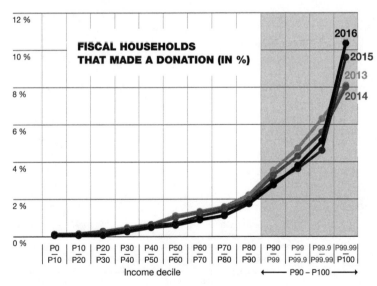

Figure 15. Percentage of fiscal households declaring a donation or subscription to political parties, by income level, France, 2013–2016

In 2016, 0.6 percent of taxpayers in the sixth income decile declared at least one donation or subscription to a political party.

an average of just 121 euros a year to political parties. And we can understand them, because unlike high-income individuals, these nontaxpayers effectively foot the entire bill for their generosity. One hundred and twenty-one euros is scarcely more than the annual fee for membership of a political party—for example, 120 euros for a member of the Green party Europe Écologie–Les Verts (EELV) whose monthly income is between 1,600 and 1,799 euros.[7]

The average donation is 210 euros for the eighth income decile, but the figure really takes off in the tenth and final decile. Here, the average size of a donation is 4,000 euros for the 0.01 percent of French people with the top incomes (Figure 16). Four thousand euros: that is more than a third of the average annual gross income of the poorest 50 percent of French people. So, if it is ever suggested that nothing prevents anyone from getting out their checkbook to support the party of their choice, the comeback is that something certainly does prevent it: their income.

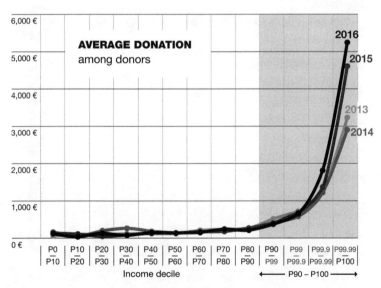

Figure 16. Average size of donations and subscriptions to political parties, per donor, by income level, France, 2013–2016

In 2016, among taxpayers who declared at least one donation or subscription to a political party, each taxpayer in the first income decile contributed an average of 122 euros to political parties.

Who could earmark *a third of their annual income* to the funding of political parties?

Since 2013, this unevenness has grown continually worse, so that in 2016 the average donation among the 0.01 percent of top income-earners in France reached 5,245 euros. Note that this is not far short of the permitted ceiling for donations. Once again it suggests that, if there were no upper limit, the sums donated by the superrich would be much greater (which is indeed the case in countries that have no ceiling).

Another way of approaching the uneven private funding of political life would be to look at the distribution of the donated sums per donation decile (Figure 17). The average donation by the top 10 percent of donors is nearly 2,000 euros. For the bottom 10 percent of small donors it is twenty-three euros. In other words, the average donation by the 10 percent of very large donors is more than eighty-four times higher

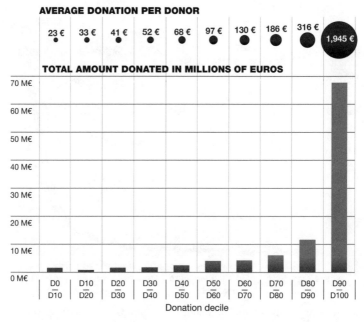

Figure 17. Average donation and total sum given in donations and subscriptions, by donation decile, France, 2013–2016

In 2016, the average size of the top 10 percent of donations was 1,945 euros. Altogether, the top 10 percent of donations amounted to 67.8 million euros.

than the average donation by the 10 percent of very small donors. At the level of the ninth donation decile, the average donation is only 316 euros. So, it is clear that the inequalities really explode only at the very top of the scale, where each year the 10 percent of very large donors donate an average of nearly 68 million euros, or two-thirds of the total sum given in donations. By comparison, the income of the top 10 percent of French people amounts to 35 percent of all income in France.

When we come to the real superrich, we find that their donations are even more concentrated. The 1 percent of top donors alone contribute to the tune of 27.6 million euros, accounting for a quarter of the total donations. Finally, if we consider only the 0.1 percent of megadonors, the total amount of their contributions averages 6.97 million euros.

What is the conclusion? The richest sections of society donate more than the middle and popular classes to political parties, and the gap is particularly marked in the case of the superrich. The richest 10 percent of French people account for more than 53 percent of the total in donations and membership fees handed over to political parties.[8] That is higher than their share of total incomes (33 percent).[9] The richest 1 percent contribute 12.4 percent,[10] the top 0.1 percent account for 3.87 percent, and the top 0.01 percent for 1.4 percent. To be sure, we are still well short of the level of political inequality in the United States, where, according to data compiled by Adam Bonica, fewer than 25,000 donors (0.01 percent of the American population) contributed 40 percent of the funding during the 2016 presidential campaign.[11] But in the United States there is no longer any upper limit on donations. Is that really the road we wish to take? If the 7,500-euro ceiling is abolished, it is certainly not French people with the lowest incomes who will contribute more; they are already restricted by their level of earnings. No, it is only the richest 0.01 percent, those already near the limit of permitted donations, who will be happy to add a zero or two to the expression of their generosity.

This highly uneven distribution by income group is a striking characteristic of donations to political parties. If we take donations to charitable bodies that assist persons in distress, which operate under the terms of the so-called Coluche Law of 1989, then the 10 percent of taxpayers with the highest incomes account for "only" 35 percent of the total sum of donations, which is equal to their share of total incomes.[12] When generosity is basically political, however, you might think that control has something to do with it.

The conclusion: since donations and membership fees to political parties bring an entitlement to tax relief, this means that each year the state spends much more public money satisfying the political preferences of the richest sections of society than those of the majority. And, though I risk fraying the nerves of already incensed readers, I shall now calculate the sums in question. I promise to strike a more optimistic note very soon. Unfortunately, the reality today is far from satisfactory, and it is important to face it head on. But it is also filled with happy surprises, and we shall see in Chapter 5 that politicians, too, know how to innovate when they have to come up with a more equal public funding of democracy. Part Three of this book, in particular, will offer some solutions. In the end, we will find a positive way out of the present crisis of representation.

The Realities of Private Funding: When the State Spends Much More for the Most Advantaged

The total amount of tax spending in France for donations to political parties averaged a little more than 56 million euros a year over the period from 2013 to 2016.[13] That 56 million euros is a nice round figure; it could almost be one euro per adult head of the population—except that, as we can clearly see from its distribution by income level, equality is not at all what this is about.

If there were perfect equality among taxpayers, what would the picture look like? Let us begin with the year 2016, when tax expenditure stood at 48 million euros (less than in previous years because of a fall in the total number of donations and their average size). If all 37 million taxpayers had benefited equally, this expenditure would have been 1.3 euros per head. But remember that each year fewer than 300,000 French people declare a donation to a political party (291,000 in 2016). This means that for more than 36 million taxpayers, the tax expenditure in question was quite simply zero. Figure 18 presents the average fiscal expenditure by income level for each year. The French state spends literally nothing for the least advantaged citizens, and next to nothing all

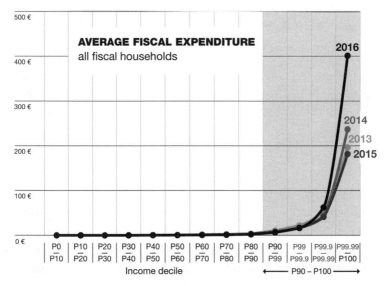

Figure 18. Average fiscal expenditure by income level, all taxpayers, France, 2013–2016

In 2016, the French state spent an average of 400 euros in tax relief associated with donations to political parties, for each taxpayer among the 0.01 percent (P99, 99–100) of people with the highest incomes.

the way up to the ninth income decile; in 2016, the average tax expenditure for French people in the ninth decile was 2.20 euros (still better, you may say, than the 0.29 euros for taxpayers in the fifth decile). By contrast, in 2016 the state spent an average of 400 euros per taxpayer for the 0.01 percent of French people in the highest income bracket—a disparity that has only increased with time.

I should add that I am here looking only at donations to political parties, but everything suggests that if we had the same data for contributions to election campaigns (totaling 8 million euros of government tax spending in an average year), they would further reinforce the fact of this inequality.

What happens when we consider only the 291,000 French people who contributed to a political party in 2016? Had there been equality at least within this small group, everyone would have received 165 euros. But even that is asking too much. To begin with, 48,000 donors benefited from no tax reduction; do not forget that, unfortunately, the French tax system is such that all citizens who pay no income tax are effectively excluded from the tax benefits associated with donations.

What of the remaining 243,000 taxpayers? They shared a tax reduction of 48 million euros, and that, too, in an extremely uneven way. Tax expenditure received by the donors among the 40 percent of French people with the lowest incomes averaged 73 euros in 2016. Compare that with the average of 3,900 euros that went into the bank accounts of donors belonging to the wealthiest 0.01 percent of French people (Figure 19)[14]—fifty-three times more! Each year the state spends several thousand euros per taxpayer to help with the expression of political preferences for the very rich and a few dozen euros, if anything, for the political preferences of the vast majority of citizens. As we shall see, that comes to little more than one euro per adult in direct public funding.

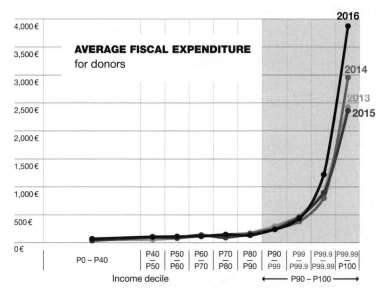

Figure 19. Average fiscal expenditure by income level, taxpayers who made at least one donation or paid at least one subscription to a political party, France, 2013–2016

In 2016, the French state spent an average of 3,876 euros in tax relief associated with donations to political parties, for each taxpayer among the 0.01 percent (P99, 99–100) of people with the highest incomes who made at least one donation or paid at least one subscription to a political party.

Consequently, in democracy as it functions today, there are three categories of citizens: plutocrats, the supposed sponsors of democracy, who in reality get the state to pay for them; activists, who give their own money and time to political parties but are forgotten in the state's fiscal handout; and "ordinary citizens," who may be said to benefit indirectly from the few cents of public subsidies that the state pays to parties in their name, but who ultimately are the big losers in terms of representation.

The picture becomes very clear if we finally consider the distribution of total tax expenditure (Figure 20). On average, this rose to 56 million

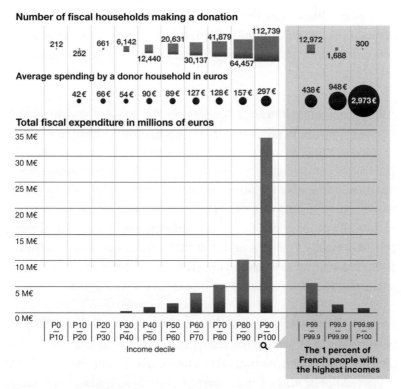

Figure 20. Total fiscal expenditure and number of fiscal household beneficiaries, France, annual average 2013–2016

During the 2013–2016 period, the French state spent in tax relief associated with donations and subscriptions to political parties an annual average of 33.5 million euros for taxpayers with the top 10 percent of incomes (P90–P100). This fiscal expenditure benefited 112,739 fiscal households.

euros a year between 2013 and 2016, out of which 33.5 million euros (approximately 60 percent) benefited the 10 percent of French people with the highest incomes.

Let us recap. The average donation to a political party by one of the 0.01 percent of French people with the highest incomes is today greater than 5,000 euros. A total of 3,300 euros is ultimately paid by the state, and only 2,700 euros by the taxpayer. The average donation to a political party by the 10 percent of French people with the lowest incomes is twenty-three euros—and they pay every last cent of it. In 2016, then, the state paid more than 29 million euros to the wealthiest 10 percent in tax relief associated with donations to political parties—that is, more than twenty-one times more than it spent for the least well-off. And it spent as much for just 0.01 percent of citizens (a little over 1.4 million euros) as it did for the whole of the disadvantaged half of the population.

The Realities of Private Funding: An Extremely Concentrated Pattern in Germany, Italy, and the United Kingdom

The highly detailed data to which I had access for France are not systematically available for other countries. Nevertheless, there are other sources that can help us plot the concentration of donations to political parties in a number of European countries, beginning with Germany. The advantage of these sources is that, above a certain amount, the donor's identity is most often publicly known. This can reveal some very interesting facts, particularly in the case of corporate donations.

Germany: A Country of Mass Parties or Company Parties?

In Germany, political parties report each year the total amount of contributions received from individuals (donations + contributions by those in elected public office + membership fees); these are broken down into sums below 3,300 and sums above 3,300 euros (the threshold after which individuals are entitled to a tax rebate). On average, for the whole of the period from 1994 to 2015, contributions above 3,300 euros represented scarcely more than 9 percent of the total received in individual donations by political parties. In 2015, their total amount (for all parties combined) was approximately 24.4 million euros, compared with nearly 200 million euros for all individual donations below 3,300 euros. The majority of these donations (nearly 55 percent) correspond to membership fees, and more than a quarter to contributions from members in elected public positions.

The aggregate sum of donations above 3,300 euros may seem relatively low, but it should be noted that, as a percentage of the total of individual donations, it has been continually increasing in recent years—from 7.4 percent in 1994 to 12.5 percent today, for political parties as a whole (Figure 21). More surprising at first sight is the fact that sums above 3,300 euros represent a larger share of total individual donations for parties on the left of the spectrum, such as Die Linke or Die Grünen (the Greens), than for parties on the right. But the main reason for this is that a party like the Greens is funded mainly by contributions from members in

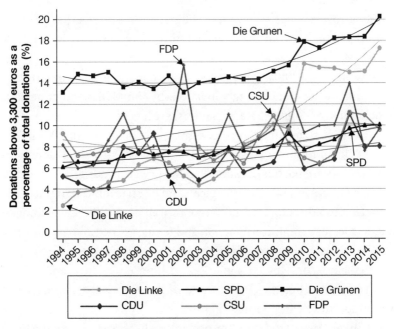

Figure 21. Share of donations above 3,300 euros in the total sum received in individual donations by political parties, Germany, 1994–2015

In 2015, 20 percent of total donations received by Die Grünen were above 3,300 euros.

elected public positions, and that these are mostly in excess of 3,300 euros a year. Thus, Tarek Al-Wazir—who chaired the Greens' parliamentary group between 2000 and 2014—gives 15,000 euros a year to his party. As we shall also see in the case of France, it is often elected officials who contribute on the left, whereas it is the rich who donate on the right.

In Germany, there is a strong fiscal incentive for small contributions, and the rich donors are mostly not individuals but companies. This becomes clear if we turn our attention to donations above 10,000 euros. For in Germany, it is compulsory for parties to publish a list of donations above 10,000 euros at the end of each year, with not only the amount of each donation but also the identity of the donors.[15] In 2015, the grand total of donations above 10,000 euros—from both individuals and companies—came to 13.4 million euros.[16]

Despite the increasing number of donations above 10,000 euros, their total amount, though peaking in election years, has remained fairly stable over time (Figure 22).[17] As for the average size of donations above 10,000 euros, this has fallen slightly during the same period (hovering around 45,000 euros in the 1980s but now more in the region of 20,000 euros).

Since the early 2010s, a majority of these donations has regularly come from individuals. But although donations by companies and professional associations (or employers' associations) are less important cumulatively, their average size is much greater (thus, 49,000 euros in 2015 for employers' federations, against 15,000 euros for individual donations). Some sectors are particularly active in the private funding of democracy: the mechanical, metal, metallurgical, and electrical industries (a highly export-oriented sector in Germany), as well as the chemicals industry and, to a lesser extent, construction and textiles. Since 2000, professional organizations in the mechanical, metal, metallurgical, and electrical industries have contributed some 18.2 million euros to the funding of German political parties,[18] and those of the chemical and pharmaceutical industries nearly 6 million euros.

It is likely that the data I am presenting here greatly underestimate the contributions that companies and employers' associations make to political parties. According to an investigation published in 2017 by Deutsche Welle (the German international radio station), many compa-

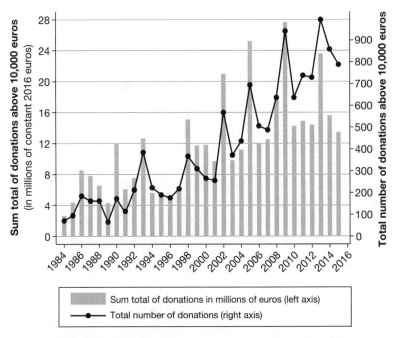

Figure 22. Sum total of donations above 10,000 euros and number of donors, Germany, 1984–2015

nies use a loophole in the German legislation to conceal a large part of the money they donate.[19] While companies are legally required to declare all their donations above 10,000 euros, many get around this obligation by making a series of smaller contributions. The article gives the example of the Deutsche Vermögensberatung Holding consulting company, which, when its subsidiaries are taken into account (Deutsche Vermögensberatung AG, UBG Unternehmensberatung & Betreuung GmbH, and Allfinanz), allegedly donated 403,000 euros to the Christian Democratic Union (CDU) in 2013, without having to declare this as a large donation because it was broken down into multiple donations by the various subsidiaries. It would also be possible to categorize as corporate donations the sums paid by its founder, Reinhard Pohl, who contributed as much as 220,000 euros in 2013. We should point out, of course, that there is nothing "illegal" in this: all these political contributions display the greatest respect for the letter of the law. Questions may be asked, however, about whether they respect its spirit.

Despite this limitation of the official data, it is interesting to study the way in which donations above 10,000 euros break down. In 2015, for example, the great majority (80 percent) ranged from 10,000 to 20,000 euros, and 14 percent involved sums between 20,000 and 30,000 euros. Some, however, reached 100,000 euros or more, as was the case with two donations of 100,000 each from the German carmaker Daimler (one to the Social Democratic Party [SPD], the other to the CDU) and the donation of 195,000 euros that the financial services company Deutsche Vermögensberatung AG made to the CDU.

In the end, which parties profit most from donations in excess of 10,000 euros? Systematically over the past thirty years, the CDU has been the principal beneficiary of these large donations (Figure 23), and it is interesting to note that this "advantage" is particularly marked in years

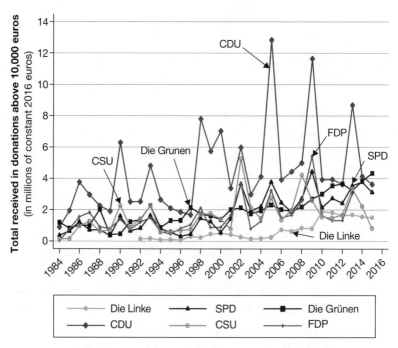

Figure 23. Donations above 10,000 euros, total amount received by each political party, Germany, 1984–2015

In 2013, the CDU received a total of 8.7 million euros in donations above 10,000 euros. The total for the SPD was 3.4 million euros.

when national elections are held. Since the turn of the century, however, the SPD has been catching up. As I briefly mentioned before, companies and employers' associations in Germany tend to fund the main parties simultaneously. And as we shall see again in the case of the United Kingdom and the United States, parties on the left (which have historically been mass parties representing the preferences of the popular classes—a feature of the SPD, in particular) have sought in recent decades to capture private donations and to give them priority over membership dues. This is the new oligarchic tendency of modern democracy. It is not that workers become more bourgeois when they are elected—they no longer stand as candidates in the first place—but that party programs move rightward to satisfy the preferences of their new financial backers. In Germany, the ruling SPD under Gerhard Schröder went so far as to lower the marginal rate of income tax and to exert a downward pressure on wages. We know the consequences today, in terms of purchasing power and the squeeze on working-class living standards.

Since I was talking above about tax expenditure associated with donations, let me conclude this rapid survey of Germany with an estimate in this regard. Fiscal spending in Germany depends, as it does in France or Italy, on the amount of the taxes paid by donors.[20] On the hypothesis that the sum total of donations below 3,300 euros gave rise to tax relief of 50 percent, the conclusion is that, over the period from 2012 to 2016, the state spent a maximum yearly average of just over 104 million euros in tax reductions associated with contributions to political parties—or 1.55 euros per adult.[21]

It may be noted that this fiscal spending per adult is quite similar to what we see in France (56 million euros a year, or 1.08 euros per adult, in tax exemption for donations to parties), despite the fact that France's more generous fiscal policy allows a 66 percent rebate for donations to political parties, up to a maximum of 7,500 euros.

Nevertheless, in Germany there is no ceiling on donations either by individuals or—even more problematically—by companies. I shall return in Chapter 7 to the fact that a number of companies contribute several hundred thousand euros a year to political parties, and that many do so regardless of the parties' political colors. What does a company hope to gain when it sends out two checks at the same time, to the SPD and the CDU—if not influence? But for the moment let us finish our global survey of private funding. Before we speak of the excesses, let us also show a little optimism. For while Germany suffers from deregulation of the private funding of democracy, it has known how to innovate in relation to public funding.

Long Live the Berlusconi Family!

In Italy, regulation of the private funding of democracy developed only recently—and, paradoxically, at a time when public funding was being questioned. A ceiling on permitted individual and corporate donations, as well as a requirement that they should be transparent, was introduced only in 2013.[22]

For the 2014–2016 period, since political parties now have to report all donations above 5,000 euros, their accounts allow us to study the concentration of donations.[23] I shall therefore consider all donations between 5,000 and 100,000 euros, the maximum permitted amount. Let us note at once, however, that it can be rather easy to play around with this ceiling. I include Berlusconi in the "Why not bust the ceiling?" family, since Papa Silvio got upset that he could no longer donate millions to his party in election years.[24] In 2015, no fewer than six Berlusconis contributed the maximum permitted amount of 100,000 euros to Forza Italia: Silvio, of course, but also his daughters, Eleonora, Barbara, and Marina, his son Luigi, and his brother, Paolo. And the same was true of part of the family in 2016. As if that were not enough, the family corporation Fininvest also contributed 100,000 euros in 2015, before it tightened its belt in 2016 and reduced this to 99,900 euros.

Let us stress again that the figures I have just given reflect only the new reality of the concentration of donations in Italy; until 2014—although we unfortunately lack the details—contributions could rise as high as seven figures. On average, in the years between 2014 and 2016, the sum total of donations above 5,000 euros was 11.9 million euros: 95 percent, both of the number of donations and of the total amount donated, came from individuals; 40 percent ranged between 15,000 and 20,000 euros; but a number of donors—as we have just seen in the case of Berlusconi—contributed up to the ceiling of 100,000 euros (Figure 24). In 2016, the ten largest donations to parties (2 percent of all

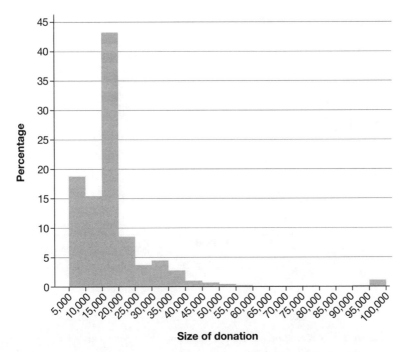

Figure 24. Distribution of donations above 5,000 euros to political parties, Italy, 2014–2016

donations) alone accounted for 10 percent of all 472 donations above 5,000 euros.

The majority of these donations above 5,000 euros were destined for the Democratic Party—the main beneficiary of the "2 per thousand" system—which received an annual average of over 7.8 million euros (Figure 25). Once again, in Italy as in Germany, the Left in government is not afraid to appeal for private funding, and under Matteo Renzi it was the ruling Democratic Party that loosened the labor market (with its "Jobs Act") and made the conditions for young people a little more insecure. Forza Italia and the Northern League almost pale in comparison, with total donations below 3 million euros, and the sums received by other parties are very low indeed. The Democratic Party receives many more donations above 5,000 euros than other parties, but the average value of its donations (17,000 euros) is lower than that of the average donation received by the Northern League or Forza Italia (more than 21,000 euros each).

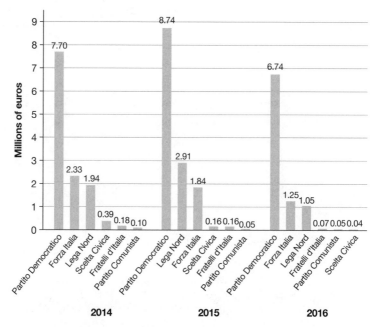

Figure 25. Total amount received in donations above 5,000 euros, by political party, Italy, 2014–2016

The reader should not be surprised at the absence of the Five Stars Movement here. I noted above that this party rejected any form of public subsidy for political parties—including the reimbursement of campaign expenses under the old system as well as today's "2 per thousand" system—and that this position meant it did not have to comply with the legal requirement of transparency (since the movement did not have the formal status of a party). Not much inclined to transparency anyway, Five Stars does not publish a list of the donations it receives in excess of 5,000 euros.

God Save Our Parties (from Clubs and Other Donors)

Let us finish this tour with the United Kingdom, where, in contrast to Italy, there is no ceiling on either individual or corporate donations, but where, as in Germany, the amounts of the largest donations must be published online, together with the identity of the donors. To be precise, it is obligatory to communicate to the Electoral Commission—which has published them online since 2001—all contributions above a certain limit to political parties and their local branches, whether these are made in one or several payments. The amount was £5,000 sterling until 2009, and since then it has been £7,500.[25] Furthermore, in any given year, a natural or legal person that has already declared a donation must declare all contributions above £1,500 (£1,000 until 2009).

The wealth of data on the Electoral Commission website include public subsidies in the category of "donations." In order that the results should be comparable with those we have seen for other countries, I shall concentrate solely on individual and corporate donations, excluding from the scope of my analysis not only public subsidies but also financial contributions made by the trade unions (very important for the Labour Party) and "friendly societies," as well as donations coming from other political parties. I have also chosen to classify donations by foundations and "unincorporated associations" under the heading of donations by private persons, since wealthy individuals are most often behind such associations. In particular, more and more donors in the United Kingdom act through unincorporated associations so that they do not have to reveal their identity—a practice rather like that of the super PACs in the United States. There is certainly nothing illegal about this, but again it diverges from the spirit of transparency rules. It has long been a specialty of the Conservative Party: between 2007 and 2017, the National Conservative Draws Association—a Conservative lottery organization—donated nearly 8.8 million euros to the party.[26] Labour, too, is increasingly going in for it, however; it is a sign of the times that left-wing parties heed the siren song of donors with fat checkbooks. Hasn't Matteo Renzi been described as "the Italian Tony Blair"?

I have been analyzing here only donations to political parties—not, for example, those given directly to parliamentarians. The end result is that, between 2001 and 2017, there were 39,960 donations—an average of 1,900 a year, with an average value of 21,400 euros—and 28,500 donors (Figure 26).[27] In 2017, the total amount of these donations reached 57.7 million euros.

How important were the smaller of these sizable donations in comparison with the larger? To answer this question, I studied—as before in the case of France—the distribution by decile of donations (Figure 27).

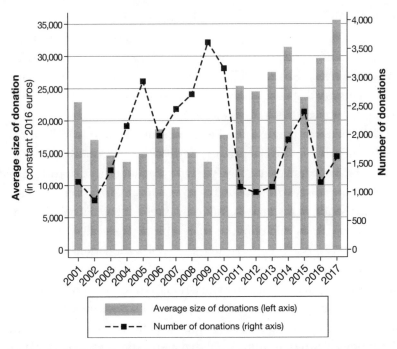

Figure 26. Total number of donations to political parties and average amount of donation, United Kingdom, 2001–2017

In 2017, the average donation by the largest 10 percent of donors was in excess of 229,000 euros. The equivalent figure for the smallest 10 percent of donors was 1,700 euros. In other words, the average donation by the largest 10 percent of donors was more than 135 times greater than the average donation by the smallest 10 percent of donors. In 2017, the top 10 percent together gave 37 million euros, or more than two-thirds of the grand total of donations. This level of concentration is quite similar to what we found in France.

We can study the extent to which the concentration of donations varies among the different parties. For the year 2017 and for each of the five main parties, I have calculated the percentage of the total sum of donations represented by the largest 10 percent of donations. It clearly emerges that—as we saw in the case of Germany—the donations are more concentrated for parties on the right of the political spectrum. Thus, in 2017, whereas the largest 10 percent of donations together ac-

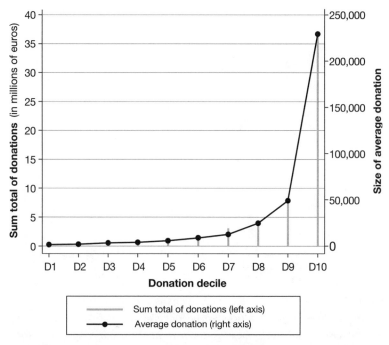

Figure 27. Average donation and total amount paid in donations to political parties, by donation decile, United Kingdom, 2017

counted for 66.3 percent of the total sums donated to the Conservative Party, the equivalent proportion for the Labour Party is "only" 51 percent (Figure 28).

Donations, then, are not politically neutral, especially above a certain amount. Everything suggests that both companies and wealthy individuals tend to favor parties whose economic programs are advantageous to them: that is, the most conservative parties, with an economic policy geared to exports, labor market flexibility, lower marginal rates of taxation, and so on. On the opposite side, the Left has historically consisted more of "mass parties," which benefit from membership dues and, to a lesser extent, from the contributions of members elected to public office. Has this been enough to offset the relatively low level of large private contributions? In other words, are parties of the Right everywhere richer than parties of the Left, or do the models differ from country to country? This is the question we shall consider next.

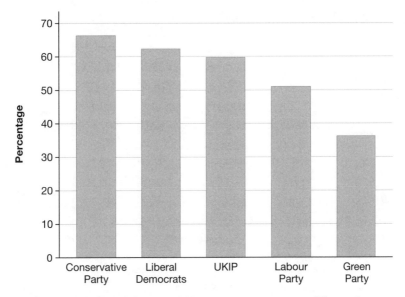

Figure 28. The largest 10 percent of donations as a percentage of the total received in donations, by political party, United Kingdom, 2017

In 2017, the total amount of the largest 10 percent of donations received by the Conservative Party came to 66.3 percent of the total received by the party in donations. The corresponding share for the Labour Party was 51 percent.

The Public Funding of Private Preferences Makes for Rich, Well-Endowed Parties of the Right

In the end, how much do the various political parties and campaigns receive each year from a few thousand donors supported in their generosity by government fiscal policies? Let us begin again with the case of France, before turning to the other European democracies.

Political Parties French-Style: On the Left, Elected Officials Contribute; On the Right, It's the Rich Who Give

The total amount of donations and membership dues received by political parties in France came to 101 million euros in 2013, 84 million in 2014, 91 million in 2015, and 95 million in 2016 (or 1.80 euros per adult).[28] We are talking here not only of private individual donations but also of membership dues and contributions from members elected to public office.

The sums in question have been relatively stable since 2008, having been higher in the first half of the same decade (Figure 29). Over the period as a whole, donations accounted for 26 percent of private contributions to the parties, membership dues for approximately 34 percent, and contributions from elected officials for 40 percent.

Does this distribution vary between the different parties? Figure 30 shows the average relative importance of the three sources of income throughout this period (1993–2016) for the five main parties. Different models come very clearly into view. For the parties of the Left—the Communist Party, the Socialist Party, the Green party Europe Écologie–Les Verts—the contributions of elected officials are very much to the fore, accounting respectively for 62 percent, 52 percent, and 50 percent of the total "donations" in the broad sense of the term. On the other hand, such contributions account for only 13 percent of the total donations to the Front National and 12 percent to the Republicans. Do politicians of the Right elected to public office forget to pay their tithe to the party?

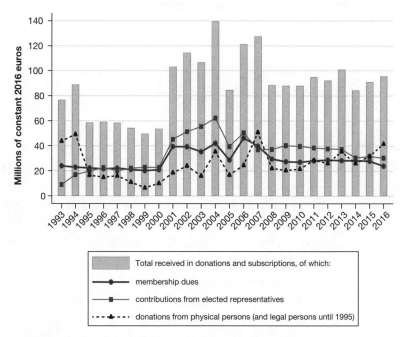

Figure 29. Donations and subscriptions to political parties, total sums by source, France, 1993–2016

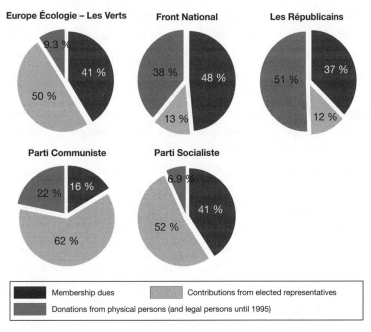

Figure 30. Distribution of donations, subscriptions, and contributions to political parties, France, by party, averages, 1993–2016

Evidently these differences reflect the existence of rules defining the share of their income that elected officials are expected to pay. The Communists—in a historical peculiarity that has survived through the decades—hand over their official compensation in full to the party, which then makes a compensatory payment in return. In the Socialist Party, while local groups are allowed some discretion, the rule is that members elected to public office pay approximately 10 percent of their official salary. At the national level, deputies and senators pay 500 euros a month—note that the percentage applies only to "direct" remuneration, and parliamentarians effectively double their income with the sums they receive in expenses—while the contribution is 650 euros for members of the European Parliament. This "10 percent" rule in the Socialist Party is by no means peculiar to France. In Belgium, for example, each elected representative must also pay the party 10 percent of his or her gross remuneration from political offices. Belgium's most interesting handover system is probably the one operated by the Parti du Travail de Belgique (PTB), a historically Marxist-Leninist party it is tempting to compare to La France Insoumise (Unbowed France); it decided that each of its elected representatives should keep the "workers' wage" he or she had before being elected, and that anything on top of this should be paid to the party.

Now that we mention it, what of La France Insoumise? I would love to answer the question, but unfortunately I lack sufficient competence in investigative journalism. Research reaches its limits when transparency doesn't enter the picture. Not only do the statutes of La France Insoumise make only passing reference to fixed contributions; when the political movement is asked about its handover rules, all we are told is "Ask Jean-Luc Mélenchon [its leader] directly." Yes, that's right, Jean-Luc Mélenchon is apparently the only person capable of saying anything on the subject. Monsieur Mélenchon, if you ever read this book . . .

Still, we should add that Emmanuel Macron's new world of La République en Marche (LREM) is hardly more transparent and that its appetite for money is doubtless more pronounced. True, no one has gone so far as to tell me that it comes under the sole authority of King Macron, but as I write these lines (in late February 2018, eight months after its deputies took their seats for the first time) the sums that LREM representatives pay to their party amount to precisely zero. While the LREM statutes mention, among its annual revenues, "the handover of monetary compensation paid to elected officials," they also note that "the dues paid by members who hold one or more elective offices entitling them to monetary compensation, or who perform a function in government, correspond to a fraction of the net monetary compensation received by them in the course of the year. That amount is fixed each year by the executive bureau."[29] It would appear from its deliberations, however, that the said executive bureau has still not managed to agree on the size of that fraction; its discussions of the matter are sadly not public, but walls have ears and journalism can offer a helping hand here. What is certain is that our roped lead climbers are in no hurry to pull everyone else up with them.

What of the rules applicable to elected representatives of the parties of the Right (I mean, those to the right of LREM)? The Républicains do half as well, so to speak, as the Socialist Party; their elected representatives have to hand over only 5 percent of their monetary compensation—although this percentage is not fixed in any official party document. Ah, the joys of transparency! The Far Right performs no better: they just hang up if you broach the matter on the phone, and it receives no mention in the statutes of the Front National.

So, if our elected representatives leave us in the dark, how can we discover what they hand over to their respective parties? I had fun doing a little cross-multiplication—certainly not a perfect solution, and one I would not have had to do if the parties displayed greater transparency. For 2014 and 2015, I calculated for each party the total amount of the remuneration paid to its members in elective office (number of deputies multiplied by deputies' salaries, plus number of senators multiplied by senators' salaries, and so on, taking into account all elective public offices). Then I compared this total with the contributions that elected representatives paid to their parties (as reported in party accounts), which allowed me to obtain a way of measuring the proportion they handed over. The results are truly striking: while Communist parliamentarians pay more than half of their monetary compensation to their national party (local representatives contribute to departmental funding associations[30]), and those of the Green EELV pay one-third, this share declines as one moves right along the political spectrum (Figure 31). Particularly stark is the case of the Républicains, who do not even abide by the low figure of 5 percent that they have announced. Indeed, it is tempting to take the propensity of elected representatives to contribute financially to their party as a measure of the position they occupy on a left-to-right political axis. And given the discussions within the LREM—which, let us not forget, is a businessmen's party—the president's party risks finding itself too close to the Républicains for comfort.

The lack of transparency on this matter is particularly damaging because it fuels the distrust of overpaid politicians and plays into the hands of populist discourses, just when we should be having a full and meaningful debate on the nature of political remuneration, its ideal scale, and its role as a source of party funding.

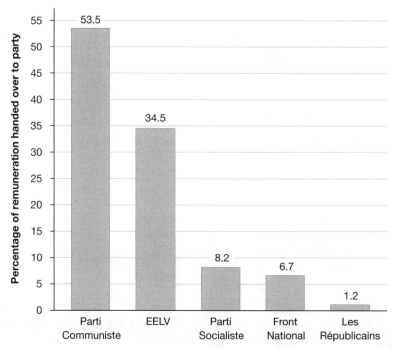

Figure 31. Percentage of official remuneration that elected representatives handed over to their political party, France, by party, annual averages 2014–2015

Once again, it may be useful to take a look at Italy and its Five Stars Movement, an emblematic element in the wider crisis of democracy and its public funding. Instead of handing over part of their public remuneration to their party (or nonparty), members of the movement have decided to pay half of it into a special fund for the financing of small and medium-sized businesses (the Fondo Centrale di Garanzia per le Piccole e Media Imprese, administered by the Ministry of Economic Development). Why? First of all, their decision fits into the populist Five Stars critique of the existing party system, which, not surprisingly, denounces the overpayment of parliamentarians. Thus, the movement argues for a halving of present levels of remuneration and has chosen to apply this idea to itself right here and now, effectively requiring its parliamentarians to hand over half of their pay to the state.

In practice, however, not all its parliamentarians show the same enthusiasm in fulfilling this obligation. Each month they are supposed to
publish online the transfer orders for their payment of half their remuneration to the SME Fondo Centrale, but some—such is the beauty of
new-style movements—soon realized that it was enough to take a screen
capture of their transfer order before deleting it without further ado. The
whole business ended in a scandal, since it quickly became clear that the
sums received by the Fondo Centrale fell short of those in the transfer
orders declared by Five Stars parliamentarians. It was all a little reminiscent of the payments that Republican parliamentarians in France
made to their party.

On the other hand, the idea of dividing political remuneration by two
and handing half to the state rather than the party coffers also reflects
a strong conviction in the Five Stars Movement that we need to look at
more closely. The movement considers that it can live entirely on the
many small donations that it receives, and it is indeed not uninteresting
to reflect on this as a way of funding political parties, instead of one
based on a small number of fat corporate or individual checks. But to
replace the present system with genuine "crowd-funding" presupposes
some regulation of private funding—and the Five Stars Movement takes
issue only with the public funding of democracy. It seems to me preferable to reform the existing "2 per thousand" system, so that each citizen
is allocated the same number of euros to fund the party of his or her
choice rather than a sum that depends on income. This is the idea behind
my proposal for Democratic Equality Vouchers. The Five Stars Movement, however, campaigns not to reform the "2 per thousand" but to
abolish it. And it does so partly for a bad reason, since the party's fine
words suffer from its lack of transparency. In rejecting the "2 per thousand" system, the Five Stars Movement avoids having to publish its accounts, with the result that all we know of the small donations it receives
is what it tells us about them. It would be easier to take it at its word if it
made its accounts public, as the other parties do.

But let us return to France, where two models of party funding are
clearly apparent. Parties on the left of the spectrum (Communists, Socialists, and Ecologists) depend mostly on contributions from members
in elective public positions, whereas those on the right—particularly the

Républicains—rely for the most part on individual donations. Can you spare some change, ladies and gentlemen? After all, it won't cost you much, because the state will pay two-thirds of it anyway. In the end, what do these two models of contribution mean in terms of hard cash?

Poor French Parties?

You might think that, with just 676,000 euros in donations in 2016, the French Socialist Party is badly off; things certainly did not augur well for its presidential campaign in 2017, especially in comparison with the Républicains (who notched up 7.45 million euros around the same time) or the super-youthful En Marche! (which, in its first year, gave the game away by mobilizing 4,962,730 euros in private money). Yet we should remember that the Socialist Party's trifling private donations were supplemented by more than 11.1 million euros in contributions from members in public positions and 5.7 million euros in ordinary membership dues. To study the financial health of political parties, we therefore need to take into account all the dimensions of "private money." What counts is not only the total value of the party's resources but also their origin. For, in terms of representativeness, it makes a huge difference whether a party relies on the dues of tens of thousands of members or on the checkbooks of a handful of megadonors.

How do French parties manage in comparison with others in Europe, such as the British, German, Belgian, Italian, or Spanish? Are the left / right differences with regard to party funding replicated elsewhere? To answer these questions, I first identified "the Left" and "the Right" in these countries as a whole.[31] Then I calculated, for the different variables of interest, the average annual amount over the 2012–2016 period (which corresponds to the last election cycle in France).

Let us begin with the total amount in donations that the different parties receive from individuals and companies. (Here "donations" does not include membership dues or contributions made by members in elected public positions, which will be considered separately later.[32]) Several things emerge clearly. First, in the countries as a whole, parties on the right receive much more from private individuals and companies than do parties on the left (Figure 32). This will doubtless not surprise readers, but we should stop to think about it for a moment. For it means

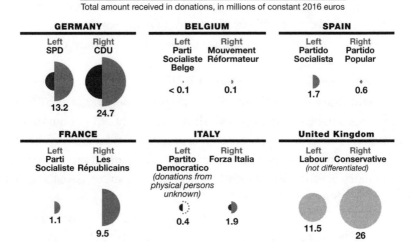

Figure 32. Total annual sum of donations (in millions of euros) received by the main political parties of the Left and Right, averages 2012–2016, international comparison (United Kingdom, Germany, Italy, France, Spain, and Belgium)

that, in all countries where donations entitle donors to a tax reduction, the government funds parties on the right more than those on the left. It also means that, because of private funding, parties on the right have a systematic electoral advantage over their counterparts on the left (a phenomenon I shall document in Chapter 8).

Another unsurprising but noteworthy result is that, in countries without a ceiling on donations—particularly the United Kingdom and Germany, where corporate and individual donations can flow freely—the total amount of money received by parties in donations is far higher than in countries such as France or Belgium where the private funding of parties is much more tightly regulated. The massive divergences between countries clearly do not stem from their population size: the Conservative Party received an annual average of 0.53 euros in donations per British adult in the 2012–2016 period, and the CDU 0.37 euros per German adult—that is, respectively, 2.8 and 1.2 times more than the French Republicans (0.19 euros per French adult).[33]

In Italy, corporate donations have been limited since 2014 to 100,000 euros a year, but it may seem surprising that they are still on the low side.

Unfortunately, the likely reason for this is that because of new transparency requirements, some donations are being passed under the table. This does not mean, of course, that there should not be transparency—on the contrary, I think that France should compel parties to publish a list of donations above a certain level and to disclose the identity of donors, as is already the case in Germany, Italy, and the United Kingdom. But there is an urgent need to give more powers to commissions in charge of the regulation of private funding.

More or less everywhere, therefore, parties on the right benefit to a greater degree than their counterparts on the left from the largesse of private donors—but this is especially the case in countries like Germany and the United Kingdom, where such generosity is not subject to regulation. But are the parties richer as a result? In France, as we have seen, contributions from elected representatives have enabled parties to compensate for the shortfall in private funding. But what of other Western European countries? Figure 33 shows the average annual contribution that parties receive from elected representatives in the different

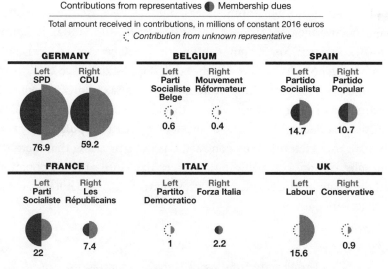

Figure 33. Annual total received by main political parties of the Left and Right (in millions of euros) from elected representatives' contributions and membership dues, annual averages 2012–2016, international comparison (United Kingdom, Germany, Italy, France, Spain, and Belgium)

countries. A number of points stand out. First, contributions by elected representatives and membership dues are an exact mirror-image of private donations; in all the countries, left-wing parties rely much more than right-wing parties on these sources of funding. Second, the German parties—*on the right as well as the left*—are mass parties; it is a phenomenon endlessly commented upon, studied, dissected, and analyzed since the days of Maurice Duverger,[34] and it shows up very clearly here in the importance of membership dues. The equivalent of approximately 0.80 euros per German adult is paid each year to the SPD by its members, and 0.60 euros to the CDU. In the United Kingdom, the Conservative Party is not a mass party; proportionately to the adult population, it is the party that receives the least in membership fees. The Labour Party, historically an offspring of the unions, receives more than 15 million euros a year in membership dues—that is, 0.32 euros per adult. But times are changing, and since 2015 private individual and corporate donations have been a more important source of revenue than membership fees for the Labour Party.

Finally, let us note the important role of legislation. Income from the general membership is so high in Germany not only because the parties have large numbers of members, but also because the state offers major encouragement through tax subsidies for individual donations below 1,650 euros. Spain comes second only to Germany in terms of its members' generosity per head of the adult population; since 2007, members of a political party have been entitled to a tax allowance equal to the amount of their subscription, up to a total of 600 euros a year. Both the Socialist Party (PSOE) and to a lesser degree the Popular Party benefit from this exemption. By contrast, it is not surprising that membership subscriptions are so low in Italy, given that unlike private donations and the contributions of elected representatives, they do not attract any fiscal advantage.

The Private Funding of Election Campaigns

Up to this point, we have been focusing mainly on donations to political parties. Let us now round off this survey of the private funding of democracy by looking at how things stand with election campaigns. In countries like France that use a single-member constituency system, a number of citizens contribute financially by donating directly to their chosen candidates. Regrettably, the French fiscal data do not allow us to differentiate taxpayer donations to election campaigns from other donations; they are grouped under the broad category of "donations to other public-interest entities," which includes, for example, donations to corporate foundations, academic foundations, and the Foundation of France.[35] We can, however, obtain aggregated information about the total size of these donations from the campaign accounts of the various candidates.

Campaign donations vary widely between types of election—local polls elicit more than others—but also from year to year (Figure 34). For example, candidates in the presidential election of 2012 received much more in donations (a total of 9.3 million euros) than candidates in the presidential election of 2017 (4.7 million euros). The comparison between

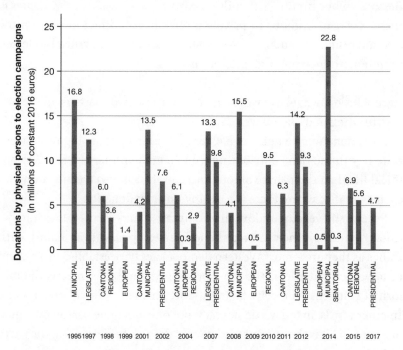

Figure 34. Donations by physical persons to election campaigns, France, 1995–2017

Nicolas Sarkozy (nearly 6 million euros in 2012) and François Fillon (just 6,600 euros, or nearly 100 times less!) is very striking in this respect. Are we talking about a "primary" effect? After all, the Republican primary in 2016 allowed the party to collect 9.4 million euros (more than it cost to hold), and the profit went into the campaign account of the winner, François Fillon. He therefore had no need to embark on a new round of fund-raising, especially as—if we add a Penelope effect to the primary effect[36]—it might not have been so easy.

Beyond these variations, French people donated an annual average of 12 million euros in private money to finance campaigns during the last electoral cycle (2012–2016).[37] In contrast to donations to political parties, the private funding of elections (12 million euros) is thus much lower than the public funding (52 million).

If we add together donations to political parties and donations to candidates, a total of 113 million euros in private money flows each year into the operations of political democracy in France—only just less than the total public funding (119 million euros). As we shall see in Chapter 8, these scores of millions in private money have a direct impact on the election results of candidates—as well as the policies pursued by elected representatives—from the different parties.

In conclusion, what have we learned from these two chapters on the private funding of democracy?

First, donations to political parties and campaigns are highly concentrated, with the rich contributing a much greater financial share to political life than their share of total income. This is also true in countries such as France where there is a ceiling on such donations.

Second, however paradoxical and unfair it may seem—at least to ordinary citizens, since the real beneficiaries appear quite happy with things as they are—most Western democracies have established a system of tax relief that allows the most privileged, but by no means the majority of citizens, to receive state support for their political preferences. In other words, in today's democracy, not only does one person not equal one vote, but it is the poorest who pay for the rich to ensure that the party of their choice comes to power.

Third, this is a very long way from being politically neutral. It comes as no surprise—or anyway we are by now used to it—that citizens do not contribute at random to the different parties. In all countries, parties on the right tend to receive more than those on the left in donations from individuals and, where permitted, companies. To be sure, this difference is partly offset by the fact that elected representatives and party members contribute more toward the left end of the political spectrum; but in the end, parties on the right tend to be better off financially than their counterparts on the left.

If all this were not enough, we shall see in the next chapter that donations to candidates and campaigns are by no means the only way that the most privileged sections of society have of influencing the political process. There are many other, often less regulated, ways, beginning with the funding of think tanks and the purchase of media outlets.

4

Beyond Politics: Private Funding
of the "Public Good"

AS WE HAVE JUST SEEN, the private funding of electoral democracy today involves three worrisome aberrations. First, not only do the richest sections of society contribute the bulk of this funding; it is governments that actually pay out a large part of what the richest (and only the richest) spend. Second, this funding gives a major advantage to conservative parties over others that are supposed to be a little less conservative. Third, this funding—which in many countries comes from companies as well as individuals—is partly reflected in the public policies adopted by governments (on the right as well as the left), although in theory these are supposed to take the preferences of the majority into account. Some might be tempted to speak of a new form of "corruption," pointing to Philip Morris and the tobacco lobby in Germany as an example of the "cancer" of money eating away at the electoral lungs of democracy. Without going that far, we can be sure that, in many present-day democracies, euros have a greater say than people.

Nor are these aberrations peculiar to the direct funding of political parties and campaigns. For a citizen eager to influence the result of elections, as well as the terms of the public debate, there are other potentially effective (and often even less regulated) channels of intervention, beginning with think tanks and media outlets. If the battle at the polls is hard to win, why not win the battle of ideas at an earlier stage?

Are Think Tanks a Disguised Form of Private Funding of Democracy?

In most countries—even those where donations to political parties and election campaigns are highly regulated—there is no limit to the sums that can be donated to political foundations and other think tanks.[1] And to say the least, these laboratories do not always glow from the transparency of their accounts.

In some cases, it has been clearly established that foundations must not campaign directly. In France, for example, only "parties" or "political groups" as defined in the electoral code—which are obliged to respect the legal rules on funding and transparency—are permitted to finance campaigns in any way at all. De facto, however, foundations participate in the democratic debate, sometimes greatly influencing it through the dissemination of ideas, the publication of studies and reports, or a highly visible media presence. They also tend to define their role as one of animating public political debate.

Once again, we shall begin our study of the question in France, before turning to other countries, particularly Germany, which has developed an interesting system of public funding for foundations linked to political parties. We shall also consider the case of the United States, where the grip on the "public interest" exerted by "philanthropists" has assumed staggering proportions, and then link the whole question up with media funding, another playing field dear to the hearts of the privileged.

Political Foundations French-Style, between Public Subsidies and Private Donations

Which are the principal French think tanks? If you have ever lived in France, you will probably know their names from the regular appearance of their leading figures on TV shows. From left to right: the Gabriel Péri Foundation, created on the initiative of the Communist Party; the Jean Jaurès Foundation, historically associated with the Socialist Party but independent of it; the Terra Nova Foundation, also active on the center left; the Foundation for Political Innovation (Fondapol), which situates itself on the center right; the Montaigne Institute, farther to the right on the political spectrum; and the Foundation for Public Administration and Policy Research, the ultra-liberal herald of the end of the state. We should also add the Concorde Foundation, geared to small and medium-sized enterprises and the world of industry; Europa Nova, a think tank concerned with Europe and a kind of little sister of the Robert Schumann Foundation; the Political Ecology Foundation, backed by the Green Europe Écologie–Les Verts (EELV) party; the Nicolas Hulot Foundation, whose eponymous backer, a former minister and defender of the environment, is a great lover of high-polluting vehicles; and the Res Publica Foundation, presided over by Jean-Pierre Chevènement.

Most of these think tanks are legally recognized as "public utility foundations": that is, they may receive donations not only from taxpayers (who are entitled to a 66 percent tax rebate[2]) but also from companies; meanwhile, since 1995, political parties and candidates have no longer been permitted to receive donations from companies in France. Donations to think tanks attract a 60 percent reduction in corporate and income tax (up to a limit of 0.5 percent of turnover). Let us note in passing the bad faith of the Foundation for Public Administration and Policy Research (IFRAP), registered since 2009 as being of public utility, which proudly brandishes the fact that it receives no public funding (supposedly a sign of independence) yet heavy-handedly insists on its website, using a tax deduction simulator no less,[3] that it is possible to offer tax exemption on donations. Is fiscal spending not a form of public funding? You would not think so from the budgetary papers of the French Finance Ministry. To be sure, it is an indirect form, but no less real for all that—and anyway, it is always curious to hear claims of "independence" when the one issuing those claims essentially relies on funding from private enterprise.

A certain number of these public utility foundations also receive direct public subsidies, either as what are commonly known as "prime ministerial subsidies" or (until their replacement in 2017) as special state subsidies available for allocation by members of the National Assembly and Senate (*la réserve parlementaire*).[4] The former, allocated at the discretion of the prime minister's head of cabinet, are quite sizable for a number of foundations: more than 1 million euros a year for Fondapol and 1.7 million euros (in 2016) for the Jean Jaurès Foundation. Not all foundations are in the same boat, however—far from it. Terra Nova, for example, received only 30,000 euros in 2013 and 2014 and still has to make do today with 200,000 euros a year, nearly nine times less than the Jean Jaurès Foundation (Figure 35). (The reader may wonder why the Montaigne Institute does not appear in this figure: it is not an oversight on my part but reflects the fact that this think tank does not receive direct public subsidies.) Moreover, although the sums are published online,[5] there is a complete lack of transparency about the way in which they are allocated. It is therefore understandable that some think tanks, not knowing the precise reason why their subsidies are lower than others, may sometimes feel unfairly treated. In this regard, France might have some lessons to learn from Germany, where, as we shall see in a moment, the public funding of think tanks is governed by precise rules.

As for transparency, it took some years before the "parliamentary reserve" allocations became public knowledge, although it was long considered legitimate in France for parliamentarians to have envelopes filled with public money to use as they saw fit.[6] The Jean Jaurès Foundation is again the great beneficiary, with a total of 668,000 euros received in 2016 (Figure 36).[7] The Concorde Foundation pales into insignificance beside it, having received a mere 3,000 euros for its "development of a plan for the country's recovery" (thanks to none other than Sarkozy's former defense minister Gérard Longuet!). Some think tanks are therefore much better endowed than others. The gap between Terra Nova and the Jean Jaurès Foundation is another striking example of this.[8] But is it not perhaps a blessing in disguise? When the "parliamentary reserve" was discontinued in the summer of 2017, it left the best endowed foundations struggling to make ends meet. A difficult backlash.

In the end, even the richest French think tanks, the Jean Jaurès Foundation and the Montaigne Institute, are relatively poor in comparison with their counterparts in Germany; neither has had a budget over 4 million euros during the past five years (Figure 37). These think tanks are also very poor in comparison with the political parties. To take just one example, the Jean Jaurès Foundation, with its resources of 2.5 million euros a year, is twenty-three times less well-endowed than the Socialist Party; whereas the resources of the German political foundations are not far short of those of their respective parties.

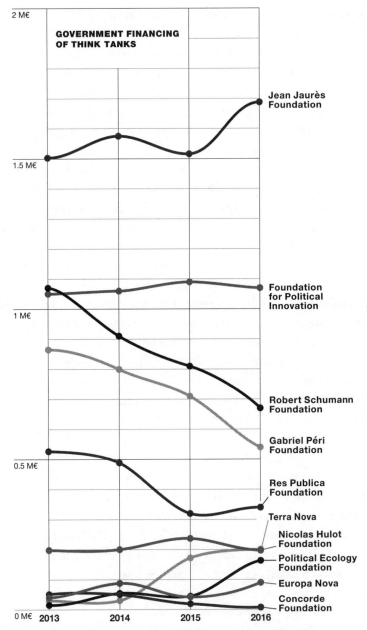

GOVERNMENT FINANCING OF THINK TANKS

2 M€

Jean Jaurès Foundation

1.5 M€

Foundation for Political Innovation

1 M€

Robert Schumann Foundation

Gabriel Péri Foundation

Res Publica Foundation

0.5 M€

Terra Nova

Nicolas Hulot Foundation

Political Ecology Foundation

Europa Nova

Concorde Foundation

0 M€ 2013   2014   2015   2016

Figure 35. French government's financial input into associations (prime minister's fund), annual amounts received by principal think tanks, 2013–2016

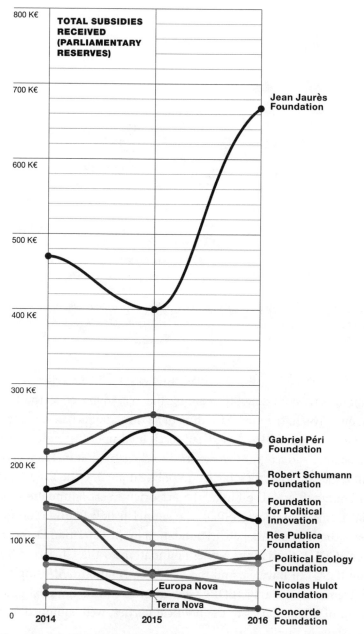

Figure 36. Subsidies received from parliamentary reserves by French think tanks (in thousands of euros), 2014–2016

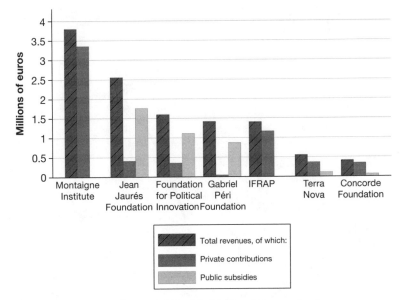

Figure 37. Revenues of principal French think tanks, annual averages 2012–2016

Germany's Rich and Institutionalized Think Tanks

Germany is without doubt the country that has advanced farthest—and most quickly—in the public funding of its think tanks (the famous *parteinahe Stiftungen*). They have been receiving important state subsidies since as long ago as 1967.[9] In contrast to the situation in France, these think tanks are directly attached to political parties: the Rosa Luxemburg Foundation to Die Linke, the Friedrich Ebert Foundation to the Social Democratic Party (SPD), the Heinrich Böll Foundation to the Greens, the Konrad Adenauer Foundation to the Christian Democratic Union (CDU), the Hanns Seidel Foundation to the Christian Social Union (CSU) in Bavaria, and the Friedrich Naumann Stiftung to the Free Democratic Party (FDP). The German think tanks should be thought of as ancillaries to the political parties, well equipped to hold center stage in public debate.

The German think tanks are also much older than their French counterparts. Whereas the main political foundations emerged in France around the year 2000,[10] some of the German ones date from well before the Second World War.[11] The Friedrich Ebert Foundation, for example, was established in 1925.[12] Of course, their roles then were not exactly the same as they are today. They took the form of political academies, with education a very large part of their mission, and this dimension actually became more pronounced after the Second World War, when they developed a large number of civic education programs. At the origins of the Konrad Adenauer Foundation (created in 1964) lies the Christian Democratic Center for Civic Education, which was founded in 1956 and soon turned into a political academy.

The main distinguishing feature of these German think tanks is the size of their resources, which come largely from the public subsidies they receive.[13] Most of the funds are allocated out of federal budgets, particularly those of the Interior Ministry, the Foreign Ministry, the Ministry of Economic Cooperation and Development, and the Ministry of Culture. Unlike in France, where public subsidies are left to the discretion of parliamentarians or the prime minister's office, the funding of political foundations in Germany depends on precisely defined arrangements. The six political foundations share the allocated budget on the basis of their average respective results in the four previous federal elections.

In 2017, 581 million euros of public money were paid to the German political think tanks (Figure 38), whose annual subsidies had been constantly increasing since the middle of the 2000s. If we compare the annual averages for the 2012–2016 period, we can see that Germany spends a sum three times greater on the public funding of political foundations (509 million euros) than on the funding of political parties (152 million euros).

How much does this represent for each foundation? In the 2012–2016 period, the Friedrich Ebert Foundation (associated with the SPD) received an annual average of 150 million euros (Figure 39); though not strictly comparable, this was seventy-one times more than the public subsidies paid to the Jean Jaurès Foundation (associated with the French Socialist Party), whose 2.1 million euros comprised an average of 1.6 million from the state and 513,000 from the "parliamentary reserve." In fact, 150 million euros are also sixty times more than the total resources

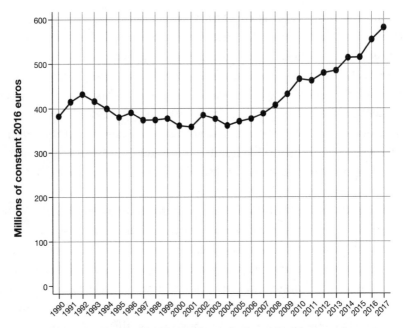

Figure 38. Total amounts of public funding of political foundations, Germany, 1990–2017

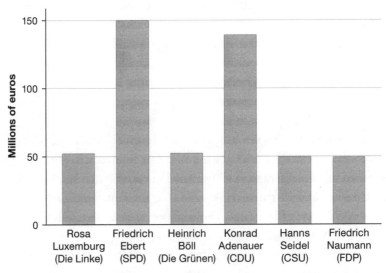

Figure 39. Public subsidies received by the principal German think tanks, annual averages 2012–2016

of the Jean Jaurès Foundation in France; it is a completely different ball game. More surprisingly, those 150 million euros make the German political think tanks much richer than the largest American political foundations (which I shall look at in a moment).

But although the German think tanks are richer, everything indicates that they are less "free." Their role has been largely institutionalized, and much of their funds is in effect allocated to international cooperation and foreign policy, rather than to German public debate and inputs into party election platforms.

I have calculated for the 2012–2016 period the sources of public subsidies to the German political foundations (Figure 40). More than half the total amount is paid by the ministry of economic cooperation and development: in other words, it serves to support the "diplomatic" role of German think tanks abroad. Thus, each of the two main German political foundations, the Friedrich Ebert Foundation and the Konrad Adenauer Foundation, has around sixty offices. Another 9 percent of the public funds in question come from the foreign ministry, mainly to allow the think tanks to disburse study grants.

Nevertheless, the German model of funding political foundations is extremely interesting, and it is clearly more satisfactory in terms of

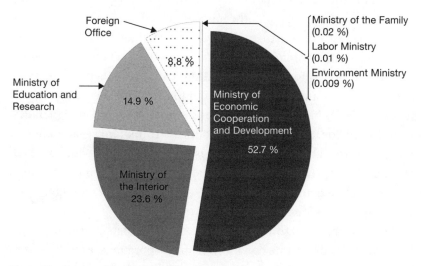

Figure 40. Sources of public subsidies received by political foundations, Germany, annual averages 2012–2016

transparency than the French funding systems involving a "parliamentary reserve" or the prime minister's stash of money.

In Spain, too, the think tanks are attached to political parties—the Fundación para el Análisis y los Estudios Sociales and the Fundación Humanismo y Democracia for the Popular Party; the Fundación Pablo Iglesias, the Fundación Jaime Vera, and the Fundación Ideas para el Progreso for the Socialist Party, and so on[14]—and they also receive public subsidies by virtue of such activities as cooperation with Latin America or the study of politics, sociology, and culture. To be sure, the sums in question are lower than in Germany, but between 2012 and 2016 Spanish political foundations received an annual average of just over 2 million euros in public subsidies.[15]

American Political Foundations and the
Private Capture of the Public Good

Whereas in Germany political foundations largely live off public subsidies, one is tempted to say that in the United States they define themselves "against the state."[16] In the Introduction, I already noted that a number of foundations depend on the readiness of self-proclaimed philanthropists to pursue the public good—a readiness that goes together with an unwillingness to pay taxes. To cut a long story short, the state is seen as ineffectual and philanthropists as defenders of a (better-defined) general interest; the aim, then, is to reduce the weight of the state as much as possible—and therefore the amount it can raise in taxes—so that private (theoretically nonprofit) foundations can spread their wings. There are tens of thousands of foundations in the United States today, in sectors as varied as health, education, research, defense, and foreign policy. Here I shall concentrate only on "political" think tanks—and only on the main ones in the field—but there is evidently a much wider problem when a wholly private definition of the public good is being substituted for a collective definition. We shall return to this in a moment, when we discuss the hidden face of philanthropy.

America's political think tanks, like the whole of its charitable sector, live essentially on private donations from corporations, as well as from wealthy individuals and other foundations. But we should be under no illusion. In the United States, as in France, private donations to foundations also involve (indirect but sizable) public funding. One irony of this is that the think tanks in question, though usually with strong political leanings, often declare themselves to be "strictly nonpartisan," so that tax exemption can be claimed under provisions covering donations to entities with the status of foundations.[17]

To what extent do these think tanks benefit from the largesse of private donors? I shall focus here on the main political foundations in the United States: on the liberal, progressive side, the Brookings Institution and the Center for American Progress; in the center, the Center for Strategic and International Studies (CSIS) and the independent Council on Foreign Relations; on the conservative side, the American Enterprise Institute, the Heritage Foundation, and Americans for Prosperity (AFP, the political organization of the billionaire Koch brothers, who have been funding ultra-conservative movements for decades, and whom we shall have occasion to meet again); and farther right still, the Mises Institute (which rejects the "conservative" label) and the libertarian Cato Institute. The annual accounts of these foundations—which do not always let in any light—make it hard to differentiate their various sources of income. But let us take a closer look at their total annual revenue (Figure 41).

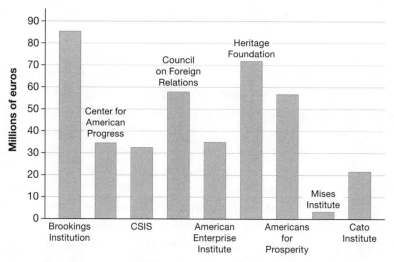

Figure 41. Revenues of principal think tanks, United States, annual averages 2012–2016

It seems clear that even the "poorest" of these American think tanks, the academic Mises Institute (named after Ludwig von Mises, the Austrian American economist from the first half of the twentieth century), is as rich as the richest of the French think tanks (the Montaigne Institute), with an annual average income of 3.3 million euros. As for the other American think tanks, the orders of magnitude quite simply defy any attempt at comparison. The income of the Brookings Institution, the Heritage Foundation, and Americans for Prosperity is in the tens of millions of euros.

The growing importance of foundations is not a phenomenon peculiar to the United States. I have given the example of the Council on Foreign Relations, but I could equally well have mentioned Chatham House (the Royal Institute of International Affairs) in the United Kingdom or Civitas (also in the United Kingdom), an ostensibly independent think tank that, in reality, has a strong right-wing leaning. Often, the development of foundations is thought of as a parallel process to the decline of the welfare state—as if, faced with the "crisis of the state," it was necessary to replace it with a new kind of "market" supposedly not oriented to profit.

The Hidden Face of Philanthropy

We have just briefly surveyed the world of political foundations, a side of the private funding of our democracies that is too often overlooked. This neglect is all the more problematic because even in countries where the spending of political parties and the donations they receive is subject to regulation, foundations have a free hand to receive and spend donors' money. It is as if these juggernauts of public debate did not affect the electoral process in any way. One euro more on the side of money in weighing up votes.

To this we need to add that marvelously packaged tax-avoidance strategies most often lie hidden behind the radiant face of disinterested charity and its marvels of generosity; that in many cases public money serves to finance private interests; and that, worst of all, everyone applauds it.

Massive Misuse of Public Money for Private Profit?

Here is a revealing story if ever there was one. French citizens are supposed to thank their lucky stars: not only does the minister of labor, Muriel Pénicaud, have everything you would expect to find in a great minister, not only is she an active figure in civil society who knows all about the food industry (she used to work at Danone) as well as the great shows of Las Vegas (where she promoted the "Business France" image and campaigned for the current French president); on top of all that, she is an artist. By day she is said to have a golden touch in dismantling workers' rights, and by night she is an acclaimed photographer without equal. Does not such a talent deserve to have a gem cut specially for her? Don't worry, Muriel Pénicaud may have worked a few years at virtualizing the world, but she still has her feet on the ground. Well aware of her skills, she created a special "endowment fund" (*fonds de dotation*),[18] Le Fonds Sakura, with a mission "to promote, support, and develop activities in the public interest." For example, Sakura supports La Maison Laurentine, a "center of discreet art,"[19] which for some years has had the good taste to exhibit the artworks of none other than Muriel Pénicaud. They say that if you want something done, it's always best to do it yourself.

You may ask why a little artistic chit-chat on the side should be a problem. Well, Muriel Pénicaud was not content to create the Fonds Sakura; she also deposited a lot of money in it—670,000 euros to be precise.[20] And in France, donations to endowment funds entitle the donors to tax relief of 66 percent.[21] In other words, Muriel Pénicaud saved more than 442,000 euros in taxes from financing a foundation to exhibit her own artistic output—sakuras may be cherry trees in Japanese, but does that mean money grows on them?—and from misusing public money for private interests. We should be clear that such misuse is perfectly legal. But that is the whole problem: the creation—and continuation—of a system that allows the rich to get the state to pay two-thirds of the bill for their political preferences and artistic activities, with money received from other taxpayers. Surely there is something amazing about a system that benefits the private artistic ambitions of a minister of labor but does not make such benefits available to the media, because they are not permitted to claim endowment fund status.

Let us note another paradox. When a government decides not to increase, but to reduce, the tax burden on the richest people in society—as Emmanuel Macron did in 2017 by abolishing the ISF solidarity tax on wealth—it usually leads to a *decline* in private donations to public interest bodies. Yes, a decline not an increase, even though the rich emerge from such a reform even richer (since they pay less in taxes). Is there not a contradiction here? No—not when you realize that the rich do not usually donate out of the goodness of their hearts; if that were the case, they would give more when they accumulate more. The fact is that their main motive is usually to avoid paying taxes. So, if the ISF no longer exists, they no longer need to donate to reduce their ISF tax bill, and they do less charitable work as a result.

Deductio ad Absurdum

Is this peculiar to France? Unfortunately not. In the Introduction I noted that the Chan Zuckerberg Initiative, apart from being a nonprofit foundation, provided a number of tax benefits that made it a huge boon for the founder of Facebook. David Yermack, in an article aptly titled "Deductio ad Absurdum," has perfectly documented the absurdity of the American system, which allows rich CEOs extensive tax relief for donating stock to their own "private family foundations."[22] Yermack further shows that these donations—which do not come under the law on "insider dealing"—most often occur just before a fall in the price of the company's shares. According to his results, a number of CEOs fraudulently backdate their donations so as to augment the personal tax benefits they derive from them. Not only does US legislation mean that these "generous" benefactors enjoy tax relief; they also do not have to pay the capital gains tax to which they would be liable if they simply sold these shares.

The many complex tax benefits that come with donations to foundations in the United States depend on, among other things, the form of the foundation in question. Here I shall try to outline the present state of play, but the reader who is short of time may fast-forward to the next section, where I more straightforwardly propose an end to these regressive and antidemocratic systems. (As for millionaire readers in search of loopholes, they would do better to seek their tax lawyers' advice while there is still time—if they have not done so already.)

In the United States, nonprofit organizations benefit from a number of tax exemptions. For some of them, known as 501(c)(3)s or "public charities," the contributions they receive qualify the donating individuals or companies to deduct them from their taxable income.[23] What does this mean in practice? Let us imagine I am a rich, unmarried American woman straight out of *Gossip Girl* or *Sex and the City*, whichever you prefer. Thanks to my outstanding talents in mergers and acquisitions, my annual income is in excess of $1 million. Above $500,000, this is taxed at a rate of 37 percent. In a (well considered) burst of generosity, I decide to make a donation of $100,000 to the Salvation Army. This $100,000 is deductible from my taxable income and therefore saves me $37,000 in taxes, so that the donation actually costs me no more than $63,000. I have stressed in previous chapters the injustice of a system of tax incentives linked to political donations and campaigns in various countries—a system conceived for the most advantaged groups in society. Donations to political parties do not entitle donors to tax relief in the United States, but we find there the same injustice—and the same regressivity, with the poorest paying more than the richest—in the case of foundations. Imagine, for example, that my annual income was only $8,000, and that I was therefore liable to a marginal tax rate of 10 percent. Not only would I not be able to donate $100,000 to the Salvation Army; even if I gave $100 dollars, the cost to me would be $90 dollars, whereas it would be $63 dollars to my millionaire alter ego. The system differs in details from the French and Italian systems, but it has a similar general effect.

To this fiscal injustice associated with the 501(c)(3) should be added many other openings available to rich Americans hungry for influence. After all, although donations under 501(c)(3) are tax-deductible, they have two major drawbacks: public foundations, at least on paper, are not allowed to take part in electoral politics, and the donations they receive are made public. By contrast, donations under 501(c)(4)—that is, to "social welfare groups"—may not be tax-deductible, but they can be kept secret. The foundations themselves are exempt from taxes and are permitted to engage in politics (with the condition, again only on paper, that this is not the main reason for their existence). Perhaps you have already heard of "dark money groups," a term popularized in Jane Mayer's excellent book *Dark Money,* in which the American journalist investigates the secret funds of the Right, beginning with Charles and David Koch and their petrochemicals fortune that is the second largest in the United States. These billionaire brothers spend millions on the Republican Party and on ultraconservative think tanks that will champion their ideas, particularly an end to all forms of government.[24] Mayer lists the numerous opportunities for the megarich in the labyrinths of American philanthropy, from 501(c)(4) to the famous "donor-advised funds," an unrivaled formula for those who wish to erase all trace of a financial contribution. When we read her description of the Donors Trust—probably the largest of these funds, which redistributed $750 million between 1999 and 2015—we cannot help wondering when American democracy ceased to exist. For not only do donor-advised funds create an entitlement to tax relief; they do not have to distribute money immediately, still less to disclose the provenance of the donations they receive. And as if that were not enough, another instrument—the 501(c)(6) or "business league"—is increasingly used by self-styled American philanthropists, beginning with the Koch brothers. These "leagues" have two advantages: the lack of any transparency regarding the identity of donors, and tax exemption for part of the donations (considered as membership fees, under the rubric of professional expenses).[25]

Note moreover that, while these deeply inegalitarian tax deductions for charitable contributions have been introduced on the basis that the philanthropic sector will combat inequality and eliminate the most basic injustices in our societies, it turns out that in the United States—which has more than 1.5 million public charities—charitable giving is more frequently about the pursuit of individual projects than a mechanism for redistribution. This has been demonstrated by Rob Reich, who points out that "in some cases, philanthropy actively exacerbates social inequalities in a way that seems fundamentally at odds with certain egalitarian aims of social policy."[26] Why is it so? Because while some charitable donations provide for basic needs, many are oriented to higher education or the arts and do not constitute support for the needy. Reich takes the example of private funding for public schools. Given that "wealthy schools and school districts can raise substantially more money than can schools that have high concentrations of poor students," the consequence of local education foundations is to worsen existing inequalities in public funding between schools and school districts—not to speak of the fact that this happens with the support of the state through tax subsidies for charitable donations.

What if it was decided collectively that those who earn and / or own the most should also pay the most, instead of naively assuming that they will make charitable contributions to the collective effort? For even if this were true and they contributed the equivalent of what might be expected from truly progressive income and inheritance taxation, they would do it in line with their own preferences, not to satisfy the collective preferences. The key point is that collective preferences should be expressed at the ballot box, in accordance with an egalitarian and democratic logic of participation, not in the elitist boardrooms of secretive foundations. As things stand today, however, the growing role of private money in the democratic process means that collective preferences no longer translate directly into the choosing of governments and public policies—hence those absurd tax niches that weaken the state and benefit only a minority of the population. Economic inequalities reinforce political inequalities, which in their turn reinforce economic inequalities. It is a vicious circle, which the political scientists Martin Gilens and Benjamin Page have superbly tracked and documented in the case of the United States.[27]

Philanthropy against Democracy?

We can go further and follow the line of investigation in the excellent book by Robert Reich and others on philanthropy in democratic societies (or rather, in the United States—this restriction being the only possible criticism of their work).[28] To what extent, they ask, is there not a contradiction in the very idea of philanthropy in a democracy? For what is philanthropy if not the stentorian voice of a few plutocrats, whereas democratic societies are supposed to be the locus of civic equality? If philanthropy means giving more votes to a few individuals on the pretext that they have larger purses, then it conflicts with the definition of democracy: "one person, one vote"—however large the purse.

Philanthropy is, or at least has become, a power—the power of money. It would like to present itself as a doer of good, but in reality it is arrogant and, for most people, threatening.[29] In a society where public goods were no longer provided by the state but by a handful of philanthropists, the great majority of citizens would be dependent on the good will of those billionaires. It would be necessary to go and beg for public goods; indeed, that is sometimes necessary today, as museum directors or university presidents faced with massive cuts in funding will tell you. Fundraising has become a profession to be learned, the supplicant an entertainer one invites to add a little sparkle to ego-drenched dinner tables. In a properly functioning democracy, where the superrich pay their taxes and Parliament debates how large the taxes should be and what they should be used for, the public authorities deliver public goods in line with the preferences of the median voter.

Perhaps most startling of all is the fact that, although foundations are subsidized by public money, they are not responsible to anyone (or only to their executive boards, usually consisting of not much more than the founders and their children or closest friends[30]). Foundations are not responsible to "clients," as corporations are, for example. They sell nothing but give instead: who could complain about that? Nor—need we say it?—are philanthropists in any way responsible to citizens. Sure, they claim to act in the public good, but that does not mean they comply with any electoral or other democratic principle. Philanthropists do not have to give an account of themselves to anyone. In their way, they are autocrats with no fixed term of rule, exempt from even the illusion of an election that presidents claiming to represent the people's will have to undergo in Russia or Egypt.

I repeat: they have no fixed term of rule. The most amazing, and not the least frightening, development is that foundations in the United States can exist *in perpetuum*. And when we see the speed at which their wealth piles up—particularly since the higher the capital endowment, the higher the interest rates it enjoys[31]—there is a danger that their light will never fade and that their weight in our democracies will become more and more significant. That is a very real danger—if it is collectively decided that that is how things will be. But there is an alternative way to go, which would involve limiting the lifespan of foundations, profoundly reforming the tax benefits to which they are entitled, and democratizing the operation of their executive boards.

So, are the ideas of democracy and philanthropy incompatible? Or, to put it another way, does the spread of philanthropy threaten the basic democratic principles of our societies? I think the answer to both questions is yes—and I hope to have persuaded you of this. But let us switch sides for a moment and consider Robert Reich's argument, in the third chapter of *Philanthropy in Democratic Societies,* that democracy and philanthropy are basically compatible. Indeed, in his view, foundations have an important role to play in democratic societies, for two reasons.

First, Reich maintains, since philanthropists are not responsible to anyone and their foundations can last forever, philanthropy promotes risk-taking and innovation, whereas governments and markets are constrained—the former by elections, the latter by investors—to make only low-risk investments that can show a visible profit in the relatively short term. In other words, only Elon Musk is mad enough—or, sorry, sufficiently free of short-term constraints and responsibility, therefore visionary enough—to want to head off to Mars and colonize outer space. I am not sure why, probably because I have seen the film *Snowpiercer,* which would dampen the enthusiasm of the most extreme techno-optimists, I do not find this argument convincing. More seriously— although the general freeze-up produced by the geo-engineering response to global warming is a fine allegory—the problem for me is the very fact that philanthropists are not responsible to anyone. The obligation that governments have, at regular intervals, to give an account of themselves to their citizens is a good thing; it reduces the danger that they will embark on senseless projects, especially as issues such as trans-humanism are too important for us not to wish society to debate them and reach collective decisions reflecting the preferences of the majority, rather than the individual choices of billionaires with a peculiar sense of morality.

Reich's second argument in favor of foundations is more interesting. In his view, whereas the state seeks to satisfy the average voter's preferences—which may lead it, for example, to support only cultural activity that appeals to the broad mass—philanthropy reflects the preferences of a small number of rich people and allows for greater "pluralism" or the emergence of an avant-garde. Long live Jeff Koons and his tulips! At the same time, however, Reich himself recognizes that philanthropists tend to be rather conservative in their tastes—and anyway, even if they were super-revolutionary, their preferences would in no way reflect those of the majority. Reich is right to stress the danger that, in wishing to satisfy the preferences of the average voter, governments may financially support only works of art that appeal to the broad mass of the population. Nevertheless, nothing forces us to stick with a system in which the state responds to the preferences of the average voter. On the contrary, each citizen (rather than just a handful of philanthropists) could be offered the chance to finance the art foundation of his or her choice—an idea not unlike the system of party funding that I propose in Chapter 10. It would make it possible to guarantee representation of the plurality of citizens' preferences, instead of settling for those expressed by a minority of rich individuals.

A Glaring Lack of Transparency

In France, foundations recognized as being of public utility—the status chosen by most political think tanks—are required to publish detailed annual reports that may be consulted in the *Journal officiel,* while in Germany the accounts of political foundations may also be easily found online. However, such transparency is by no means typical of the system prevailing in a large number of countries.

This partly explains why, in their attempts to influence the democratic process, some "philanthropists" choose to channel their activity through foundations, instead of relying on donations to political parties. In the United States, for instance, all donations above a few hundred dollars to political parties and candidates have to be publicly disclosed, more or less in real time, on the website of the electoral commission; campaign expenditure, too, must be made public. Millionaires shy about their largesse can therefore choose to do things differently and use a whole range of foundations, including the civic foundations or "donor-advised funds" mentioned above. What is ruled out is failure to innovate! In the twenty-first century, the latest craze among influence-seekers for whom money is no object is therefore to write out fat checks to nonprofit organizations—when they do not set them up directly—as a way of promoting their private preferences away from the public gaze.

We should note that even in France, although foundations of public utility publish their annual accounts online, they do not disclose the identity of those who pay contributions to them. Donations to foundations as well as to political campaigns or parties remain anonymous; even their distribution is not made public. (Between 1993 and 1995, political parties did have to give a list of corporate donations at the end of their accounts.) This is a serious lack of transparency in comparison with other democracies such as Germany, the United Kingdom, or Italy, and the French regulator seems in no hurry to make progress.

The Capture of Intellectuals

Another aberration amid this floodtide of philanthropy is the capture of intellectual milieux by private money, with a growing confusion between what counts as "science" and as "research" funded by shadowy interest groups. Often the results of such research are as dubious as their sources of finance. Naomi Oreskes and Erik Conway speak in this connection of "merchants of doubt."[32] Their book describes in great detail how conservative lobbies have attempted in recent decades to deflect and discredit researchers in fields as varied as the dangers of tobacco (no link with cancer, of course) and acid rain (no link with factory chimneys and other industrial pollution, and no consequences for our health), or in relation to the struggle against communism (a justified strategic expense since the United States could have won a nuclear war against the Soviet Union). These merchants of doubt have proven just how effective they can be, especially in the health field, when doubt gains the upper hand in a climate of controversy, and it is impossible for politics to regulate things as it should (that is, in the general interest).

Climate change is the best illustration of how private interests instill this policy of doubt. What are we to make of the fact that so few Americans are convinced of the reality of climate change? In practice this leads to political impasses, such as the US refusal to ratify the Paris Agreement of 2017 or the Kyoto Protocol before it, but also to unsustainable consumption choices on the part of disbelieving citizens. Justin Farrell has studied in detail the network of political and financial players who fuel the controversy with their skepticism.[33] Campaigns against the current, suggesting, for example, that CO_2 has beneficial effects, are funded mainly by corporations such as ExxonMobil[34]—the oil and gas giant that largely contributed to the Republican election campaign in 2016 through the Exxon Mobil Corporation Political Action Committee.

Without wishing in the least to excuse these loathsome strategies on the part of ultraconservative clubs and petroleum corporations, we should end by noting that the success of "doubt" more generally—from climate change denial to creationist theories—is bound up with the decline in public research. Here, too, private money is substituting itself for public funding: the National Science Foundation (NSF), for example, has suffered deep cuts to its budget in the last few years. In France, although the private capture of academic elites seems almost nonexistent in comparison with the situation in America, there is real cause for concern about the consequences of the collapse of public investment in universities and research.[35] The number of posts combining teaching and research in universities and elsewhere in higher education has been continually falling since 2009.

The Media: A Potentially Very Effective
Tool of Influence

Let us recapitulate. I am a billionaire, with strong political convictions that I would like to promote, especially if my billions are at stake. As a German or American, I am free to back my hobbyhorses to my heart's content. As a UK citizen, I can donate as much as I see fit to the political party of my choice, although there is an upper limit on what it can spend. As a French citizen, I am limited in the size of my contributions—but it would be unseemly of me to complain, since the richer I am, the more the state delights in adding to my kitty. And there is another large "but." Nothing stops me from contributing hundreds of millions of euros to the running of my favorite think tanks, which help, by a very slight detour, to win the battle of ideas. If I wish, I can do this without making it publicly known, since think tanks are by no means models of transparency when it comes to the identity of their contributors.

Is that enough? Well, if it isn't enough for me, I can always count on the media. And the good news, if I've got millions to spare, is that the sales are on in the information market.

Media Independence in Question

From the United States to France via Italy, or from the United Kingdom to Spain with a detour through Germany, the crisis of the traditional media has everywhere gone together with a change of ownership.[36] One constant is that, in the past few decades, more and more media outlets have passed into the hands of millionaires (or billionaires) whose main income derives from other sectors such as construction, finance, or telecommunications.

I could give many examples of this. In France, where everything took off in 2010 with the buying up of *Le Monde* by Pierre Bergé, Xavier Niel, and Matthieu Pigasse, the cable and telecoms magnate Patrick Drahi[37] now owns the newspapers *Libération* and *L'Express* (or what is left of it since the slashing of its editorial staff), as well as BFM TV, BFM Business, and RMC, all under the aegis of the SFR Group and housed in one of the four buildings of the new Qu4drans complex. This is the "content" motivating the visionaries behind the telecoms-media convergence. And it is another visionary, Vincent Bolloré, who in 2014 took over as head of Vivendi's supervisory board. Since then, his prime mission seems to have been to smash his new media toy, comprising everything from Canal+—which has lost more than a million subscribers, as well as the opportunity to broadcast high-quality investigative documentaries that its owner thought preferable to censor—through to I-Télé, or sorry, I mean CNews, since not only the audience and editors of I-Télé but even its name have disappeared since Vincent Bolloré decided to use his basic ownership rights to quash journalistic independence. The king has triumphed, to be sure, but he is naked. As for the Bouygues group—top dog in construction and telecoms but also a longstanding funder of French political campaigns—it continues to wear the TF1 media label, although it is no longer as new as it used to be.

This mix of genres and activities is far from peculiar to France. In Spain, when we look at the principal shareholders of the PRISA media group (which owns the leading daily *El País* as well as many radio stations such as Cadena SER), we find the Amber Capital hedge fund, a trio of banks (Santander, La Caixa, HSBC), and also a Mexican businessman, Roberto Rojas Alcantara, the founder and owner of the low-cost airline Viva Aerobus.[38] But we cannot speak of Spain without also speaking of Italy, since another major Spanish daily, *El Mundo,* is owned by Unidad Editorial, the Spanish branch of the Italian RCS MediaGroup, one of whose long-time shareholders—indeed, principal shareholder—was the Fiat vehicle manufacturer, until it scaled down its participation and pulled out altogether in 2016. Thus, for forty years in Italy, the leading daily *Corriere della Sera* was partly owned by an automobile group that also had a large shareholding in *La Stampa,* long considered the "voice" of Fiat's Agnelli family.[39] Media, industry, politics: the interlocking has come to seem almost natural in Italy—probably more than elsewhere in Europe—since these three facets of power have been closely associated there for decades. One need only think of Silvio Berlusconi, businessman, politician, and media magnate, who, through his Fininvest holding company, owns the Mediaset communications group that includes three television channels: Canale 5, Italia 1, and Rete 4.

In the United States, the situation is scarcely better, stretching from the spread of the Murdoch empire to the Meredith group's recent purchase of *Time* magazine (supported by the Koch brothers, whom I will not present a second time).[40] Alongside these moves, the purchase of the *Washington Post* in late 2013 by Amazon founder, Jeff Bezos, appears almost anecdotal. In this case, moreover, all is not black and white, and it has to be recognized that Jeff Bezos has recruited a few dozen journalists, at a time when his competitors have been making more and more cutbacks.

Why, you may ask, is this mix of industrial and media activities a problem? Did the Meredith group not declare that Koch Equity Development (the Koch brothers' investment fund) would have no seat on its board, and no influence on the editorial line of the group in general or *Time* in particular? I might reply—laying off on Vincent Bolloré for now—by taking the example of Bernard Arnault, who put such energy into imposing his editorial line on the daily *Le Parisien* that even its journalists publicly deplore its indulgent articles on the LVMH luxury goods conglomerate or the Carrefour supermarket chain (of which Arnault is respectively the owner and a major shareholder).[41] I could add any number of other cases of intervention by owners who seem not to understand the principle of editorial independence. But I prefer not to persist. After all, faced with such examples of trampling on the freedom of information, an opponent will always dig up some published article ostensibly against the interests of this or that newspaper owner. Do we really want to get involved in that game of Go?

The problem is more fundamental—and threefold. First, whether it is a question of family media groups or of owners active mainly outside the media sector, the protection of editorial independence is much too often left to their discretion, whereas it should be guaranteed by law and encouraged through a more pluralist ownership of the media, including by journalists as well as readers, listeners, and viewers.[42] As in the case of political foundations, the concentration of power in the hands of one man—or of him and his family—cannot augur well for the functioning of our democracies. Second, beyond the (sometimes very real) dangers of direct censorship on the owner's part, there is also the question of journalistic self-censorship. How can a journalist deal calmly with economic matters that directly affect the industrial interests of a paper's owners? How, for example, can an editor on the *Washington Post* raise the need to regulate a more and more concentrated e-commerce sector, when the owner of the paper is the founder and CEO of Amazon? To be sure, many journalists carry on regardless, but it makes their work much more complicated than it ought to be, especially when the precarious climate in their profession means that they have to fear not only for their jobs but also for the survival of media dependent on the whims and often obscure motives of their owners. All this increases the mistrust of readers, who legitimately wonder what interests may lie behind this or that article.[43] Historically, the ceiling on campaign donations in the United States was based mainly on fears of corruption or the appearance of corruption. The same should apply to the media: the problem is not only intervention by their owners but the *appearance* of such intervention, which, in sowing doubt, tends to delegitimize the work of journalists.

Third, and lastly, what does the acquisition of news media mean for billionaires with flourishing industrial activities, if, as is often the case, they are not *directly* profitable? For an industrialist who has been kept on the margins of the "world of politics"—especially in countries where the price of an entry ticket is subject to the regulations governing campaigns and parties—a media outlet is a great way of opening doors, whether those of lawmakers or regulatory agencies, Washington or the Élysée Palace, the Bundestag or the House of Commons. It can serve the same purpose as an expertly tailored tuxedo, smoothing the way up the staircase to power. To buy a media outlet for yourself is a little like funding an election campaign, except that there are no limits and no obligation to be transparent. It assures you of a place at all the tables even if you are "not very political"; you just have to be concerned about regulation of your sector of activity—or rather, have an interest in ensuring that there is none.

Do Funding the Media and Funding Parties Belong to the Same Struggle?

Often, then, it is only one step from funding the media to funding political parties—a step quickly taken by politicians who have their own media. Italy is out in the lead in this respect, from Silvio Berlusconi to Carlo De Benedetti. But it is also a step taken in many other democracies, where there is no shortage of examples of businessmen who fund both parties and media. The most "internationalist" of these is probably Rupert Murdoch, the founder and owner of the ultraconservative Fox News, and financial backer for decades of both the British Tories and the US Republicans. But some now see Murdoch as a man of the last century, preoccupied with his own succession, who may be being overtaken on his right by our libertarian figurehead Peter Thiel, the founder of Paypal. Thiel has already said that he wants to create his own TV channel to compete with Fox News, which is not sufficiently conservative for his taste. This is the Peter Thiel, remember, who funded not only Ron Paul's Super PAC in 2012 but also Donald Trump's campaign in 2016.[44]

Who are some of the other donors of Donald Trump, that peerless lover of media independence? First come the Mercers, father Robert and daughter Rebekah, who are none other than the owners of the ultraconservative (dis)information site Breitbart News, and who, not content to amuse themselves in Washington, have also pumped money into the Brexit campaign in the United Kingdom. Robert Mercer, an old friend of Nigel Farage, is a major funder of Cambridge Analytica, a firm that specialized in targeting voters on Facebook to swing the referendum in 2016 in favor of Brexit.[45] Big data, media, campaign funding: the Mercer success story would be incomplete without a political foundation. Commonly known as the Mercer Family Foundation, it is a philanthropic organization if ever there was one, interested primarily in science, higher education, and the well-being of army veterans. You can almost hear the cheers.

I could stop there. The examples are too numerous, and there is no point in listing them all. But allow me to end this American tour by mentioning Sheldon Adelson, a casino magnate and open-handed contributor to the Republican Party—and to Trump's campaign in 2016—who in 2015 bought the *Las Vegas Review-Journal,* the main newspaper in Nevada, the state from which he derives by far the greatest part of his financial income.[46] Note also that this tendency to fund the media with one hand and political parties with the other is by no means peculiar to the United States or even the rich Western democracies. In India, for instance, Subhash Chandra—who modestly presents himself on his website as "visionary, father of Indian television, and philanthropist"—is the owner of the Essel Group (with its numerous TV channels and newspapers) and a member of the upper house of Parliament (the Rajya Sabha), to which he was elected in 2016 as an independent backed by the right-wing Hindu nationalist Bharatiya Janata Party (BJP) of the present prime minister, Narendra Modi. It is a heady mix, which since 2017 has enabled Chandra to sit on the permanent committee on information technologies—a committee in charge of regulating the media![47] Nor is he the only Indian parliamentarian with media interests—far from it. The MP Vivek Gupta, for example, is founding president of the Hindi daily *Sanmarg* in the east of the country; the tycoon Rajeev Chandrasekhar, also a member of the Rajya Sabha, not only runs one of the most popular news channels in Kerala and a mass circulation daily, but in 2017 also had a hand in launching the English-language Republic TV.

So, even if everything is not black or white, even if there are always independent media and brilliant journalists working in far from optimum conditions, the overall picture is frightening enough. Democracies, did you say democracies? The real point is not so much to expose the faults as to find solutions. What should be done to face the juggernaut of often conservative media, which have become another string in the bow of billionaire ideologues already well equipped to achieve their aims?

Taking Control of the Public Media: A Bad Response to Lack of Independence in the Private Media

The Nonprofit Media Organization: I proposed this in *Saving the Media* as a truly democratic model of ownership, such that decisions no longer depend on the size of checks but are taken by executive boards consisting not only of shareholders but also of journalists and readers, where everyone has a say and the votes are more evenly distributed than the capital. This does not go as far as a purely cooperative form—one person, one vote—which, although it should be the bedrock of electoral politics, suffers from excesses of its own in the world of business. But my proposed model would make it possible to democratize the relationship between capital and power by capping the voting rights of the largest shareholders (above 10 percent of the capital, for example) in order to expand the voting rights of all the others. Apart from the media, this might also apply to political foundations: democratization of their management would make more acceptable the production of the public good by these mammoths of philanthropy.

Of course, the division of power within the enterprise—whether a media company, a political think tank, or private companies in general—is not the only issue here. Nevertheless, it should be thought of as a key block in the rebuilding of our democratic institutions. And those who see it as an attack on private property—which is not at all what it is—should reflect more on the encroachments by a few private interests feeding well off our public liberties. There may even be a willingness to go further, by limiting the size and lifespan of political foundations, as well as the amount they can receive in donations or the sums they are allowed to spend. I can already hear someone shout: "*an attack on free speech!*" But what remains of our collective freedom of expression if our votes are captured even in the ballot box? The concentration of market power is regulated almost everywhere, and so too should the concentration of philanthropy. As for the media, particularly in the audiovisual sector, regulations already exist even in the United States to define their obligations, both within and outside election periods, and to limit their share of the market. Why should some simple rules not be added to democratize the way in which they are governed?

In fact, what is the alternative? It is always possible to do nothing and accept things as they are, but then what is the point of writing (or reading) books? I am still much too young to give that up. But I am also scared of a different kind of radicalism, sometimes expressed in the struggle for media independence, which consists in using the same weapons as your opponent. Have too many media been captured by conservative forces with unlimited resources behind them? Well, let's oppose them with other media that have been captured by the forces of progress. In a way, that kind of thinking was practiced in Cristina Kirchner's Argentina or Hugo Chávez's Venezuela. You can understand the argument: If all the private media are in the hands of oligarchs bent on keeping (or removing) the Left from power, why not restore some balance by taking over the public media, at least for a time? But that cannot be the solution. In Venezuela, there were certainly plenty of aberrations in the Andrés Pérez era or during the coup d'état in 2002, which was backed by the Venezuelan bosses and media as well as the United States,[48] at a time when Chávez stood for democratic legitimacy. But nothing can justify the subsequent closure of private audiovisual media under Chávez, or the arrests of journalists under Nicolas Maduro and the gradual takeover of the main opposition media by financiers close to the regime. It was a case of going from one aberration to another. Nor, in Argentina, can one really applaud the law on audiovisual media pushed through in 2009; it may have been necessary, as it put an end to the high degree of concentration in the audiovisual sector, but the motive that led to it is open to criticism—that is, a determination to weaken the Clarín group, which had become critical of the Kirchner government.

To be sure, these few sentences are not enough, and my only aim here is to evoke the infinite complexity of certain situations. I do not claim to draw any definitive lessons. But it is important to establish the facts and to outline some perspectives that, even if they do not seem altogether good, are perhaps not the worst. In the past few years, I have been struck by the enthusiasm that the model of a Nonprofit Media Organization can arouse among committed citizens and journalists, yet also by the inadequacy of this model when faced with state violence, threats and intimidation, bankruptcies, and arrests that can cause journalists to spend more time in police stations than in their offices. With such trampling on liberties, how can it be said that better governance of the media is the solution? In Turkey, for example, the Nonprofit Media Organization seems a mere drop in the ocean beside the brutality of a government whose prisons hold the largest number of journalists anywhere in the world. In Egypt, where journalists at the independent online *Mada Masr* wage a daily battle to inform people and to keep their website going, the Nonprofit Media Organization is part of a horizon about which one might dream if it did not seem so remote from reality. And in a whole range of developing countries, where citizens do not have the means to buy papers, how can ways of funding them ever be found? Still, even the journalists at the online *Mada Masr* with whom I had the opportunity to exchange views saw the issue of governance as key to regaining media independence.

We are speaking here of the media and of political parties and foundations. Of course, the deep reforms to the funding of political life that I propose in this book, as well as moves toward a mixed parliamentary assembly representative of the social-occupational structure of society, make sense only in democratic systems that, however imperfect, provide for regular elections and the freedom for candidates to run in them. Should this be seen as the miracle solution applicable in every country, even where the rule of law is still in its early stages? I think the question answers itself. But does that mean we should consider these solutions unsatisfactory, or insufficient?

On the contrary—and I shall return to this in much greater detail in Part Three—they would mark an important advance toward greater democratization of our exhausted regimes, which, we have reason to fear—in the age of Donald Trump—could suddenly lurch into a populism from which there is no turning back. This chapter ending might be called "I'm lost whatever happens": I can already hear conservatives fulminating against "communism" and attacks on free speech, or leftists waxing vociferous against "conservatism," as if the rules of the game cannot really be changed under the rule of law. We should not fear profound legal changes to the rules of the game—changes that will, where necessary, reduce the scope for private money and therefore private interests.

Let us end with a brief mention of something that I will not have the space to discuss further in this book—*il faut choisir!*—but that is a key form of private intervention in the political process: namely, the lobby. For a long time, France thought it was free of lobbies, and indeed regulation is stricter there than in the United States, but, alas, they occupy an ever larger place in the decision-making of French legislators. And then there is the overlapping EU level: one way in which lobbyists achieve the representation of employers is through the funding of European think tanks and the capture of scientific space by private industrialists. Sylvain Laurens has shown this very clearly in the ethnographic study she conducted among EU functionaries and Brussels lobbyists.[49]

This brings us to the end of our analysis of the private funding of democracy. As we have seen, it can take a number of forms that are most often not mutually exclusive and can sometimes result in a disturbing mix. In many cases, it is the same individuals who finance parties, foundations, and media. The image of Mark Zuckerberg as president of the United States ought to unsettle us, and not only because of Facebook's legendary firepower. But many actually applaud the idea, and I hope I can help to open their eyes to what this tells us about the state of our democracies. If I had to draw a parallel, albeit on a lesser scale, it would be with Michael Bloomberg in New York, who in a way has developed the genre mix to perfection. When Bloomberg was the (democratically elected) mayor of New York, he was also one of its most generous donors. As the *New York Times* put it: the city used to pay its mayor; Bloomberg paid to be mayor of the city.[50]

One wonders what could have happened in recent decades to make philanthropy regarded as a legitimate source—sometimes more legitimate than governments—in the funding of the public good. But I think it is more important to end with a different question: What can be done to turn the tide, so that things are different in the years to come? Part of the answer must evidently come from public funding; the weight of selfish private interests can be reduced only if democratically accountable governments massively reoccupy the field of the public good. The first requirement for this is to tax private wealth instead of subsidizing the political or cultural preferences of the most advantaged sections of society. Similarly, there will never be an end to the excesses until the private funding of democracy is limited and, above all, until it is increasingly replaced with a generous, egalitarian system of public subsidies. For history teaches us that one of the hopes of democracy lies in its public funding.

PART TWO

MISSED OPPORTUNITIES

5

A Hope? Public Funding of Parties
and Election Campaigns

IN THIS CHAPTER, we shall look at the past and present forms that the public funding of electoral democracy has taken in Europe, particularly in France, the United Kingdom, and Germany, but also in Belgium and across the Atlantic in Canada and the United States. The next chapter will then examine today's threats to this system, which has been comprehensively called into question in Italy, the United States, and elsewhere. The public funding of political democracy, like democracy itself, is the worst system, with the exception of all others. But it is a system that can be improved, as long as the political will is there. If nothing is done in the coming years, there is a danger that private funding—and therefore private interests—will sweep the board, with the consequences we know for greater inequality and an explosion of populism. This is why popular mobilizations are sorely needed to create a new playing field, since the politicians in power today are often there because they knew how to profit from a withered system that they have no (personal) interest in reforming.

I admit it is hard to imagine a demonstration on the Champs-Élysées or protesters in Washington, DC, marching to the cry of "More money for our representatives!" Nevertheless, what is at issue here is the principle of equality. As things stand, a handful of superrich citizens vote twice over: once with their ballot papers and once with their purses. The vast majority have only one, "political" vote—and even that is partly captured by the weight of private funding in the electoral process. In the twentieth-first century, it is high time that the same amount of *public* money is spent for the expression of each citizen's political preferences—preferences that he or she should have the right to switch each year to new parties or groups, not only to a small set of grandee parties. And for that public money to have some meaning—and some effect—it must no longer be drowned beneath a flood of private money. Each year, all citizens and taxpayers should be able to contribute, if only with a few euros, to the emergence or persistence of the political movement most capable of defending their interests. It is on their euros, however few, that the vitality of democracy will depend. But to understand why such a radical, egalitarian redefinition of democracy has not yet occurred, and what operational form it might take, we need to begin with a history of the unsuccessful (but never pointless) attempts that have been made in various countries.

The reader should not be put off by the title of this chapter. My aim is not to draw up an inventory of pieces of legislation and to follow what happened to them over the decades. Although the law is important, it should not overshadow what really interests us: the political choices—and the implications of those choices—regarding the participation of all citizens in the political process. All too often, representative democracy is a captured democracy: one euro, one vote—except that the euros are unevenly distributed. At the risk of repeating myself: one person, one vote—that is the essence of democracy regained.

Finally, it should be stressed that there is not a virtuous European model over here and a tainted American system over there. How often have I been told, sometimes with a touch of outrage, "But that's nothing to do with what we have!" when I dared to draw a parallel between the lack of a ceiling on donations in Germany and the United States, the end to reimbursement of campaign spending in Italy and the United States, and the lack of transparency about the identity of rich political sponsors in France and the United States. "I'm all right, don't worry": that's a common refrain among European democrats. "I'm all right; and the proof is that on the other side of the mirror, in the United States, things are not all right at all." Our grim double! Radiant Dorian Europe reassured by the very existence of Gray America. So much for our perceptions.

But there are perceptions, and there are facts. First of all, it is very hard to speak of one European model: the funding of democracy varies enormously from country to country, and none can claim to have established a fully satisfactory system—far from it. How, for example, can a system in which a little over two euros per adult is spent annually (France or Germany) be considered on the same level as one in which ten times less is currently being spent (Italy)? Second, it is almost everywhere the case, in both Europe and the United States, that private money is winning, and public money losing, the electoral battle. Some European countries, such as Germany and the United Kingdom, have nothing to be ashamed of when it comes to donations received by political parties, since they are near the top in relation to the size of their population. But the choices made in Germany, especially in economic policy, are not without consequences for its EU partners as a whole, and they are probably not always unrelated to the preferences of corporations that do not think twice before reaching for their checkbook.

Third, it is important to draw the lessons of the American case, which should be seen as not so much a counterpoint as a possible future in the event that nothing is done. We should not forget history. The United States was once right up at the front in the public funding of democracy, as it was in the introduction of progressive taxation. Why was it also one of the first countries to roll them back?

The Public Funding of Democracy: Born to Die in the USA?

As early as 1907, in his State of the Union address, President Theodore Roosevelt stressed the need for public funding of election campaigns and a ceiling on private campaign contributions, including a ban on corporate donations. For him these were two sides of the same coin: the point was to ensure that no unscrupulous individual could buy himself a place in the Oval Office. The solution staring Roosevelt in the face was to ensure that Congress itself funded the principal parties. Not without difficulty, he managed to obtain a ban on corporate donations and a limitation of the political power of big business (through the Tillman Act of January 26, 1907, already mentioned in Chapter 2), but he faced insurmountable obstacles to public funding. In fact, he had expected that the innovative idea would not be approved overnight, since citizens might need time to get used to it and would at first probably distrust such public generosity toward the party apparatuses. Time, yes, but was he thinking of more than half a century?

Public funding of the US presidential election was really secured only in 1971,[1] with the Federal Election Campaign Act (FECA) and the Revenue Act.[2] This was sixty-four years after Theodore Roosevelt's address, but still much earlier than in France and Belgium (late 1980s and early 1990s), whereas West Germany, a country traumatized by the earlier collapse of the Weimar Republic, was particularly innovative in rethinking social and political democracy in the 1950s and 1960s.[3] In the United States, funding took a highly original (in a way, unique) form with the establishment of the Presidential Election Campaign Fund. What is this? Each year, every American taxpayer is able to participate in public funding of the presidential election, and of the party primaries and national conventions.

The Presidential Fund

For half a century, Americans have had the opportunity to check the following box (or boxes, in the case of a couple) on their tax return: "If you want $3 to go to this fund [the Presidential Fund], check the box. If you are filing a joint return, your spouse can also have $3 [$1 until 1993] go to the fund. If you check a box, your tax or refund won't change."[4] So, each American can choose whether or not to contribute $3 a year to the public funding of democracy.

It is not a question of choosing to support a particular party (as in the Italian system) or a particular candidate; and no tax rebate is involved, only additional spending by the federal government. The issue is funding the presidential election. Whenever a citizen checks the box, the American state has no option but to spend three extra dollars on the presidential campaign (by paying into the Presidential Fund). In other words, it is a kind of annual vote on the public funding of democracy—a surprising system when you think that, if applied to other areas of state intervention, it would imply asking citizens each year through their tax return to indicate how much they wanted to spend on education, health, or expressways. In marked contrast to the Italian "2 per thousand" system, it allocates the same amount for each citizen to the funding of political campaigns. Yet, though more promising and more egalitarian, it has never functioned very well, as we shall see.

In 1974, more than 85 million euros were paid into the Presidential Fund: that is, 0.61 euros per adult American.[5] The total rose to its highest level in 1978, when it stood at nearly 93 million euros. That is certainly a lot of money, but much less than it might have been, since there were never more than 35 percent of American taxpayers who checked a box that cost them nothing and was intended to ensure a more democratic funding of political life. One wonders whether it is not a good thing that taxpayers are not asked to vote annually on each type of government spending, since it might produce some surprising, and not always consistent, results. Besides, as we shall see in the next chapter, the sums received—and the numbers of contributing taxpayers—have been sharply declining in recent years.

Astonishing though it may seem, this system of public funding began to play an important role in the United States with the presidential election of 1976, under the supervision of the Federal Election Commission (FEC). In 1976, Jimmy Carter (the Democratic candidate) and Gerald Ford (the Republican candidate) each received $21.8 million (the equivalent of 59 million euros in today's money) for the presidential election. That was no trifle—and it was a real innovation after all the years when private money ruled. In addition, Carter received 10.4 million euros and Ford 12.5 million euros (less than Ronald Reagan's 13.7 million euros) as candidates in their respective party primaries.[6] And the national conventions of the two parties were publicly funded to the tune of 5.3 million (Republican) and 5.9 million (Democratic) euros.

The Presidential Fund therefore serves to fund three events tied to the presidential election: the primary campaigns, the national party conventions, and the presidential campaigns themselves.[7] Although the last of these have historically attracted the most funding, it is interesting to pause for a moment to consider how the funds are allocated among the three items of expenditure and among the candidates.

With regard to the primaries, the federal government has established a "matching system," whereby each dollar raised in private money creates an entitlement to one dollar of public money. In practice, then, the federal government doubles the amount of the donations received by eligible candidates, up to a maximum of $250 per donor.[8] The idea behind this is to favor a plurality of small donors. To benefit from the "matching funds," a candidate has to prove to the FEC that at least $5,000 have been raised in at least twenty different states.[9]

As to the presidential election itself, the two main candidates—in effect, the Republican and the Democrat—each receive a fixed (and equal) amount of public funds.[10] This amount is equal to the legal ceiling on election spending, and of course the funds can be used only for campaign expenditure. However, to benefit from them—and we shall see that this is an important restriction, since it creates the possibility of an "opt out" that has led in recent years to a withering of the public funding system—candidates must limit their spending to the amount of these public funds and cannot accept private contributions to their campaign. In other words, either candidates agree to limit their electoral spending in return for public funds equal to the ceiling on expenditure, or they decide to spend as they see fit—up to and above the ceiling—but bear the full cost (or generous backers bear the full cost) of that spending.

Figure 42 shows how the cap on spending for US presidential elections has evolved since the introduction of public funding in 1976. Although the ceiling has been revised slightly upward since 1976, in relation to the adult population, it has actually fallen from 0.41 euros per adult in 1976 to 0.31 euros today. Is 0.31 euros per adult a lot or very little? I imagine you will spontaneously say that it is rather little—for how can anyone "get to" voters and influence their opinion with three times less than a little euro?[11] I could reply that, until ten years ago, those tens of cents seemed enough to the candidates, and that I have never heard anyone say that the contest between Al Gore and George Bush in 2000 was vitiated by a shortage of funds (except, perhaps, funds for modernization of the ballot machinery). Interestingly, this spending cap corresponds exactly to what is in place today for French presidential elections; the ceiling on what candidates can spend in the first round is 0.326 euros per adult.[12] But there are two important differences. First, unlike

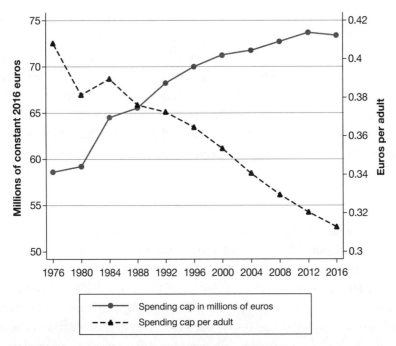

Figure 42. US presidential election, spending cap for general elections, 1974–2016

their American counterparts, presidential candidates in France cannot decide to forgo public funding in order to spend above the ceiling. Second, whereas US candidates who opt for public funding have all their expenses reimbursed, the size of the refund in France cannot exceed 47.5 percent of the ceiling on election spending and applies solely to the candidates' own contribution.[13]

In the United States, moreover, candidates from other parties can receive a smaller proportionate amount of the Presidential Fund if they obtain more than 5 percent of the vote. Those parties—defined as having received 5 to 25 percent of votes in the previous election—are considered "minor parties." The amount of public funding they receive is determined by the ratio of the popular vote they obtained in the previous presidential election to the average popular vote of the candidates from the two major parties. Thus, the Texas billionaire Ross Perot, who had scored 18.9 percent of the vote in the 1992 presidential election, received 19 percent of the Presidential Fund for the main campaign in 1996—that is, $29 million, in comparison with $61.82 million for Bill Clinton and $61.82 million for his Republican rival, Robert Dole. The law also makes allowance for new parties, or, above all, independent candidates.[14] If these win more than 5 percent of the votes, they have a right to public funding proportionate to their share of the popular vote divided by the average share obtained by candidates of the two main parties (that is, a ratio equivalent to the entitlement of candidates of "minor parties," but based on the result of the election itself rather than the previous election).

The Evolution of Public Funding

Those are the details. I hope you have followed me until now and that we can conclude this brief American survey by looking at the evolution of the public funding of democracy in the past forty years (Figure 43). The general presidential election—until 2012 and the decision of all candidates no longer to draw on public funding (to which we shall return in the next chapter)—has always been the main item of election expenditure. In 2012, only the party conventions still gave rise to a semblance of public funding; and since 2016, it may be said that in a way there is no longer any public funding of democracy in the United States. That was the year when Donald Trump was elected. But who would stick their neck out and make a connection?

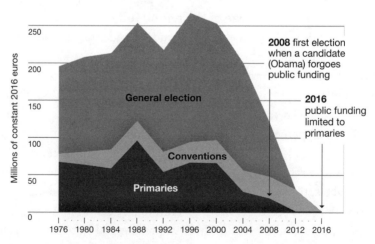

Figure 43. Public funding of democracy, US presidential elections, 1976–2016

As an annual average per adult citizen, the federal government now spends no more than 0.001255 euros for the public funding of democracy. That is 271 times less than forty years ago (Figure 44). It represents a historic setback, harsh and not subject to appeal. But it is also rich in lessons for the future.

We should note that this outcome was by no means due to a budgetary crisis forcing a reluctant federal government to sacrifice the public funding of democracy. Rather, it was politicians who chose of their own volition to sacrifice public funding—once the law, ill-conceived from the outset, gave them that possibility. Not all the resources of the Presidential Fund were spent each year, and the size of the fund therefore continually swelled. That was one weakness of the system established in the late 1970s. While the state offered citizens the opportunity to decide each year whether they wanted it to add to the fund—in other words, whether they wanted spending on the presidential election to rise or fall—the public reimbursement of campaign spending was never

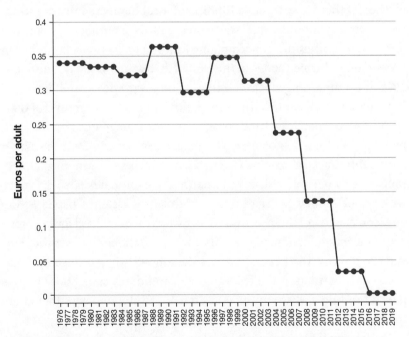

Figure 44. Public funding of democracy, annual average per adult, United States, 1976–2019

indexed to the success of that fund. The amount refunded was simply fixed by law and adjusted annually for inflation. So the chance on my tax return to vote for the public funding of elections was partly illusory, since my "vote" had no effect on the amount that candidates were authorized to spend. (Only the funds spent for the primaries vary from year to year depending on the preferences that people express, since in that case the state credits them with public money matching the amount of the private donations.[15]) To some extent, this may explain the growing lack of interest in this "presidential fund"; we shall return to it in Chapter 6.

The Funding of Local Democracy

Although the United States introduced public funding of its political process very early on, this centered on the presidential election and did not systematically extend to local elections. In the last few decades, this regrettable defect has been the subject of widespread debate and given rise to many proposals for legislation. With no result, unfortunately.[16]

Thus, if there is any public funding of local democracy, the decision rests entirely with individual states. In the 1970s, a number of states and local communities introduced public funding of their elections, but in the end only thirteen states in the United States offer it today. The forms of such funding range from "clean election programs" (candidates collect enough small contributions to qualify later for a full refund of their spending) to "matching funds programs" (the state matches private donations), but they do not apply to all local elections. In 2017, the city of Seattle introduced a system of "democracy vouchers" for municipal elections, which permits citizens to finance the candidates of their choice with public money; we shall return to this new idea in Chapter 9. The only constant in all these forms is that, as at the federal level for the presidential election, candidates qualify for public money only if they undertake to limit their spending and the amount they receive in donations. But, again as at the federal level, candidates can choose to give public funding a miss and spend as much private money as they wish, thereby undermining the very existence of public funding.[17]

Which elections are we talking about? In eleven of the thirteen states that have a system of public funding, it covers the election of the governor and his or her deputy.[18] In five of these states, it also applies to candidates running for seats in the state legislature. And in New Mexico and West Virginia, only candidates for the State Supreme Court can benefit from a public refund of their campaign expenses. Nine states also provide for the public funding of political parties.[19] Clearly the systems in place reflect great diversity. But above all it needs to be stressed that the United States has fifty constituent states plus one federal district, and that today no public funding of democracy is in place in three-quarters of these.

No public funding of local democracy, essentially no direct public funding of political parties, and the public funding of presidential elections reduced to zero: born and died in the USA.

The Development of Public Funding Systems: A Healthy Reaction to Political Scandals

While the funding of democracy developed in the United States partly in the context of the Watergate scandal—the Federal Election Campaign Act (FECA) comprised two sets of reforms, the first adopted in 1971 and the second in 1974, at the height of the scandal then shaking the American capital[20]—a similar picture was observable in many other democracies. In Italy, in 1974, the introduction of public funding for political parties came in response to a corruption scandal in which several of them were implicated. We shall return to this in the next chapter.

From Direct Party Subsidies to the Taste of Maple Leaf

Similarly in the case of Canada, where it is harder to link the Election Expenses Act of 1974 to a scandal on the scale of Watergate, the creation of the Barbeau Commission in 1964—which led ten years later to the introduction of public funding—took place against a backdrop of financial scandals.[21] An American observer might see what happened in Canada as an indirect result of Watergate, whereas someone more focused on France—and more inspired by De Gaulle—might note with amusement that the Quebecois set the ball rolling as early as 1963, with a Quebec Election Law that provided for the partial reimbursement of election spending.[22]

Which forms has public funding taken in Canadian history? The reform of 1974 introduced the partial reimbursement of spending by political parties,[23] the reimbursement of a half of campaign expenses for parties obtaining at least 15 percent of votes, and tax refunds for donations to parties. But, as is often the case, there is a quid pro quo in the shape of a cap on spending by parties and candidates.

The twentieth century saw several amendments to the legislation on party and campaign finance, and I shall not dwell here on the details of each reform (such as those of 1983 and 1996). But it is interesting to note that it was another spate of scandals—within the Liberal Party—that led in 2004 to the Federal Electoral Reform. The most notable of these was the "sponsoring scandal," in which the Liberal Party awarded tens of millions of euros in public funds to publicity and communication agencies, supposedly to counter the pro-sovereignty activity of the Parti Québécois following the 1995 referendum on independence. But these agencies, run by friends of the Liberals, did not put maple leaves on banners or other flags—which was their official task; instead, they offered three years of "free" communications advice to the Liberal Party and multiplied the donations coming into its coffers. In other words, a tried and tested system of kickbacks with multiple ramifications.[24]

By 2004, the Liberal Party urgently needed to stabilize the situation and to woo public opinion by clamping down on the role of private enterprise in the operations of political parties. However, a party needs money to function. So, the reform of 2004 introduced direct public funding of parties (not just the existing system of partial refunds of routine and campaign expenses), with a tri-monthly allocation for registered parties depending on the number of votes they had obtained in the last election. Those with 2 percent of the popular vote in the last election, or with 5 percent of votes in constituencies where they presented candidates, were able to benefit from this handout. In practice, this meant the Bloc Québécois, the Green Party, the New Democratic Party, the Conservative Party, and the Liberal Party.

How much do these direct public subsidies total each year? The figure was between 18 and 19 million euros in the 2004–2010 period (Figure 45)—

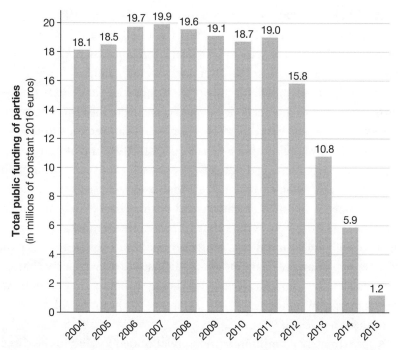

Figure 45. Total public funding paid directly to political parties, Canada, 2004–2015

which, per adult, amounted to 0.75 euros in 2004 and 0.71 euros in 2011, peaking at 0.80 euros in 2006.[25] These tri-monthly allocations began to wind down in 2011 and completely disappeared in 2015; their annual value since 2016 has therefore been zero. (We shall return in Chapter 6 to the gradual abolition of direct public funding of political parties, in Canada and Italy.)

In the end, between 2012 and 2016 the Canadian government spent an annual average of 6.7 million euros on direct public subsidies to political parties—that is, barely 0.25 euros per adult.

Direct Public Funding of Political Parties in France: A Late and Rather Modest Innovation

In France, unlike in Canada, a prime minister did not have to be caught with his fingers in the maple syrup pot before the public funding of political parties got under way. But the laws that introduced it, at the late dates of 1988 and 1990, were closely linked to cases of shady funding that had punctuated the previous decades. The regulation of 1988 also followed a whole series of reform proposals, some of which had been debated in the National Assembly but never seen the light of day.[26]

Today, the direct public funding of French parties comes in two equal parts. The first is divided among parties according to the number of votes they received in the first round of the most recent elections to the National Assembly. The second, earmarked for the funding of parties represented in Parliament, is divided each year according to the number of parliamentarians who declare their allegiance to each party in the month of November.[27] We shall see at the end of this chapter that one of the main defects of this system is that it freezes the democratic process; the cards of public funding are dealt only once every five years, since the number of parliamentarians attaching themselves to each party changes only marginally from year to year. This being so, how can a new political force emerge spontaneously—for example, as the result of a protest movement in society?[28]

Approximately 63 million euros were allocated in 2017 to the direct funding of parties in France—that is, a little more than one euro per adult (Figure 46). Over the period from 2012 to 2016, public funding averaged 67.3 million euros a year (1.32 euros per adult), a sum more than five times greater than in Canada. However, the current level of direct public funding of parties in France is barely 60 percent of what it was twenty years ago (107 million euros in 1994).

This raises the question of whether political parties are adequately funded in today's France. One is tempted to answer: it depends on the party and the year. Here it may be worth looking for a moment at the evolution of public funding received by the main French parties since the 1990s (Figure 47). It is clear from the figures that the financial health of the parties varies with their electoral success. The Républicains (originally the RPR, then the UMP) were particularly fortunate in the first decade of the twentieth century, but then came the turn of the Socialists. Now they too have been reminded that election defeats are very costly; they came close to bankruptcy and were forced to sell the party's historical headquarters in the Rue de Solférino.

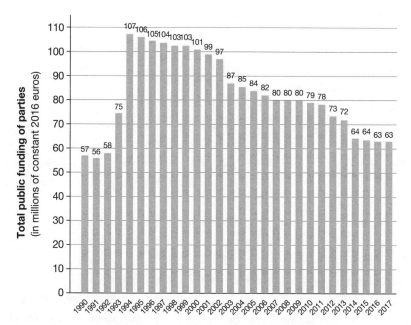

Figure 46. Total public funding paid directly to political parties, France, 1990–2017

In 2017, 63 million euros were paid in direct public funding to political parties in France.

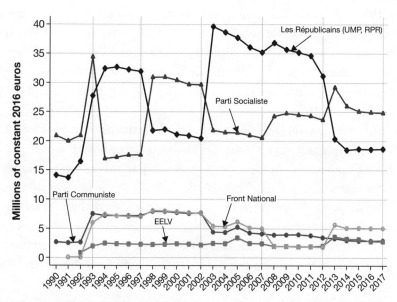

Figure 47. Annual direct public funding received by the main political parties, France, 1990–2017

It may not necessarily be an argument for greater public funding (since we might simply want them to spend less), but we should note that French political parties have run up high levels of debt in recent years. The Républicains' debt, certainly above 110 million euros following their defeat in 2012, has fallen very slowly and is still in the tens of millions. But when the Left was in power—and therefore relatively well served by the state—the Socialist Party's debt hovered around 30 million euros (more than a year's worth of public funding), while that of the Front National never stopped rising.[29]

The best way to judge how "generous" the French state is toward its political parties is to compare its record with that of neighboring European countries. Figure 48 shows the average annual amount (for the 2012–2016 period) of direct public subsidies received by the main parties in Germany, France, Italy, Spain, the United Kingdom, and Belgium. What do we find? First, the public subsidies are extremely low in Italy, where they have been phased out in recent years, and practically nonexistent in the United Kingdom, where they never really took hold except for a few subsidies to opposition parties. To make it easier to read, Figure 48 does not include Canadian political parties, but, as in Italy today, the totals there have been zero since 2016, and direct public subsidies to political parties were on average very low between 2012 and 2016. The best endowed party, the Liberal Party, then received 5.5 million euros a year (or 0.21 euros per adult), while the New Democratic Party received only 0.8 million euros (0.03 euros per adult).[30]

In international terms, French political parties do rather well out of direct public funding; only the German and Spanish parties fare much better. (The Spanish model is very interesting in this respect, although it is not often showcased.) This also contributes to the relative affluence of French parties—which, as we saw in Chapter 1, spend more than their British counterparts—despite the stricter regulation as to the size of the donations they are allowed to receive. I shall return in a moment to modes of publicly funding democracy in Germany, but I should first like to take a brief glance at Belgium.

It is in the Kingdom of Belgium that the regulator has taken the idea of democracy funded almost entirely from public money far-

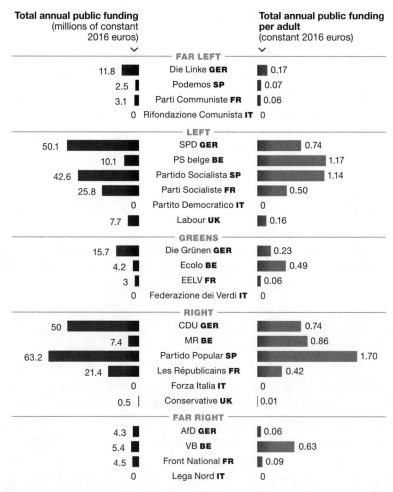

Figure 48. Total annual public funding received by the main political parties, annual averages 2012–2016, international comparison (Germany, Belgium, Spain, France, Italy, and the United Kingdom)

thest, with private donations reduced to minuscule proportions. The Belgian model is certainly not perfect, but it deserves serious attention. As we saw in Chapter 1, it has included a ceiling on election spending since 1989—the regulation of campaigns and political parties dates from almost the same time as in France. Very tight limits on private donations were introduced alongside this, but not without a quid pro quo, in the shape of an extremely generous system of party funding.[31] Thus, Paragraph 5 of the law of July 4, 1989, established a monthly public allocation for parties with at least one elected member in each of the two assemblies of the federal Parliament.[32] This allocation takes two forms: (1) a fixed annual amount of 175,000 euros for parties represented only in the Chamber or 245,000 euros for those also represented in the Senate; and (2) a public subsidy varying (as in France or Germany) in accordance with the number of votes obtained in the last election to the Chamber. Thus, parties represented only in the Chamber receive 2.99 euros annually per vote obtained, while those also present in the Senate receive 4.18 euros. These figures compare with 1.42 euros per vote for the first fraction of public funding in France or less than one euro in Germany.

Belgian parties further receive (on the model of the second fraction of public aid in France) what is called a "group subsidy"—that is, public funding depending on the number of parliamentarians in each party group. This subsidy, 60,000 euros per member of the Chamber group and approximately 22,000 euros per member of the Senate, is again much higher than the equivalents in France.

As we can see at once, the Belgian system is characterized by a very high direct public subsidy to political parties. This appears even more clearly if, instead of considering the total amounts of public aid received each year by the main parties, we relate these amounts to the total population and calculate the public funding per adult. In this light, Belgian political parties are among those that receive the greatest direct public funding. Thus, in the 2012–2016 period, the Belgian Socialist Party occupied the top spot among parties of the Left with an annual average of nearly 1.20 euros per adult, more than twice as much as the French Socialist Party but also much more than the German Social Democratic Party (SPD).[33] Only the Spanish parties benefit more from generous public funding.

Of course, the situation is far from idyllic in Belgium, particularly with regard to the relationship between money and politics; successive crises in recent years—from the Publifin affair to the Samusocial scandal[34]—or the recurrent difficulties in forming a government have kept reminding us of this. The point here is not to promote an "ideal" model, especially as the scale of direct public funding in Belgium goes together with a failure to reimburse campaign expenses (which make up a sizable share of public funding in such countries as France, Canada, or Spain). But it is interesting to note that, if we consider only direct public subsidies, political parties can function perfectly well by relying on them to provide more than two-thirds of their total revenue—which is the case with the Belgian Socialist Party, the Ecologists, or the Mouvement Réformateur.[35]

The Numerous German Debates

In Germany, the direct public funding of parties is generous but subject to two rules. First, the law stipulates that public subsidies must not make up more than a half of the total revenue of political parties—a ceiling that may restrict what a party receives, if, lacking other sufficient sources of finance, it is unable to claim the subsidy in full. Thus, in 2017, when the Alternative for Germany party might have netted 13.2 million euros in public subsidies (owing to the votes it received in the last elections and an abundance of small donations), it was in fact not allowed to receive more than 8.8 million euros (the total amount of its revenues before any public subsidies). The rule in question is strange. To the best of my knowledge, no law has ever forbidden a party to finance itself essentially out of private funding. Yet the capture of political parties by private interests is a much more real danger than a hypothetical dependence of political groups on public money. Second, each year the Bundestag sets the maximum amount of public spending that can be allocated to the funding of political parties. In 2017, that maximum was 161.8 million euros, which reduced the public subsidies available to the Christian Democratic Union (CDU; it received 48.4 million euros when it might have been entitled to 56.4 million) and the SPD (49.2 million instead of 57.5 million).

Still, Germany cannot be regarded as a "conservative" country or a laggard in the public funding of democracy; its problem has more to do with the swamping of public subsidies by unlimited private funding. To begin with, it is one of the few countries in the world to have legislated before the 1960s for the public funding of democracy. Indirect funding was established as early as 1954 in West Germany, in the form of tax relief for donations, and this was followed by direct funding in 1959. Interestingly, direct public funding was introduced on the explicit recommendation of the Federal Constitutional Court, which in 1958, being aware that tax exemption for donations benefited certain parties much more than others, had declared it to be an unconstitutional violation of the principle of equal opportunity.[36]

However, this introduction of direct public funding went through a series of back-and-forth "tweaks" between the legislature and the Constitutional Court, in which the debate centered both on the constitutionality of tax exemptions and on what could or could not be funded with public money (only campaign expenses or also current party spending[37]). Only with the law of July 24, 1967, on political parties was the refund of campaign expenses (in proportion to the number of votes obtained) finally guaranteed. And only in 1994 did the (re)introduction of general public funding on an annual basis enable parties to cope with their expenses in full.

In Germany today, the direct public funding of parties takes two forms. On the one hand, in a mechanism fairly similar to the first fraction of party funding in France, political parties that have won a sufficient number of votes receive an annual subsidy calculated according to their results in the most recent elections.[38]

On the other hand, political parties receive public funding that varies with the size of the donations they receive from physical persons. To be precise, parties get 0.45 euros in public funding for each euro in donations, up to a donation cap of 3,300 euros. Although there is no ceiling on donations from physical persons, the fact that extra public funding ceases above the donation cap of 3,300 euros testifies to a wish to encourage contributions from small donors. It is a little like the thinking behind the "matching funds" for donations made during primaries in the United States.

All in all, in the 2012–2016 period, the German government spent an annual average of 162 million euros on the direct public funding of political parties—or 2.39 euros per German adult (nearly twice as much as in France). It is an average that has remained relatively stable over time (Figure 49).[39]

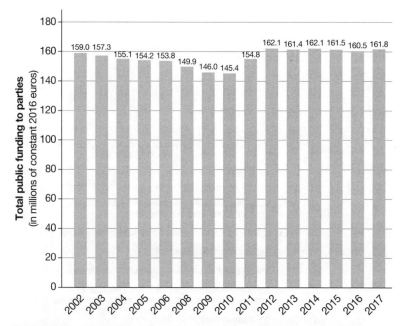

Figure 49. Total public funding paid directly to political parties, Germany, 2002–2017

In 2017, 161.8 million euros in direct public funding was paid to political parties in Germany.

Reimbursement of Campaign Expenses

While we have so far concentrated mainly on direct public subsidies to political parties, the public funding of democracy also takes another form in many countries: namely, the reimbursement of election expenses to parties and / or candidates. Indeed, in some countries this is the only form of public intervention in the process of political democracy. The reimbursement of campaign expenses was often introduced before any other form of direct party funding. In Germany, for example, it was established as early as 1967 with the law on political parties—although, as we have seen, a system of direct public funding replaced such refunds in the wake of a landmark ruling by the Constitutional Court on April 9, 1992.

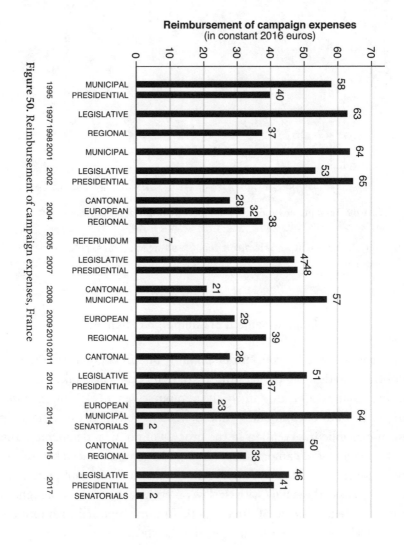

Reimbursement of campaign expenses
(in constant 2016 euros)

Figure 50. Reimbursement of campaign expenses, France

Reimbursement in France: One Adult, One Euro (One Vote?)

In France, a standard rate of reimbursement of campaign expenses, like the direct public funding of political parties, was introduced in the late 1980s. For presidential and other elections, candidates who receive at least 5 percent of the votes cast in the first round are entitled to have their personal contribution to campaign expenses reimbursed,[40] up to a limit of 47.5 percent of the ceiling set for each constituency (or, at the national level, for the presidential election[41]). The proviso, of course, is that their campaign accounts have not been rejected by the National Commission on Campaign Accounts—a fate suffered by Nicolas Sarkozy in 2012, to the great displeasure, and great expense, of his UMP party and all the right-wing activists and sympathizers who were urged to come to the aid of their unjustly condemned supreme leader.[42]

On average, how much does the French government spend on the reimbursement of campaign expenses? Figure 50 shows the total amount for each year and each election.[43] Of course, this varies sharply from one election to another (as do the number of candidates and the permitted ceiling on expenses), the costliest being the municipal and legislative elections, followed by the presidential elections.

In the last five-year election cycle (2012–2016, including legislative and presidential elections, as well as cantonal, municipal, European, regional, and senatorial elections), the total reimbursement came to 260 million euros, or roughly 52 million euros a year (one euro per head of the population).[44] Is that a lot or a little? Again, only international comparisons can help us to provide an answer.

International Comparisons

In Spain—where, as we have seen, direct public subsidies to political parties are very high—the state spent an annual average of 53.6 million euros in the 2012–2016 period for the reimbursement of campaign expenses. That was proportionately higher than in France (1.44 euros against 1 euro per adult head of the population).

The available data for Canada do not allow us to make a similar comparison.[45] Let us, however, consider for a moment the reimbursement of expenses incurred in parliamentary elections: parties are refunded

50 percent of their expenses, within a limit determined by the number of electors in the constituency, while candidates who obtain at least 10 percent of the votes are refunded 60 percent. In 2004, 2006, 2008, and 2011, government refunds for legislative elections averaged approximately 21.5 million euros to parties and 18 million euros to candidates, or in total a little more than 39 million euros (approximately 1.57 euros per Canadian adult). In 2015, when the seventy-eight-day campaign was the longest in the country's modern history, these amounts shot up to 38.6 million euros to parties and 27 million euros to candidates.[46]

Thus, when we speak of the public funding of democracy, we need to bear in mind its different dimensions, and in particular to consider both direct public subsidies and the reimbursement of campaign expenses, even if the implications of these two forms are very different. In Italy, until 1993, political parties received sizable direct subsidies; when these were abolished, the reimbursement of campaign expenses increased sharply in 1994, almost compensating in full for the loss of the associated resources.

Now, if in France we add together the direct public funding of parties and the reimbursement of election expenses, we get total annual spending of approximately 119 million euros. Per adult head of the population, this is roughly equal (2.32 euros against 2.39 euros) to the amount spent in Germany on the direct public funding of political parties.[47] This needs to be emphasized, because too often there is a tendency to insist that parties are much better endowed by the state in Germany than in France.

To be sure, taken individually, the direct public funding for parties is higher in Germany, and the parties are therefore considerably richer (partly, also, because fewer parties benefit from public funding than in France). Yet in Germany, since the mid-1990s, political parties have fully covered their own election expenses, whereas in France the state has partly reimbursed the expenses of candidates. The two systems are different, especially because proportional representation in Germany gives greater weight to parties than to candidates; few candidates run for election there independently of the major parties, whereas this happens regularly in French local, and sometimes national, elections. In France, the contribution made by parties to candidates' expenses accounts on average for only 7 percent of spending in municipal elections and 28 percent in legislative elections. Candidates cover most of their own expenses, for the very good reason that this entitles them to be reimbursed by the state.

The real difference between France and Germany lies in the subsidies paid to political foundations. As we have seen, the German state is very generous with foundations, which are in effect associated with political parties and whose funding varies with the electoral score achieved by those parties. As a yearly average, the government allocates 7.55 euros per adult to the funding of political foundations. In France, by contrast, most think tanks are not directly linked to a political party—and, above all, they receive virtually no public funding.

The main weakness of the French system is not poor funding of political parties but the conditions attached to it. In short, the direct public funding of parties in France freezes democracy—a defect also found in Germany, although in a less pronounced form. Let us end this chapter by considering this point more closely.

Public Funding French-Style: A System That Freezes Democracy

I began this chapter on a positive note, pointing out that in many countries, and for many years, governments have established a public system for the funding of political life. This is an excellent thing, because public funding can at least partly limit the need for private money (with all the control problems associated with it). But unfortunately, as we shall see in later chapters, these systems are now almost everywhere under attack.

The main weakness of direct public funding in France, as well as in other countries, is that it is almost totally decided on a five-year basis (or a four-year basis elsewhere, depending on the periodicity of parliamentary elections). This system is intended to "impoverish" parties that have just lost elections—for the years until the next elections—and to "enrich" those that just won them. On this point, the French Socialist Party, like the Républicains, will have to draw the financial lessons of the election of 2017—not, to be sure, for the first time in its history.[48] But in my view that is not the problem; there is even some logic in the idea that a party crushed at the polls should benefit less from official largesse.

No, the problem is that the existing system does not allow new political forces to emerge between two elections, unless they are capable of raising enough private money, with all the control problems I have already begun to mention. This gives a great advantage to conservative movements—or anyway to those, like En Marche! in France in 2016–2017, that are markedly on the right on economic questions. For it is obviously much easier to raise private funding for a movement that promises to abolish wealth taxes or to lower corporate taxation than it is for a political force fighting to increase marginal rates. Recent experience also teaches us that it is much easier to hire the Mutualité hall in Paris if you are En Marche! (at a cost of 25,000 euros) than if you are the Socialist Party (a much steeper 43,000 euros).[49] I shall have occasion to return to the services of GL Events in organizing such events and to the campaign expenses incurred by candidates.

So Emmanuel Macron and his rich backers willed into existence a political party that managed in just a few months to capture the Élysée Palace and the National Assembly. In an instructive contrast—the two movements emerged more or less simultaneously, almost as if the one was born out of the laws imposed by the other—the Nuit Debout protest movement against proposed labor legislation eventually lasted no more than a few nights in France. Much the same goes for Occupy Wall Street and others like it around the world. Ninety-nine percent of people in the United States can occupy the stage for only a brief moment, before . . . before they must attend to more urgent matters like earning a living. With the exception of those rightly called professional politicians—for whom politics is a profession they are paid to exercise— citizens have to work to make ends meet. And in practice that is enough to exclude them from the political process.

Political movements arising from civil society have not become political parties, because they have not benefited from the necessary resources. For a movement to take shape, campaign, and win elections, it must have access to enough funds. But how can it do this if it first needs to have won elections? There is the absurdity of the present system, which functions in a way that hugely favors parties already in place. And although, historically, the names and the alliances may have changed, the reality of the apparatuses has remained largely fixed.

For a movement to take shape, enough citizens must be able—and I say "able" rather than "willing," because many are willing but not able—to give some of their time to it. Not everyone has the good fortune to be able to organize a breakfast at the Finance Ministry. And everyone's time is short, because the pressures of work call. If movements arising out of civil society never get anywhere—except those, like the Tea Party, which are awash with private money and often express an already organized political will—it is because, for lack of money (by which I mean *an adequate system of public funding*), they cannot take control of time.

This is why, in Chapter 10, I propose that each year—not every five years—the whole body of citizens should be able to decide, in whichever way they wish, the amount of public funding to be allocated among the various political movements, including new ones that have appeared in the course of the previous year. It would be a system that incorporates electronic breakthroughs, which are more democratic, more dynamic, and better adapted to the new realities of our century.

I call this the Democratic Equality Vouchers system. Though inspired by the way in which the Italian "2 per thousand" and the American Presidential Election Campaign Fund make use of people's tax returns, the Democratic Equality Vouchers differ from them in several respects. I have drawn the lessons not only of recent innovations but also of past mistakes, to propose a more efficient and egalitarian model of public funding for the twenty-first century. In this system, each citizen allocates each year a fixed amount of public money—which is the same for everyone—to fund the political movement of his or her choice.

We urgently need to move toward this modernized, egalitarian model of public funding of democracy. For, as we shall see in the following chapters, the tendency everywhere, if nothing is done, is to call into question the unsatisfactory systems of public funding that still exist today.

6

The Public Funding of Democracy:
A System in Danger

IN THE FIRST FOUR CHAPTERS of this book, we looked at the various regulatory regimes for the private funding of democracy in Western Europe and North America, and in Chapter 5 we began to examine the ways in which political life has been publicly funded. Several salient facts already stand out. Only in certain countries (France, the United States, Belgium) were ceilings on campaign spending, regulation of private donations, and the public funding of elections and/or parties introduced more or less simultaneously, leading to systems that are nevertheless highly imperfect. In Germany, by contrast, the public funding of parties and especially political foundations was introduced ahead of other reforms, and corporate donations remain permissible and expenses unlimited. In the United Kingdom, election spending has been strictly regulated for more than 150 years, but there have never been any plans for a real system of publicly funded democracy or for a ceiling on donations. It is as if you could play with different pieces for the funding of political democracy, without having to give serious thought to its overall regulation. It is my conviction that things are not fated to remain like this. So long as citizens finally get a grip on these questions, it is possible to develop a coherent system that allows us to reshape democracy on an egalitarian basis.

If the whole mechanism is to function, each of the pieces is important. But the possibility for our democracies to function in an egalitarian manner is under attack on all sides. In Italy and the United States, a completely wrong-headed response to corruption of the existing system has reduced public funding to zero. While people on this side of the Atlantic like to think the aberrations are peculiar to the United States, the truth is that the private funding of democracy is almost everywhere winning the battle of ideas, and often the battle at the polling stations, too. In far too many cases, as we shall see in Chapter 7, politicians no longer respond to the political preferences of any but the rich. This is largely because they are chasing after dollars rather than votes, but also because the idea that private donations are about "free speech" is sweeping all before it, when rationally we should sense the danger of corruption that has been around for years. What this leads to is a polarization of political debate and the rise of populist movements.

The question "who pays what?" is essential, because if politicians chase after private funding, it is for the good reason that their campaign spending generally has a directly positive impact on the number of votes they obtain. Most often all this is entirely legal, but sometimes it takes more problematic forms. One need look no farther than the way in which supporters of Brexit used private data from the social media.

Beyond the Scandals

This book could have compiled a long list of the scandals besmirching our democracies. Money in politics, meant to be kept secret, does sometimes come to light—and we can be glad that it does. I could write about the scandals one by one, especially as some have an amusing side to them. You feel outrage, yet sometimes end up laughing.

Take the long, drawn-out Beauharnois scandal in Canada, for instance, which finally came to an end in 1929. I could begin by telling you the story of Charles and Claude de Beauharnois and the fiefdom they established in the "Belle Province" of Quebec in the early part of the eighteenth century. But it is probably better if I skip two centuries of history and move straight on to the Beauharnois Light, Heat and Power Company. In the interwar period, this company of theirs donated C$700,000 to the Liberal Party of Quebec and Canada in return for the right to divert the waters of the Saint Lawrence River and build the Beauharnois power station. In the end, though, it was the Liberal Party that came within an inch of drowning in the affair.

I could also tell you about David Lloyd George, the British prime minister who in the 1920s liberally handed out honors—or rather, sold them in return for funding.[1] But would I dare to draw a parallel with Tony Blair and the Cash for Honors affair, which saw the Labour prime minister accused of bestowing the title of lord on businessmen who had granted loans to the Labour Party?

How can I not mention the Rabelbauer scandal in Austria, whose spin-offs were worthy of a John LeCarré novel? It all began in 1980 with an attempt by Bela Rabelbauer—"the man with the suitcase," as the Austrian press dubbed him—to buy a national assembly mandate in 1980 with a donation of 10 million schillings to the Populist Party, done at night, with a suitcase, in an apartment. The scandal then led to accusations of corruption in the justice system, when it was discovered in 1985 that a public prosecutor in Vienna had dropped the case after receiving from Rabelbauer's hands an envelope stuffed with 1.5 million Swiss francs. Money, justice, and politics.

These scandals were not without their uses, since the indignation they aroused when they broke in the media made it possible to press ahead with further regulation. Politicians, especially when in power, have little interest in reforming a system that works to their advantage, and the principle of "playing by the rules" is repeatedly held up as an irrefutable argument. Thus, in only one year has the French Communist Party refused public funding, although it was strongly opposed to its introduction in the early 1980s. How could it forgo the manna of public money when all the other parties were receiving it? The German Greens, having failed to obtain a ban on the public funding of foundations, decided to create one of their own. But again, how can you blame them, especially as it can be argued that such funding is beneficial? The real problem arises when politicians give up on their principles and, sometimes with the full support of the law, play according to the rules of private money. In the United States, even Bernie Sanders artfully used private funding from interest groups such as National Nurses United—a practice that many held against him, because he once declared that he would refuse any funding from super PACs and the union in question relied on that legal resource for its campaigning. Still, Sanders's funding was clearly much more modest, and much more legitimate, than the donations that other Democratic candidates, particularly Hillary Clinton, have received from wealthy private donors.

The reader will probably wonder why I do not spend more time on the scandals associated with campaign funding that have punctuated the history of our democracies. Is it that I do not wish to stir things up too much, or even that I want to shield certain things from close attention? Am I deliberately avoiding—"such a shame that it happened"—the relationship between Nicolas Sarkozy and the openhanded Colonel Gaddafi? Or am I refusing to tell racy stories about the hydra-headed Petrobras scandal, which tainted so much of Latin American politics, because I prefer to drown it beneath a flood of figures and legislative measures that I would like to see changed?

More seriously, if I do not spend longer on these episodes, it is because I am convinced that, however useful they were in triggering further regulation, they sometimes worked more to the advantage of those in power. Once the scandals broke and the culprits were punished (if they were), the general impression was that everything had been sorted out. With the guilty in the dock and justice in the headlines, with public life cleansed on live television, Penelope would have to do more for her fat paychecks than just watch over her consort's possessions. "Hey, keep moving, there's nothing to see here." However, simply to expose scandals and introduce ad hoc regulations, without going into solutions and legislative changes, is to steer clear of the fundamental problem, which is the power of money to corrupt the democratic process. It is to refuse debate about precisely the new system that needs to be introduced—a subject that, though perhaps less entertaining than individual scandals, is much more useful in the end.

For the rot goes much deeper. The system itself is rigged. And the (legal) ways in which it works are weakening our democratic processes. The punishment of visible excesses should not distract us from the key task: to reform nefarious principles and practices. If nothing is done about them, the whole system is in danger of collapse as exasperated citizens—and far right movements that know all too well how to stoke legitimate but displaced anger—shake it to its foundations. The signs are there before our eyes, in Italy, the United States, and elsewhere.

Perhaps it is not so surprising that the two countries where the public funding of democracy is being challenged today, Italy and the United States, were among the first to introduce it in their past, however inadequately it was designed and debated, and however incomplete, and ultimately damaging, was its implementation. Their failures need to be understood and digested if we are to build a better future for our democracies.

The Italian Paradox: The Abolition of Public Funding in Response to the Excesses of Private Funding

As we saw in Chapter 2, Italy's switch to "2 per thousand" in 2014, following a series of previous reforms, established a system of private contributions to the funding of democracy. In reality, however, this was fueled by public money and organized in such a way that the state allocated far more to the expression of the political preferences of the rich than to those of the poor.

This system was designed to replace the public funding of parties, including the reimbursement of campaign expenses, which was completely phased out between 2014 and the end of 2017. Thus, the legislative elections of 2018—which saw a major victory for "populist" anti-EU parties on both the "right" and the "left"—were the first in forty years to be held without any reimbursement of candidates' expenses.[2] It is important to try to understand how things came to such a pass in Italy. For if nothing is done, a similar trajectory may ensue in many other democracies, as recent developments in Canada or the past ten years of American history illustrate.

Italy's Relatively Early System of Public Funding, Challenged Right from the Start

The public funding of parties in Italy dates back to 1974, much earlier than in France or Belgium.[3] It was established in the aftermath of corruption scandals, most notably the Oil Scandal of 1973, when a number of petroleum corporations admitted to having "funded" Italian political parties. As you can imagine, they had done this not out of generosity but to influence the regulation of their sector, particularly with regard to pricing policies. At a time when the prices charged by oil-producing countries were going through the roof, it was vital for the corporations to ensure that they could pass on the increase to consumers, plus a little extra if possible. This meant that the state and its taxation policy had to show understanding in a troubled period. Money has its reasons, after all.

Beginning in 1974, Italian public funding took two forms that should not come as a surprise: the annual funding of political parties represented in Parliament,[4] and the reimbursement of election expenses. This funding entailed that parties were forbidden to receive funds from public enterprises, and that they had to make public—and to publish in their annual accounts—the size of donations above a certain threshold that they received from private enterprises or individuals.

The new system was not enough to put an end to the corruption of Italian politics; much more would have been required to see off the Mafia. Indeed, the corruption burst into the public limelight in 1992 with the "Tangentopoli" scandal.[5] The uncovering of this system of corruption and illegal funding of political parties came in the wake of the "Clean Hands" (*Mani pulite*) operation, a massive judicial investigation in the 1990s initially conducted by the public prosecutor's office in Milan and later extended to the whole country.[6] It eventually led to the explosive break-up of the Italian party system, with the disappearance of such historic parties as Christian Democracy (which had proposed public funding in 1974 as a way to end the corruption of political parties), the Italian Socialist Party, the Italian Social Democratic Party, and the Italian Liberal Party. For some political scientists and historians, the year 1993 marked the beginning of the "Second Republic" in Italy.[7] Will the election of 2018 mark the passage to a "Third Republic?" Only history will tell.

Paradoxically—since Tangentopoli had suggested that regulation and public funding were woefully inadequate—the scandal also led a majority of the population to favor an end to the public funding of political parties. In 1993, a popular initiative, the "abrogative referendum," was to abolish entirely the public funding of political campaigns and parties.[8] The "yes" camp, supporting its abolition, swept the board (90 percent of votes, on a 77 percent turnout), and Paragraphs 3 and 9 of Law No. 195/1974 on the public funding of parties were duly repealed. Could a different result have been expected, at a time when party structures were being scorned, reviled, and rejected with disgust? Probably not. In the TV series *1992*, broadcast light years later in 2015, it was almost possible to feel some sympathy for Pietro Bosco (the Northern League deputy and ex-combatant in the Gulf War, now nauseated by the old world of the First Republic), or even for Leonardo Notte, the publicity man serving Silvio Berlusconi's business, and then party, affairs.

I shall not dwell here on all the intricacies and all the parliamentary tricks that ensured that, despite the vote in 1993, the Italian state continued to fund political parties directly—and quite generously—for more than twenty years.[9] Thus, following the 1993 reform, the reimbursement of campaign expenses increased to such an extent that the total public funding of political parties scarcely diminished at all, despite the end of direct funding (Figure 51).

When the book *La Casta* was published in 2007, a new wave of protests—almost as large as those during the Tangentopoli scandal—shook the Italian political landscape.[10] How, to quote from the title, did the "caste" of politicians become untouchables? The investigation by two *Corriere della Sera* journalists was not unrelated to the surge in popularity for Beppe Grillo and the Five Stars Movement, one of whose main proposals was to wind down the public funding of democracy in Italy. Presenting itself as a nonparty, Five Stars meanwhile refused to accept the public funding to which it might have been entitled.[11]

The End of Public Funding in Italy

The famous comedian had his way on this point: Italy decided in 2014 to close down its whole system of public funding and to replace it with a private funding system—or, to be more precise, with a system in which public money would be used to fund parties in proportion to the preferences expressed on taxpayers' returns. It was a Pyrrhic victory, however, since the new system merely strengthened the *casta* that it was designed, on paper, to topple. It turned out that a (certainly imperfect) direct public system was to be replaced with a private system in which the rich contributed more (voted more with their wallets) and the poor paid their bit without having their political preferences taken into account. For, whether it was question of the "2 per thousand" or of donations to parties, the amount spent, as well as the tax deduction to which it gave rise, was proportional to the amount paid in taxes. How did people not see this? The most astonishing aspect is that we seem to have grown used to this regressive system of public funding of private political preferences—almost as if we accepted that in the future the rich will vote twice and the poor only once, or not at all.

In Italy today, if we leave aside the "2 per thousand" system, the state spends the very modest sum of 0.00 euros a year for the public funding of political parties. Figure 51, which shows the evolution of public funding since its introduction in 1974, illustrates the dangers associated with its disappearance. Whereas from 1974 to 1993, the real size of public funding

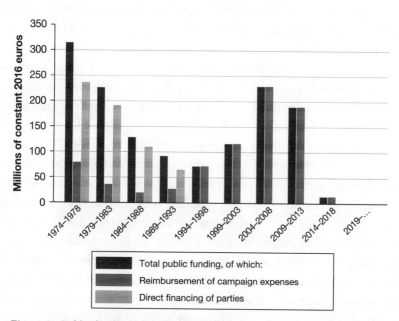

Figure 51. Public funding of political parties, Italy, annual averages 1974–2018

On average, between 1984 and 1988, the Italian political parties received 189 million euros a year in public funding, of which 109.26 million was in direct public subsidies and 19.78 million in reimbursed campaign expenses.

(adjusted for inflation) continually declined, the year 1993 saw the collapse of a party system plagued by corruption. It was in 1992, 1994, and 1996 that the Northern League recorded the highest election results in its history (8.6, 8.4, and 10.8 percent of the vote for the Chamber of Deputies). The system of public funding was gradually reconstructed (with abuses, to be sure) between the late 1990s and the turn of 2014, the year when its abolition was announced. In 2018, for the first time since 1974, Italian political parties had to manage without direct subsidies or any reimbursement of their campaign expenses for legislative elections. Of course, this alone cannot account for the victory of extreme parties in the March elections, but we may note that the League (the old Northern League) then obtained 17.4 percent of the vote and conclude that this new, even less regulated world of politics is itself questionable.

Some will say that the "2 per thousand" is a system of publicly funding parties that has simply replaced another system. I have already highlighted its limitations, and especially the fact that, while based on public money, it caters mostly to the private political preferences of the richest sections of society. But even if it is regarded as a viable alternative to direct subsidies and the reimbursement of expenses, what do we find? The establishment of the "2 per thousand" in 2014 barely compensates for the collapse in public funding since 2009 (Figure 52). Back in 1974, when it was decided to introduce a system for public funding of the electoral process, the idea was to allocate eight euros per adult to it each year. Subsequently, even during the political crisis of 1993, it never really fell below two euros a year per adult, and in 2009 it climbed back over five euros. But then it nose-dived to 0.28 euros per adult in 2016 and has remained at zero since 2017. The "2 per thousand" yields a trifling sum (barely 0.31 euros a year per adult) in comparison with what used to be allocated to public funding; this cannot be considered a serious system for the public funding of democracy. Remember the comparable amounts spent in France, Germany, and Spain (even if we just take direct subsidies and omit the reimbursement of campaign expenses): respectively 1.32, 2.39, and 4.20 euros per adult, or four to fourteen times more than in Italy. How are parties supposed to operate with so few public funds? The answer is all too evident: they have to go knocking on the door of private interests.

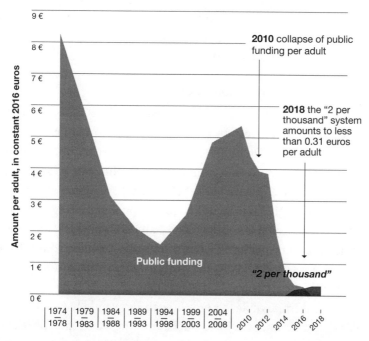

Figure 52. Amount of public funding of democracy, per adult, Italy, 1974–2018

In other words, we must get used to the idea that, at least for the time being, Italy seems to have given up funding its electoral process with public money. When is a democratic rebound likely to happen? We need to learn from the setbacks in Italy and America, which both express the same unfulfilled yet instructive resolve to establish an egalitarian democracy.

The American Case

In the United States, following a history in some ways reminiscent of Italy's, the last few years have witnessed an end to the federal system of publicly funded democracy. As we saw in Chapter 5, this essentially involved the reimbursement of campaign spending by candidates in the presidential election. There was always a possibility that the system would collapse, since public funding was never obligatory; candidates always had a choice between opting in (at the price of a ceiling on expenditure and a ban on private donations) and opting out (with the freedom to spend unlimited sums).

Obama's Fault?

Through 2004, all candidates in the general presidential election opted for public funding and reimbursement of their campaign expenses. Then, in 2008, Barack Obama became the first to give up this public funding, so that he could spend more than the limit of $84.1 million (which his opponent, John McCain, adhered to).[12] Obama's decision in 2008 marked the beginning of the end for the public funding of democracy in the United States, and since 2012 all candidates in the general presidential election have systematically rejected public funding. To repeat: their aim in doing this has been to avoid any constraints on the total amount they can spend.

Of course, it is impossible to know how things would have turned out if Barack Obama had not declined public funding—and thereby broken one of his campaign promises—in 2008. Perhaps Mitt Romney would still have chosen to cross the Rubicon himself four years later; perhaps, by spending more, he would have achieved the Republican dream of making Obama a one-term president. But although we cannot know what would have happened, it is distressing to observe that it was a Democratic candidate who cast the first stone at public funding—an edifice that has now totally crumbled.

Barack Obama's choices during his two terms scarcely improved the situation. True, he was not responsible for Citizens United—the Supreme Court ruling in 2010 that shattered all the constraints on corporate and other private funding of elections in the United States. But what he can be blamed for is that in 2012, having staunchly opposed the ruling and come out in public against the very existence of super PACs, he encouraged his supporters to make donations to the super PAC, Priorities USA Action, that backed his campaign.[13] How was that to be interpreted if not as downright cynicism? "Sure, there shouldn't be any super PACs, but all the same, don't forget to contribute to mine!"

Similarly, in 2014, Barack Obama decided to end the public funding of national party conventions, which until then had been subsidized by the Presidential Fund.[14] On April 3, 2014, to be absolutely precise, the president signed the Gabriella Miller Kids First Research Act, which abolished the right of party national committees to draw on the Presidential Fund for their election campaigns. No doubt it was a cause for rejoicing that pediatric research would from then on be properly funded in the United States, but why should this have been to the detriment of the public funding of elections? Above all, why should it have been flaunted in such a way as to suggest that the public funding of elections was not worthwhile, as if the money spent on this in the past had been wasted at the expense of more fundamental public goods? I specified the date of the act, April 3, 2014, not to bore the reader with superfluous details but to underline the historical irony. The day before—on April 2, 2014—the US Supreme Court ruling in the *McCutcheon v. Federal Election Commission* case had relaxed a little more the campaign funding rules by removing the ceiling on individual donations.[15]

A Climate of General Mistrust

We should bear in mind, however, that Barack Obama made these political decisions in a long-growing climate of general mistrust, which the Democratic president had not had the courage to confront. Almost from the outset, the Presidential Fund system had been the victim of its own unpopularity—which proves, in my eyes, not that all such systems are doomed to failure, but, on the contrary, that it is necessary to look closely at how they work if a more effective and more widely accepted system is to be developed.

Figure 53 shows, for each year since its creation in 1974, the percentage of taxpayers who chose to contribute to the Presidential Fund. Since it cost citizens nothing to check the fund box on their tax return—an easy-to-see box in black and white—one might have expected the percentage to be very high. But that was by no means the case. The percentage has continually declined from a peak of 35 percent (in 1977) to a bare 5 percent today. To what extent is this due to a simultaneous collapse of confidence in American political institutions? It is, of course, impossible to trace a causal link between the two phenomena, but it is interesting to note the strong correlation between falling numbers of contributors to the fund and the collapse of confidence in political institutions,

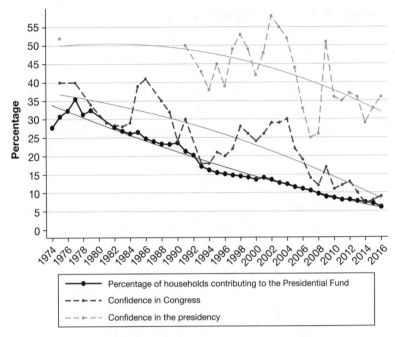

Figure 53. Contribution to the Presidential Fund and level of confidence in the institutions (Congress and presidency), United States, 1974–2016

particularly Congress (which fell below 10 percent in 2013). Confidence in the presidency is higher but also more volatile, albeit with a similar, though less pronounced, downward trend. In 2016, barely 35 percent of Americans expressed confidence in their president. These figures fell again in 2017 in the first year of the Trump administration, and although it was unclear how they would evolve in September 2018—as the French edition of this book went into print—there is likely to be a further decline in confidence, given the unpopular and erratic nature of many of the decisions taken by Trump since his investiture.

Thus, while the turnout in US presidential elections has varied between 50 and 60 percent over the past forty years, only a small minority of voters express—through their tax return—a wish that the election should be funded by public money. Furthermore, this minority is unrepresentative of the population as a whole. If we consider the percentage of contributors by income level, we find that the lowest-income Ameri-

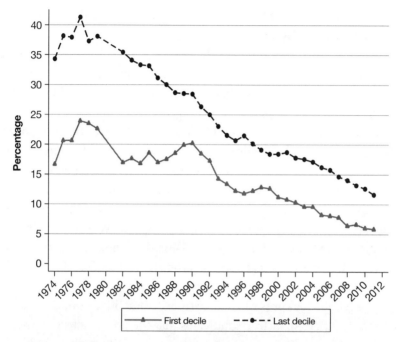

Figure 54. Contribution to the Presidential Fund by income level, United States, 1974–2011

cans (the first decile of income distribution) have always chosen in much smaller numbers than the richest tenth decile to contribute to the Presidential Fund (Figure 54).[16] Today, the difference between the two groups is nearly six percentage points, and although the richest Americans seldom contribute to the fund, the percentage of those who do so is twice as high as in the lowest income group. Interestingly, however, the propensity to contribute in the two groups has followed parallel downward trends ever since the 1980s.

It is worth trying to understand why the fund is so unpopular. Clearly, if we look at Figures 53 and 54, this is not linked to the fact that presidential candidates (Democrats since 2008, all candidates since 2012) have chosen to miss out on public funding; the unpopularity of the fund goes much farther back. At the end of this chapter, I shall discuss the arguments that may be made against the public funding of presidential elections; it seems to me that most of them, if pursued to their logical end, do not hold water. But it is impossible to ignore a general sense of the uselessness of political parties. Why, people say, should we fund party full-timers (who for the most part have never really worked, who think only of power, and so on—the list is well known) when we could use the same sums of money to run schools or hospitals? I think that the first weakness of the US Presidential Fund is that it has not offered American citizens the choice of party that they wish to finance. To "politicize" the fund, by allowing them to decide whether their $3 should be used to fund the Democratic or the Republican Party (or any other party, for that matter), would be a first step toward restoring part of its effectiveness. In a way, this is the idea behind my proposed Democratic Equality Vouchers: each citizen can choose to indicate on his annual tax return the political movement to which he would like his seven euros of public money to be allocated (but it could be three euros in the case of the United States—the precise amount is not important here).

The second weakness of the existing Presidential Fund is that, although the tax return clearly indicates that there is no effect on the individual's tax liability, a number of citizens may still think it would cost them something to check the fund box and therefore prefer not to do so. This would suggest that more (and better) efforts should be made to communicate with citizens about the opportunity that is being given to them.

Finally, as we have seen above, the most astonishing feature of the fund established in 1974 is that it has never linked the size of the fund (determined by citizens' contributions) to the size of the reimbursements (since the ceiling on expenses in the presidential election is set independently of the success of the fund). This inevitably creates the sense of a pointless gadget, or, worse still, makes citizens feel that they are being led up the garden path. How can one fail to understand the mistrust of people who are attributed an illusory power?

Inadequate Public Funding?

Although it may seem paradoxical, I also think that the public funding of democracy is dying in the United States because it is too weak: in other words, candidates have given up using it because the public reimbursement of campaign expenses was too low. As we saw in the previous chapter, the (never high) ceiling on spending by presidential election candidates—in relation to the adult population—has been continually falling since the middle of the 1980s, whereas campaign costs have been continually rising during the same period. The ceiling on expenses per adult head of the population was, it is true, not so different from the level observable in France. But the problem lies in the nature of the expenses incurred. For if US presidential candidates were really to campaign in the French style, the first requirement—not necessarily a bad idea, though difficult to realize in view of deep-rooted practices—would be to make it impossible for parties and candidates to buy TV or radio publicity slots. This would not, of course, remove the campaign from the wide range of screens, but it would give each candidate free (and carefully regulated) airtime.

If the spending cap had been two or three times higher, we still cannot know the extent to which candidates in recent years would have chosen to forgo public spending so that they could spend more private money; the original sin of public funding American-style is that it is always possible to opt out. But it is worth noting that, in today's United States, even a Bernie Sanders did not draw on public funding ("primary matching funds") during the 2016 primaries because he did not want his spending to be constrained.[17] Had he accepted public money, he would have had to commit to spending no more than $10 million on the primaries. And in the end, Bernie Sanders raised more than $228 million dollars for his campaign and spent nearly $223 million of them![18] That was more than twenty times higher than the ceiling . . .

I have deliberately taken the example of Bernie Sanders, because he is one of the most fervent advocates of a reform of US electoral campaign funding; not only did the senator support the Fair Elections Now Act on the floor of Congress,[19] but he also refused to have a super PAC behind his campaign (something on which Obama soon gave way). Should he be reproached with spending much more than the limit of $10 million? You might spontaneously answer "yes," but things become much more complicated once you consider the structure of the donations he received. In fact, 59 percent of the contributions received by the senator from Vermont in 2016—a total of $135 million—consisted of "small sums" less than $200. If it could be ensured that each candidate in elections was *really* reliant only on small donations—I say *really* because, as we briefly saw in the case of Germany, the practice of "slicing up" large donations is very widespread—then the use of private funding would evidently be much less of a problem than it currently is. However, the reality of campaign donations is that they are constituted not by a multitude of small sums but by a handful of individuals who contribute the vast majority of the funding, including in countries such as France, where the maximum permitted donation is comparatively low in international terms.

What can be done? First, the ceiling on donation size could be made much lower: 200 dollars or euros, for example, which is the dividing line today in the United States between large and small donations. Second, direct public funding could be introduced, so that all citizens are able to express their political preferences without having to pay anything directly themselves. Not everyone has a spare $200 to give a candidate, but everyone should be able to make his or her voice heard in a legitimate manner—including financially.

The Public Funding of Democracy: A System Everywhere under Threat

In both Italy and the United States, the system of publicly funding democracy has been almost entirely dismantled in recent years. What is most disturbing is that, apart from the direct implications for each country—as we shall see in the next chapter, the United States in particular has entered a circle of self-perpetuating political and economic inequalities—this reflects a more general tendency in today's world.

In Canada, Repeated Conservative Attacks

In Canada, for instance, on the pretext of spending cuts needed to meet the financial crisis, the ruling Conservatives tried in 2008 to dismantle the annual public funding of political parties. This move triggered a major political crisis in the government coalition, until the Conservatives finally backed down for a time. But in 2011, only three weeks after forming a new government, they voted to eliminate the tri-monthly funding allocations, which were duly whittled down to zero by 2016. In

Canada today, at the federal level, all that remains is the reimbursement of campaign expenses.

It is remarkable that in Canada the Conservatives were the ones who systematically challenged and eventually eliminated the direct public funding of political parties. Why was this? The amounts that the Conservatives receive in private donations give them a great financial advantage over the Liberals and other parties, and the existence of substantial public funding did a lot to offset this. In 2015, the Conservative prime minister, Stephen Harper, made an edifying statement on this matter. While some were questioning the need for a particularly long and costly election campaign of seventy-eight days, he declared: "In terms of the advantages this party has, in terms of the fact that we are a better financed political party, a better organized political party and better supported by Canadians, those advantages exist, whether we call this campaign or not!" And he concluded that it was essential that the campaign "money comes from the parties themselves, not from the government resources, parliamentary resources, or taxpayer resources."[20] That says it all.

In the United Kingdom, Tight Public Funding

We have seen the winding down of public funding in countries such as the United States or Italy, where it existed for decades, and its decline in a country such as France, where it was introduced much more recently. But in some countries there is nothing to challenge, since no real system of public funding was ever created. In the United Kingdom, for example, there has never been a real system of direct public subsidies or reimbursement of campaign expenses, and despite extensive debates in the past, such a system has not featured for a long time in discussions of how political parties and election campaigns should be funded.

To be absolutely precise, there is public funding of parties in the United Kingdom, but it does not add up to much and takes three forms that seem amazing in comparison with other countries: Policy Development Grants (PDGs), Short Money, and Cranborne Money. Let me briefly describe them, so that it is clear what they involve.

Policy Development Grants were introduced quite recently, in the framework of the Political Parties, Elections and Referendums Act

(2000). The idea is to assist parties financially in the preparation of manifestoes for parliamentary elections, as well as for EU or local elections, by subsidizing their research and development (R&D) activities. Each year the various parties share the subsidy, which has a total value of £2 million sterling, and for this purpose they must make an application to the Electoral Commission. Why only £2 million? Obvious answer: to limit the total amount of public subsidies to political parties. The proof? The R&D spending by all parties before 2000 was £1.5 million, funded out of their own resources. The report on party funding published in 1998 by Lord Neill of Bladen recommended the creation of this subsidy. It can hardly be said that, by allocating just £2 million of public money, the government changed the game in any real way.

More interesting is the Short Money introduced in 1975, which is available to all opposition parties that won at least two seats (or one seat + 150,000 votes) in the House of Commons at the previous elections.[21] The name "Short Money" does not express the small amounts involved (although it could), but rather the fact that it was introduced by Edward Watson Short (Baron Glenamara), who was the leader of the House in 1975.[22] These subsidies are intended to cover the annual expenses that opposition parties incur in carrying out their parliamentary functions; the UK Parliament features a "shadow cabinet," made up of the most important MPs in the main opposition party. Similarly, since 1996 the two main opposition parties in the House of Lords have benefited from a public subsidy in the shape of Cranborne Money (so called after Lord Cranborne, leader of the House of Lords when it was introduced).

These public subsidies have been refined several times since the mid-1970s, but the discussion today centers not so much on their possible extension to all parliamentary parties—particularly the ruling party—as on the need to cut costs by scaling down the money allocated to them. Moreover, the expenses scandal in 2009—when MPs and members of the House of Lords from the three main parties were indicted for claiming expenses to which they were not entitled[23]—did not help to popularize the idea of spending more taxpayers' money on the processes of political life.

When will the United Kingdom see a real debate on limits to the private funding of democracy and the establishment of substantial public funding? As things stand, the main obstacle has to do with the role of the trade unions: the Conservatives are prepared to limit the size of donations as long as the union funding of political parties (essentially the Labour Party) is similarly capped; the Labour Party would like to restrict individual and corporate donations but to exclude union subsidies from such regulation. Bad faith on both sides ends up blocking everything. It is to be hoped that electoral shocks, such as those associated with Brexit, will lead politicians and other citizens to think again about the role of private interests in the electoral process, and about the best way to regulate it.

Public Funding of Democracy against the Costs of Running the State

In Part Three, I shall make the case for Democratic Equality Vouchers, a way of publicly funding democracy that would be financially more generous, and radically more equal, than systems currently in operation. It would also, of course, entail such further measures as a drastic curb (or total ban) on private funding and a complete rethinking of the forms and timing of public funding, in the light of past experiences and with a view to streamlining the democratic process and renewing the forces present in it.

To those who think that this clashes too much with the almost universal cooling toward public funding systems, I would make two points straight away. First, the present system is no longer operational and is leading everywhere to major distortions; the preferences of citizens— your preferences—are no longer being represented. We shall consider this failure more in later chapters: we need to be aware of it, and of the need for reforms that it implies. In this respect, I am not swimming against the current. I am fully aware of the imperfections of the present system. But I do not think that the solution lies on the side of nihilism. What is necessary is not to destroy but to rethink.

Second, I want to forestall the (sometimes demagogic, sometimes naïvely honest) criticism that it would be better to spend public money on hospitals or education than on political parties. This was Obama's approach in 2014 with his Medical Research Act, which took away the resources that used to go to the public funding of democracy and allocated them to cancer research. The sums of money that I have in mind for the proposed Democratic Equality Vouchers are calculated on the basis of what is currently spent (in France, for example) on the funding of democracy. I am not suggesting an increase in the grand total, but rather a fairer and more efficient allocation—for example, by ending the regressive tax deductions highlighted in Chapters 2 and 3. Thus, in France today, the state spends each year approximately 175 million euros on the funding of political democracy: 67 million on the direct funding of parties, 52 million on the reimbursement of campaign expenses, 56 million on tax relief associated with donations to parties, and 8 million on tax relief for donations to electoral campaigns. I think that these 175 million euros would be much better spent if they took the form of Democratic Equality Vouchers, each to the value of 3.55 euros, which all adults could allocate to their chosen party simply by checking a box on their annual tax return. I even show that, with a reallocation of existing resources and no extra public spending, the value of one Democratic Equality Voucher could easily rise to 7 euros a year per adult citizen.

I will also permit myself here to mention an important point that will become clearer in the next chapter. To leave democracy in the hands of private interests, by failing either to limit the size of private donations or to subsidize the operations of parties with efficiently allocated public money, would have very real consequences for our politicians and for the decisions they make in office. It would therefore have very real policy consequences for the taxation of high incomes or bequests and for the sums of money allocated to education or public hospitals. To put it in another way: a little more public money to fund political democracy, as part of a wider reform of the funding of democracy, would certainly not lead to a fall in the resources for schools or hospitals through some kind of substitution effect (the sums in question are not comparable), but it might have the positive effect of increasing future public expenditure for the benefit of the majority, whose preferences would finally be heeded.

In the end, how much does the running of the state cost today? If we simply take the "public authorities" in France, the annual spending totals 992 million euros (991,742,491 euros, to be precise, or 19.20 euros per adult), of which 103 million goes to the presidency of the Republic, 518 million to the National Assembly, 324 million to the Senate, and 35 million to the Parliamentary Channel TV station—to which should be added 12 million euros for the Constitutional Council and 1 million for the Court of Justice of the French Republic.[24] The running of all the ministries and their cabinets accounts for further annual spending of 117 million euros, of which 27 million goes to the prime minister's office.[25] If we also included the state advisory and supervisory functions, this would add another 663 million euros to the bill (405 million for the Council of State and other administrative jurisdictions, 40 million for the Economic, Social, and Environmental Council, 217 million for the Court of Auditors and other financial bodies, and less than 1 million for the High Council of Public Finances). In total (and please excuse the spate of figures), the annual cost of running the state therefore comes to nearly 1.8 billion euros, or 34 euros a year per adult head of the population. This covers only a limited number of functions, roughly corresponding to the pay of the elected politicians who govern us (ministers, deputies, senators, and their advisers), but not the total expenditure they have to approve and assess (total public spending accounts for nearly one half of gross domestic product, or approximately 20,000 euros per capita).

In other words, if two or three euros per capita are spent for the funding of political life, this means that ten times less is being spent to organize democratic deliberations and choices than to remunerate the work of those who govern us (and 10,000 times less than the expenditure we ask those politicians to manage in our name). To those who want to reduce this public funding to zero, I would ask this: Is it not normal that the equivalent of 10 percent—or more—of the sums paid to those who govern us should be allocated to the people's democratic decision-making in the election of its rulers? I would also say this: do not fear to draw the lessons of history, to learn from what has been happening elsewhere in Europe and on the other side of the Atlantic. We shall look more closely at the aberrations produced by decades of deregulation in the United States. But if private money now has the upper hand there, it is also because there is no longer any public funding. To fund democracy out of the public purse, and to do it in such a way that everyone has an equal say—no more, no less—is the best means to relegitimize the work of those who govern us and to restore a bond of trust between citizens and politicians.

7

Are America's Aberrations
a Danger for Europe?

FRANCE SHOOK for a few moments in 2016, responding to the Trump tsunami on the other side of the Atlantic. Coming as it did after the Brexit vote, was it another harbinger that the Front National would be in power before long? The elections of 2017 soon reassured French people and allowed them to go about their business again, perhaps a touch chauvinistic in their prompt insistence that France was decidedly not America. The wave of populism threatening to engulf the world had come up against the solid, stubborn wall of Gallic intelligence. Ah, nothing like a bit of good old nationalism!

In the United States, it's obvious, the weight of money and lobbies has corrupted the democratic process; few know that it has a system of public funding of democracy (the Presidential Election Campaign Fund), or that this has been cut adrift by private funding—and by a real disenchantment with political parties. In the United States, of course, but in France and the rest of the world? We have just seen that Italy is the country that has gone farthest in challenging the public funding of democracy. But the Canadian Conservatives' dismantling of the trimonthly public allocation of funds to political parties goes in the same direction. And in France today, the three main political forces present themselves as anti-parties: La République en Marche constantly explains that it pits itself against "yesterday's world"; La France Insoumise declares on its website that it does not have "the structures of traditional

political parties"; and the Front National has always refused to place itself on the right-left axis or to compare itself to other parties. Cause or
consequence of the denigration of parties?

Fewer than 10 percent of French people today have confidence in political parties new or old. It is only one step for most of them to reject
any further funding of parties with their tax money, especially as recent
scandals involving parliamentary assistants and campaign expenses
(whether suspected under-invoicing by Olivier Ginon's GL Events
corporation during Emmanuel Macron's presidential campaign, or
suspected over-invoicing by Mediascop during Jean-Luc Mélenchon's
campaign) have helped to fuel distrust of politicians as serial misusers
of public funds. That further step could one day be taken with no real
awareness of what is happening, in a sudden lurch into a world where
private money is king. For what we have seen in previous chapters is that
democracy involves some costs (the running of parties and election expenses) and that, if public subsidies do not adequately cover those costs,
generous private donations from a privileged minority will take over and
fuel the electoral machine, creating a major danger of corruption and
capture.

In France in 2017, many thought that the unexpected election of the
young president Emmanuel Macron would end the populist wave and
signal the beginning of the renewal of Western democracies. How do
things look a couple of years later? The first point to make is that the
French electorate has never been so divided in its perceptions of a president. All the opinion polls tell us that he is greatly appreciated by the
richest and most educated strata, but massively rejected by the poorest
and those with the least formal education. This is only a reflection of the
economic policy he pursued during the first months of his five-year term.
It was a policy of tax breaks for the well-off, that is, for those who funded
his campaign and must not be allowed to regret it. As for all the rest,
they were supposed to make do with a personal housing allowance worth
five euros less a month.

What is so frightening is that the present balance in America could
become the new normality. Do we not already see signs of this in Germany? The purpose of this chapter is not to stop readers from sleeping
at night, but to open their eyes to the yawning precipice before us and

to show how we have come to this pass. Then we might take the necessary steps so that we do not have to deplore the growing influence of private interests, and so that we feel happy at having again made the idea of representativity a full and living reality. Perhaps, on reaching the end of this book, readers will no longer be able to conceal a hopeful smile at the thought that solutions exist, and that these are neither particularly costly nor particularly difficult to implement.

We shall analyze the anti-egalitarian drift in the American system and the dangers presently weighing on Germany and the rest of Europe. The point is not to present a litany of complaints, but to map out the necessary stages on the road to solutions: Democratic Equality Vouchers, a complete remake of the public funding of democracy, and a new mixed assembly that introduces social representation as a component part of the national parliament, bringing its membership and its decisions more into line with the social-economic reality.

Decades of Deregulating Political Democracy

Private money has not always had the upper hand in American political life. If we speak today of the "new gilded age," alluding to the exponential growth of economic and political inequalities on the other side of the Atlantic, it is because an earlier "gilded age"—from the end of the Civil War to the early twentieth century, marked by unprecedented economic growth and a culture of rampant corruption—gave way for a few decades to a progressive and more egalitarian era. According to the history books, that Progressive Era came to an end with the crisis of 1929. But it continued in the 1930s with Franklin Roosevelt's New Deal, and, in respect of the regulation of the democratic process, I would be tempted to prolong it until the mid-1970s.

I have already mentioned Theodore Roosevelt's hopes and his early ambitions to bring about political reform. I have also noted the scale of the system established between 1971 and 1974, right at the end of the period and probably too late to bear its fruits. It was a system partly inspired by initiatives in a number of other countries. One might say "Bravo!"—except that the expression "the beginning of the end" has never been as meaningful as it is in the American case. No sooner was it introduced than it was dismantled: that is the story of the publicly regulated funding of political life in the United States. The Supreme Court plays the grim reaper here: for a long time it opposed the imposition at the federal level of income taxes and a minimum wage; and it has constantly upheld the idea that money and expression are one and the same thing, thereby undermining public regulation of the private funding of democracy.[1]

Money: A Most Peculiar Conception of Free Speech

The US Supreme Court began its gradual demolition of the rules of private funding in 1976, with its judgment in the famous *Buckley v. Valeo* case.[2] This declared unconstitutional the ceiling on candidates' contributions to their own campaigns. What were the consequences? Long before the days of Trump, it allowed the billionaire David Koch to spend more than $2 million during the 1980 presidential campaign, simply by running for vice-president on the Libertarian Party ticket. As a candidate, he was able to spend as much as he liked. As an ordinary citizen, he would have been constrained by the official ceiling on individual campaign donations.

But the Supreme Court did not stop there. In the same judgment, while it upheld the limits on individual contributions to a candidate or party, it ruled as unconstitutional any ceiling on "independent" spending; in other words, so long as an individual or group did not directly run in an election, and so long as it was not acting in coordination with a candidate but simply wished to support or oppose him, it was free to spend as much as it liked. Only corporations and unions were not permitted to do this in 1976. Private individuals were therefore restricted in the size of their direct donations to a candidate: "hard money" was capped but not campaign expenses; "soft money" had its limits removed. Why? Because the US Supreme Court used a highly restrictive definition of corruption as involving a quid pro quo, "something for something else." In other words, when a citizen contributed directly to a candidate's campaign (by donating something), there was a risk of corruption since something would be expected in return. But that risk did not exist—according to the Supreme Court—if the citizen spent money directly to express her preferences. In that case, since the candidate did not receive anything, she could not give anything in return. It was just a form of self-expression for the citizen who spent the money.

I would like to emphasize this point, as the distinction seems far from self-evident to anyone who is not an American citizen. In the United States, I may campaign independently for the candidate of my choice; so, if I am a fan of Michelle Obama and I want to see her win the Democratic primary in 2020, nothing stops me from paying for my own TV ads in support of the candidate, although the degree of tolerance may vary if the messages become too explicit ("Vote for Michelle!"). On the other hand, the size of the contributions I can make to Michelle Obama's campaign—let's say "Michelle for America"—is strictly limited, since in the case of such direct contributions there may be a suspicion of corruption, but certainly not in the case of indirect contributions. The Supreme Court reaffirmed this position in 2012 with its "Citizens United" decision (to which we shall return): "When Buckley identified a sufficiently important governmental interest in preventing corruption or the appearance of corruption, that interest was limited to quid pro quo corruption." However, the Court ruled, independent spending—that is, independent of the candidates and their campaigns—is nothing other than a form of political expression; it cannot, therefore, cause either corruption or the appearance of corruption. In France, by contrast, only political parties or groups are permitted to receive donations or to engage in electoral spending—a restriction that may appear onerous but is essential to the effective control of campaign funding.[3]

Lastly, the Supreme Court abolished limits on total campaign expenditure as early as 1976, with the result that today it may be necessary to spend more than a billion dollars to become president of the United States. Who wants to try their luck?

It is interesting to examine the Supreme Court's arguments for killing off the regulation of private electoral funding. Everything was done in the name of the sacrosanct freedom of speech, and information.[4] The basic reasoning is quite simple—which is not to say that it is not wide open to criticism. The first point: in a democracy, citizens should be able to make informed choices (no quarrel about that), and so the First Amendment, which guarantees free speech, is central to the conduct of election campaigns. Each candidate must be able to convince people of the merits of her ideas, the virtues of her candidacy, and so on. I imagine you agree with that, too. But what role does money play in all this? The ability to defend your ideas, and more generally to wage a campaign, comes at a high price—one that has been climbing higher and higher in the modern world. (In the 1970s, the Supreme Court had in mind the cost of radio and television advertising, but also of publicity pages in the press; today, we would also think of the costs associated with online campaigns.[5]) Therefore, the Court argued, a ceiling on the spending of candidates effectively limits their freedom of speech; for money helps them to express their ideas—and is even an indispensable requirement. This brings us to the second point: a limit on election spending is tantamount to a limit on public debate, whereas debate should be, in the Supreme Court's words, "uninhibited, robust, and wide open." This is where we begin to disagree. For how can a debate be "wide open" if some, but not others, can spend money on it without having to think twice? The openness is clear for the wealthiest candidates, but the smaller fry are in danger of being trapped in the scrum.

Since 2010, moreover, the scrum has had two props. Individuals are permitted to spend what they like as long as they do not give money directly to a candidate; and corporations are permitted to do the same, being considered as "individuals" whose freedom of speech is protected by the First Amendment.

When Corporations Become Individuals, Protected by the First Amendment and Unrestricted in Their Election Spending

And to think that it all began with a film: *Hillary: The Movie*—or rather, *Hillary: The Movie, Season 1,* since we need to think back to 2008, when the former First Lady made her first bid to become the first female president of the United States. It was a movie with a charge, produced and distributed by the unforgettable conservative group Citizens United. When watching the film (which I do not advise), you might be tempted to rename it *Hilarious the Movie,* so poor is the argument and so third-rate the direction. You start to shake when you are told that Hillary probably comes closest to a "European socialist," without a knife between her teeth (because the special effects budget was limited).

But you laugh less when you learn of the consequences that this 90-minute documentary had for American political life, opening the way as it did for the unrestricted corporate funding of election campaigns. A little backward tracking shot.

Since 1907 and the Tillman Act, US law has prohibited direct corporate contributions to election campaigns. It is an important piece of legislation, but it is also worth mentioning that for a long time its restrictive effects were rather minor. Throughout the twentieth century, what corporations were not entitled to do was draw directly on their resources to finance election campaigns. But it was quite permissible for them to campaign through a political action committee—even without creating a political action committee of their own. No doubt this was already too complicated for Citizens United, the conservative association that made such a song and dance about it all. What has this to do with *Hillary,* the movie?

Not content with having produced this documentary, Citizens United decided in 2008 that it would pay the Comcast cable operator $1 million to distribute it free to its subscribers—and that it would pay the million dollars straight out of its cash funds, thereby contravening the regulations in place. (Citizens United did this despite the fact that it had a political action committee of its own, which it could perfectly well have used for the purpose.[6]) The aim, then, really was to test out the "Justices," the not-so-young judges appointed for life, whose previous rulings led Citizens United activists to believe that they had never been closer to hitting the nail on the head. And in fact, in its ruling in the *Citizens United v. the Federal Election Commission* case, the Supreme Court did declare unconstitutional all the bans then in place, thereby conferring on corporations the status of "individuals," which allowed them, with the protection of the First Amendment, to spend as much as they liked. To put it in another way: according to US constitutional and case law, corporations are today individuals who, as individuals, must be able to express their opinions freely; they may therefore spend their money as they see fit during election campaigns, since money is a form of speech.[7] On this new, baroque conception of corporations as people, I would recommend Adam Winkler's excellent book *We the Corporations,* which relates how corporations in the United States finally won their civil rights.[8]

The only restriction allowed by the Supreme Court was that corporate spending must remain "independent."[9] As we have seen, however, this completely artificial distinction between "hard money" and "soft money" is in no way an obstacle to the tide of private money washing over the American electoral process. Little known in Europe, this ruling from 2010 transformed the terms of the debate and forces us today to rethink everything.

To finish off the already shaky semblance of regulation still standing in the 2010s, a Supreme Court decision of 2014 in the *McCutcheon v. Federal Election Commission* case dismantled the federal limits on two-year aggregated campaign contributions. (The cap on contributions to each candidate remains unchanged, but for how much longer?) Thus, since 1990, the combined total spending of candidates in the three major US elections (presidential, congressional, and senatorial) has been continually increasing (Figure 55). In 2008, the year that saw the election of Barack Obama (the first to refuse public subsidies so that he could spend

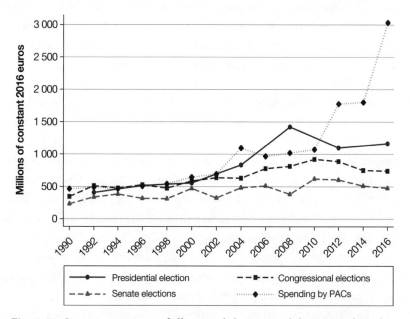

Figure 55. Campaign expenses of all national election candidates (presidential, congressional, and senatorial), United States, 1990–2016

In 2008, the total campaign expenses of all candidates in the presidential election (primaries and general election) amounted to 1.36 billion euros.

beyond its limits), the expenditure of candidates alone, leaving aside independent spending by PACs, came within an inch of the threshold of 1.4 billion euros[10] (or 4.78 euros per adult American). Even more striking for this period—and largely reflecting the result of the above Supreme Court decisions—is the evolution of spending by PACs, which shot up from 500 million euros per two-year electoral cycle in 1990–1992 to more than 3 billion euros in 2016–2017. All in all, in 2016–2017, more than 11.50 euros per American adult went each year on election spending—with the results that we know.

Democratic Rebounds

In this downward spiral of American political democracy, in which both Democrats and Republicans now seem inclined to sign Faustian pacts with the devil, the movement has not always been uninterrupted. The early twenty-first century, particularly after the scandal that engulfed Enron (which for years made extremely high donations to election campaigns),[11] witnessed a democratic rebound all the more interesting for its bipartisan nature in a context polarized along party lines. The Bipartisan Campaign Reform Act (or McCain-Feingold Act) of 2002 restricted the use that political parties could make of "soft money," especially for "issue ads." It also put an end to a certain hypocrisy that had been present until then, by stating that corporate TV or radio ads in a pre-election period should be considered "normal" campaign publicity even if they did not clearly say "Vote for X" or "Vote against X." This entailed that such publicity could not be paid for directly out of corporate funds—which was not at all to the liking of Citizens United. When we reread the text of this act today, it seems like nothing more than common sense. And yet, such meager provisions survived only for a few years against the constant pounding they received from day one. We see how important the Supreme Court nominations were under the Reagan, Bush Sr., and Bush Jr. administrations, and how important it is to limit and regulate the power of judges in France and Europe.

In the United States, then, money really does seem to have swept the board, at least for a time. The Citizens United ruling paved the way for unlimited corporate funding of election campaigns. As far as individuals are concerned, even transparency is no longer a requirement: super

PACs and other associations that do not disclose the identity of their donors—from the 501(c)(4) through "donor-advised funds" to the 501(c)(6)—can spend to their heart's content, and away from the public gaze.

Should we surrender to the Mercers, Kochs, Bloombergs, Simons, and other billionaires of this world, who may be media magnates and are always rich donors? What is needed today is for citizens to mount a real democratic counterattack. Who would have said, just a few years ago, that more than a million Americans would demonstrate in favor of tighter gun controls? Everything encourages me to think that a million or more would mobilize to demand restrictions on corporate and individual contributions to election campaigns. Such a level of popular support will be essential to bring about change. Today, in the face of lobbyists and the Supreme Court—and of contradictions that mean a cap on donations can go against their own short-term interests—lawmakers often seem alone and isolated. But perhaps tomorrow, with the support of hundreds of thousands of Americans, enough energy can be gathered to make things happen.[12]

Why would Americans mobilize in the thousands, or even millions? The simple answer is that it is in their interest. The consequences of decades of deregulation are painfully obvious: American politics caters to the preferences of the rich. Unless public opinion really shakes politicians up, they are most unlikely to move. The answer to the evident lack of representation is certainly not mass abstention. Nor is it the Tea Party—what a paradox that an outfit that, more than any other, lives off handouts from conservative plutocrats (the same ones who fight for ever greater deregulation of the economy and pay ever less in taxes) should serve as a receptacle for the frustration of unrepresented low-income citizens! The solution, rather, is greater regulation. And if that requires a change in the Constitution, then so be it. One way or another, there is an urgent need to uncouple free speech from the private funding of elections.

Let me insert here a short parenthesis on supreme courts and other constitutional councils.[13] As the American case clearly shows, these supposedly independent bodies have in many cases become real democratic anomalies; their members are accountable to no one and make or unmake laws in accordance with thoroughly personal interpretations of the Constitution.[14] On the one hand, you have elected representatives who, though far from perfect, derive their democratic legitimacy from the ballot box and theoretically enact laws representing the preferences of the majority. On the other hand, there are the judges, sometimes appointed for life (as in the United States, which in this respect has curiously chosen to follow the papacy in fashioning its democracy) and cheerfully presented as neutral experts above any political considerations. But there is nothing more political in today's France than the Constitutional Council; it may not have launched into the thorny issue of the funding of political democracy, but it displays a stunning activism in fiscal matters. Progressive social security contributions levied on all types of income? Out of the question. Relief on employees' contributions for low earners? Out of the question. Fiscal transparency for the multinationals? Out of the question. A "Google tax"? Out of the question. And what about the proposal to abolish the solidarity tax on wealth (ISF)—or rather, to change it into a tax on real estate (which comes to the same thing), involving a breach of equal treatment between different categories of wealth? Well, then its positive judgment shoots straight through, since the public interest is all that matters to our dear judges. The fiscal decisions of the Constitutional Council are in reality political and ideological decisions, which testify to a conservatism mostly without any basis in the Constitution, and which the judges try to pass off as the result of purely legal reasoning.

This is not peculiar to France. The Constitutional Court in Germany is just as egregiously conservative in its rulings on fiscal matters. In 1995, for example, it deemed any direct tax above 50 percent to be unconstitutional,[15] whereas the highest income tax rate in the United States and the United Kingdom had been above 80 percent for decades without infringing the rule of law and democratic principles—on the contrary. Was the decision purely legal? The neutral Paul Kirchhof—the irreproachable jurist who delivered the Court's decision—appeared again in 2005 to propose a flat tax of 25 percent on the highest incomes, at a time when he was being tipped to become Angela Merkel's finance minister. The flat tax corresponds to a quite peculiar vision of fiscal equality, which some prefer to disguise as a legal principle because they could never persuade voters to support it in a democratic debate. In the end,

Merkel lost some votes because of Kirchhof and thought it wiser to dispense with his services. He was obviously better equipped to assert his views in the arcane world of constitutional courts and convoluted legal squabbles than on the terrain of political democracy.

I am not saying it is wrong to uphold the principle of tax equality. Indeed, it is essential to defend it, as the yardstick by which the constitutionality of our laws should always be measured. But today it is also essential to transform the Constitutional Council in France (or its counterparts in other countries) and to limit the scope of its arbitrary powers. Many ideas have already been floated in this direction. Dominique Rousseau, for instance, proposed that the Constitutional Council should be converted into a Constitutional Court, with the power to verify constitutionality only *a posteriori*.[16] More fundamentally, he supports a reform in the way in which its members are appointed, so that this would take place in accordance with two criteria: legal competence and parliamentary confirmation.[17]

Politics in the Service of the Superrich

Why should we be worried about the deregulation of political democracy in the United States during the last few decades? One reason, of course, is the frenzied campaign spending, which has reached levels of indecency reminiscent of football transfers in Europe. Who dares to mention the exact figures anymore? They leave us dumbfounded, as if, past a certain number of zeroes, they lose all meaning. But even more frightening is the fact that the preferences of the rich and superrich are more clearly reflected than those of low-income groups in the course of government policies. The minority outweighs the majority by far in today's United States.

Democracy by Coincidence

Wealth buys influence. One might have suspected as much, but on reading Martin Gilens's fascinating books, especially *Affluence and Influence,* all you can do is exclaim: "Have things gone that far?" For what Gilens shows—on the basis of survey results over several decades—is

that, when the (economic, political, or social) preferences of the rich and
the poor diverge, there is no longer any connection between government
decisions and whether or not the poorest sections of society oppose
them.[18] In other words, even if 90 percent of Americans among the
"bottom 50 percent" want the minimum wage to be increased at the federal level, it is enough that the "top 1 percent" oppose it for such a measure to stand no chance of adoption. The bottom line is that, while the
minimum wage has stood still since the election of Ronald Reagan—
apart from a few ad hoc adjustments under Clinton and Obama—its
purchasing power has declined by more than a third since the 1970s.
And what goes for the poor also goes for the middle classes, who have
been steadily losing out to the richest groups in society. So, whether it
is a question of higher taxes on millionaires and billionaires or an increase in the minimum wage, the support expressed by the lower and
middle classes counts for nothing: the superrich have only to deem them
unsuitable in modern times for them to drop off the political agenda.
And what applies to economic and fiscal policy also holds for cultural,
social, international, and other policies—in short, for all the fields of
government action.

This is not to say that most of the policies implemented by governments do not correspond to the preferences of the majority of citizens;
if that were the case, a revolution might be in the cards. De facto, policy
decisions are often in line with public opinion, but that is only because,
in general, the preferences of the richest sections of society coincide with
those of the rest of population. It is not because the poorest want x or y
that politicians decide to give them x or y; the only, or the main, reason
why they do so is that the superrich want the same. The legalization of
abortion and the US intervention in Iraq, for example, were two policies that met the preferences of both the poorest and the richest groups
in society. Martin Gilens and Benjamin Page describe this as "democracy by coincidence." Should we be satisfied with it?

As Gilens and Page emphasize, the problem with democracy by coincidence is that fortunate coincidences can very quickly turn into an
unfortunate tyranny. And even if it does not come to tyranny, can we
really speak of democracy? In a way, we are coming back to the question of philanthropy: a handful of billionaires who are more capable than

the majority of deciding for the majority, no doubt because the radiance of the Money God illuminates their preferences.

But Why Do Citizens Vote against Their Own Interests?
From Conflict over Values . . .

Instead of looking down on people who do not vote, we might try to understand them. Why go to the polls, after all, if democracy has already been captured? At least we can refuse to legitimize the electoral masquerade by casting our vote.

What is more difficult to grasp—for the researcher, but also the citizen, that I am—is why the representation deficit throws hundreds of thousands of citizens into the arms of right-wing populists, especially in the United States, where the most striking thing about populist movements is their economic and social conservatism. Let us say I do not feel represented as a low-income citizen of rural America, someone suffering from the economic crisis, the pollution of my rivers, an inability to give my children the education they need to achieve success, or my parents the social care they need to live a decent life; and suppose I am right to feel this, because of a representation deficit that has been well documented. Why, then, do I vote more and more for parties that want to make the rich pay even less in taxes, to unravel the welfare state a little more, and to deregulate the industrial sector so that it can expand without having to worry about environmental safeguards? To put it in a nutshell, why do I vote against my own interests?

Attempts to answer this question are fast becoming a literary genre of their own in the United States—and I say this without any sarcasm, since books that dissect the working-class vote are mostly fascinating. Countless social science researchers—and numbers of journalists as well—are going off to meet Tea Party voters to try to understand what motivates them—a return to their origins for some; a real discovery of an alien milieu for others.

In a sense, Thomas Frank opened the way in 2007 with his bestseller *What's the Matter with Kansas?*, in which he investigated why the electors of the small Midwest state of Kansas should for years have steadily voted for the Republicans, if not for ultraconservatives and the Tea Party farther to the right.[19] Kansas lies geographically in the middle of

America's "heartland," now frequently and derisively called "flyover country" by the coastal middle classes, a region marked by depopulation and a declining, aging, and disadvantaged population.[20] It is one of the least unequal states in the United States (although everything is relative: the richest 10 percent now haul in 41.9 percent of the total income, and the richest 1 percent capture 16.2 percent, in comparison with 35 percent and 11.1 percent respectively in France). But while this is doubtless to be welcomed, it also means that the idea of taxing the rich more heavily has less support than in New York State, where the average annual income of the top 1 percent is over $2 million (against just under $1 million in Kansas).[21] The highest US incomes—as well as the highest net assets—are not found in Kansas but elsewhere; people in Kansas frown upon those "Others" because of their lack of values, regarding themselves as more "deserving." But they see those "Others" only on TV or the big screen, where images of an unfamiliar America are constantly relayed to them.[22] All they know about the America of New York and California is that it votes Democrat.

In a way, therefore, political conflict is converted into identity conflict: there are "them" and there are "us." The identity conflict is not a race conflict (although, as we shall see, the racial dimension is by no means absent from American political debate); nor is it necessarily a conflict between Americans and foreigners; nor is it a religious conflict, of the kind that some seek to stir up in Europe, particularly in relation to Islam. But it is a conflict between Americans. From the perspective of the professional classes in Boston or San Francisco, it looks like a conflict between the future and the past, between educated cosmopolitans and rubes and hicks who stubbornly "cling to guns or religion," to use Barack Obama's controversial phrase. In reverse, it can look like a fight between those who drink their coffee plain and the snobs, pseuds, and liberals—in a word, Democrats—who order macchiatos and all kinds of flavorings.

This coffee argument may strike you as anecdotal,[23] but Thomas Frank has shown just how significant it is for an understanding of why Americans with everything to gain from big government—high-quality public education, a better healthcare system, and so on—vote instead for Washington to reduce taxes and to spend and redistribute less. For them, government is the "evil," the embodiment of all the Others who do not represent or understand them. It is a value conflict, and it is on the ground of values—not economics—that the Tea Party has won over its electorate.

It has done this by convincing the "left behind" that the present crisis is above all a moral crisis,[24] reflecting the decay of an America facing cultural decline for which the "flyover" jet-set is mainly responsible. In fact, it was on the abortion issue that the ultraconservative Republicans won their first electoral battles in Kansas, before finally losing control of their own party to the Tea Party. Anti-abortion, deeply religious, and anti-intellectual, the conservatives won at the polls by shifting the terms of the political debate: what had previously been a class conflict became a conflict over values. Their great victory was to redefine class relations around the concept of "authenticity," whereas until then it had been wealth that defined social classes.[25]

One cannot but hail their skillful political maneuvering. For the great advantage of cultural class conflict is that the most deprived groups in society can have a sense that they are winning. Economically, they have already lost and see no possible way forward; the policies of the Republicans, who cut marginal tax rates and block increases in the minimum wage, certainly offer them no solution. The disadvantaged also have a sense that their children have lost the economic battle; the American dream is now a long way off, not having survived a period in which the likelihood that children would earn more than their parents plummeted from 90 percent in 1940 to just 50 percent fifty years later.[26] But on the "cultural" terrain of authenticity, those at the bottom of the ladder can aspire to victory. Take the rejection of abortion, which—beyond the religious dimension—has become a moral and cultural value in conservative discourse. The problem has been reformulated in terms of "merit": on the one side are "deserving" Americans, ready to accept adversity and even an unwanted child; on the other side are the decadents, who put their own pleasure above everything else.

. . . to the Hard Economic Realities

This conflict over values should not blind us to the economic distress that the most deprived social groups experience. The fact that political

debate has shifted to cultural issues has not conjured away the funda-
mentals of class conflict—on the contrary. To win back the voters seduced by right-wing populists, it would appear necessary to refocus the
debate on economic questions. Unfortunately, too many in the "New
Left," as Richard Rorty lamented in the 1990s, themselves gave "cultural
politics preference over real politics," retreating into the academy to
fight over words rather than wages.[27] In the United States over the past
forty years, the economy has grown (cumulatively) by 59 percent. That
seems a good record—much better than France's over the same period
(39 percent). However, that 59 percent conceals enormous disparities: for
the richest 10 percent, the cumulative growth rate for the period was
115 percent (685 percent for the top 0.001 percent!). But the bottom half
of the population saw the size of its economy fall by 1 percent. For the
50 percent of people with the lowest incomes, not only was there no
growth, but the situation actually worsened.[28]

So, it is at the economic level that we must try to understand the pro-
conservative vote in the red states. With this in view, the political scientist Katherine Cramer went off to talk with voters in Wisconsin, a small
state south of Lake Superior, which, like Kansas, is relatively poorer and
less unequal than the rest of the country.[29] It is an overwhelmingly rural
state—hence the "rural consciousness" that Cramer places at the heart
of her analysis. Rural consciousness and resentment: the two concepts,
in her opinion, make it possible to understand why the most disadvantaged voters—who would be the first to benefit from greater redistribution—vote systematically against higher taxes and welfare.

There is some reality in the rancor that "rural people" express toward
"urban people";[30] their resentment is at least partly grounded in economics.[31] I have already noted that America's economic growth in recent decades did not benefit the least advantaged groups—on the contrary. We are not just talking of naïve voters or, worse, irrational people
fed on reality television and *The Apprentice* (the reality game show that
made Trump famous on the small screen), ready to be seduced by appeals to their racism and other base instincts. No, the voters in question are largely rational, and their resentment has an economic basis.
They ask legitimate questions: Who benefits from what? Who deserves
it? Who has power? Who is responsible? And they cannot be satisfied

with the answers. Certainly they have no power, because they are no longer really represented. They do not have power, and the people with the power ignore them. No account is taken of their preferences.

But in that case, why are they not in favor of higher taxes on the rich and therefore—since money buys power—the powerful? Why do they not aim for money and power to be redistributed together? Why do they not vote "on the left," for candidates who promise greater redistribution? This is where the concept of "merit" becomes central again. For in the eyes of these Midwesterners, most of them whites, any redistribution and any measures of social protection are benefiting primarily poor people, who do not deserve to benefit from them—what the French Right would call *les assistés,* welfare recipients. The deserving good folk of Kansas or Wisconsin, who uphold the value of rural hard work, do not benefit. Of course, they are wrong to think that they are victims of redistributive injustice—for example, that they pay more than their fair share of taxes yet benefit relatively less. But they are right in thinking that they have been left behind—because that is what has happened to them in the last few decades of economic growth. However, the Others who have stolen its fruits are not poor people like themselves but the men and women with money.

This kind of talk reminds one—though never explicitly—of the language used by the sociologist Arlie Russell Hochschild, who has perfectly grasped, this time in Louisiana, the core of deeply rooted frustration inside average white males.[32] It feels as if their whole lives have been spent standing in line, waiting for their turn to come on the social ladder that embodies the American dream. They queue up, patiently, and what do they see today? They see all the "minorities" overtaking them: first women, then blacks, then homosexuals, handicapped people, and so on. Everyone, except people like themselves. Alone and destitute in their queue, they feel enraged against a state that always seems to trample on the "little guys." What are they left with? God.

Do not smile. The point here is not to justify racism, homophobia, or sexism, but to try to understand. Why in Louisiana, where all of the (low) economic growth between 2009 and 2013 was captured by the richest 1 percent, did citizens vote massively for the Tea Party? In her 2016 book, *Strangers in Their Own Land,* Hochschild puts a lot of stress on

202 THE PRICE OF DEMOCRACY

environmental policies. It is another way of focusing our attention on what seems inexplicable voting behavior. Why do those who suffer the most from industrial pollution—and who benefit most from government protection and measures to limit pollution and its toxic effects—nevertheless vote for a party that opposes the social state and favors the large corporations that pollute the most? How can we account for this paradox? The answer is that, as the popular classes see things in Louisiana, Kansas, or Wisconsin, regulations hit the weakest members of society, while the strongest escape their effects.

This whole sense of injustice and value conflict is fueled by the reality of a representation deficit, both in the political world (as we saw from the work of Martin Gilens, in particular) and in the media. For the working classes, their general absence from the mainstream media is compounded by the vicious contempt that the "liberal elites" direct at them when they deign to look at them for a moment. I think that the Left, in the broad sense of the term, will be unable to win back this popular vote if, beyond purchasing-power or unemployment, it fails to tackle head-on the whole issue of representation. This will form the core of the proposals I make in Part Three. Of course, it is necessary to develop a strict framework for private individual and corporate donations. But working-class voters will partly see this as just one more case of regulation, just one more invasion of their liberty (even though the most deprived groups largely lack the means to contribute financially to election campaigns[33]). A regulatory framework must therefore go together with a democratic revolution with respect to political representation. This is why it is essential for the popular classes to enter Parliament; only then will there be an end to their resentment.

As we shall see in Chapter 11, whether we take France, the United Kingdom, or the United States, the working classes (both blue-collar workers and employees) are the great absence on the benches of Parliament, even though they still make up more than a half of the active population. This partly explains why a large number of citizens feel unrepresented—a situation that they suffer rather than choose, since, other things being equal, they tend to prefer a working-class to a managerial candidate when they are given the choice—and it has direct consequences for the kind of policies that are eventually adopted in

Parliament. This is why I support the idea that a proactive policy affording better popular representation in Parliament should be legally guaranteed. I therefore propose replacing the present national assemblies with mixed assemblies, whose members will be elected under a proportional party-list system with at least 50 percent of the candidates from the popular classes (workers in manual and office jobs or without secure employment).

The End of Class Conflict and the Abandonment of the Democrats

If whole swathes of rural America have turned in recent years to populist movements, particularly the Tea Party and now Donald Trump, this is partly due to the perception of a moral crisis. They see themselves as left behind and deserving of better, while the urban liberal elite tries to impose top-down regulation and unwanted forms of redistribution.

This does not mean, of course, that the economic battle and the struggle against inequalities should be abandoned—quite the contrary. The victory of the Tea Party in the United States is a victory for those who managed to shift the terms of the debate by replacing class struggle with cultural warfare. But above all it is a defeat for the Democrats, who were the first to withdraw from the terrain of class struggle. Thomas Frank shows this exceptionally well.[34] In the course of the last few decades, the Democrats have abandoned the workers, but they have also stopped attacking the aberrations of Wall Street; one need only think of Hillary Clinton's speeches at Goldman Sachs or Citibank, which probably brought in a lot of money but also cost her dearly. There is little doubt that those speeches went easy on the abuses of the financial world—otherwise the Democratic presidential candidate would not have obstinately refused to make them public. They were meant to flatter the egos of those who paid handsomely for her interventions, as well as to treasure the interests of potential contributors.

Why did the Democrats abandon class conflict? Partly to net more campaign contributions from the rich. The worst is that they were doubtless successful in those terms. In 2016, Hillary Clinton raised more private money for her campaign than Donald Trump did for his—and spent more money too. She won the battle of electoral resources, but then fell flat at the polls. Having largely turned her back on the popular classes, she ended up losing their vote.

We might ask what has led the Democrats in recent years to pursue a strategy that it is tempting to describe as harebrained. Thomas Frank suggests an interesting answer, although one would have liked him to give some empirical evidence for it: namely, that during the years in between elections (when they are not advising candidates) the Democrats' advisers—or strategists—spend their time lobbying. In other words, they work for the corporations that will subsequently fund the candidates' campaigns. It is what is called covering all the fronts at once—a conflict of interests might be another way of putting it—with the unfortunate exception of the social front.

The Democrats too wanted, and fought for, the model of economic growth that America has seen in recent years, without showing any concern about inequalities of distribution. It is true that, at the national level, there can be some cause for pride in America's relatively high growth rates, especially if compared with Europe, but they have profited only a tiny minority. The works of Thomas Piketty and Emmanuel Saez have shown that, since the end of the economic crisis, the richest 1 percent have captured more than a half of economic growth in the United States.

I do not agree here with Larry Bartels, who seems to lay the explosion of all inequalities at the Republicans' door.[35] I am completely with him when he highlights the role of policy changes since the end of the Second World War in the surge of economic inequalities; these were not an inevitable result of globalization and technological advances, as some like to claim, but flowed from a series of economic policy choices.[36] What Bartels overlooks, however, is that if lower to middle incomes increased faster under the Democrats than under the Republicans, they nevertheless—*even during Democratic administrations*—increased much more slowly than the highest incomes. Under the Republicans, top income groups creamed off nearly the entirety of economic growth. Under the Democrats, they creamed off the great majority of it. OK, that is less than everything, but the effect was ultimately the same: a widening of inequalities.

So, not everything is the Republicans' fault. The Democrats are also to blame, perhaps more so, since they claimed to be defending the interests of the most deprived. (The Republicans stuck to their usual place in class relations, on the side of the large corporations and the super-rich.) The Democrats applauded economic growth, failing to take action that would lead to its being shared around equally. In this way, they fueled the vicious circle of inequalities.

Political and Economic Inequalities:
A Dangerous Vicious Circle

The growth of economic inequalities fuels the growth of political inequalities; and the greater the political inequalities, the more numerous are the policies that lead to even sharper economic inequalities. Thus, as a direct result of the deregulation of American political democracy, the share of the very rich in contributions to election campaigns has skyrocketed since the 1980s. According to data gathered by Adam Bonica, 0.01 percent of the US population contributed 15 percent of funding in 1980.[37] But the figure had climbed to 40 percent by the time of the 2016 presidential election—much more than the share of annual incomes (4.3 percent) and even total wealth (10.7 percent) controlled by the richest 0.01 percent in the United States.[38] This soaring inequality in election contributions is a direct consequence of the rise in economic inequalities; Adam Bonica and Howard Rosenthal have perfectly documented this from the political contributions of the wealthiest 400 Americans.[39]

Of course, the structure of donations varies from one candidate or party to another. As we have seen, 59 percent of the donations received by Bernie Sanders during the Democratic primaries consisted of small donations less than $200, whereas for Hillary Clinton small contributions accounted for only 19 percent, and larger contributions for more than 53 percent, of her total campaign resources.[40] Even for Barack Obama, donations of $200 or more accounted for 44 percent of his total resources in 2012.[41] With the explosion of inequalities, both Republicans and Democrats "benefit" more and more from the generosity of the ever richer superrich. For although I have spent more time so far on the conservative billionaires—for good reason, since the methods of the Koch brothers or the Mercers are the most objectionable—the

Democratic Party, too, has plenty of moneyed supporters, the best known being Warren Buffett and George Soros. This is not without dangers—for the Democrats as well as the Republicans.

The Grip of Money That Almost Turned against the Republicans

In effect, an ever tinier minority of individuals are providing the sustenance for political parties. The times are long gone, in the immediate postwar period, when political theorists raised questions about the survival of mass parties in various countries. Maurice Duverger, the pope of French political science, drew a distinction between (German) mass parties and (French) cadre parties.[42] Today we would have to add the category of "captured parties," whose principal resource is the checkbooks of the megarich 0.01 percent. I say this in all seriousness, since the key questions in the running of any political group are: Who holds the power? To whom are the power-holders responsible? What means do they have for taking action? What resources do they depend upon? If money becomes the principal means of power and the only necessary resource—apart from activists and cadres—it plays havoc with the customary balance of forces.

Thus, the hyperdependence of the Republicans on a mere handful of megarich, beginning with the Koch brothers, eventually had negative effects for the Grand Old Party.[43] To put it simply, "traditional" Republicans ended up losing control of their own movement, as financial dependence on the Koch brothers for the running of the party and the funding of candidates reached a point where, in an exceptional, though hardly unpredictable, turnaround, the two men could decide on anything in contradiction to the majority party line.

"Traditional" Republicans lost control of their movement, but they also lost elections. It was impossible for the political preferences of a handful of Kansas billionaires to reflect those of the Republican electorate. In 2012, in the tight grip of the "Kochtopus," the Republicans chose neither the best presidential candidate nor the best political message; they went for the candidate of money, Mitt Romney, and the message of money. As Larry Bartels has shown, if Republican voters turned away from Romney during the election campaign, it was because they saw that the former governor of Massachusetts cared more about people with money than people without.[44] From this point of view, the remark that the Republican candidate let slip about the 47 percent of Americans who are nontaxpayers and welfare recipients (and about whom he therefore did not have to care) was the kind of political hara-kiri you don't see often in life.[45]

The extreme dependence on ultraconservative billionaires did not end with the choice of candidates and political message. As we shall see, even in the running of election campaigns, and particularly the use of private data to microtarget electors, the tentacles of the Koch brothers wrapped themselves around the Republican National Committee. Whereas it used to handle its electoral data internally, it is now forced to rely on a database that the Kochs developed themselves and that is marketed by their data analytics company i360.

Why, you may ask, do the Republicans not simply end the chokehold by cutting off the moneyed tentacles? The reason is that, *in the current state of regulation,* Republican candidates cannot do without them. It is almost impossible to run in even a local primary today without having first raised hundreds of thousands of dollars. Money has become the new form of disenfranchisement, and only a few pockets are deep enough to provide the necessary sums. A change in the law is required to break the tentacular grip.

Donald Trump is in a way an exception: his personal fortune allowed him to evade capture by the Kochtopus; and when the brothers withheld their support for his candidacy in 2016,[46] he did not fail to lay into them on Twitter, also describing the Republican establishment, with his well-known moderation, as the "puppets of politics."[47] (It is hard to disagree with the latter term, by the way, given the relationship that the Republicans have had for years with the billionaires.) But Trump did not show any special merit in refusing to bow and scrape before King David and King Charles; a multibillionaire himself, he did not need them and went on to put up 25 percent of his own campaign funds.[48]

A Trap the Democrats Do Not Avoid

Although on the Democrats' side, there is no organization as powerful as the Koch empire towering over the Republican Party, "philanthropy" is a snare that can trap them at election time. Many commentators have explained Hillary Clinton's unexpected defeat in 2016 by her closeness to financial circles. And the (equally unexpected) success of Bernie Sanders in the Democratic primaries reflected a drive by significant sections of the electorate to link up with the party's historical values. As we have seen, the Democrats have abandoned those historical values— particularly class struggle—to satisfy the preferences of the Wall Street traders, Silicon Valley engineers, and Google or Twitter developers who have become its main financial backers.

The problem is that the preferences of such individuals, whose annual incomes stretch (at least) into six figures, do not correspond to those of the popular classes and labor unions. On social questions, the wealthy contributors to the Democratic Party are more liberal than those who fund the Republicans: they are for equal marriage, resolutely defend abortion when it comes under attack, and sometimes even support strict firearms control. On economic questions, however, they are extremely conservative, in some cases as much as their Republican counterparts. Taxation just happens to be one of those cases. For, as good philanthropists, they are always happy to give—to a political party, a charitable organization, a good cause, and so on—but mostly oppose any increase in taxes. Consequently, Democratic politicians have humored them with historically low marginal rates of taxation, over and against the preferences of the traditional Democratic electorate, so much so that the latter eventually deserted them in droves.

I mentioned Hillary Clinton above, but on this score Barack Obama—who spent endless hours during his presidency raising funds from the rich—bears an enormous share of the responsibility. To quote from the *Washington Post* in July 2014, "Regardless of what is going on in America and the world, one thing has become certain about President Obama's work schedule—there will always be fundraisers."[49] According to the paper's figures, during his first term, Obama hosted 321 fundraising events, compared with 80 for Reagan, 137 for George H. W. Bush, 167 for Bill Clinton, and 173 for George W. Bush. This might be seen as the continuation of an upward trend over decades, except that things only really took off under Obama, a Democratic president, so virulent in his hostility to Citizens United,[50] who might have been expected to reverse the trend instead of amplifying it. What is more, his fundraising naturally took place among well-off sections of society rather than the popular classes and had the effect of widening the gap between these and the Democratic Party.[51] This also helps to explain Obama's relative economic conservatism during his two terms, which did not witness any reduction of inequality in the United States. Given the time he spent on the road collecting money, it is tempting to ask whether he was capable of doing his presidential job properly.

From Germany to the United Kingdom:
An American-Style System?

In the United States, then, all the dikes have burst in the last few decades; nothing holds back the torrent of money, whatever its origin, and even the transparency of donations has been swept away.[52] Both the Republican Party and the Democratic Party appear to be in the grip of money, and politicians on both the left and the right no longer seem to answer the preferences of any but the rich. Should this be regarded as an American peculiarity? I will show that, on the contrary, these aberrations now threaten the whole of Europe, beginning with Germany.

Lack of Transparency in Germany

Ways of funding political democracy rarely make it to the front page in Germany's leading press organs.[53] When we probe deeper, though, we may well wonder about a certain whiff of scandal that surrounds the political process there. As far as funding is concerned, the workings of German democracy have a lot more in common with the American than the Belgian or French system, and private interests—particularly those of the large industrial groups—play a not insignificant role. The point here is not to denounce the German system as less virtuous than the French, but to take the measure of everything it involves. For Germany's industrial choices, including an aggressive export orientation, have consequences for European countries as a whole.

What is the German model exactly? On the one hand, as we saw in Chapter 5, Germany has a historically innovative system for the funding of political parties and associated foundations. On the other hand—and this is more surprising, since many other countries match public funding with the regulation of private funding—there is a complete absence of regulation concerning individual and corporate donations, with the exception of a transparency requirement. This brings us to one of the key points in our enquiry: the links between money and democracy have never been fully, or calmly, considered in the light of historical and comparative experiences. Germany has therefore broken new ground in some areas, while showing itself to be very retrograde in others. It is a country where there is no ceiling on the amounts that political parties can spend (in election campaigns or more generally), or on the donations they are permitted to receive. Yet each year huge sums are devoted to the funding of parties there.

The only legal obligation relates to transparency. The accounts of political parties, published each year on the Bundestag website, must include a list of all donations above 10,000 euros as well as the identity of the donors. These data are far from perfect, to be sure, since many companies use their subsidiaries to "slice up" their donations into sums of less than 10,000 euros apiece, so that they do not have to declare them; there is also quite a long delay between the time of the donation and the point at which the public is informed of it. But on these matters Germany does much better than France, for example—where the public does not know who gives how much—and with a little political will it would be easy enough to plug the hole in the legislation. Furthermore, all donations in excess of 50,000 euros have to be declared each month, and a special page on the Bundestag website lists them in something close to real time.[54]

The transparency requirement was introduced very early in postwar Germany. On paper, it goes back to 1949 and the adoption of the Basic Law of the Federal Republic, Article 21 of which stipulates that political parties must make public any sizable donations they receive. In practice, it was necessary to wait a little longer, since the Basic Law noted that the details of how parties should publish their donations would be established by a special law on parties, and the German parliament did not enact that law until nearly twenty years later, in 1967.

Beyond these legal niceties, what has been the reality on the ground? We have already seen that German companies and employers' associations contribute very generously to political life in the country. With regard to their motives, perhaps the most striking feature is their tendency to contribute to more than one party at once, on both the right and the left.

In every single year between 2008 and 2015, the specialty chemicals company Evonik Industries AG—whose chairman of the board of directors, Werner Müller, is a former minister of economics and technology—donated tens of thousands of euros to the Christian Democratic Union (CDU, a period total of 575,000 euros), the Social Democratic Party (SPD, a total of 669,000 euros), and the Free Democratic Party (FDP), as well as making regular payments to the Christian Social Union (CSU) and the Greens (surprising though it is that they accepted money from a company that makes most of its profits from chemicals). Why did it finance all the parties in this way—observing symmetry even between the CDU and SPD, the main rivals for power?

It would be tempting to ask the same question to directors of the Daimler carmaker, which between 2008 and 2015 donated a million euros to the CDU, the same to the SPD, and from 300,000 to 400,000 euros each to the CSU, FDP, and Green Party—the left-wing Die Linke being the only significant party "overlooked" in this largesse. Or what about Deutsche Bank, which gave 200,000 euros to the FDP and an identical sum to the CDU in 2009—despite the fact that it was a tricky year financially, when the government came to the assistance of German banks? Was it a corrupt quid pro quo? One thing in return for another? Anyway, that is how it looks.

It's funny that German corporate donations to political parties are rather like Christmas gifts: they all happen on the same day. This appears clearly in Figure 56, a screen capture from the Bundestag website, where we can follow the policies of the Allianz insurance giant in 2006—though they are peculiar neither to Allianz nor to 2006—which on August 28 and 29 donated simultaneously the sums of 50,000 to 60,001 euros to each of five German parties: the SPD, CDU, CSU, Alliance 90 / The Greens (Bündnis 90 / Die Grünen), and the FDP. Obviously it was the day they got their checkbook out!

Many readers will probably be saying that such figures in the thousands—not millions—of euros are a long way from America's

Party	Donation	Donor	Receipt of donation	Notification of donation
Abbreviation	Euros	Name, Address	Date	Date
SPD	60,001	Allianz AG, Königinstraße 28, 80802 München	29.08.2006	31.08.2006
CDU	60,001	Allianz AG, Königinstraße 28, 80802 München	28./29.08.2006	04.09.2006
CSU	60,001	Allianz AG, Königinstraße 28, 80802 München	28./29.08.2006	05.09.2006
BÜNDNIS 90/ DIE GRÜNEN	60,001	Allianz AG, Königinstraße 28, 80802 München	28./29.08.2006	31.08.2006
FDP	50,001	Allianz AG, Königinstraße 28, 80802 München	29.08.2006	31.08.2006

Figure 56. Donations by Allianz Corporation to German political parties in 2006, screen capture

hyperexcesses of inequality, and that Germany remains a promising model. But I think we should take the German excesses seriously, too, with all the donations coming from large, mostly export-oriented corporations. They may explain, at least in part, the German obsession with trade surpluses, even when these take economically irrational proportions and have had the consequences we know for the collective organization and functioning of the eurozone since the crisis of 2008.

A Little French History

Of course, what I just called "German excesses" have nothing cultural about them; they stem from the law, or rather from the absence of laws imposing strict limits. In France today, companies are not permitted to make donations to political parties or campaigns. But they were in the early 1990s, and what we see in the data from those years is scarcely more heartening than the present situation in Germany.

I have collected for the years from 1993 to 1995 (the only ones for which such data are available) a full list of corporate donations compulsorily recorded in the accounts of political parties, together with—and this is the most interesting—the names of the corporate donors.[55] More than 2,500 private corporate donations were received by parties in 1993, and more than 3,000 in 1994. They benefited all the major political movements, but the conservative Rassemblement pour la République (RPR) was well in the lead with 1,932 donations between 1993 and 1995 (a total of 138 million euros, including 64 million in 1993 and 62 million in 1994), followed by the Socialist Party (1,196 donations and a total of 98 million euros); the "Parti Républicain," the Communist Party, and the centrist Union pour la Démocratie Française (UDF) paled in comparison, with 5.6, 3.8, and a little over 2 million euros respectively.

So, which companies displayed particular generosity to the French political parties? The top four consisted of Bouygues, Vivendi (then called the Société Générale des Eaux), Financière SAE-Fougerolle (better known today by the name of Eiffage), and La Lyonnaise des Eaux—all of them under contract to the state and / or local communities. Here I am talking only of contributions to political parties, but there were also numerous corporate donations to election campaigns; in the next chapter, I shall have occasion to consider, for example, the exceptional generosity of companies in the Hauts-de-Seine department bordering on Paris.

Between 1993 and 1995, the Bouygues group in all its forms—that is, Bouygues, Colas (a public works subsidiary), Sacer (a road haulage subsidiary), and so on—donated to no fewer than twenty-eight political movements, from the Radical Party to the Parti Républicain, including the Communist Party, the Socialist Party, and, of course, the RPR. It is not that the group changed its political preferences over time; it gave a good greasing each year to the whole range of political palms.

The good old checkbook again. . . . So, what we see in France in the early 1990s with Bouygues or Vivendi, but also Alstom and JC Decaux— nothing illegal under the regulations of the time—bears a strong resemblance to the present situation in Germany. What conclusion may we draw? The only way to change corporate practices is through new legislation; if companies are allowed to donate as much as they see fit to political life, they will continue to do just that. Why would Philip Morris deprive itself of the opportunity to persuade German politicians that nothing should be done against the ravages of tobacco? Why would German carmakers give up the means they have to keep diesel models running? Why would the banks fail to insure themselves politically against the risk of collapse? I could give more and more examples, but there is no point. You will have understood that, to fight against the weight of private interests, particularly industrial interests, in the democratic process, the first part of any solution is to prohibit companies from making financial contributions.

The British Middle Way and the Danger
of Oligarchic Capture

Such a prohibition is no more to be seen in the United Kingdom than in Germany, but the British system is nevertheless much more restrictive: while there is no cap on individual or corporate contributions, the ceiling on election expenses is very low. This was recently brought home to the campaigners for Brexit, who, it is claimed, spent more than the permitted amounts in 2016.[56]

As we saw in Chapter 3, donations in the United Kingdom used to be very concentrated: the top 10 percent of donors accounted for more than two-thirds of donations. The main point I want to make here, though, is that the United Kingdom is symptomatic of another excess in the current system: the role played by the money of oligarchs, particularly Russian oligarchs. I am not thinking of football clubs or the like—although much could be said about them—but of the funding of political democracy. According to Transparency International, the many Russian assets invested in London in recent years serve as a great machine for the laundering of dirty money.

Not only are these assets being invested in the British capital; they also flow into the coffers of political parties. Foreigners are not allowed to fund parties or election campaigns in the United Kingdom (or in many other countries—even the United States, where the free-speech conception of money stops with physical and legal persons of American nationality). But many Russian oligarchs have acquired British citizenship, which the United Kingdom is happy to grant, often in exchange for their financial investments, and so they are free to act generously in funding the political process.[57] A couple of revealing examples: Lubov Chernukhin, wife of the former Russian finance minister Vladimir Chernukhin, has made donations totaling no less than £514,000 to the Conservative Party since 2012, the last recorded one having been £161,600 in September 2017; Alexander Temerko, a businessman who made his fortune in the energy sector and worked for Yukos (the Russian oil company long controlled by Mikhail Khodorkovsky) before acquiring British citizenship in 2011, made no fewer than forty donations to the Conservative Party between 2012 and 2017, with a total value of more than 500,000 euros.[58] In exchange for what? That is indeed the question. Temerko is a member of the Conservative Party, but that would be one hell of a membership fee.

Since we are talking of the money-politics nexus, let me conclude this excursus on the United Kingdom by mentioning Lakshmi Mittal, a well-known businessman who specializes in steel and has generously subsidized the Labour Party in recent years. According to information on the Electoral Commission website, he has given no less than 6.8 million euros to the Labour Party since 2001.[59] For love of Tony Blair? As many commentators noted in 2002—although it did not prevent Mittal from continuing to donate, in increasing quantities, over the following years—it is tempting to make a connection between his generosity and a letter that Blair sent to the Romanian government supporting Mittal's purchase of a steel plant that was up for sale. Tony Blair had to explain himself on the matter before the UK Parliament.

I highlighted above that the Democrats in the United States have abandoned class conflict. The truth is that the Labour Party has done the same in the United Kingdom—like causes produce like effects.[60] It is not that people's experiences and perceptions of class have changed in recent decades; they have not.[61] Class has not disappeared; if anything, the concentration of wealth has increased in the United Kingdom since the 1980s,[62] and the average income of the poorest fifth of the population has shrunk by 1.6 percent in 2018.[63] The reason, rather, is Labour's deliberate move to the right under Tony Blair—a move at least partly due to its increasing reliance on large donations from wealthy individuals and firms.[64]

From the Excesses of European Regulation to Hopes from Elsewhere

The most disturbing aspect for the future is that, even if the British government decided to get a grip on things and tighten its regulation of the private funding of democracy—why shouldn't it after all, since a century and a half ago it pioneered the capping of campaign expenses?—it would be in danger of running up against EU legislation. The reader may rest assured that we will shortly move on to some solutions. But here is one last piece of bad news: Europe has decided to follow the path of the United States in equating money with free speech. Why? Obviously to blow away the regulations limiting private money in politics.

When Europe Undermines the Regulation of Private Funding

The European Union's most visible intervention on the funding of political parties and campaign expenses was undoubtedly the 1998 judgment of the European Court of Human Rights (ECHR) in the *Bowman v. United Kingdom* case.

In brief, the ECHR ruled that the ban on paid political advertising was a violation of the freedom of expression. What exactly was at issue? A certain Mrs. Bowman, the executive director of the Society for the Protection of the Unborn Child, was prosecuted in the United Kingdom for the distribution of anti-abortion leaflets during the campaign period preceding parliamentary elections—leaflets that contained information about the views of local candidates on the subject. Since 1983, under the "Representation of the People Act," it had been illegal in a pre-election period for any unauthorized person to spend more than £5 for the purpose of conveying information to voters in support of one or another candidate (the regulation of campaign expenses necessarily involves defining who is and who is not authorized to spend).

Although Mrs. Bowman had been prosecuted for the same offense several times before in the United Kingdom, the ECHR decided on this occasion to acquit her. It did so in the name of free speech—on the grounds that limits on spending must be compatible with the freedom of expression protected under Article 10 of the European Convention on Human Rights. In fact, the ECHR held that laws restricting the distribution of leaflets in a pre-election period were a total barrier to Mrs. Bowman's wish to publicize certain information that might influence people to vote in favor of an anti-abortion candidate. Why, the court asked, should she be prevented from spending money in this way, when there was no restriction on the freedom of the press to support or oppose any ideas or candidates? The ECHR concluded that the restriction in question was not justified by the stated objective of preserving equality among candidates, and that it was therefore in violation of Article 10 of the Convention.

The main problem with this judgment was the way in which the Court drew a parallel between, on the one hand, freedom of the press (regulated by rules defining what is a press organ), journalistic freedom and ethics, the ownership and governance structure of the media, and so on, and, on the other hand, the freedom of individuals to spend their money on political publicity—for example, by printing and distributing leaflets—which potentially had no limit other than their monetary wealth. This false track inevitably recalls the one followed by the US Supreme Court, which, in the name of free speech and on the strength of a completely personal interpretation of the Constitution, effectively decided that, whatever the wishes of the electorate, Congress had no right to legislate to restrict the weight of private money in political campaigns. For the moment, the ECHR decision is of limited reach and may easily be underestimated, but we need not wait for further ECHR or European Court of Justice rulings before we begin to get seriously worried.

A Good for an Evil? On the Corruption
of Brazilian Political Life

Let us end this chapter with a potentially more positive trend. In Brazil, companies have long been the main sources of income for political parties, both officially (through donations) and unofficially (through kickbacks). This is not because of political convictions or even the goodness of their hearts, but because the "return on their investment" has been very substantial. Political science researchers have shown that, in 2006, companies specializing in public works obtained an average increase in the value of their government contracts more than 14 times higher than the amount of their donation to a successful Workers' Party candidate in the federal parliamentary elections.[65]

This helps us to understand the origins of the Petrobras scandal that has tarnished the Brazilian political class; there is a lot to be gained from such types of behavior. And just as we thought we had seen everything, an even greater scandal has broken out in the last few years, this time sullying the whole political class in Latin America. The roots are still Brazilian, though, since it is the giant BTP Odebrecht conglomerate that stands accused of greasing the palms of politicians of all stripes throughout the region. The pattern is all too familiar by now, involving kickbacks to political leaders in return for the allocation of public markets. And the scandal has spread to Venezuela, Argentina, Colombia, Guatemala, Mexico, Honduras, and Peru (where President Kuczynski has been forced to resign).

The good news—for there is some in this banal story of corruption—is that the scandals have led to radical reforms, with a ban in 2015 on corporate donations in Brazil and the introduction of a system of public funding for political parties. The full program has yet to be implemented in a chaotic political context, and it is too soon to evaluate it properly. But the rules being proposed seem ambitious—about time too! Moreover, the new system is being established at the very moment when Western democracies are gradually dismantling their public funding systems.

It is quite possible that, in the near future, we will see a similar movement in the other large emerging democracies—particularly in India, where candidates' expenses have skyrocketed in recent years.[66] Corruption scandals have also been on the rise, leading to growing public distrust. The Modi government has announced several times that it is going to take action and introduce new regulations, but so far nothing concrete has happened—there have even been some disturbing retreats from earlier timid legislation. The Brazilian case shows that it is never too late, and that crises and scandals can end in a salutary new awareness. Faced with these questions after decades of fumbling and failure in the richest parts of the North, the democracies of the large emerging countries might perhaps prove to be the most innovative in the future.

8

The Price of a Vote: From Local Elections
to General Microtargeting

THROUGHOUT THE PREVIOUS CHAPTERS, we have surveyed the rules governing election campaigns in Western Europe and North America, paying special attention to the limits (or absence of limits) on campaign funding and candidates' expenses. In France since the late 1980s, unlike in the United States today, election expenses have been subject to major legal restrictions; not only are candidates unable to do what they like with their money—they cannot, for example, buy themselves a series of TV ads—but they are also prohibited from spending more than a certain amount fixed by law. In the 2017 presidential campaign, candidates who ran in the first round could not spend more than 16.851 million euros, and those who made it to the second round were limited to 22.509 million euros. In the legislative elections, the rules on campaign spending are a little more complex, since they involve a fixed limit of 38,000 euros per candidate plus 0.15 euros per resident of the constituency.[1] Thus, whereas a candidate in the second constituency of the Hautes-Alpes department (centered on the city of Briançon) could spend no more than 47,930 euros in 2017, the total rose to 61,300 euros for a candidate in the fifth constituency of Loire-Atlantique.[2] There are similar tight restrictions on spending in local elections: the limit for municipal elections, for example (in all constituencies with more than 9,000 residents[3]), ranges from 1.22 euros per resident for the first 15,000, 1.07 euros for 15,001 to 30,000 residents, and so on. (I will spare you other superfluous details, but I wish you the best of luck if you plan on winning a city hall and want to work out how much you are permitted to spend.[4]) In 2014, a candidate in the municipal elections at Bourg-en-Bresse (Ain department) could not spend more than 53,312 euros; that may not sound like much, but it was a lot more than the ceiling in neighboring communes (15,676 euros in Gex, for example).[5] And remember that in France the permissible amount that anyone may donate to a candidate is very low (4,600 euros per campaign) and that since 1995 no direct corporate donations have been allowed.

So, a few tens of thousands of euros for an election—sometimes even less. That must sound ludicrous to readers who recall the hundreds of millions of dollars available in American campaigns. But does it mean that money plays no role in election results in France, that campaign spending has only a marginal influence on whether a candidate will be elected? Does it similarly imply that we should not care about campaign spending in the United Kingdom, where the spending limits faced by the candidates are even lower?

I will begin by showing you that, *even in France and the United Kingdom,* election spending has a real impact on the votes obtained by candidates. Then we shall try to understand why. After examining what candidates do with their money in France, the United Kingdom, or the United States—from traditional campaign meetings to the microtargeting of electors on social media—we shall see that, contrary to a widespread idea, new technologies have neither made it easier for new candidates to emerge nor led to a lowering of campaign costs. Online campaigning is an expensive business, and it can pay big dividends. Since 2004, in the United States, the victorious presidential candidate has always been the one who spends most of his or her electoral resources online; the difference between Donald Trump and Hillary Clinton is striking in this respect. We shall then bring Part Two to an end, and the time will come for us to turn to solutions. Based on the aberrations and innovations reviewed in the past eight chapters, these will offer the possibility of recovering an idea of democracy as "one person, one vote."

How Campaign Spending Influences Voting Behavior

I studied the influence of campaign spending on election results in a research and data collection project conducted with Yasmine Bekkouche on France and Edgard Dewitte on the United Kingdom.[6] We looked at the role of money in the political process during the past decades—a focus that was particularly important for several reasons. First, economic and political research on these questions continues to suffer from a strong US bias, with the result that, although there is no lack of factual material about the growing and disturbing weight of money in US elections, very little is known about the effects of election spending elsewhere in the world.[7] And second, France and the United Kingdom are interesting from this point of view precisely because the tight limits on campaign spending might lead one to suppose that it does not have a major influence on voting behavior. America is America, so no danger in Europe? It was necessary to investigate whether this was true.

On the basis of the National Commission on Campaign Accounts and Political Funding (CNCCFP) archives and electoral data, Yasmine Bekkouche and I began by constructing a new database of all funding associated with legislative and municipal elections in France since the early 1990s.[8] More specifically, our data cover four municipal elections (1995, 2001, 2008, and 2014) and five legislative elections (1993, 1997, 2002, 2007, and 2012), as well as the campaign spending and election results of approximately 40,000 candidates. The new database I constructed with Edgard Dewitte covers all the UK general elections since 1857, including detailed expenses for 34,000 candidates. In both cases, the results are astonishing.

Very Uneven Resources among Election Candidates

The first striking feature is that both the amount of campaign spending and the origin of campaign funds vary widely among candidates, mainly—but not only—according to their political party.[9] As highlighted in Chapter 3, in practically all the democracies of Western Europe, parties on the right received much more each year in individual and corporate donations than parties on the left. This inequality is also found at the level of election campaigns. Figure 57 shows the average size of

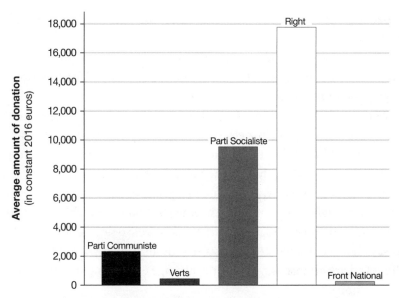

Figure 57. Average donation received by candidates in legislative elections, by political party, France, 1993–2015

donations received by candidates of the different parties in the French legislative elections. On average, candidates on the right receive 18,000 euros in private donations—that is, more than the average total expenses of an election candidate (a little under 15,000 euros). By comparison, Socialist Party candidates receive less than 10,000 euros, Communist Party candidates 2,300 euros, and those from other parties less than 500 euros.

It might be thought that municipal elections—where many candidates run as "independents," and votes often depend more on local factors than on the national political context—would be characterized by greater "equality" in the donations received by candidates. However, this is not what we see in the data. As in legislative elections, candidates on the right are the best endowed with resources; they receive on average 3,400 euros more in private donations than candidates on the left, while those on the far right and the far left receive hardly any donations at all. What are the consequences? Being better funded, conservative candidates spend more than their opponents. The extra private money might have been reflected in a smaller contribution by their parties to campaign expenses, but again this is not the case—for one simple reason. The parties of the Right are themselves richer and can do more to help their candidates. Besides, since election spending is usually a highly effective instrument for winning votes, why should candidates deny themselves any opportunity to increase their chances of success?

In the end, the 3,400 euros of extra donations that right-wing candidates receive for municipal elections in France are immediately translated into additional revenues, so that the candidates have on average 4,200 euros more than their left-wing opponents and are therefore able to spend more. Similarly, in the case of legislative elections, the total revenues for a right-wing candidate average 53,000 euros, which is 12,200 euros more than for a Socialist Party candidate. Some might be tempted to say that the difference is only a few thousand euros, but those few thousand are almost as much as the average expenses of a candidate in the elections.

Interestingly, the only item in the revenues that is lower for a right-wing than for a left-wing candidate is the personal contribution. In fact, what is called "personal contribution" corresponds to the part of campaign expenses that a candidate can have reimbursed, so long as he or she has received enough votes (at least 5 percent of the total) in the first round. In other words, the candidates of the Left as well as challengers from smaller parties take more of a personal financial risk than their counterparts on the right when they run in elections, and in many cases they have recourse to loans. (This comes as a surprise when we think how highly parties of the Right tend to value individual risk-taking.[10]) Moreover, since candidates cannot claim a refund for more than 47.5 percent of expenses, it is very rare that their personal spending rises above that ceiling. Not everyone is Donald Trump, ready to pay out of his own pocket to ensure an election victory. Nor, of course, does everyone have companies he can harness in defiance of any notion of a conflict of interests.

On average, then, right-wing candidates in both municipal and legislative elections receive more than their opponents by way of private donations, and they spend more per elector on their campaigns. The main consequence of this is an extra boost to their total vote.

Election Results Partly Determined by Campaign Expenses

The main result of the research projects I conducted on France with Yasmine Bekkouche and on the United Kingdom with Edgard Dewitte is as follows. Campaign spending on such things as communications, public meetings, leaflets, or door-to-door canvassing has a direct impact on the number of votes candidates obtain in both municipal and legislative elections. This emerges very clearly from Figure 58, Figure 59, and Figure 60a–d, which demonstrate that, for legislative and municipal elections in France as well as for general elections in the United Kingdom, there is a strong correlation between a candidate's percentage of the first-round vote and her percentage of total election spending in the electoral district (each point on these charts stands for a candidate). In general, the greater the amount by which one candidate's spending exceeds that of other candidates, the higher is her share of the first-round vote.[11] This fit is strikingly similar across the years (it holds for the first half of the twentieth century as well as for the twenty-first century) and across countries (notwithstanding the fact that the United Kingdom and France have different electoral systems).

Of course, correlation is not the same as causality, and many factors may be involved other than a direct causal effect of spending on votes. For example, a more promising candidate might obtain more donations (money goes to money, and therefore to winners) as well as more votes because she is popular, not because her spending has brought in more votes.[12] Well aware of this problem, we proceeded in the following way to identify the causal effect of spending. First of all, we isolated the effect of a variation in spending on the number of votes received by a candidate by introducing an "other things being equal" clause: that is to say, we checked a systematic preference for the Left or the Right in voting behavior, as well as the popularity of the different parties in the election year under consideration, against the social-demographic specificities of each electoral district (occupational categories, educational levels, age groups, and so on).[13]

We concentrated mainly on the impact of "exogenous" variations on the revenues of candidates: that is, variations determined by factors external to the district or candidate in question, such as the 1995 French

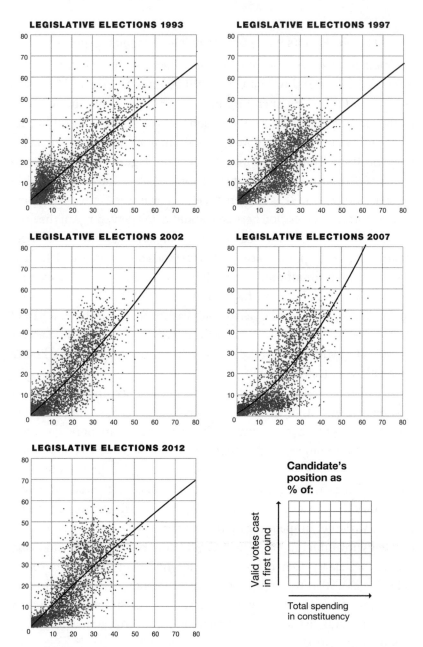

Figure 58. Correlation between campaign expenses and voting score, legislative elections, France, 1993–2012

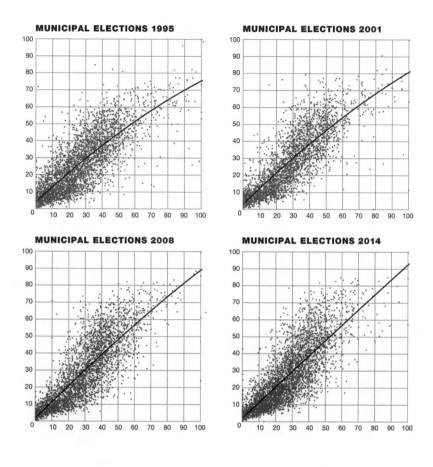

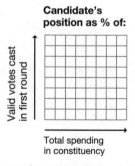

Figure 59. Correlation between campaign expenses and voting score, municipal elections, France, 1995–2014

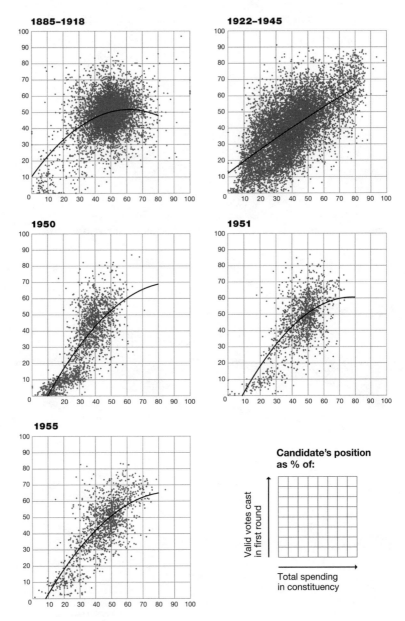

Figure 60a. Correlation between campaign expenses and voting score, general elections, United Kingdom, 1885–1955

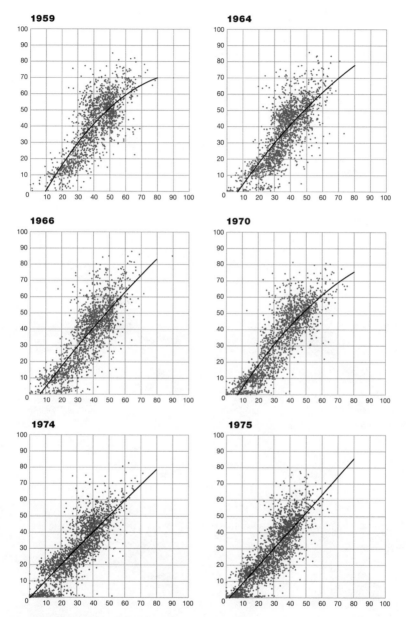

Figure 60b. Correlation between campaign expenses and voting score, general elections, United Kingdom, 1959–1975

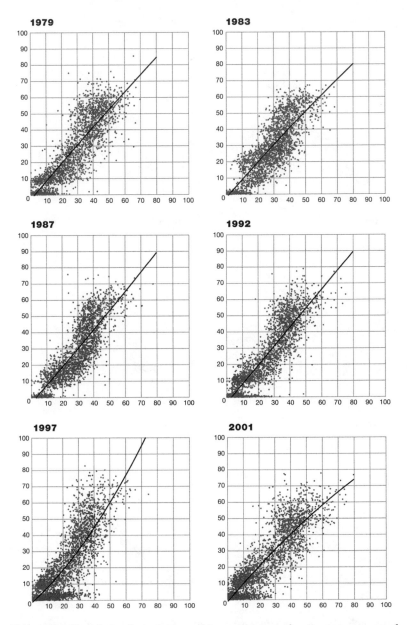

Figure 60c. Correlation between campaign expenses and voting score, general elections, United Kingdom, 1979–2001

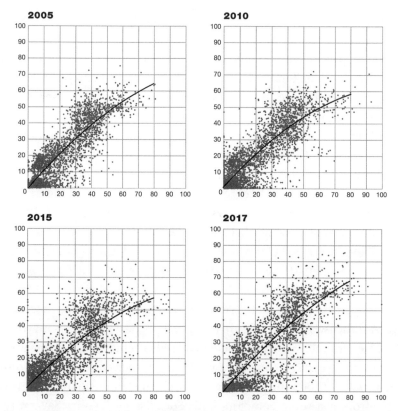

Figure 60d. Correlation between campaign expenses and voting score, general elections, United Kingdom, 2005–2017

legislation that prohibited corporate donations to election campaigns. That sudden and unexpected reform led to a huge fall in the resources available to some candidates but not others, even in geographical areas with the same characteristics and for candidates in the same political party. It is therefore a near-perfect natural experiment, and the results speak volumes.

According to our estimates, the price of a vote in France is roughly six euros for legislative elections and thirty-two euros for municipal elections. This implies that the average of 8,000 extra euros in private donations received by candidates of the Right gives them an advantage of 1,367 to 2,734 votes over candidates of the Left in legislative elections (depending on whether the gain is at the expense of the Socialist Party or another party). That works out at 3 to 6 percent of the votes cast in the first round of the elections. In other words, if there were no cap on spending, private money could easily alter election results. A few euros, one vote. And don't forget that the state (that is, the taxpayer) picks up some of the bill, since two-thirds of the value of a rich person's donation comes out of the public purse.

This effect is all the more problematic because the extra spending is done mostly on the right of the political spectrum; the implications would be different if it were at random that Socialist, Republican, Communist, and other candidates received and spent more than their rivals. But what we see is that the perennial Conservative legislator Patrick Balkany—and not his Socialist rival Gilles Catoire—received more than 1.7 million francs (353,000 euros) in 1993 for his election in the fifth district of the Hauts-de-Seine department, 98 percent of it from private companies, at a time when the ceiling on expenditure was 500,000 francs![14] And we know that there is perhaps more to this than meets the eye. Another well-known figure is Alain Juppé, who served as mayor of Bordeaux from 1995 to 2004 (incidentally, also being French prime minister for two years, starting in May 1995). He received more than 1 million francs (222,000 euros) in donations, of which more than two-thirds came from just seven companies; his Socialist rival, Gilles Savary, received less than 80,000 francs from companies, and the other six candidates nothing at all.

The Strange Defeat Explained?

Perhaps there is justice in this world, however. The new legislation banning corporate donations in 1995 was applied for the first time in the national elections of 1997. Patrick Balkany, who may have sensed a change in the wind—and had anyway been disqualified from standing for two years—gallantly gave up his place to his wife Isabelle.[15] But the poor lady had probably not expected the corporate manna to dry up, and she ran for election with a mere 148,000 francs in donations, more than ten times less than her spouse had received four years earlier. In the end, with scarcely more resources than her two main rivals, Olivier de Chazeaux and Catherine Lalumière, she did not even make it through to the second round.

Beyond the case of the Balkanys, the effect of election spending on voting behavior is such that it may largely explain the "strange defeat" of the Right in the legislative elections of 1997, just four years after the Socialist Party debacle in 1993, and two years after Jacques Chirac's clear victory in the presidential election of 1995. The ban on corporate donations affected only candidates who had received corporate donations in the past—mostly on the right, and only some of them. Whereas the average size of corporate donations received by a candidate in 1993 had been 8,600 euros (representing approximately a quarter of the total of private donations), the median donation had been zero. In other words, more than a half of candidates had received no corporate donation in 1993—and were therefore unaffected by the reform—but candidates on the right had received an average of 40,000 euros from that source!

Like the Balkany couple, these candidates were generally incapable of recovering from the ban introduced in 1995. On average, one extra euro in corporate donations received in 1993 is associated with a 0.46 euro fall in the total revenues of that candidate between 1993 and 1997. In other words, the data tell us that the total revenues in 1997 of a candidate who had received corporate donations worth 100,000 francs in 1993 averaged only 54,000 francs. Such a drop may be explained by the fact that the 1997 elections took everyone unawares; no election had been expected before 1998, until Jacques Chirac surprised even people in his own party by announcing the dissolution of the National Assembly in April 1997 and the holding of elections in May. In making this decision, he felt sure of winning the legislative elections. But he was mistaken. Our results allow us to see that at least part of the reason for this was that candidates of the Right, used to raising money from private companies, did not have enough time to find new donors. They therefore obtained a lower score than they would have done in the absence of the ban, since the new state of their finances meant that they could not spend as much as they had anticipated during their election campaigns.

The nature of our estimates is such that they remain imprecise—we cannot replay the elections in a laboratory—but it would seem from the data available to us that the total impact of the funding reform may have swung several dozen constituencies from the Right to the Left, by a sufficient amount to determine the overall election result. For we should remember that the Socialist Party won by a very small margin, with 255 seats (plus thirty-five for the Communists and seven for the Ecologists) against 251 seats for the ruling Rassemblement pour la République (RPR)–Union pour la Démocratie Française (UDF) coalition.

Thus, despite the existing ceilings on election expenses and the limits on private donations, money plays an important role in European politics, sometimes even a decisive one for the result of elections. Despite or *because*. Whereas the existing literature obtains conflicting results regarding the impact of campaign expenditures on votes, this may be due to the fact that this literature has centered mostly on the United States, where campaign spending is not capped. Hence, given that candidates' expenditures keep growing in US elections, the diminishing returns of spending may dominate—what is the value of one additional dollar in television advertising when you have already spent over a million? On the other hand, in countries such as France and the United Kingdom, where spending is limited, the marginal returns of campaign spending are actually positive. Obviously, this does not mean that money matters less in places with no regulation. The absence of campaign finance limitations adversely affects electoral competition; in the United States, as of today, candidates by and large need to be wealthy to run. This means that, even in countries such as France and the United Kingdom, the role of money in politics has to be further reduced. To lessen this role in the future and to make our democracies more representative, there would have to be tighter limits on private money and a more equitable system of public funding. These will be the themes of Part Three.

Statistical Regularities and Freak Accidents

I would stress that, although a few additional tens of thousands of euros—or mere thousands in small constituencies—may be enough on average to swing an election, it will always be possible to find counterexamples. So, when I say that the price of a vote is thirty-two euros in French municipal elections, I am talking only of a statistical regularity—an average that by no means implies that high spending is always a guarantee of victory. The Koch brothers learned this to their detriment in the presidential election of 1980: David Koch could run for the vice presidency alongside Ed Clark on the Libertarian Party ticket and immediately spend more than $2 million, but this was not enough for the party to win more than 1 percent of the vote.[16] However, the Koch brothers learned some lessons from the experience. Since then, they have decided to go about things differently, creating and pouring millions into numerous think tanks (as we saw in Chapter 4). Money counts in politics, but only if you put it on the right horse.

I could mention any number of other "statistical irregularities," including such examples in France as that of Benoît Hamon in the 2017 presidential election (who was well funded but attracted few votes) or Nicolas Sarkozy in 2012. But I am sure you can think of some yourself. We can see the importance of systematically analyzing data, to raise the debate to a general level rather than the back-and-forth exchange of anecdotes, examples, and counterexamples that allows anyone to come up with arguments against the regulation of campaign expenses. Systematic data have now been collected and used in the case of French and British elections, district by district, and the results are clear.

Lastly, let us note that this statistical regularity—which I established together with Yasmine Bekkouche and Edgard Dewitte—rests solely on data relating to official funding and registered as such. But I am by no means unaware that not only in France or the United States, but also in India or Brazil, there is a lot of what Jane Mayer calls "dark money": that is, campaign influxes—and outflows—that by definition do not appear in my data. Nor am I unaware that election accounts often lack transparency—the commissions in charge of analyzing them (the CNCCFP in France and the Electoral Commission in the United Kingdom) regularly reject a certain number—and that the resources of these commissions, which have been sharply reduced in recent years in France, need to be given a considerable boost. The significant effect of election spending on voting behavior that we were able to identify underestimates the scale of what happens in reality, but it still testifies to the important role of money in the electoral process.

Thus, it would be rather naïve to suggest that French political parties and election campaigns benefited from corporate donations only between 1988 and 1995. We know that, before the law of 1988 came into effect, there had been numerous transfers, including unauthorized ones, between companies and parties,[17] and that corporate kickbacks to political parties in return for the award of public contracts were never an Italian peculiarity (which is, indeed, why regulation was finally introduced in France). Such practices have been amply documented in André Campana's excellent book, *L'Argent secret,* as well as in the works of Éric Phélippeau, who draws a picture, based on Sciences Po press kits, of the hidden funds paid by corporations to political parties in 1993.[18] Similarly, it would be naïve to think that, since companies no longer have the right to fund parties and campaigns, they have actually stopped doing it. We do not need to delve into relations with Libya, but simply bear in mind all the simple (and illegal) devices still open to corporations—from good old bribes to violations of the spirit of the law, such as encouraging employees to donate with a company credit card and to pocket the associated tax relief in exchange for the service rendered. Besides, hidden campaign funding includes not only corporate gifts but also individual donations. I am thinking, at random, of Nicolas Sarkozy's visits to the L'Oréal heiress, Liliane Bettencourt.

Despite all the visits and bribes, despite the millions of euros that neither shrewd researchers nor supervisory authorities are able to track down, the official data alone reveal that money has a significant impact on election results. On average, higher spending for a candidate means that he or she obtains a better result. How is this to be explained?

The Role of Money in Politics—From Campaign Meetings to Social Media

I can see you raise your eyebrows. If, without being an activist or member, you have always voted (at least in national elections) for a political party, *your* political party, you may find it difficult to make a link between what candidates of that or other parties spend and how you vote. After all, your vote is a matter of course. Would a few euros be enough to swing it? Surely not—the very idea seems to jar. Yet, before each polling day, many voters have not yet decided whether they will vote at all or for which candidate they will cast their ballot. It is on these undecided citizens that election campaigns concentrate their efforts and their spending, since there is some hope of swinging their votes. In which ways? There is no lack of possibilities, and candidates often show proof of originality.

Advertising Culture

The nature of campaign spending varies enormously from country to country, depending first of all on what candidates are permitted to spend. In the United States, one of the main objects of spending is TV advertising, which may take either of two forms: "positive" publicity, to "sell" candidates and their programs, or—more surprisingly—"negative" publicity directed against their rivals.[19] For example, instead of vaunting the merits of Hillary Clinton's program on climate change (such as her Clean Energy Challenge worth $60 million), her "negative" campaign publicity attacked the indecency of Donald Trump and his reckless judgments. And on the other side, Trump's TV advertising frequently focused on Hillary Clinton and her alleged corrupt practices.[20]

Everything—or rather, anything—can be said: that is the best way of summing up US election campaigns; anything can be said, so long as you have the means to buy airtime, and enough voters' brains are available. And since this is America, all is in the name of free speech. It may be amusing to recall that, at least with regard to television, things might have worked out differently. For in the United States as in France, election campaigns are regulated by an "equal time rule." The famous Section 315 of the Communications Act requires TV and radio stations to treat all candidates equally.[21] This could have meant that they were required to "offer" the same speaking time free of charge to each candidate, but it actually gave rise to a completely different interpretation: if a channel sells airtime at a certain price to one candidate, it must agree to sell the same airtime to other candidates at the same price.[22] Boom! The signal was given for election spending to take off. Too bad for anyone who could not afford to buy a quarter of an hour of celebrity. That is how America defines free speech and equality.

Donald Trump's spending on TV and other publicity in 2016 came to more than $198 million, or 55 percent of his total spending, while Hillary Clinton's amounted to $352 million, or 58 percent of her total spending.[23] This massive recourse to radio and television as campaign tools is far from unique to the United States. In Canada, for instance, if we take spending in the past four parliamentary elections (2004, 2008, 2011, and 2015), we see that on average the parties allocated 39 percent of their campaign spending to audiovisual advertising (Figure 61).[24] There are notable differences among the parties, however, the two main ones, the Conservative and the Liberal Party, generally having greater recourse to TV and radio to try to win over voters. In 2015, the Liberal Party spent 18.9 million euros on TV and radio advertising during its successful campaign.

In France (as well as Belgium and the United Kingdom), regardless of any cap on spending by candidates and parties, the kind of sums seen in North America could not be deployed in election campaigns, since electoral advertising is not permitted on radio or television. That saves millions of euros from the beginning. But this does not mean that candidates do not have recourse to publicity in these Western European

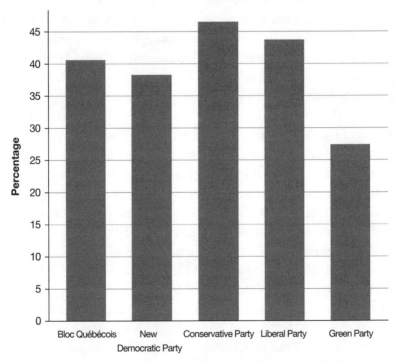

Figure 61. Percentage of campaign spending devoted to TV and radio advertising, by political party, legislative elections, Canada, averages 2004–2015

countries, only that they have to "content themselves" with other media supports. For a long time, the only other option was "printed propaganda," but now there are also "telephone campaigns" and—a new form that may eventually prove the most effective—online publicity. In 2016, Donald Trump devoted $85.7 million to online advertising, and Hillary Clinton approximately $32 million. What are we talking about exactly?

On the one hand, there is the kind of straightforward publicity on the internet and social media that you can see every day of the week, except that it is political rather than commercial. On the other hand—and this is one of the real novelties of recent years—there is the sponsoring of tweets and Facebook posts (which appears in the "post boost" or "post promotion" categories of candidates' spending). Finally, and although candidates tend to be more discreet about this, there are the "fake followers" bought on Twitter and on Facebook or Instagram. Of course, these are very hard to quantify precisely, especially as digital robots (the famous "bots") have now joined fake human followers, that is, real individuals, often located in India or Pakistan, whose job it is to "like" their clients' posts; it seems to have been established that both Trump and Clinton had a significant number of robots among their millions of followers on Twitter[25]—as did Obama before them. Nor is this phenomenon confined to the United States; French politicians also evidently make use of fake Twitter subscribers. Countless companies specialize in selling "friends" and other followers on social media; I advise readers in need of digital affection to try searching online for "How to Become Twitter Famous." But it will be at their own peril, since companies that specialize in detecting fake subscribers are also legion.

This recourse to a variety of fake subscribers obviously creates manifold problems, yet it remains a legal gray area in most democracies. In my view, it has become an urgent matter to regulate such practices. On the one hand, they should be clearly recognized for what they are: an attempt to manipulate the electoral process. There is very little difference between the use of "fake followers" to boost public perceptions of a candidate's popularity and the publication of rigged opinion polls, for example. In France, election surveys are regulated by law and placed under the supervision of a special Survey Commission.[26] Why should fake friends on social media—the new barometers of public opinion—not be subject to the same regulation? On the other hand, the recourse to fake subscribers poses problems of privacy. For how are these fake followers constructed? The chief way is through information taken (one might say stolen) from the profiles of real followers, who are not asked for their real opinions. So, @reader—you whose eyes are now open to what is going on—have you already come across your digital twin @ Reader, who uses not only your name, with a slight alteration, but often also your profile picture?

Facebook and Big Data

Nowadays, social media are used not only as a publicity support or mirror for boosting the popularity of candidates for public office, but also as a campaign instrument, an informational tool, for teams seeking to conquer new voters.[27] In Chapter 4, I briefly noted the possible role that the American billionaires Robert and Rebekah Mercer played in the Brexit referendum victory in the United Kingdom, through the precise targeting of voters on Facebook. But such practices are increasingly common and occupy a growing place in the spending of candidates for public office (or anyway, of those who have the money to spend). Many campaigns use information posted on social media to try to "hack" the electorate, as Eitan Hersh shows in his excellent book.[28]

Media coverage of the Cambridge Analytica affair in the spring of 2018 finally sparked off public debate on the ways in which political campaigns misappropriate information about citizens that ought to be purely private. After the Brexit referendum, it came to light that data stolen by Cambridge Analytica had been used during the Donald Trump campaign to target American voters. Whether or not this helped to swing the election in Trump's favor is not the issue; rather it is the urgent need for regulations to ensure that such attempts at manipulation do not recur in the future.

Of course, hundreds of millions of euros would not be enough to get all French (let alone American) citizens to open their doors to canvassers, and it is not a new idea that party campaigners may use precise data about the electorate to fine-tune their efforts. Eitan Hersh traces such use of electoral registers back to the late nineteenth century. But what has changed with the digital revolution are the scale and the resourcing of this practice. Citizens may rightly be frightened at the quantity of information circulating about them on which campaigns can potentially draw, especially as much of it, though supposedly private, is described as "commercial."[29]

Thus, in the United States today, Democratic Party campaigns rely on the constantly updated Catalist database, which contains hundreds of items of information about each voter at the national level.[30] All in all, since the creation of Catalist in 2006 (as a for-profit business, we should note), election candidates or their electoral committees have spent nearly 4.1 million euros to have access to these data.[31] To this should be added all the campaign spending whose main beneficiary has been NGP VAN, the user interface that the Democrats employ to contact their electors: 67 million euros since 2013, an average of 4.1 million euros *a year* between 2007 and 2017.[32] We are looking at an immense financial effort to take the greatest advantage of new voter-targeting technology.

Not to be outdone, the Republicans have access to the Voter Vault database, which, together with its user interface, is operated by the party internally. This is an important difference, which means that while the Democrats use an independent for-profit company, the Republicans for a long time relied only on their own resources. I say "for a long time" because most Republican candidates now use the i360 company, whose database, developed by the billionaire Koch brothers, contains a detailed portrait of 250 million American consumers and more than 190 million registered voters.[33] Koch brothers: 1, Republican National Committee: 0. Didn't I say that too much reliance on a few billionaires can lead you seriously astray? Since 2011, more than 4 million euros have been spent on this company, including nearly 2.6 million in 2016 alone.

Dangers of Microtargeting

Let us pause for a moment to consider a simple, but often overlooked, normative question: Is it a good thing that political movements of any kind can possess large quantities of data from electoral registers? On the "yes" side, it might be said that, if this information helps politicians to be more in touch with their voters' preferences, it will serve the people's needs, and that, at a time when we rightly lament the widespread disconnect from politics, anything likely to increase voter turnout can only be good. On the "no" side, the first point to make—remember the work of Martin Gilens and Benjamin Page reviewed in Chapter 7—is that politicians today tend to respond less than in the past to the preferences of the majority. Data are for winning elections; preferences are about humoring those who fund the acquisition of data.

Imagine a world in which politicians can perfectly microtarget voters. What does that imply? Quite simply, those politicians will in the end heed the preferences only of those who help them swing the vote. It's a little like with rich donors: if money is all that counts for an election, and if a handful of billionaires can contribute more to my campaign financially than millions of voters, then I may as well target all my campaign efforts—and all the policies I implement—toward that handful of megarich supporters who can ensure I am elected. It is the argument from effectiveness—which, of course, turns against the argument from democracy.

In his book, Eitan Hersh develops a further argument that should weigh on the "no" side of the scales. Campaigns use mainly public data to target voters—or rather, data made public following a legislative decision, and within the United States itself what is public or not varies widely from state to state. Consequently, there is a real conflict between the administrative interests of politicians (one of whose tasks is to protect the private lives of citizens) and their political interests (which push them to make as much information as possible publicly available, so that they can themselves use it in their campaigns). It is important that citizens be aware of this, because politicians are not going to tie their own hands all by themselves.

The End of Intermediaries?

The growing weight of electoral spending on social media also testifies to the growing importance of a direct relationship between politicians or legislators and ordinary citizens. It is as if institutional mediation in the shape of political parties, as well as mass media and labor unions, has lost the trust of citizens and is no longer necessary—or worse, is actually pernicious. Some of the most popular parties today, beginning with the Five Stars Movement in Italy, define themselves as anti-parties;

they feature a rejection of the old vertical structures of existing parties and a strong desire for horizontality (surprisingly allied, it must be said, with a certain leader cult).

This is not the place to discuss the advantages and disadvantages of horizontality; we shall consider the question of participatory democracy at length in the next chapter. But we do need to stress one important point. Some would have us believe that, in this new world beyond intermediation, money plays no more than a marginal role in politics; that the age of big spending, high-maintenance parties, campaign headquarters, and expensive rallies is gone forever; and that there is therefore no longer any need for a cap on campaign spending. But that is a wrong conclusion. Publicity on social media, online videos, YouTube channels, voter targeting, the recruitment of one or more "community managers": all this comes at a price, and the price is high. Ask Jean-Luc Mélenchon how much his holograms cost him!

I have calculated, for the last four US presidential elections, the percentage of each candidate's campaign spending that was spent online— on items ranging from the creation of a website through voter targeting on social media to the sponsoring of Facebook posts and other kinds of e-publicity. Figure 62 presents the results. Interestingly, the winner in all elections since 2004 has been the candidate who allocated the larger share of his or her campaign funds to online spending. In this respect, Barack Obama was the first real innovator: at nearly 13 percent, his online spending in 2008 was colossal in comparison with the old school campaign of John McCain that same year. Also striking is the wide gap between the rival campaigns in 2016: whereas Hillary Clinton spent less than 6 percent on internet publicity and other online campaign costs, the equivalent figure for Donald Trump was nearly one-quarter. No less remarkable is the fact that, in the last three UK general elections (2010, 2015, and 2017), UKIP (UK Independence Party) candidates spent on average more than one-fifth of their campaign funds on advertising, mainly on the internet, compared with less than 10 percent for the Liberal Democrats and around 12 percent for the Conservatives and the Labour Party.

As I said in Chapter 4, government control over public media does not seem the right way to correct the imbalance in favor of the private

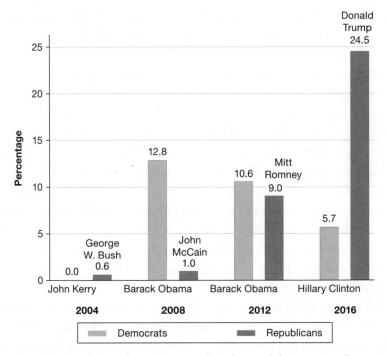

Figure 62. Percentage of campaign spending that candidate spent on the internet (online advertising and so on), presidential elections, United States, 2004–2016

media empires. Similarly, the creation by political movements of their own media will not solve the democratic problem with which we are presently confronted. To be sure, political movements are fully justified in wishing to create new communications media, such as YouTube channels, that enable them to reach their supporters directly and even to enlarge their base. Jean-Luc Mélenchon in France now has his own YouTube channel, with nearly 400,000 subscribers;[34] and Bernie Sanders also created one during the Democratic primaries in 2016. (But in the United States, YouTube is mainly used to broadcast election advertising that viewers have to see before they launch a video—a more effective way of reaching them than TV ads, and less of a drain on campaign spending.) Politicians are right to want to diversify the social media, so that they can know their electorate better and reach out to them. But that cannot be a substitute for independent political and general news media. A candidate's YouTube channel cannot be considered a news medium; it is nothing other than a means of communication. Today, journalists who work for the news media need to have their independence protected, both from private shareholders seeking to promote their industrial interests and from political parties seeking to disseminate their ideas.

Campaigning in the Old Way

Let us not forget what might be described as the good old campaigning methods, beginning with public meetings and rallies. For although I have said a lot about new technologies, public meetings are still a key pillar of election campaigns, not only locally but even more generally in countries where candidates are not permitted to buy airtime.

It is also interesting to note that in France, where candidates are not allowed to engage in TV advertising, election meetings can be a powerful means of televisual publicity in the age of round-the-clock news channels. This is one of the reasons why they play such an important role. For example, Jean-Luc Mélenchon's rally in Lyon on February 5, 2017—with a simultaneous hologram double in the Paris suburb of Aubervilliers—attracted more than 18,000 curious spectators,[35] but that was very little compared with the average of 637,000 viewers (or the cumulative 1,440,000) who followed the meeting live on the BFM TV news channel.

What is the relative weight of these different forms of spending in France? Figure 63 presents the spending by category of the five main candidates in the presidential election of 2017. For the candidates as a whole, public meetings were the principal item by far—above all for Jean-Luc Mélenchon, with his costly holograms, and for Emmanuel Macron, despite the sizable discounts he received. Next came payments for services, which were largest in the cases of Macron and Benoît Hamon, and less significant for Mélenchon, who, in a legal though socially questionable practice, used external providers rather than put a part of his team on the payroll.

If we now consider all eleven candidates in the 2017 presidential election as a group, taking the average percentage represented by each category of spending, the importance of advertising still stands out (Figure 64). More surprisingly, communications advice occupies a lower

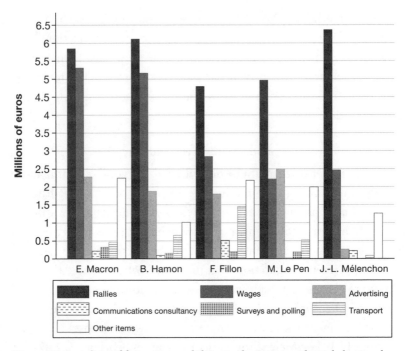

Figure 63. Spending of five main candidates in the 2017 presidential election, by spending category, France

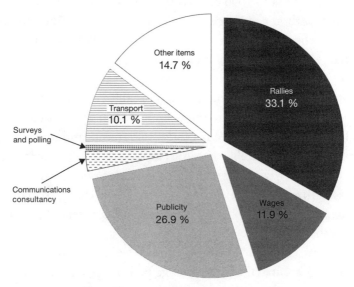

Figure 64. Relative weight of spending categories (average of all eleven candidates), France, presidential election of 2017

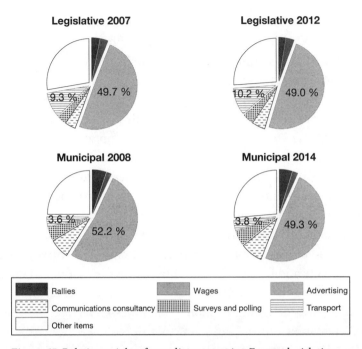

Figure 65. Relative weight of spending categories, France, legislative and municipal elections

place than one might have expected, except for poor François Fillon, who had to deal with the business of Penelope's dubious remuneration.

A final point in this review of election spending, however, is that the great weight of public meetings is peculiar to presidential elections. It does not apply to local contests, including parliamentary elections, where advertising (or "printed propaganda," as it is known) is by far the largest item, as Figure 65 shows for the most recent legislative and municipal elections.

Funding Democracy and Election Spending: The New Property Qualification

Democracy is one person, one vote. Or at least it should be.

Apart from the question of women around the world and blacks in the United States,[36] self-styled democracies for a long time set strict conditions, particularly related to income and assets, for inclusion in the electorate, and other restrictions were often in place to limit the number of citizens permitted to run for public office. The justifications given for such practices were many and various, since rulers never lack the imagination to legitimize the power in their hands. One common argument, for example, was that to allow only property-holders to stand in elections was a way of guarding against corruption.

This is no longer the case today. And yet, what has Part Two of this book told us if not that the present system seems to revolve around a plutocratic conception of democracy? One euro, one vote. The private funding of democracy has become the new "property qualification."[37] It seems difficult to characterize the system in any other light. To be sure, there are no longer formal barriers to participation: everyone is permitted to vote and to run for office. But the representation deficit takes a more perverse, because less transparent, form insofar as campaign contributions partly determine election results and—even graver—the reality of representation.

What is the difference between the "double vote" law of June 29, 1820—which allowed French voters who paid the highest taxes to vote twice[38]—and the present situation under which the richest groups in society can express their political preferences two, three, or even four times through the medium of electoral spending? The only difference is the hypocrisy of the existing façade, which claims to give everyone the same weight in the democratic process, much as the shroud of educational merit is used to make us believe that inequalities are just.[39]

In the French and similar systems, not only are the rich allowed to vote more than once, but the taxes of all the less well-off are used to finance the multiple votes of the rich. It is a kind of reverse redistribution, which can also be found in different forms in Italy and Canada.

Let us stop lamenting. It was important to establish how things stand today in our democracies; that has now been done. Yes, money captures the democratic process, placing a question mark over the very reality of representation. Yes, this is directly reflected in the public policies that are pursued on a daily basis—policies that, mirroring the ultra-flexibilization of the labor market or the multiple tax breaks given to the rich, put the preferences of the rich into effect, against the interests of the least well-off. Yes, the political choices of the past few decades have led in both Europe and North America to a paradoxical system in which the majority vote on paper, but an ever smaller (and richer) minority actually decide.

But the time for lamentation is over—especially as it is possible for us to act.

Yes, we can change things and save democracy from the grip of money that is not only tolerated but promoted by the regulations in force today. Yes, we can save democracy from all the populisms that have chosen the path of rejection, the worst response to the crisis of representation.

How can we do this? I will try to provide some answers in Part Three, which is given over to solutions. The first urgent task is to reshape the public funding of democracy by making it more reactive and more in keeping with the realities of the twenty-first century. In the internet age, four or five years are not needed to create a political movement: a new one can take shape in just a few months. But if it is not given proper support, a burst of democratic energy may run short of funds and peter out. Public funding must be placed on an equal, democratic, and annual footing. This is what I propose with the idea of Democratic Equality Vouchers worth seven euros each, which each citizen is entitled to receive and can allocate to a political movement simply by marking the appropriate choice on his or her tax return. This modernized public funding would have to go together with strict limits on private funding—otherwise, all its democratic impetus and beneficial effects would be drowned beneath a flood of private donations.

The equality of all citizens in the funding of democracy is a first essential step to solve the representation crisis. But the crisis is such that it would not be enough. It is necessary to go farther and use the instruments of the law-based state, so that tomorrow the men and women who represent us are more like the great body of citizens. This could happen through the introduction of genuine social representation in the national assembly. In Chapter 11, I propose that this should become a mixed assembly where, along with deputies elected in the ways existing today (in France, a simple, constituency-based, first-past-the-post system), a third of the seats are reserved for members elected by proportional representation on lists consisting of at least 50 percent working-class citizens (in fixed jobs or in insecure forms of employment). In other words, the composition of the assembly would reflect the social-economic reality of the country, in a manner not unlike that of the male-female parity lists already in use for regional elections in France. For in order to combat today's representation deficit, the twenty-first-century legislator must match the citizens whose interests he or she is supposed to represent, no longer chasing after money but trying to convince the majority by means of argument. The laws that such a legislator enacts will no longer address the preferences of the rich and only the rich, but will correspond to those of the great body of citizens.

PART THREE

LET'S SAVE DEMOCRACY!

Reshaping Political and Social Democracy

9

Has the Last Word Been Said?
From the Illusion of Permanence
to the Novelty of Democratic Vouchers

PARTICIPATORY DEMOCRACY, cooperative democracy, deliberative democracy, permanent democracy, semi-direct or civic-tech democracy, 2.0 or 3.0 democracy, random selection democracy—there are certainly plenty of proposals on how to rebuild our political systems. Many researchers, politicians, and ordinary citizens participating in public debate have given thought to the question of democracy, particularly representative democracy. "One person, one vote": the very expression seems dated, and low voter turnouts tell us how deeply rooted is the popular distrust today. Has the last word really been said? Is it too late in the day? No, I don't think so. There is much more to be said—for the simple reason that the history of democracy is just beginning. What are our few decades of apprenticeship in electoral democracy, when weighed against all the past, and especially future, centuries of human history?

Not everything has been said, and it is important to begin by reviewing the existing proposals for participatory democracy, as well as the successful and many unsuccessful previous experiments. This will help us to construct a truly innovative model for twenty-first-century democracy, one that draws on the lessons of the past so that we can better prepare for the future.

I know only too well that summaries in a few paragraphs, sometimes in a few lines, risk not doing full justice to the ideas developed by various authors. But I will take the risk anyway. I cannot do without the support of their thinking, but nor can I allow it to have an ossifying effect. For the foundations of democracy are both collective and dynamic.

With a boldness enhanced by the sense of risk, my own proposals will follow next. In Chapter 10, I propose a completely new basis on which to fund the political process—and I hope you will give me a fair hearing. If I place the funding of democracy at the center, it is because the current system has been corroded by money; democracy will fulfill its promise of equality—at the ballot box but also in the representation of people's preferences—only if the funding problem is solved at the outset. This is not a sufficient condition, but a necessary and urgent condition. Of course, to speak of fiscal matters and the public funding of political democracy is not very "sexy," and the kind of activists who have fought historically for democracy—the men and women who hand out leaflets each week at street markets or metro station entrances and who attend branch meetings several times a month—might accuse me of staying aloof from the reality of political representation. What is the point of focusing on the relative weight of private and public money in election campaigns, when what matters on the ground is to convince voters one by one? Although the commitment of such activists is sincere and important, and although they devote tremendous energy to it at the expense of family life and leisure time, the present workings of the democratic process mostly end up nullifying its effects. What counts in politics is money: our votes have a "price," and that is why more and more politicians respond to the preferences only of the richest groups in society (those who contribute *financially* to their election campaigns) and not at all to the preferences of their own party activists, who give up so much of their time.[1] This is the reality that we must address, and in doing so we should not be scared of the figures involved. Democracy has a cost, and if we no longer want the rich to "bear" this cost—and to benefit from everything they get in return—then, well, we have to think in terms of its being borne by the public purse.

To be sure, the democratic revolution that I propose in this book cannot end with the question of funding. It is equally urgent to improve how everyone is represented. Here it seems to me necessary—as I discuss in Chapter 11—to reshape the functioning of political democracy in accordance with the model of social democracy. In particular, the reconquest of electoral democracy—against the extremes and against populism—cannot happen without a profound reform of our parliamentary system. And my proposal, in short, is to introduce an element of social representation into a dual and sovereign parliamentary assembly. To put it simply, this would guarantee the presence of the popular classes (employees, blue-collar workers, those without secure employment) in the National Assembly, Parliament, or Congress, from the benches of which they are presently missing. We shall see that their absence is not without consequences: it directly affects the legislation that is adopted or rejected in France, as well as in the United Kingdom and the United States. But before we go into details, we must run through the various proposals for democratic renewal that already feature in public debate.

Oh yes, if you skim this page again and see there is no mention of "the internet," well, there is really no reason to be surprised. True, it is not there. But if what you are asking for is Web 2.0, I am more than happy to agree: I never tire of using the social media, sometimes, I must admit, to the detriment of efficient, optimal use of my own brain time. But the internet is a tool. It is not *the* solution. Those with the power are only too happy to let people amuse themselves online; it allows them to express their preferences on paper (or rather, on the screen), giving them the illusion of participation at the very moment when the die is cast.

I am not unaware of the power of this tool. In fact, I showed in Chapter 8 the growing sums of money that parties and candidates spend on it during election campaigns. Nor am I unaware that the internet has partly altered the parameters of the electoral battle—negatively, in the spinoffs from the misappropriation of private data on the social media, but sometimes also positively, by permitting the online mobilization of young people, who, put off by traditional forms of activism, feel drawn to the idea of doing politics differently. The internet makes it possible to mobilize underrepresented constituencies; Alexandria Ocasio-Cortez tailored her 2018 tech-savvy campaign to Latino and younger voters, with a strong presence on social media. The internet also makes it possible to mobilize small donors, sometimes by directly winning their support on the social media; that is partly how Bernie Sanders was able to do as well as Hillary Clinton financially during the Democratic primaries of 2016. Would the Five Stars Movement in Italy have had such success just twenty years ago, before the internet became a ubiquitous tool of communication? And was not Jean-Luc Mélenchon's unexpected showing in the French presidential election of 2017 partly linked to his mastery of the social media? A candidate rather "badly treated" by the traditional media—who gave as good as he got—was able to reach out to citizens more easily through the social media.

But make no mistake, this new technology in no way solves the central problem of campaign finances. I have been told by some politicians that it is no longer so essential to regulate the funding of election campaigns, because in the internet age it is possible to campaign with a few cents and lines of code—in other words, that campaigns awash with money no longer have any advantage over campaigns starved of private funds. But that is false—as I showed in Chapter 8. Sure, advertising online costs less than on TV, but in the internet age the cost of campaigning on the internet can prove very high indeed.

The battle for democratic equality will not be won through some online app that brings politicians virtually closer to their constituents. Such gadgets can sometimes be fun, but all they offer is an illusory participation. The reality of participation will be acted out in a remodeled Parliament; and equality will stand a chance only once the sluice of private funding has been closed.

From Continuous Democracy to Permanent Democracy

But let us begin at the beginning, with the proposals already made to breathe new meaning into the idea of democracy. And before we set out on a little world tour, allow me to linger for a while in the French Hexagon. Here, the historian Pierre Rosanvallon is undoubtedly the author who has thought most about the history and future of democratic government. As he puts it, in terms that summarize what we have seen up to this point: "Our regimes are democratic, but we are not governed democratically."[2] Of course, Rosanvallon is referring not to the funding of the democratic process but to the representation deficit that he highlights in his critique of the French presidential system; he evidently prefers a representative parliamentarianism to the personalized presidential model. But the most fascinating aspect of his study of changes in contemporary democracies is his analysis of the "desocialization" of politics.[3] For Rosanvallon, the party system no longer has any representative function; whereas political parties for a long time animated public debate and served to express social identities, they seem today to have been reduced to the residual function of selecting candidates[4]—a development largely due to their professionalization, which entails that social groups have long ceased to identify with them. As I will show in Chapter 11, this is not so surprising if we think that political parties no longer mirror the reality of the social groups in contemporary society. Only the UK Labour Party has for a long time had workers in its representative echelons, although this characteristic was already being eroded in the mid-1980s.

I cannot but agree with Rosanvallon's conclusion, although I would add, as an alternative explanation, that the identification deficit has its roots in a failure of representation. How could I—as a group or simply as an individual—identify with a political party on the left or right that, once in power, responds only to the political preferences of the lucky few? How could I see as mine a party that devotes more time and energy to convincing the rich to fund its candidates than to mobilizing what has survived of its members' energies?

Rosanvallon speaks of society as having been "forgotten." And he proposes that it should be rediscovered through a process of "continuous" or "permanent" democracy, in which citizens are called upon to express themselves at all times, not only at elections. He suggests, for example, that democratic debate should give greater consideration to citizens' petitions.[5] I, too, think that citizens should be able to express themselves more regularly than once in four or five years, and this is why I propose—in order to give new dynamism to the expression of political preferences—that they should have the option each year to fund the political groups to which they feel closest. But I also think that, for such a society to be rebuilt, allowance should be made for genuine representation within its legislative bodies—in other words, that society should be brought into the Parliament, so that it is allowed to express itself directly in the political sphere. As we shall see in a moment, although citizens' petitions are a good idea, they usually fail because a flood of private money and corporate lobbying determines the ultimate fate of this expression of the people's will.

A Representative Social Assembly

The legal theorist Dominique Rousseau also champions the idea of "continuous democracy," albeit in different forms from those advocated by Pierre Rosanvallon.[6] In particular, he has more to say about the incorporation of a social element into the legislative process, arguing for the creation of a Social Assembly.[7] This would be a deliberative body, expressing the will of civil society, alongside the Congress and the Senate (in the French context, such an assembly would take the place of the existing Economic, Social, and Environmental Council). Its members would be elected in such a way as to take into account "the productive forces in economic and social life, the broad sectors of activity, . . . and the forms in which those forces and activities are organized."[8] The novelty of this idea is that, by making it a deliberative (not simply consultative) body, Rousseau gives this third chamber the character of a "genuine" assembly. It is a pity, however, that he does not follow his argument through to the end; in particular, he does not discuss in detail how pieces of legislation would proceed through the different chambers, and he does not consider the question of which chamber would have primacy. But we cannot really judge the importance of such a Social Assembly unless it has been decided which of the chambers will have the final say in the event of disagreement. We can only assume that Rousseau would uphold the existing primacy of the National Assembly in the French context, which would limit the scope of the reform.

Rousseau is right to think that social forces should be given deliberative powers, but in my view he should allow himself to be more "radical." For his idea to take on its full meaning, it would be preferable to bring the representation of the social directly into the existing Parliament or Congress—which is what I propose with a mixed assembly. Otherwise, the kind of Social Assembly advocated by Rousseau might end up as an illusory form and lead to disappointments.

The Failed Example of Venezuela

Some readers may think they can hear strains of a Venezuelan tune in this proposal for political representation of the social. But let me make it clear that, as I see it, the failure of Venezuela's constituent assembly elected in 2017 is not the failure of occupational representation as such; rather, it is a further symptom of the gradual breakdown of the Maduro regime and the "Bolivarian" experiment. We should not extrapolate from it to condemn the idea of better minority representation, especially as the precise form that I propose (and here, as in so many other questions, the devil is in the detail) does not have much in common with the one tried out in the Caribbean oil-producing country.

What happened exactly in Venezuela? After Nicolas Maduro proceeded with the election of a Constituent Assembly in July 2017[9]—an event boycotted by the opposition—it took over (in August) most of the legislative powers held by the National Assembly,[10] effectively giving the president's party full authority to rule the country. Since then, Venezuela has been sliding a little more each day into dictatorship.

But why mention this development in a book on democratic renewal? The reason is that—if we leave aside a political context that, today in 2018, on the eve of early presidential elections again boycotted by the opposition, can only serve as an example to avoid—the way in which the Constituent Assembly was elected is full of interest. One part (364 members elected by universal suffrage) represented territorial constituencies where each vote was based, as usual, on a residential qualification, while the other part (181 members) represented social groups and minorities: 173 from sectoral categories (farmers, students, pensioners, workers, handicapped people, company directors, and so on) and eight from indigenous communities. Each elector voted twice: once in her local constituency, and once by virtue of her social group attachment. It was a way of combining political and social representation at the heart of one and the same assembly.

Such dual representation—which in a way is what Dominique Rousseau proposes, as well as being one reading of what I propose in the final chapter of this book—could add up to a veritable democratic revolution. In a different context from today's Venezuela, it could permit the rediscovery of a "forgotten society," though with an important change in the way people vote. For although I agree that everyone should vote twice—once locally by universal suffrage and once by proportional representation for lists reflecting the reality of social groups—I do not think that there should be two different electoral colleges. In other words, I do not think that each individual should vote by virtue of his or her social group attachment; separate electoral colleges of this kind are a democratic aberration and have never really been established anywhere, except in extremely tense historical contexts (such as Bosnia, with its separate Croat, Serb, and Muslim electorates, or colonial India, with its Hindu and Muslim electorates) or for the representation of highly specific minorities such as the New Zealand Maoris. What is necessary is that all citizens should vote for lists under a system of proportional representation (PR) that reflects the reality of social groups, including 50 percent members of popular socio-occupational categories (employees, blue-collar workers, and the whole group of workers without secure employment). There is a similarity here to the "gender parity" lists for regional elections in France or to the Tunisian gender parity law,[11] except that the active intervention would be in favor of the working classes rather than women.

In the case of Venezuela, the other major limitation—to say the least—of the electoral system proposed for the 2017 Constituent Assembly was that political parties were barred from running candidates for the "occupational" seats. Clearly this was a way for the regime to exclude the opposition and to ensure that a large number of seats were occupied by members of socio-occupational groups close to the ruling party (since only such groups could run candidates). The same kind of manipulation can be found in many of the puppet assemblies featuring in the constitutions of "real-world socialism," including that of China today, where far-fetched types of social representation are invented to circumvent universal suffrage and to keep the existing parties in power. However, these shams should not stop us from going further: the idea of better social representation is certainly not a bad thing in itself, as long as it is based on transparency, universal suffrage, and the right to stand as a candidate.

The Right to Petition and to Hold Referenda
Based on Citizens' Initiatives

In practice, how should citizens be able to express themselves outside election periods? It is a question asked by numerous researchers as well as governments, and specific measures have already been introduced in a number of countries. Italy, for instance, has gone a long way in the practice of permanent democracy and—as we saw with the elimination of public funding for political parties—has had frequent recourse to referenda on the basis of citizens' initiatives. People's votes of this kind are also commonly held in Switzerland, as we saw recently in the (fortunately unsuccessful) attempt to abolish national broadcasting license fees.

People's Referenda and "Recall" Procedures

What are referenda on the basis of citizens' initiatives? Although their forms vary from country to country, they may be generally defined as referenda organized on the initiative of a section of the electoral body, where everything depends on the size of that section.

In Italy, the people's referendum was made part of the Constitution of 1948.[12] It is what is known as an "abrogative referendum": it can be held only to repeal a law or part of a law.[13] The proposed change must come from at least 500,000 electors, or roughly 1 percent of the adult Italian population.[14] For the result to count, a majority of the electorate must take part in the vote—a requirement that often leads to the rejection of a proposal, even if it obtains a majority of the votes cast.

In Switzerland, the referendum based on a citizens' initiative—which is called a *votation* in French—can be traced back to the establishment of "optional referenda" in 1874 and the introduction of people's initiatives in 1891. These may take several forms. If, within the hundred days following the adoption of a law in Parliament, 50,000 citizens sign a text requesting a vote by the whole electorate, the law can come into force only if the voters approve it ("optional referendum").[15] Or, any elector who collects 100,000 signatures may propose a change to the Constitution (citizens' initiative referendum).[16] In Switzerland, these two practices are very popular—the appropriate word here: between 1848 and 2010, 167 optional referenda and 158 people's initiative referenda were held. (A new "general people's initiative" introduced in 2003 allowed 100,000 citizens to request the adoption or revision of a federal law—not just a change in the Constitution.[17] However, this possibility was eliminated in 2009 without ever having been used.)

Switzerland is often cited as a model in France, where the popular initiative referendum has been the object of debate for many decades.[18] However, the popular initiative referendum has existed de facto in France for a number of years. You didn't know? That's not surprising, since the relevant measure, introduced during the constitutional revision of 2008 but only in force since January 1, 2015, is such that it was taken up for the very first time in 2019.[19] For, instead of "simply" providing for a referendum to be held if enough citizens mobilize on the question at issue, it requires that at least one-fifth of members of Parliament should first table what is called a "referendum law." Hence the name "shared initiative referendum"—not "popular referendum." Nor is there anything "popular" in the fraction of the electorate that has to file the request: no fewer than 10 percent, or 4.7 million citizens.[20] In other words, another fine but unworkable promise.

This is why the idea of a genuine popular initiative referendum comes up again at each presidential election in France. In 2017, it was part of the program of five candidates, including Jean-Luc Mélenchon—who did not, however, specify the number of signatories that would be required—and Marine Le Pen—who supported the idea of a popular initiative referendum with at least 500,000 electors behind it. Mélenchon went further and suggested that citizens should be able to call referenda themselves, adding that they might even be able to propose legislation. His institutional program also had at its core the principle of a "recall referendum based on a citizens' initiative," which would allow elected representatives to be removed before the end of their term.

Although the idea of a "recall referendum" may seem quite radical—or even "populist," to judge by the words often used to defend it ("Out with them all!" for example)—everything depends on how it would actually work. The possibility of "recall" has existed for decades in parts of the United States,[21] most notably in California, and it is interesting to look at the reasons that led to its introduction there in 1911. There is talk today of a new "gilded age," but, as we saw earlier, the term was first applied to the explosion of inequalities in the United States around the turn of the twentieth century, which was when recall provisions were introduced to fight endemic corruption and the growing economic and political dominance of a handful of large corporations. The economic giant of the time was not called Google or Facebook, but rather the Southern Pacific Railroad.[22]

Recall petitions were periodically organized throughout the twentieth century, but until 2003 all of them failed for lack of signatures.[23] The number required in California for a vote to be held on a petition is equivalent to 12 percent of the voter turnout at the preceding election, somewhere around 1 million in total. Yet in 2003, the recall procedure initiated against Governor Gray Davis, just eleven months after his election, led to his replacement by the political newcomer Arnold Schwarzenegger.[24]

The Illusion of Direct Democracy and the Semblance of Representation

If recall procedures are still very rare—at least in the United States, though less so in Latin America—we may wonder how much they and other popular electoral initiatives are illusory and how much they involve real direct democracy.[25] Or, to put it in another way, how much do such instances of participatory democracy really help to solve the problem of the representation deficit? Do they not anyway create other problems, particularly with regard to the legitimacy of the vote?

Take the example of the abrogative referendum. To what extent is it legitimate that a vote by a small number of individuals can lead to the repeal of laws passed by the elected representatives of the majority of citizens? Of course, the answer to this question largely depends on the percentage of citizens required for the referendum to take place: 1 percent as in Italy or 0.7 percent as in Switzerland is very different from the 10 percent threshold often discussed. The higher the threshold, the more the referendum may be considered legitimate; but too high a threshold may mean that the whole procedure is unworkable (as we can see from the French case). You may say that a sufficient number of signatures does not necessarily result in abrogation: the proposal still has to secure a majority at the ballot box, where all citizens are called upon to express their will. But the problem is that all too many citizens do not bother to turn out, not being much concerned about the issues on which they are asked to vote. In Switzerland, for example, although people's votes are a common occurrence, the numbers of those participating in them are usually very low. From this point of view, the Italian option of requiring a 50 percent turnout for a referendum victory is extremely interesting: direct democracy then means that a majority of citizens are involved in saying "yea" or "nay."

Is this enough to legitimize abrogative referenda or the holding of votes based on citizens' initiatives? Most opponents of these tools of direct democracy warn against populist aberrations and argue that they threaten to lead to greater political polarization. In this connection, the Swiss popular initiative "against the construction of minarets," resulting in a referendum held in November 2009, gives us food for thought.[26] The two key questions here are the legitimacy of a majority "yes" vote that contravened such a basic right as religious freedom, which one might have thought would be guaranteed under the constitution; and the character of what citizens intended, and what information they had at their disposal, at the time when the vote was held. Did the Swiss really express themselves for or against minaret construction, or did the debate center more on the issue of immigration? As to the information available to citizens at the time of the vote, this is by no means a problem only for popular initiative referenda; we need only think of the Brexit referendum, when no one was clear about what would happen if the "no" vote won (nor is anyone very clear about it today, three years later). Important political debates usually call for deep deliberation and involve multiple formulations and amendments that cannot be reduced to a simple "yes" or "no."

In 2016 in California, voters in the presidential election also took part in a number of popular initiative referenda; the media focused mainly on the marijuana issue, but there were also several highly technical questions that were surprising to find in a people's vote. Take, for example, Proposition 52: "Continued Hospital Fee Revenue Dedicated to Medi-Cal Unless Voters Approve Changes."[27] Is it really credible that voters—not the legislature—are best able to decide on the allocation of hospital revenue and on ways to fund health insurance for the poor?

We need to ask, then, whether advocates of popular initiative referenda should not address the question of expertise. Without siding with partisans of technocracy, I think it is necessary to ask whether citizens have the capacity to vote on certain technical matters. Let us be clear: it is not at all a question of their capacity "in the absolute," but rather of their capacity as citizens at a particular point in their lives, with all the constraints such as limited time to absorb relevant information. Evidently, each citizen can acquire this capacity—for example, by becoming a parliamentarian. If parliamentary representation was introduced in our modern democracies, it was precisely because technical expertise is necessary in various fields, and because it takes time to consider a draft law, to digest its complex implications, and to propose improvements.

But let us suppose for a moment that there is a magic formula for practicing direct democracy, through people's votes on issues about which citizens have the expertise to decide in an informed manner. Would that be an appropriate and sufficient response to the representation deficit? The answer has to be no (I almost feel like adding: unfortunately). Let me try to explain why.

Imagine that a popular initiative has obtained enough signatures for a referendum to be held. What happens next? The referendum campaign itself—which can cost a lot of money. But when a campaign costs a lot, in comparison with the statistical average, victory usually goes to those who have spent the most (remember the results in Chapter 8). What does that mean? Well, if the opposition is well organized, ready to spend what it takes and to mobilize the usual kind of lobbies, the answer is that, sad to say, nothing is likely to change in the end. In Switzerland, between 1848 and 2010, 44.3 percent of "optional referenda" and 90.5 percent of popular initiative referenda had negative outcomes.[28] To take just one (striking) example, a referendum proposal in 1984 "against the abuse of banking secrecy and the power of the banks" was rejected by 73 percent of voters; the amount spent by the UBS bank alone on press ads in favor of a "no" vote was ten times more than the total funds available to the committee organizing the initiative (800,000 Swiss francs).[29]

This brings us back to where we started: to the need for the regulation of election spending. Without that, popular initiative referenda do little more than give "the people" the illusion that it can express itself freely between two elections,[30] when in reality the dice are loaded from the start. The same holds true for the "recall" procedure. I mentioned above the vote in 2003 in California that led to the removal of Governor Gray Davis, just eleven months after his reelection. Was that a "people's vote?" On the contrary. The campaign was not launched by an ordinary man on the street, a California citizen rightly dissatisfied with the governor's record. No, the person behind it was Darrell Issa, a superrich businessman and Republican politician, who spent no less than $2 million to collect the required hundreds and thousands of signatures.[31] A multimillionaire with two motives and no particular concern for the public interest. On the one hand, Darrell Issa never concealed that he would have liked to replace Gray Davis—a pity that in the end he had to withdraw in favor of the Terminator. On the other hand, he saw the point of the exercise as being to swing California over to the Republicans, but although his campaign, "Rescue California, Recall Gary Davis," centered on the $38 billion hole in the California budget, it has to be said that the deficit kept growing and growing under Schwarzenegger's governorship. He came first among 135 candidates in the election to replace Davis, paying by far the most ($13.4 million) to see off his rivals.

Perhaps you will say that all this is well and good but only anecdotal. However, the *causal* impact of election spending on the success of popular initiative referenda has been systematically evaluated for California in the period from 1976 to 2004. John M. de Figueiredo and his coauthors have shown that spending in favor of a citizens' initiative strongly increases the probability that it will be adopted.[32] The weight of money again, as always.

So, you can see what I am getting at. My point is not that the citizens' petition is a bad thing in itself; it is a tool of direct democracy that can be usefully discussed. But it would be wrong to see it as the solution to the representation deficit. As long as the problem of campaign funding has not been solved, citizens' initiatives will be captured initiatives. Sure, people can go to the polls more often, but the die is already cast when it comes to any real regard for their preferences. And their lack of power is compounded by the hypocrisy of suggesting that they can at last make meaningful decisions. This complete blindness to the issue of funding is, in my view, the big mistake made by numerous theorists of direct democracy (or "permanent" or "continuous" democracy, as it is sometimes called). But it must be settled first before real progress can be made in linking up with the people and restoring a genuinely representative dimension to our democracy.

Equally mistaken are all those who focus only on voting systems. Again, it is not that the question is unimportant—it would be good, for example, to have a strong element of proportionality in parliamentary elections in France or the United Kingdom. Yes, it might also be worth thinking about alternatives to proportional representation and first past the post. The "Borda" method, whereby voters rank all options or candidates in order of preference instead of having to choose just one, might help to raise political participation and to reduce the polarization of debate. An alternative vote system is already in use in Ireland for the presidential election, and in Australia for legislative elections.[33] But again, the debate on voting methods should not make us forget that, unless the question of election funding is solved, the finest system in the world will not redeem the capture of democracy and the fact that elected representatives cater overwhelmingly to the rich.

Since No Conqueror Believes in Chance, What If We Tried Random Selection?

There is another option, however, which is regularly evoked by researchers, politicians, and the new democracy activists, and which has given rise to many experiments in recent years: *random selection*. If the aim is to end the capture of the electoral process and to solve the representation deficit, then why not put our trust in chance? Why not replace our current legislative assemblies with parliaments consisting of randomly chosen citizens? With a sufficient number of members, chance would guarantee representativeness—and if there were no longer elections, all the negative features associated with them would disappear.

Bingo?

To understand the beauty of such a system, it is not necessary to go back to the often-cited example of ancient Greece. Present-day Iceland will do nicely, with its participatory experiment (between 2010 and 2013) in the rewriting of its constitution.[34] First, the government brought together a representative panel consisting of 950 randomly chosen citizens (the National Forum), which met on November 6, 2010, and formally stated the principles that should underlie the new constitution. Then a twenty-five-member constituent assembly was elected from civil society. Many political scientists have studied this experiment, beginning with Hélène Landemore, who sees it as a success despite the fact that in the end the new constitutional text was not adopted. In her view, the multiple versions of a constitution drafted by the twenty-five representatives of civil society were "better, smarter, and more 'liberal'" than the one produced around the same time by a group of seven government experts. In particular, they were much more open to the rights of religions and laid greater stress on the importance of having a genuinely democratic society.

Beyond this Icelandic example, Landemore has developed a number of arguments in favor of participatory democracy and random selection, her key idea being that of a "collective intelligence," or "democratic reason."[35] The intelligence of a group of individuals, she argues, will always be greater than the combined intelligence of all the individuals in the group, since inclusive decision-making permits the emergence of "cognitive diversity" (for example, different viewpoints on the world or different perspectives), and such diversity is itself a key element in the emergence of collective intelligence. In other words, what is important in determining the quality of decision-making is not so much the intelligence—or IQ—of each member of a group, but rather their diversity. It is this diversity that ultimately determines the IQ of the group. And even if, taken separately, individuals are not competent in such and such a field, cognitive diversity enables the group to be competent by virtue of discussion and the different perspectives that each member brings to it.

This concept of "collective intelligence" has given rise to numerous empirical experiments; the researcher James Fishkin, in particular, has tested out "collaborative" or "deliberative" polling in various places around the world. These often fascinating experiments, from Australia through the United Kingdom and Italy to China and Thailand, which are described in his book *When the People Speak,* point to a number of lessons for the renewal of our democracies. Among the most noteworthy of these is that deliberation by a group of citizens reflecting the country's diversity leads to changes in attitudes, as the citizens become better informed, more concerned, and ultimately expressive of more moderate opinions than those they held at the outset.[36] When we see today the extreme polarization of political life in the United States, where it sometimes seems to have become impossible to enact a law, one cannot but be tempted by this idea of deliberative democracy.[37]

For my part, I think that deliberation—above all, the giving of high-quality, independent information to the largest number of people—must be at the heart of discussions about solving the current crisis of representation. "Diversity" is also a key concept: no one can be competent *ex ante* in all matters that come up for deliberation in a parliamentary term; some will be knowledgeable about economics, others about environmental questions, but no one can be expected to have expertise across the full spectrum of issues. The combination of deliberation with a diversity of representation—and therefore of points of view—helps to ensure a higher quality of democratic decisions. However, I think we can do better than random selection, and this is why in Chapter 11 I argue for a mixed assembly with a guaranteed degree of social parity, but which maintains the principle of election.

Why Random Selection Is Not the Solution

Many arguments have been put forward against random selection. I shall not review them all here, especially as I think some of them are not altogether convincing. But, of course, what comes to everyone's mind is the question of competence. To borrow a formulation from Myriam Revault d'Allonnes, people do not want to "appoint *just any citizen* without a particular qualification";[38] election, by contrast, allows citizens to be chosen on the basis of competence. As we have seen, however, advocates of random selection show that competence emerges "collectively," so a first answer would be to say that the question is not the competence of each citizen chosen by random selection. More important, we must not distort the thinking of those who support randomness: what they propose is not usually to select citizens at random from the electoral register, but only citizens who wish their names to be fed into the machines that do the random selection. This implies that only those who feel capable of exercising the burden of authority can be chosen at random. Bernard Manin eloquently points this out in the case of Athenian democracy.[39]

Furthermore—and Manin also clearly explains this in detail— random selection does not entail absence of responsibility. In ancient Athens, it was current practice to initiate proceedings "on grounds of illegality": that is, any citizen could proceed on such grounds against a proposed law or decree submitted to the citizens' assembly, or even against a law or decree that had already been adopted. If the courts then ruled in favor of the complaint, not only was the decision of the assembly quashed, but its initiator was penalized with a fine. By all accounts, this encouraged legislators—though randomly selected—to be attentive in discharging their functions, especially as such proceedings were a common occurrence.[40]

The most telling argument against random selection seems to me the following. Election together with social parity offers a superior solution, because it allows us to build on our collective capacity to listen to different candidates, to watch them debate with one another, and to choose the ones who seem most suited to represent us and play a useful part in collective deliberations and parliamentary decision-making. To choose representatives is not only, or even mainly, to choose the most competent individuals; it is to choose those most suited to take part in complex debates on a wide range of issues, many largely unforeseeable at the time when they were elected. It is this capacity to listen and debate that parliamentary candidates have to display in an election campaign, and the replacement of all that with a game of dice would seem to bespeak a kind of democratic nihilism. Random selection foregrounds the capacity of any human group to debate and deliberate—but, paradoxically, it also deprives virtually all citizens of their right to discuss and decide who should eventually be entrusted with voting on laws. Random selection may be used for specific decisions; one thinks of people's juries for certain courts or of "consensus conferences" required to reach an agreement on urban planning projects. But to make it the principal means of constituting the assembly that votes on legislation would be to surrender our collective capacity to delegate that highest of all rights.

To sum up, the debate on random selection highlights a real problem concerning the nonrepresentation of whole social groups in classical parliamentary elections. But it does not provide the best solution to the problem. A preferable way forward would be to maintain the elective principle while introducing a minimum of representation for different social groups, as I shall argue in detail in Chapter 11 with my proposal for a mixed assembly with social parity.

Democratic Vouchers

Fortunately, I am by no means the first to underline the importance of stricter regulation of election spending and contributions. But it has to be said that this question, rightly central in American debates, hardly features at all in political discussion in France or Germany, although, as we have seen, private money plays a not insignificant role there.[41] In previous chapters, I have looked at the writings of legal theorists such as Timothy Kuhner, Robert Post, and Richard Hasen who have dissected and excoriated recent decisions of the US Supreme Court; they mostly also put forward clear proposals on how to reverse the Supreme Court decision that changed everything in 2010, the "Citizens United" ruling. In the same vein, political scientists such as Benjamin Page, Martin Gilens, and Larry Bartels do not stop at highlighting the uneven attention paid to the preferences of American citizens; they also propose ways of ending it and support the idea of better regulation of election finances. Each in his way is fighting for a ceiling on both private contributions and campaign spending, and above all they advocate the elimination of super PACs. (If I have one criticism of their efforts, it is that they focus entirely on the American case, whereas the problems they raise exist, in different forms, in many other democracies.) In the book they published in 2017, Page and Gilens actually emphasized the need for public funding of elections, in order to break up the weight of private money.[42]

To keep the attention of all my readers, albeit at the risk of not doing entire justice to all these authors, I shall pause here on just one of these proposals that strikes me as particularly interesting and echoes the ideas I develop in Chapter 10: that is, the proposal for democratic vouchers.

A Way of Making Citizens Equal

How can citizens be made equal in relation to the funding of political democracy? One solution might be to give everyone a democracy check or voucher at election time, with a face value of, say, ten, fifty, or one hundred euros, which they can use to fund the campaign of their chosen candidate. The man behind this original proposal in the United States is Lawrence Lessig, a legal specialist in intellectual property rights, who in recent years has become one of the main supporters of the fight against lobbying and corruption in American political life.[43] He also put himself forward in 2015 as a candidate in the Democratic presidential primaries, but unfortunately had to withdraw because he did not garner sufficient voting intentions (and therefore sufficient prospects of funding). This strategy for winning power was part of his campaign to end political corruption: that is, elect a president, or more generally politicians, whose sole aim is to restore the proper functioning of representative democracy in the United States.[44] They would be what he calls *referendum politicians:* men and women whose task is "simply" to reform the funding of political democracy and to (re)establish political equality—and who resign once this is achieved.[45]

But let us return to the democracy voucher. Lessig's idea is to give each citizen a democracy voucher worth $50 that she can use to fund the candidate or candidates (Senate and House of Representatives[46]) of her choice. During the nine months preceding the election, candidates would be able to collect these vouchers—from citizens whose support they had won—in order to fund their campaign. Would all candidates be able to benefit from them? In Lessig's model, they would first have to show that they had sufficient public support, for example by collecting a certain number of $5 contributions.[47] More important, they would have to undertake not to accept private donations higher than $100.

Some readers might wish to go further, in accordance with the presidential fund model described in Chapter 5, so that candidates opting for the public system would be banned from also accepting any private money. But my preference would be for a third solution that did not leave it up to candidates to choose between public and private funding—otherwise, there would always be a danger that public money was eventually ground beneath the weight of private contributions. If private funding was simply banned, the benefits of democracy vouchers would be open to all candidates. Lessig does not go this far, because his development of solutions is in a way constricted by the rulings of the Supreme Court. It so happens that I am writing this in France, where money has fortunately not yet been defined as a form of "speech"; nor has it in most other European countries, even if we have to be wary of the decisions of the European Court of Human Rights. Even in the United States, it is generally agreed today that the recent decisions of the Supreme Court are much more "political" than "juridical." And so we may hope that, if things work out well under a future Democratic president, the Court will eventually decide that it may not have been justified to define corporations as individuals or money as speech.

Am I being too optimistic?

What If It Worked? A System Already in Place in Seattle

I do not think so. One piece of evidence is that such democracy vouchers have already been introduced in the United States. Since 2017, each citizen in Seattle who is on the electoral register automatically receives through the mail four $25 democracy vouchers (or a total of $100), which she can then give to her chosen candidates in municipal elections (for the posts of mayor, city councillor, and attorney general).[48] To participate in this system of public funding, candidates must first have obtained at least 150 contributions (each with a minimum value of $10 and a maximum of $250) for the post of attorney general, 400 contributions for at-large members of the city council, and 150 contributions for city council districts. The point of this is to guard against a proliferation of "non credible" candidates.

Candidates who wish to benefit from these democracy vouchers must agree to respect the strict spending limits and to receive no contributions above $250 (excluding the value of the vouchers).[49] Interestingly, candidates who choose not to take part in the democracy voucher program are also subject to a strict limit ($500) on the donations they receive from a given individual. And yet, Seattle is in the United States!

In case you are wondering, Seattle finances these democracy vouchers through a property tax that should bring in $3 million a year. A little economic equality on top of political equality! On average, the program costs property-owners $11.50 a year.

The other good news is that these democracy vouchers work. Six candidates have benefited from them since they were introduced in 2017, and nearly 46,000 vouchers have been used with a total value of $1.1 million in public funding.[50] Moreover, candidates who choose public funding do not seem to have suffered at the polls—on the contrary. The city attorney candidate Peter Holmes, for example, who opted for democracy vouchers (and received 5,885, with a total value of $147,000), was reelected with a large majority (73 percent of the votes) against his rival Scott Lindsay, who stayed out of the program.[51] And Teresa Mosqueda, who ran for the city council and signed up for the democracy vouchers, also emerged victorious; her rival in the home stretch, Jon Grant, also chose such funding, unlike most of the other candidates in the primaries.[52]

We should note that, before this program was launched, the campaign donations for Seattle city elections were very concentrated: in 2013, a mere fifth of donors contributed more than $500, but their donations represented more than 55 percent of the total funds raised for the election.[53] The introduction of democracy vouchers, however, made it possible to diversify the donor profile. A study by the Win / Win and Every Voice organizations compared the structure of donations for candidates using the vouchers program in 2017 with that of donations for candidates in the mayoral election (when the program was not yet in place).[54] And what they found was that there were more contributions from citizens with modest incomes (less than $50,000 a year) in the former than the latter case (14 percent against 9 percent of the total number), and symmetrically fewer contributions from very well-off citizens (earning more than $150,000 a year) for candidates who opted for democratic vouchers than for those who did not use public funding (13 percent against 27 percent). The democratic voucher program also made it possible to mobilize many more young voters and donors—which is a good thing, since the younger generation are on average less politically committed than their elders. It would seem that innovative forms of public funding might make a difference in this respect.

Of course, the implementation of the program did not proceed altogether calmly, and conservative groups—as one might have expected—took legal action against it in the name of "free speech"! It is always surprising for an outside observer to witness the degree to which this concept, so essential to the functioning of our democracies, is distorted in the United States. After all, it seems difficult to put up a rational argument that public funding, which enables the poor to express their political preferences, actually limits the free speech of the least advantaged sections of society. Fortunately, in November 2017, a Superior Court judge in King County ruled that the democracy voucher program was legal.[55]

So, why should this path not be pursued? I certainly think it is a possibility: there is nothing to lose, and it would anyway be better than the present situation.[56] But I also think—as we shall see in the next chapter—that the annual funding of political groups out of tax revenue is preferable to this kind of democracy voucher system, which has the defect of focusing only on elections and election candidates. In my view, parties have a role to play in the period between elections, by expressing the preferences of their supporters, by reflecting about the future, and by drawing up electoral programs and platforms; a system that focuses exclusively on candidates threatens to polarize public debate to an even greater degree. The system introduced in Seattle is also extremely complex and forces candidates to collect the vouchers one by one in paper form; at least an electronic version could have been devised in the twenty-first century.

Under the reform that I advocate, each citizen would state on her annual tax return the name of the political movement to which her seven euros of public funding should be allocated. The funding would be equal, fluid, and transparent.

10

Toward a Democratization of the "Private" Funding of Democracy and a New Way of Publicly Funding Parties

THE DEMOCRATIC REVOLUTION THAT I propose in this book stands on two legs. The first, to be considered in this chapter, is a complete overhaul of the way in which political groups and election campaigns are funded; that and that alone will make it possible to end the corruption eating away at our electoral systems, and the representation deficit affecting the great majority of citizens. The second, to be addressed in the final chapter, is the replacement of existing parliaments with mixed assemblies, which, through an element of social parity, would ensure the representation of both the social and the political sphere.

But let us take things step by step. The first measures in this chapter may strike you as being rather technical and insufficiently ambitious. But they are simple to implement and are really the least we should expect from a moderately reformist government aiming to achieve a minimum of political equality. In particular, I propose a complete reform of the fiscal dimension of the private funding of democracy, so that the poorest in society no longer pay for the richest. The reform would have two key planks: (1) a strict ceiling on permitted donations; and (2) the transformation of tax deductions (which apply only to tax-paying households) into a system of tax credits (open to all), or ideally into a system of matching contributions paid directly to beneficiary organizations. There would be nothing revolutionary about this: indeed, it would take its inspiration partly from systems already in place in such countries as the United Kingdom. Above all, it is a commonsense measure consonant with fiscal justice, against which no convincing argument can be made. A refusal to adopt it, and especially a refusal to transform tax deductions into universal tax credits, would mean saying openly that the political preferences of the rich should be favored over everyone else's.

Next come my more "radical" proposals, which in my view are indispensable, even if they demand a little more courage and political will, as well as a real effort at innovative thinking. In particular, I argue for the complete elimination of tax deductions for private contributions to political organizations (members can still contribute up to a modest ceiling, but without being entitled to claim a tax reduction), and in their place the introduction of a system for the public funding of political movements based on Democratic Equality Vouchers (DEVs). This new system entails the equal representation of citizens' preferences and a recognition of the dynamic character of the political process in the twenty-first century. Political parties are no longer fixed entities: movements come and go; a protest can become a political phenomenon in the space of a few weeks. And in order to ensure that they are not captured by private interests, *public* funds should be made available for them to take shape and—why not?—to have a presence all the way to the polls.[1] Thus, whereas in most countries the public funding of parties is rigidly tied for four or five years to their success at the previous elections, I propose that it should be reviewed and updated on an annual basis; citizens will decide each year, through an entry on their tax return, which parties or even newly emerging movements they wish to finance. This is not exactly a "recall" procedure, but it can give a little yearly wake-up call—and open the way for new ideas to take a political form more quickly.

You may be wondering in what way these measures are radical. (If you aren't, I am glad to hear it, because it probably means you are already in part convinced.) On the one hand, for such a reform to happen, it will be necessary to convince the majority of citizens that there is a value in spending public money to fund parties in which they, regrettably, no longer have much trust. Nowadays that is no easy task—just look at Italy, where citizens expressed themselves *en masse* for the elimination of public funding (a mistake that, I hope, they will decide to reverse). Second, for such public funding to have real value—by which I mean, for it to switch our democracies away from "one euro, one vote" to "one person, one vote"—it must go together with much stricter limits on private funding than those currently in force. Perhaps there would even be a complete ban on private funding (although the negative result of that might be to prevent the development of activist parties, when the aim is to dislodge the power of sponsors), or at least a ban on all contributions above quite a low ceiling of 100 or 200 euros a year, in order to encourage activist commitment, while ensuring that the sums involved do not lead to any real inequality of rights and privileges within the party. And to achieve that, of course, there has to be a struggle against the power of lobbies and other private interests.

Fiscal Rules for Private Funding That Mean the Poor No Longer Pay for the Rich

If the idea of democracy is to regain some meaning, the first and most urgent task is to do away with the tax deductions for political donations that exist in France, Canada, Italy, Spain, Germany, and elsewhere. As we have seen, they benefit only people liable to pay income tax, and the higher their taxable income, the greater the benefit.

One idea might be simply to abolish all such deductions—to contend that there is no reason why private donations to fund political democracy should attract a fiscal advantage. Tax breaks for political contributions are far from being universal; they disappeared a long time ago in the United States, for example. And I must confess that in a way their straightforward elimination seems to me the most promising course, especially as, in limiting the associated fiscal expenditure, it would free up further resources for a more ambitious public funding program. In a country like France, an average of 64 million euros (or 1.23 euros per adult) are spent each year on tax relief for the rich, in return for nothing more than their contributions to political parties and election campaigns. It would seem preferable if this same sum allowed each French citizen to allocate one euro a year to the political movement of his or her choice. I shall return in a moment to the details of what I propose.

Allow me first to consider a slightly more conservative course, whereby some tax advantages would be retained for private donors to political parties and election campaigns. This immediately raises the question of how to end the indefensibly regressive features of the present tax system—not only in relation to the funding of political democracy, but also with regard to the whole range of donations to foundations. Two possibilities present themselves: the first and simpler would be to replace tax deductions (that only benefit citizens liable to income tax) with tax credits (that benefit everyone irrespective of his or her income), thereby placing all citizens on an equal footing in the monetary expression of their political preferences; the second option (perhaps preferable to that method of delayed refunds in the following year) would be a more direct form of state intervention involving matching contributions.

Equal Expression of Political Preferences through the Replacement of Tax Deductions with Tax Credits

Mr. President or Mr. Prime Minister, do you really think it desirable that the state each year spends much more on funding the political preferences of the rich than those of the poor? No? Well, I have the solution, an extremely simple one, and I imagine you will agree without batting an eyelid to a reform that makes the funding of political contributions more democratic.

The reform I have in mind would simply replace tax deductions (applicable, by definition, only to people sufficiently well off not to be exempt from income tax) with tax credits (applicable to all households, irrespective of their tax liability). For individuals who do pay income tax (or for those whose tax credit is greater than their tax liability), the tax credit will involve a refund from the Internal Revenue Service. If we take the example of France, the real cost of a 600-euro donation for an individual with an annual taxable income of 90,000 euros is currently 240 euros, while the real cost is 600 euros for an individual whose taxable income is ten times smaller.[2] Tomorrow, under my proposed reform, the cost will be 204 euros for individuals with the highest and lowest incomes alike. The former will see a tax reduction of 396 euros, the latter will receive a check for 396 euros from the tax authorities. That is what is known as fiscal justice—and note that here I am talking only of equality, not of progressive taxation.

A fiscal measure of this kind seems to be the strict minimum, but that does not mean it is sufficient. For a tax credit, like a tax deduction, will remain proportionate to the size of the donation—which usually means to the donor's income. In France today, the ceiling on donations to political parties is 7,500 euros; so, even if the actual cost of a 7,500-euro donation was "only" 2,500 euros for each French citizen, how could someone on the minimum wage, however politically committed, devote nearly a fifth of his annual income to the funding of political democracy? In fact, 2,500 euros may be a much more "incidental" expense for a citizen whose income is in the tens of thousands. It therefore seems to me illegitimate that the state should be more "generous" to the richest citizens when it comes to (financial) participation in democracy.

Replacing Delayed Tax Reductions with a System of Matching Contributions: The Dual Benefit of Transparency and Simplicity

From this point of view, the second reform that I propose here presents the same difficulty: that is, a danger that the richest will contribute more than the poorest, since they have more money at their disposal. But it does have significant advantages in comparison with tax credits. The idea is to replace the current tax deduction system with something like the British system of Gift Aid. Instead of giving individual donors the benefit of tax deductions—usually with a year's delay, moreover—the state would, at the time of a donation, directly match it by paying a sum equivalent to the value of the tax deduction to the various political parties, organizations, or groups.[3]

Imagine again the case of a 600-euro donation, where donations to political parties entitle donors to a 66 percent tax reduction. In the present system, such a donation entitles the richest individuals to a tax reduction of 396 euros, and the poorest to a zero reduction. In a tax credit system such as the one outlined above, the 600-euro donation entitles the richest to a tax reduction of 396 euros, and the poorest to a 396-euro check from the tax authorities. In a system based on matching contributions, nothing happens that directly affects the donor, but the political party that receives the donation benefits from an additional payment of

396 euros from the tax authorities. The operation is revenue neutral as far as the tax authorities are concerned, but for the donor it has the merit of simplicity. He or she does not need to make complex financial calculations that involve paying part of the funding upfront in expectation of a refund at some later date.

The UK Gift Aid system, which was introduced in 1990, really took off in 2000, when the minimum sum required to qualify for it (until then £600 sterling) was removed.[4] As things stand today, the system allows charities to claim 25 pence extra from the government for each pound they receive from donors who sign up to it: that is, 20 percent (the basic rate of income tax) of the total sum of £1.25. In other words, the government makes a matching contribution equal to the tax relief that the donor would otherwise have received. And at first sight it has been a success, since the United Kingdom comes second only to the United States in the amount given in charitable donations.

How does this system work in practice? Charities ask the tax authorities (HM Revenue and Customs) for the matching contributions by submitting a form with the names of donors and the size of donations; they then receive the sums due to them within a period of four to five weeks. Although the system is different, the spirit of UK Gift Aid is quite similar to the German system of matching donations to political parties, since, as we have seen, the public funding received by German political parties reflects not only the number of votes they obtained at the previous election but also the size of donations from physical persons; parties receive 0.45 euros in extra public funding for each euro they receive in donations (up to a donation limit of 3,300 euros).

I should make it clear that my idea is to take inspiration from UK Gift Aid, not to reproduce it. For in my view it has a number of defects, beginning with the fact that political parties in the United Kingdom are not considered to be charities and therefore cannot benefit from the system. Furthermore, the Gift Aid system has another dimension in addition to the matching contribution that I have just described.[5] This second dimension, which should be eliminated to ensure greater fiscal justice, means that better-off taxpayers—who pay higher marginal rates—can claim tax relief on their donations equal to the difference between the highest rate (40 or 45 percent) and the basic rate (20 percent) of income tax. Thus, in addition to the 25 pence that goes automatically to the charity, a taxpayer who is taxed at 40 percent can benefit from personal tax relief of 25 percent for every pound donated. Nor is this the only inequality built into Gift Aid as it operates in the United Kingdom, since the donor must pay enough in taxes for his or her donation to entitle the charity in question to claim a matching contribution; if a taxpayer donates 80 pence to a charity, that charity can claim the extra 20 pence if and only if the donor's tax liability is greater than 20 pence.

By contrast, in the system I advocate, any contribution of 80 pence to a charity would automatically entitle it to receive a matching contribution of 20 pence from the government, whatever the amount that the donor pays in taxes. Nor would more affluent taxpayers further benefit from personal tax relief. Such a system has a number of advantages over ones based on tax deductions or tax credits. First, it is more expeditious: charities would have to wait only a few weeks before they received the government contribution, whereas fiscal mechanisms usually take effect only after a one-year delay. Second, it cuts down on tax fraud, since taxpayers no longer have an incentive to declare donations they have never made.[6] True, the foundations—or political parties—might have an incentive to cheat, by declaring donations they have not received in order to claim associated public funding. But the work of Kimberley Scharf and Sarah Smith shows that, at least in the United Kingdom, there is more of a tendency to under-declare donations.[7] The main reason for this is the complexity of the existing system, which means that charities have to enter on a form each individual sum and each donor's name, even for the smallest contributions. However, such complexity is by no means inevitable: we are living in the twenty-first century, and a fully computerized system could handle everything at very low cost.

This being said, a system of matching contributions would still suffer from a limitation I have already pointed out. Although the real cost of a donation would be the same for all donors—as it would be in a system based on tax credits—everything suggests that individuals with a low taxable income would find it difficult to contribute more than a few dozen euros, whereas the more affluent might continue to pay out in the thousands. In other words, even if the two reforms have the merit of ending the regressive character of the present system, the richest income groups will on average still donate much more than the poorest (and give conservative parties the benefit of greater electoral resources). Why is this so? Because they have the means to do it. This implies that the state will continue to spend much more each year to ensure a hearing for the political preferences of an affluent minority rather than for those of the majority of the population—unless, that is, the generosity of the rich proves to be totally tax-related, and they simply stop donating once they are deprived of the associated fiscal advantages.

For these reasons, I think we need to go further and adopt a new system of public funding—one that finally ensures the equality of all citizens in the expression of their political preferences.

A New Model of Public Funding Based on the Equal Representation of Private Political Preferences

A First Revolution: Democratic Equality Vouchers (DEVs)

Let me now spell out the features of the system I propose. Each year, when completing their tax returns, all citizens choose the political party or movement to which they want to allocate the sum of public funding they are entitled to claim. In a way, it would be an Italian-style system, but with the essential difference that each citizen, *whatever his or her income,* would dispose of the same amount of public funding. It would provide for the complete equality of all citizens in the expression of their political preferences, whereas the existing Italian system, as we have seen, allocates much more public money to fund the political preferences of the rich.[8]

The key question we must ask as citizens—even if we are under no obligation to settle it here once and for all—is how much public money we want to be spent each year on the funding of democracy. Or, in other words, what amount of public funding do we want to be assigned to each citizen? Let us take the case of France, with its current adult population of 52 million. As a yearly average, the French state spends a little more than 183 million euros on the funding of democracy (67 million in direct payments to parties, 52 million in the reimbursement of campaign spending, 56 million in tax relief associated with donations to political parties, and 8 million for donations to campaigns), which amounts to 3.5 euros per citizen. A minimal, zero-cost reform might involve taking a fresh look at our whole system for the public funding of political democracy and replacing it with Democratic Equality Vouchers (DEVs) worth 3.5 euros each, to be given annually to all citizens. They would take the form of electronic vouchers, since everything would be done through the mechanism of the annual tax return.

I think we can be more ambitious, however. As I pointed out in Chapter 6, the functioning of the French state costs 1.8 billion euros a year, or 34 euros per head of the adult population. And if we are willing to pay for those who govern us to do so in the best conditions, we should also be willing to pay for them to be chosen in the best way possible. So, let us imagine that we save a mere 10 percent on the expense of running the state and allocate it instead to the public funding of democracy; then every French person could benefit each year from a Democratic Equality Voucher worth seven euros.

Is seven euros a lot or very little? To begin with, in the model I propose in a French setting, the seven euros would be fully funded: it would not require any additional spending, and no existing funding would be fundamentally deflected from its original purpose. What today serves for the funding of political democracy would serve in my model for the funding of political democracy; but—and this is the key point—the political equality of citizens would meanwhile have been revived.

In a comparative perspective, we can say that seven euros is less than what Germany spends per adult for the public funding of its political foundations. As we have seen, those foundations also play a role in diplomatic representation. But if we just concentrate on political democracy, then the direct funding of parties and tax relief for donations together account for nearly four euros of spending per head of the adult German population. So, four euros might be the value of a Democratic Equality Voucher in Germany; or, as in France, a more ambitious target might be to economize on the funding of political foundations and / or the cost of running the state, thereby allowing the value of one voucher to be raised to seven euros. In Spain, even without fiscal expenditure (which is very low[9]) or the funding of political foundations, the government currently spends more than 5.60 euros per adult on the public funding of its democracy. There too, we are not far from my proposal of seven euros.

As to the United States, although public funding has been allowed to wither away, the system created several decades ago provided for the allocation of $3 per taxpayer just for the funding of presidential elections. The calculations are quick to do: even if we take into account only federal elections (presidential and congressional)—although local elections are also very important in the United States and should really be taken into account—the spending of candidates in the 2016 presidential election amounted to only 47 percent of total expenditure.[10] So, if public funding were allocated as a function of private spending, we would be talking about total funding on the order of $6.40 per taxpayer—not so far, in spirit, from our seven euros per citizen. Now, $6.40 per American adult comes to a total of $1.5 billion, which is the very amount spent by all the candidates combined in the presidential election of 2016, and much less than the spending by PACs and super PACs.[11] What I propose is that the same amount should be allocated, not in tens of millions of dollars by an ultra-privileged minority, but in the form of Democratic Equality Vouchers issued by the government to each of its citizens.

Just think—seven euros a year per head of the adult population to recover the basic principle of democracy: one person, one vote.

The Democratic Equality Voucher in Detail

Seven euros to allocate each year to the political movement of your choice. Let us now get down to brass tacks: what is a political group? I ask this as a thoroughly practical, not rhetorical, question, because no one wants the public funding to be diverted to sundry associations that have no intention of taking part in elections. At the same time, the conditions attached to it cannot be too restrictive, since one of the aims of the reform is to introduce a greater fluidity that allows the rapid emergence of new political movements. It cannot be required, for example, that a political group should have previously run candidates in an election. I would therefore make the following proposal (but I repeat, nothing in this book is meant to be set in stone: the point is to open things up for debate, not to issue strict rules from on high). For a political group to benefit from public funding in the form of Democratic Equality

Vouchers, it must receive vouchers from at least 1 percent of citizens (which in France would work out to approximately 520,000 vouchers and in the United States to 2.6 million). This 1 percent threshold seems perfectly reasonable: it corresponds to the least restrictive conditions existing today for the triggering of a popular initiative referendum.[12]

What happens if a political movement receives a certain number of vouchers, but not enough to trigger the release of public funding (that is, less than 1 percent of the DEVs)? In such cases, the total number of vouchers that citizens have decided to allocate to the movement will be considered null and void. After all, one of the options offered to citizens is precisely not to allocate their seven euros to any given party, and it is important to allow for the possibility that some will consider no party or movement worthy of their support.

In the system I propose, if a citizen decides not to use his or her DEV for the current year, it will not simply be lost as a result. Sizable public funding of democracy is important, and so all the finances earmarked for DEVs should be devoted to the good functioning of political democracy. The issuing of DEVs does not give citizens the right to decide how much the state should allocate each year to the public funding of democracy—that is decided "higher up," when the legislature sets the value of each voucher. What the DEVs do establish is a rule for the annual allocation of this funding to citizens in accordance with their political preference. What are the criteria, then, for the allocation of Democratic Equality Vouchers that citizens have chosen not to assign to a political movement? I would propose that any sums not directly assigned through the take-up of DEVs should be distributed among the existing political parties in line with their results at the most recent general elections (as is already the case today for the public funding of political parties).[13]

Such an allocation rule has many advantages. On the one hand, it provides for a certain stability of the system: by creating a more or less assured four-to-five-year funding base for parties that took part in the last elections, it reduces the volatility of an entirely annualized funding system. This way of presenting the argument may appear paradoxical, because one of the reasons for the introduction of DEVs was that citizens should actually use them, not that most of the vouchers should go to waste and feed back into the present system, whose major defect is to ossify the public funding of democracy.[14] However, given the historical experiences analyzed earlier in this book, it seems unlikely that all citizens will spontaneously get involved in politics to choose the party of their dreams. They must be encouraged and given a sense of their responsibility. But if they do not get involved at this level, public funding should not simply disappear as a result.

On the other hand—and for me this is the key aspect—not only can a DEV system greatly facilitate the emergence of new political movements; it may also be seen as a "soft" kind of recall referendum. The point of this would not be, at some moment, to topple a government elected by the majority (we have seen that such referenda have sometimes been captured by private interests with little concern for the public good), but to signal dissatisfaction by reducing the funding for a particular movement, perhaps with the eventual result that it either drops out of the picture or sets out to win back public support. This "soft" approach would favor democratic dialogue with all citizens (who have to be convinced), not with a handful of rich donors.

Another advantage of this public funding scheme is that Democratic Equality Vouchers involve a kind of recall referendum that applies not only to government parties but also to opposition parties. Clearly, citizens are regularly dissatisfied with the political opposition, and in my system they are able to express this every year. It is a crucial possibility because it means that at election time—when citizens are called to the polls—they will have a choice between parties that reflect their preferences more than they would otherwise do. In all likelihood, they will then vote more and abstain less—another clawing back of democracy, which will really come into its own when the political preferences of the majority, not those of a minority, receive proper attention.

An Innovative Measure That Can Shorten the Time It Takes to Fund Democratic Bodies

The system of Democratic Equality Vouchers therefore has many advantages, beginning with the restoration (or should I say establishment?) of equal representation for private preferences through a second vote built into people's tax returns. Beyond this indispensable democratization of the funding of political democracy, Democratic Equality Vouchers will make it possible to place the funding of political movements on an annual basis. One of the main accusations against the present system is that the time between elections is too long, that citizens can express themselves only once every four or five years. Democratic Equality Vouchers will be a tool of permanent democracy, enabling citizens to express themselves each year while ensuring the stability of the government. (It would obviously be unhealthy for elections to take place every year; a degree of stability is necessary for a government to implement a policy.)

But apart from enabling citizens to express themselves at more frequent intervals, the system I am describing would facilitate the real emergence of new political forces between elections. As things are today, a political force that appears between two elections has no effective claim on public resources; the most it can hope for is that its score in the next elections will give it access to subsidies for a few years. But, of course, that can happen only if it survives until the next election and does not, as is often the case, disappear before it has been able to spread its political wings. Another option would be to rely on private funds, but in practice that favors the emergence of conservative forces. Political movements with a more left-wing profile tend to have a brief surge, before they disappear again.

Why does a lack of money cause them to disappear? I have repeatedly stressed that elections cost a lot—but so too does the life of a party. What is a political party, over and above the attractive force of its ideas? I have spoken with numbers of activists, members, and sympathizers, on both the right and left of the spectrum—well-intentioned citizens who use their free time to advance their ideas. But they also know that those ideas need an "apparatus" to shore them up. Nowadays, the word "apparatus" has negative connotations, but what does it actually mean? Offices—and therefore finances. A website, pamphlets, banners, and so on—therefore finances. Women and men—therefore finances. Nor do those women and men have to be full-timers: labor representatives, for example, get time off to deal with union business, and it might be possible to provide "time credits" for members of political movements that benefit from public funding (that is, from Democratic Equality Vouchers).

Here too, it seems important to inject fluidity and innovation into the system.

A System Preferable to "Church Taxes" or
Seattle-Style Democracy Vouchers

Allow me to state clearly what Democratic Equality Vouchers are not. My proposal may set some readers thinking of the German "church tax," but although the two systems operate through people's tax returns they are in fact completely different. In Germany, citizens who are attached to an organized religion have part of their income tax allocated to the funding of its expenditure. However, this is not at all the same as public funding of religion. The state deducts income tax at source on behalf of each religion, which even pays a small percentage back to the state to offset the extra costs involved for the tax authorities.[15]

The difference between the German system and public funding of religions appears clearly if we compare the German "church tax" with the Italian "8 per thousand." In Italy we really are talking about public funding, since part of each citizen's tax payment is allocated to the organized religions; even if citizens decide not to use their "8 per thousand" to select a particular religion, the corresponding amount is still deducted and paid to the various religions in accordance with the aggregated preferences of other citizens. In Germany, by contrast, citizens may choose not to be associated with any religion, in which case they simply pay no "church tax" at all; the outcome is financially neutral for the state, but considerably reduces the resources of each religion. Increasing numbers of Germans are in fact "leaving" their religion so as not to pay this additional tax—hence the inclination of some German religions to adopt an Italian-style system that will guarantee them annual funding irrespective of the size of their congregation.

The system I propose here is much closer to the Italian "2 per thousand," but with a key difference that bears repetition: a Democratic Equality Voucher is a fixed sum allocated to each citizen by the state. It therefore guarantees the equality of citizens in the funding of political life, whereas in the "2 per thousand" system the funding of each citizen's preferences varies as a function of the taxes that he or she pays. Moreover, in cases where citizens express no choice, the resources of the Democratic Equality Vouchers are still allocated to the public funding of political life, not on the basis of the preferences expressed by those who do choose a party, but by referring to the results in the most recent elections in order to ensure a degree of stability in the system.

In a way, Democratic Equality Vouchers are reminiscent of the French "union voucher" (*chèque syndical*) system, a mode of labor union funding tried out from 1990 at the insurance giant Axa, which, though never widespread, was adopted by such organizations as the Union of National Social Security Funds, cancer research institutes, the now-defunct catering corporation Score, and the Casino supermarket group. However, there are two major differences. First, these union vouchers are funded by the organizations themselves, whereas the Democratic Equality Vouchers are a system for the public funding of democracy that the state runs for the benefit of citizens. Second, and perhaps even more important, my proposed system has an open, universal, and flexible character unlike that of the German church tax or the Italian "8 per thousand." In Germany, it is in practice quite complicated to stop subsidizing your chosen religion or to change to a different one: it is not enough to check a box on your tax return, as in Italy; you have to make a request to the religious authorities and follow a strict procedure. Moreover, in both Germany and Italy, the Muslim religion is still completely excluded from these systems of public funding, for various reasons linked to the fact that the public authorities have not managed to identify a unified organization or representative figures comparable to those in the Christian and Jewish religions (or at least that is the official explanation). The whole issue is a complex one, and it would take us well beyond the framework of this book to consider possible solutions. But I would emphasize that my proposal for Democratic Equality Vouchers makes sense only if the procedure for choosing a party to support is thoroughly open and flexible, so that everyone has a free choice and is able to change it every year by checking a box on their electronic tax return.

Finally, Democratic Equality Vouchers certainly bear a strong resemblance to the democracy vouchers proposed by Lawrence Lessig and first introduced in Seattle. But they also differ from them in some respects. Why do I think that public funding should operate through people's tax returns instead of being distributed at the time of elections? On the one hand, the tax return route obviates some of the real risk associated with Seattle-style vouchers, which is that electors will sell them and candidates buy them for hard cash. Lessig does discuss this danger and suggests quite a complicated way of limiting it: namely, citizens should have the option of canceling the allocation of their democracy vouchers for a period of twenty-four hours. But even if this removed any possibility of commodification, it seems to me that the annual public funding of parties through Democratic Equality Vouchers is still a better way to go. For Lessig's democracy vouchers are centered on the funding of election campaigns, whereas in my view the funding of political parties and groups—especially new ones—should be designed to operate also outside campaigning periods. Parties are not meant to be just election machines; they should be thought of as platforms that assist the advance of public debate, not only during election periods but also between them.

Should We Be Afraid of Transparency?

I can already hear voices arguing that such a system for the public funding of political democracy carries with it a danger to individual privacy. But there are several reasons why this is not the case. First—and as a taxpayer, you are probably well aware of this—citizens already disclose huge amounts of information about themselves on their annual tax return, without wanting it to be made public. Nor is it made public. The tax return rests upon a system that protects everyone's privacy; citizens have confidence in this system today, and there is no reason why they should lose it simply because of an extra box on their return relating to Democratic Equality Vouchers.

Second, we have seen that a number of taxpayers—a little under 300,000 in today's France—donate money every year to political parties and declare it on their tax return. To be sure, they have to enter only the amount of the donation, not the name of the party that benefits from it. But they must keep the receipts from party offices and make them available to the tax authorities in the event of an audit. (Historically, and still today in some countries, taxpayers had to attach the receipts to their actual return—a possibility that might be preferable since it would cut down on the fraudulent declaration of nonexistent donations.) In other words, the tax authorities already have at their disposal all the information they need about who contributes to such and such a political party or election campaign. This is not a problem, because the information is protected.

Third, the wish to preserve at all costs the anonymity of donations to parties and campaigns in today's France is inconsistent with the recent progress that Germany and the United Kingdom, for example, have made on the transparency of private funding. In these and other countries, all donations above a certain (often low) threshold have to be made public, and information concerning them is often made available online in near-real time. This makes it possible to limit eventual conflicts of interest, since journalists or other citizens are more cautious about "return favors." France still has a lot to do in these matters. In the United States, in the successful experiment with democracy vouchers in Seattle, you can find online a list of the individuals who have allocated their democracy vouchers and the names of the candidates who have benefited from them; I do not think we need to go that far, but the ending of systemic corruption requires greater efforts to be made in the direction of transparency.

Let us note finally that, in the UK Gift Aid system described at the beginning of this chapter, charities have to compile a list of all the donations they receive and to forward it to the tax authorities along with the donors' names and addresses. This does not mean that such data are not protected, because it is one thing to communicate information to the tax authorities and quite another to make it public. The Inland Revenue is not Facebook, and that can only be welcomed.

From the Ban on Private Funding to the Ceiling on Electoral Spending

So, what should be done to ensure that public funding—and the innovation of Democratic Equality Vouchers—is not swamped by a surfeit of private money? The simple solution is to ban private funding, or anyway its excesses.

In many countries, for excellent reasons, private corporate donations to parties and election campaigns are prohibited. Recently, as we have seen, they have even been outlawed in Brazil, a country that cannot be said to be in the forefront of the struggle for democratic equality. I think that such bans should be introduced wherever they do not yet operate— first of all in Germany, where the weight of the export sector in the funding of political life is not without consequences for the rest of Europe. Big business has managed to convince successive German governments to pursue a totally export-oriented economic policy, and this has gravely weakened the stability of the eurozone.

In France, corporate donations were authorized in the early 1990s, but then a new regulation prohibited them in 1995. By all accounts, this reform caused an outcry before it was finally given the go-ahead. Similarly, in Spain, having been permitted from 1987 to 2014, corporate donations were prohibited in a move to clean up the workings of political democracy. It is high time that such a reform was adopted in Italy, Germany, and the United Kingdom—for the good of each of these countries, as well as for the sake of equilibrium within the European Union.

But a ban on corporate donations will not be enough; it is necessary to go further and cap individual donations. In some countries—again including Germany and the United Kingdom—these are subject to no legal restriction, and an upper limit will have to be set for the first time. It should be much lower than the ceilings in Spain (50,000 euros per party and 10,000 euros per campaign) or Italy (100,000 euros per party, although the case of Berlusconi showed that this is easy to circumvent) or France. An annual limit of 7,500 euros on individual funding for all parties is much too high: it introduces huge distortions by tying the political weight of individual preferences to the size of the donor's income.

I therefore propose an annual ceiling of 200 euros on the donations that each citizen is permitted to make to political parties—a ceiling that will be introduced also for the funding of all campaigns. Two hundred euros: that is the figure mostly chosen as the dividing line between small and large donations. It is more than the average donation by French taxpayers in the first decile of income distribution (122 euros), and more than membership fees to political parties. But it should help to make the political weight of citizens more equal.

What case could be made against a 200-euro ceiling on donations? The free speech argument does not seem to hold any water: money is not a form of political discourse, and it is to be hoped that even the US Supreme Court will change its mind on this. In France and other countries where ceilings have been introduced, it is good that people think some limit is necessary on the scale of private funding. The commonest argument in favor of a low ceiling centers on corruption, and were that the only consideration perhaps 200 euros would seem too little. Could you ever get an election candidate to make promises for a mere 200 euros? However, as we have seen throughout this book, the danger or the appearance of corruption is not the only reason why it is necessary to limit private donations. The main one is democratic equality. Each citizen should be given the same weight, so that he or she can benefit from the same degree of representation. The key objective is that it should once again be possible to define democracy as "one person, one vote." And that requires that no one, by contributing a larger sum of money, can buy extra votes to influence a party or candidate.

Limits on Campaign Spending

Of course, as I said at the outset, elections cost a lot. That is why limits on private funding must go together with generous public funding of political parties, as I propose with a system of Democratic Equality Vouchers worth seven euros per adult head of the population. But it will also be necessary to cap election spending—as is already the case in France and the United Kingdom.

In the United States, as well as in Canada, some definition of permitted expenses will have to be worked out, the first step being a major reform (or even prohibition) of electoral publicity on TV and radio, including in the more loosely regulated periods between election campaigns. Not only is this very expensive—which largely explains why electoral spending is so high across the Atlantic—but it also has pernicious effects on the whole electoral system. In particular, we know that negative publicity against rival candidates, which is widely used in the contemporary United States, demobilizes citizens and makes them less inclined to vote.[16] How can anyone want there to be rules for the democratic process that have the effect of lowering turnout? It would be wrong to think that the rules are set in stone, and, as I pointed out in Chapter 8, the recourse to extremely costly TV ads is to some extent an accident of history; things could have worked out differently, and airtime could have been allocated free of charge as in other countries. Nothing prevents a change of course; the United Kingdom, for example, had to wait until 1990 for a ban on campaign advertising on radio and television.

Such publicity is not allowed in France, but a profound reform of the time allocated to candidates will be necessary there. As things stand, the funding of political movements partly freezes the democratic process— since access to funding is defined only once every five years—but the rules governing speaking time in legislative and presidential campaigns suffer from the same problem. What is the situation regarding the pres- idential election? First, we need to distinguish between the so-called in- termediate period (from the publication of lists of candidates to the launch of the official campaign) and the thirty-day official campaign it- self (two weeks for the first round, then another two for the second round).[17] Today, the principle of "equitable" speaking time prevails during the intermediate period.[18] What does this mean in practice? It means that, under the supervision of the Conseil Supérieur de l'Audiovisuel (CSA—Higher Audiovisual Council), the speaking time of the various parties during the "intermediate" campaign must reflect the extent to which they are representative of the French political landscape, as well as their capacity to demonstrate their intention to run candidates. There are three criteria of a party's "representativeness": its results in the most recent elections; the number and position of elected officials that it claims to have; and the evidence of opinion polls.[19] In other words, the allocation of speaking time during the intermediate period heavily depends on the number of MPs a party obtained five years earlier. The official campaign, on the other hand, operates in accordance with the principle of "equal speaking time" for the candidates.

As to parliamentary elections, the French electoral code stipulates that—for the broadcasting of video clips—the parties with formally con- stituted groups in the National Assembly shall together have a total of three hours for the first round, while parties without such groups may each have seven minutes' broadcasting time provided they can show that at least seventy-five candidates are running in their name. So, another big bonus for the victors—of five years ago! It is like a statement that new parties cannot emerge between two elections—or rather, a guarantee that, if any do emerge, they will not cast too much of a shadow over our politicians basking in the sun.

Such a system cannot function—or at least cannot be considered satisfactory—in a democracy on the move. Besides, the system is not (or is no longer) working, as we saw in the 2017 legislative elections, when the rules were modified. In May, Macron's "En Marche!" movement initiated a Priority Question on Constitutionality (Question Prioritaire de Constitutionalité) before the Constitutional Council, contesting the distribution of airtime between the parties (it received only seven minutes under the electoral code, as did La France Insoumise) and demanding that the equal treatment of political parties should be respected.[20] The Constitutional Council ruled that the law should give to parties not represented in Parliament a total broadcasting time proportional to their representativeness,[21] whereupon the CSA allocated thirty-five minutes to En Marche! for the first round, instead of the initially planned seven minutes. The CSA also increased airtime for the Front National and La France Insoumise, setting it at 31.5 and 24.5 minutes respectively.

The rules governing speaking time should not only be changed and updated, but also—ideally—written into the Constitution, so that parties in power cannot tinker with them as their short-term electoral interests dictate. One solution might be to use the taxpayer allocations of Democratic Equality Vouchers to estimate the popularity of political movements at election time, but of course that is far from being the only option. It would not solve the problem of ensuring equal access to the media, but nor should this stand in the way of any advance. What is sure is that in the twenty-first century election results from five years ago cannot determine the funding of political parties or the speaking time available to candidates.

To conclude, I would like to emphasize that one of the main advantages of Democratic Equality Vouchers is that they would end the unequal representation of citizens' preferences. My proposed funding reform has two pillars: the yearly issue of Democratic Equality Vouchers, a generous form of public funding that gives equal weight to all citizens; and strict limits on private funding as well as electoral spending. If politicians no longer have to rely on a small number of rich donors for their living, but can draw on a small fraction of the taxes paid by the general population, everything suggests that their policies in power will no longer follow the preferences of the rich.

This first revolution seems to me essential if we are to achieve democratic equality. But it is not sufficient: the funding question, however important, cannot alone provide an answer to the crisis of democracy. As a necessary complement, a mixed assembly must ensure that elected deputies are more representative of society as a whole. This is the subject of the next chapter.

11

Toward a Mixed Assembly: Social and Political

HOW CAN the idea of democracy as "one person, one vote" become a tangible reality again? Or, to put it in another way, how can democratic equality be guaranteed? The first requirement is to revolutionize the funding system, through the introduction of Democratic Equality Vouchers (DEVs) and the strictest regulation of any form of private funding. The aim is not only to ensure that each citizen can allocate equal funding to the expression of his or her political preferences, but also to eliminate the most undesirable consequences of the present system. Politicians today heed only the preferences of the richest sections of society. Tomorrow, instead of focusing only on those who fund them, they will listen to the views of the majority who elect them. The very essence of democracy will be put back on the map.

But that will not be enough; an indispensable second reform must focus more directly on the question of representation. Today, to elect the parliaments that exist in many countries, each citizen theoretically votes in his or her local constituency on the basis of "one person, one vote." In practice, however, some social groups are almost entirely excluded from the ranks of those elected. What is sorely lacking is any representation of the electorate as it really is, particularly of its different social classes. With the general decline of labor unions—which for decades were the bearers of social progress—the working classes lost whatever foothold they had in Parliament and found their preferences ignored by elected politicians; they became invisible twice over, as it were. Now they must regain representation, by entering the Parliament in person. This is what I propose with the creation of new parliamentary seats for "social representatives"—or, more concretely, the election of a substantial number of parliamentarians (at least a third, but why not a half or more?) by proportional representation, on lists with at least 50 percent employees and blue-collar workers, or workers without secure employment (corresponding to the share of these groups in the active population). As an immediate result, workers would become much more numerous than they are today on the benches of national parliaments, with major practical consequences for policymaking. For, as we shall see, the socio-occupational origin of representatives—and especially the job they had before entering politics—directly influences how they vote on legislation. Only such a radical proposal will make it possible to end the exclusion of the popular classes from our political institutions. We can no longer be content simply to deplore this deeply rooted exclusion, which ends up undermining our democracies from within and encouraging toxic votes. The question of social parity needs to be tackled at the roots, as in the case of male-female equality (although that came too little and too late).

But let us take things in stages. I would like to begin by briefly reviewing the tremendous role played by labor unions throughout the twentieth century, especially in the establishment of a welfare state and the reduction of inequality. Those social movements cannot be considered separately from political parties; indeed, in some countries, unions and parties have historically had very close links with each other. Yet social democracy is not political democracy: it has its own rationale, and I think it is time we took some inspiration from it.

Lessons and Limitations of Social Democracy

When people speak of "democracy," what they usually have in mind is electoral democracy: that is, the election of our political representatives. But democracy routinely takes another form as well, which is sometimes more successful: the social democracy expressed in ballots held by labor or trade organizations. Unions and parties are the two dimensions of representation.

In many countries today, beginning with France, unions are doing somewhat better than parties: they have a more favorable public image and a larger number of members. For example, 27 percent of French people have confidence in labor unions. That may not seem many, but it is three times more than the 9 percent who express confidence in political parties.[1] In the United States, trust in labor unions has risen since 2013, from 20 to 26 percent.[2] This obviously does not mean that all is well with the unions—and in this chapter we shall see the negative consequences associated with their decline. If they were really in good shape, it would probably be a less urgent priority to bring an element of social representation into our legislative bodies by changing the rules for the election of some of their members. Nevertheless, unions have suffered less than other "democratic institutions"—beginning with political parties and the media—from the public disenchantment noticeable in the past few decades.[3] While politicians and journalists are seen as out of touch with the realities and incapable of addressing the average voter's concerns (which they anyway do not share), union officials benefit in a way from the fact that they are more representative. In today's France, employees and blue-collar workers make up a little more than 48 percent of the active population,[4] yet they provide fewer than 3 percent of parliamentary deputies, only just ahead of the United States (2 percent) and not far behind the United Kingdom (5 percent). By contrast, half of union representatives are of working-class origin. Social democracy therefore fares much better than political democracy in terms of being representative—and I say "fares better" advisedly, because the representation deficit among politicians is something chosen rather than passively experienced, and it has a direct influence on policymaking.

Social democracy fares better, and we should therefore take inspiration from it. Besides, if we look back at the history, it seems almost impossible to think of political parties separately from social movements, if not actually from labor unions. As Daniel Schlozman shows very well, social movements and mass-membership parties emerged simultaneously with each other, at the dawn of modern democracy.[5]

Today, with democracy in crisis, we urgently need to return to that reality and to place the conditions for social progress back at the heart of discussion.

Between Closeness and Separation: The Complex Relationship between Unions and Parties

When Daniel Schlozman writes of the simultaneous emergence of social movements and political parties, it is not France but the United States that he has in mind. In France, although there are obviously very strong links between unionism and political commitment, the history of the relationship between the two facets of democracy was, to say the least, chaotic—and understandably so. Unions were first legalized in 1884, when a distinction was made between the specialized defense of professional interests and the general defense of political interests.[6] Political parties, though tolerated, continued to be denied official authorization. Why, you may ask, were unions legalized but not parties? According to Stéphane Sirot, this was due to a wish on the part of the state to retain its monopoly on decisions regarding the general interest. The state therefore provided for a unionism that protected a clearly defined field: labor performed in "the study and defense of economic, industrial, commercial, and agricultural interests."[7] It recognized unions because they were less alarming vehicles of change. Right from the beginning, however, unions brought with them a program for the transformation of society, conceived in terms of the general interest and not only the field of work.[8]

Only in 1901, with the law on the right of association, did political parties really acquire legal status in France. But whereas in 1884 the state had made the (bizarre) choice to separate the defense of professional interests from the defense of political interests, in 1906 it was the unions that asserted their independence from political parties. The Amiens Charter is considered the text that founded labor unionism in France, on a rather unconventional basis at least in international terms.[9] Whereas in Britain, the Labour Party came into being because of a decision by the unions to provide themselves with a party structure, and whereas the unions in effect "codetermined" Germany after the Second World War, they chose in France to fight for their independence.[10]

At least, that's how it has been on paper. In reality, some French unions were for a long time structurally linked to political parties—one thinks particularly of the General Confederation of Labor (CGT) and the Communist Party[11]—and even today there are strong links between political and union activism. Florence Haegel has perfectly documented this in the case of the Ligue Communiste Révolutionnaire.[12]

As a rule, however, there has been a division of roles between the unions (wage negotiations, social protection, and so on) and the political parties (running candidates in elections so that they can vote for or against legislation). This model, enshrined in the Amiens Charter, had its rationale especially in a rapidly developing industrial world, where wage-earners needed strong workplace representatives to negotiate on equal terms with capitalist owners. But in a world marked by deindustrialization, Uber-ization, and other forms of micro-entrepreneurship, where there is also a growing disenchantment with politics, this separation would no longer seem to apply. The employees and blue-collar workers whose rights are defended by labor unions are no longer represented in the political arena. But they would be represented (by social movements) in the kind of mixed assembly I propose. Such an assembly would open its doors to workers elected under a list-based system, and everything suggests that it would be not only traditional parties but also new movements or even the unions themselves that would draw up the lists.

Learning from the experiences of other countries, where unions are closely linked to political parties, I have arrived at the conviction that we need to have a mixed assembly, with both social and political representation. In the United Kingdom, union members used to pay dues automatically to the Labour Party, which had come into being as the political expression of the unions.[13] And when Margaret Thatcher set out to weaken the Labour movement in 1984, she made it more difficult for the unions to continue funding the party.[14] But as we shall see, until the mid-1980s the close links between party and unions expressed themselves in a strong presence of workers on Labour's parliamentary benches.[15]

The problem is that today there are few workers left in the UK Parliament—a phenomenon out of all proportion to their declining share in the active population. What is the explanation for this? It cannot be un-related to the fact that, from the late 1980s on, private donations to Labour never stopped increasing; whereas until the middle of the de-cade, they accounted for barely 10 percent of its total revenue in donations and membership fees, today they make up more than half (Figure 66). This growing weight of private donations is due partly to their quanti-tative increase since the early 1980s, but partly also to the collapse of union contributions since 1986 following the measures taken by Mar-garet Thatcher.[16] With less of a financial presence, workers have been gradually shown out of the door of the political process. But although the rise of private money began well before the arrival of New Labour, we should note that it accelerated in 1997 after the turn inaugurated by Tony Blair. As we saw in Chapter 7, he did not hesitate to support the demands that the industrialist Lakshmi Mittal made along with his gen-erous contributions to the Party. Hence the need today for an active

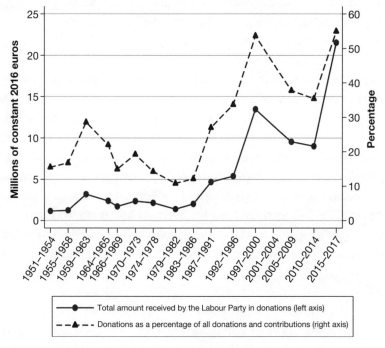

Figure 66. Evolution of private donations to the Labour Party, United Kingdom, 1951–2017

policy to change direction; for unless something is done, there will soon no longer be a single worker in the UK Parliament, just as there is already none in the French National Assembly.

The link between the financial health of labor unions and parties of the Left—and the political consequences of the weakening of that link—is far from being a British peculiarity. It is also found in the United States, for example, where the unions have for years been the main funders of the Democratic Party.[17] And in the United States as in the United Kingdom, when Republicans / Conservatives have sought to weaken their Democratic / Labour rivals, they have blocked the conduits between union and party coffers.

In the United States, this has taken the form of so-called right-to-work laws. While the National Labor Relations Act in 1935 had significantly protected the right to form unions in the private sector, the Taft-Hartley Act of 1947 curbed these advances and enabled individual states to introduce "right-to-work" laws. These removed the obligation for workers, both unionized and nonunionized, to pay "agency shop protection,"[18] thereby allowing individuals to benefit from collective bargaining and union representation without having to pay union dues. The direct result was a considerable weakening of the unions' financial base.

James Feigenbaum and his coauthors have studied the impact of right-to-work laws in a number of US states between 1980 and 2016.[19] According to their estimates, the resultant weakening of the unions led to a 3.5 percent drop in the electoral score of the Democratic Party in presidential elections (as well as a fall in voter turnout) and a worsening of its results in elections to the House of Representatives and the Senate. The mechanism was evident: the right-to-work laws reduced union contributions by 1.25 percent, and the Democratic Party was unable to make up the shortfall through other sources of funding. And, as we have seen, the candidates with fewer funds have less chance of winning an election.

The Weakening of Unions as Vehicles of Social Progress

In various countries, then, conservative forces have killed two birds with one stone, weakening both the unions and the parties on the left of the political spectrum. And insofar as the Left has relied on contributions from private sources, it has abandoned the class struggle and turned away from redistributive issues. Workers have seen their social representation crumble with the decrease in union membership, while their political representation has all but disappeared along with their presence in national assemblies. It has to be asked whether these same trends do not threaten social progress itself.

After all, workers' movements have been the principal vehicles of progress in the past centuries. One need only think of the so-called Scandinavian model of social protection: in Sweden, for example, the welfare state came into being through and with the labor unions. In Germany, the law has stipulated for decades that employees should have the same number of seats as shareholders on the boards of companies with a workforce of 2,000 or more, and a third of the seats in those with 500 to 2,000. That means real co-management at the enterprise level. And although my proposals in this book mainly relate to "codetermination" at a political level—through the entry of workers into Parliament as "social representatives"—I also think it is necessary to introduce democracy at the company level, in countries such as France and the United States, where it is absent today.[20]

Even in the United States, where the role of unions is less central than in Europe—hence the lesser development of the welfare state and the higher degree of inequality—their impact was for decades far from insignificant. Benjamin Radcliff and Martin Saiz have shown that the strength of the workers' movement was one of the main historical determinants of economic "liberalism" (in the American sense of left-oriented economic policies).[21] According to their estimates, from the 1960s to the 1980s, social allowances for dependent children, educational spending, and progressive taxation were all greater in states with a high rate of unionization. Above all, the rate of unionization played a greater role in the adoption of socially progressive measures than did the presence of the Left in government.

We can now understand why the political environment is less of a factor than the strength of the social movement. In the kind of political system that has prevailed in the past few decades—and that still prevails today—politicians *on both the right and the left* have been captive to private interests and the preferences of the most advantaged sections of society. It is a point I have made above more than once, particularly in Chapter 7. Labor unions, by contrast, do not have to raise funds for their own election campaigns—in fact, for a long time in the United States or the United Kingdom, they played a major role in funding the operations of political parties.[22]

Unions do not fight only to defend their interests at the company level; no, they also represent the wider political interests of the disadvantaged.[23] In relation to political parties, they serve important functions as financial contributors, grassroots mobilizers, and sources of influence; they help to write election platforms, conduct lobbying activity, and so on.

But unions, though the last bastion of working-class representation, occupy a weaker position today in the three key arenas of struggle. They are weaker politically, because the parties of the Left have abandoned the class struggle and eroded their historical links with social movements; weaker financially, because conservative parties, in countries such as the United States and the United Kingdom, have made repeated attacks on their funding model; and weaker socially, because they were not really prepared for the wage-labor model to run out of steam. Social equilibrium has long been based on people working for a wage, but how is social dialogue to be organized, how are the interests of new workers without secure employment to be defended, when the rules of micro-entrepreneurship demand compliance?[24] There are no magic formulas, but I have proposed here the direct representation of labor—in all its forms—in Parliament or Congress, with a third of parliamentarians elected by proportional representation on lists containing at least 50 percent employees and blue-collar workers. In this category, I would also include all the new precarious workers, since the point, of course, is to represent better not only wage-earners in insecure jobs but all forms of insecure labor, whatever the employment status of the low-income workers. This solution has two advantages: it returns the question of social progress to the parliamentary benches for dialogue and debate; and it makes it possible to reduce part of the working-class representation deficit in the national assembly.

Solving the Problem of the Lack of Representation

We have seen in previous chapters that, partly because of the present system of funding the democratic process, politicians no longer heed the preferences of their constituents, but only those of the richest sections of society. Some do not even really know their constituents, spending less and less time among them. Many do not actually care what their constituents want.[25] Nor do they bear any resemblance to them. This twofold representation deficit fuels resentment and the rise of populist movements. Large numbers of citizens have the impression that politicians never see them; they feel they have become invisible, particularly in rural areas in the United States or in many popular districts in France.[26] They feel they are not represented.

It is true that, in "representative" democracy, representativeness can have a dual meaning. On the one hand, to what extent are our representatives actually *representative* of citizens? To what extent do they "resemble" them in terms of education, income, property, and so on? On the other hand, to what extent do the decisions made by our representatives actually represent the preferences of the majority (rather than those of a privileged minority)? We have seen from various studies, especially of the American data, that politicians largely tend to heed the preferences only of a privileged minority.

Hence the importance of the first conception of representation— although, obviously, the aim cannot be perfect representativeness, since that would entail random selection and the loss of all hope that we can choose the best equipped people to represent us. We can, however, aim for a situation where our elected representatives at least partly reflect the diversity of our societies. And as we shall see, we are a long way from such a mirror, even a distorting one.

Politicians in Our Likeness?

In theory, politicians are defined as "people's representatives." In practice, they rarely belong to the people they are supposed to represent. There is nothing new about this, of course, but the gap has grown so wide in recent years that the accumulated wealth of cabinet ministers features on the front-page headlines (and cannot but fuel the collapse of public confidence in politicians). In the United States, the combined wealth of the cabinet nominated by Donald Trump after his election was greater than that of tens of millions of Americans combined.[27] According to *Forbes* magazine, Trump's first cabinet, with a combined wealth of $4.3 billion, was the richest in the history of the United States.[28] Trump himself, who has a talent for the pithy phrase, put it perfectly at a rally in Iowa in June 2017: "I love all people, rich or poor, but in those particular positions, I just don't want a poor person. Does that make sense?"[29]

Emmanuel Macron, who loves fine clothes (earned by sheer hard work, of course), would probably not have dared to use such language, but one imagines that he would not really disagree. In any case, his own first government, with its many millionaires, is not far behind Trump's. According to figures published by the High Authority for Transparency in Public Life (HATVP), twelve of its thirty-two members are millionaires. And the personal fortune of Muriel Pénicaud, one of its leading lights, who, as we saw in Chapter 4, knows how to exploit all the tax loopholes, has risen to 7.5 million euros.[30] That's only a few hundred thousand euros more than Macron's first ecology minister, Nicolas Hulot.

This unrepresentativeness is far from peculiar to ministers; indeed, it is in some ways even more disturbing in the case of elected representatives. In the United States, Nicholas Carnes has documented the predominance of white-collar professions in Congress.[31] In the year 2000, when employees and blue-collar workers represented 54 percent of the national workforce, they accounted for barely 2 percent of members of Congress; and no Supreme Court judge or president since the end of the Second World War had been an employee or manual worker before assuming public office. This is certainly not a recent development, since no more than 2 percent of congressmen have ever come from the ranks of the working class.[32]

In the United Kingdom, in the immediate postwar period, employees and manual workers accounted for as much as 17 percent of Members of Parliament—much less than their share of the active population, but more than the corresponding percentages in the United States or France (Figure 67).[33] This relatively significant representation was unique to the Labour Party—I noted earlier its close historical links with the unions. In fact, the percentage of Labour MPs coming from the working classes

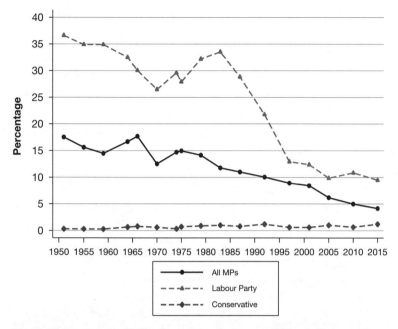

Figure 67. Percentage of MPs who were workers or employees before entering Parliament, United Kingdom, 1951–2015

remained above 25 percent (even rising above 35 percent in the early 1950s) until the end of the 1980s, whereas the comparable figure for Conservative MPs was never higher than 1.2 percent. As working-class representation collapsed within the Labour Party—a phenomenon linked to its growing dependence on private individual and corporate donations as opposed to membership dues—so too has it gradually crumbled in the House of Commons over the past thirty years. Today, a little under 5 percent of MPs had a working-class job before they entered the UK Parliament.

In the French National Assembly, the great majority of deputies are drawn from the higher socio-professional categories. Managerial staff, higher intellectual professions, and intermediate professions alone account for 80 percent of deputies (including 20 percent for managers in the private and public sectors).[34] In 2017, there were only fourteen private-sector nonmanual workers (less than 2.5 percent) in the National Assembly, whereas such workers today account for 27.4 percent of the active population in France. Deputies are also much more likely than the average population to be university graduates.[35] As for manual workers, they are literally absent from the assembly.[36] Not only did no deputy have such an occupation at the time of his or her election; there are only three former manual workers among the French representatives: Alain Bruneel (Communist Party), who worked in a textile factory from the age of fourteen and was retired at the time of his election; Dino Cinieri, a former steelworker, who had also retired when he was set to work on the assembly benches; and Denis Sommer, a former worker at Peugeot and a secondary teacher at the time of his election.

This pattern is far from new. Figure 68 shows the percentage of private-sector manual and nonmanual workers in the National Assembly

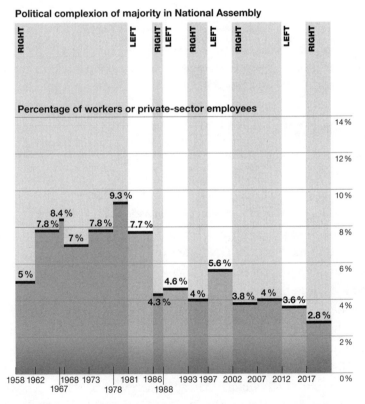

Figure 68. Percentage of deputies who were workers or private-sector employees before entering the National Assembly, France, 1958–2021

for each legislature of the Fifth Republic in France.[37] This percentage has never been higher than 10 percent, and although it rose slightly in the 1960s and 1970s, it has been declining ever since. Also worthy of note is that, with the exception of the eleventh legislature (1997–2002), which saw a very small rise in the percentage of workers, the Left's record during its periods in government is no better in this respect than that of the Right.

Finally, we should note that politicians in today's France form a professional political caste—not only because those in power sometimes desperately cling to it, but also because (as Julien Boelaert, Sébastien Michon, and Étienne Ollion have shown, on the basis of years of investigating changes in French political life) anyone who wishes to assume national office must have already spent many years in politics.[38] The latest legislature is obviously an exception in this respect, which should probably be seen more as characteristic of a particular moment in history rather than as the beginning of a new trend. Although 75 percent of the

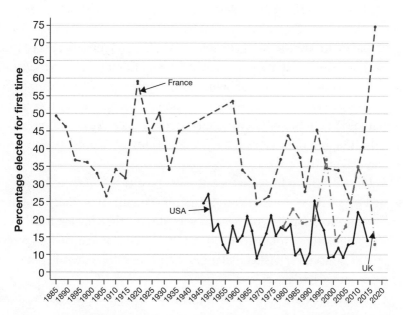

Figure 69. Legislative elections, percentage of representatives elected for the first time, France, the United States, and the United Kingdom, 1885–2017

membership of the National Assembly was renewed in 2017,[39] the long-term, systemic tendency in the Fifth Republic is for newly elected members to constitute less than 45 percent (Figure 69); this may not seem much, but it is not a low figure in comparative international terms. In legislative elections since 1980, the percentage of deputies elected for the first time has averaged 40 percent for France, 23 percent for the United Kingdom, and a mere 14 percent for the United States.[40] In any case, variations in the rate of renewal change nothing in the essential fact that certain social categories are never represented.[41]

A Representation Deficit More Passively Undergone Than Actively Chosen

Why, then, are the working classes so little represented among elected politicians in France or the United States? Does the situation reflect a shortage of candidates, so that workers simply do not put themselves forward to be elected? Or—at the risk of being politically incorrect—should we conclude that voters are not keen on working-class candidates and consider them to be incompetent? Did not Donald Trump in the United States—like Silvio Berlusconi in Italy years before him—campaign on the theme that his personal financial success was proof of his capacity to run the country? It is a pity that no journalist asked him to explain why in reality he underperformed the financial markets, as John M. Griffin has clearly shown. For if Trump in 1976 had simply invested his $200 million in investment products linked to an index mainly centered on real estate,[42] he would be twice as rich ($23.2 billion) as he is today ($10 billion) as a result of his actual investments. Upsetting for a financial genius, no?

Let us take this a little further. If voters really do prefer to be represented by senior executives rather than less qualified workers, judging the former to be more competent, why should they have a fixed percentage of workers imposed on them in the Parliament or Congress? Why go against their wishes and impose representatives they do not trust and do not wish to have?

I will not spend time answering this question at a philosophical or ethical level—for the good reason that what it assumes is not in fact the case. Voters do not prefer the richest candidates. On the contrary, they have a preference for working-class candidates, identifying with them more and considering them to be just as qualified. Nicholas Carnes and Noam Lupu have shown this in their investigations, not only for the United States but also for Argentina and the United Kingdom.[43] When voters are asked to choose between a manager or senior executive and a working-class candidate (an ordinary factory worker, for example), they express no preference in the United Kingdom or Argentina (all other things being equal) and a slight preference for working-class candidates in the United States. Why? Quite simply, they do not think that executives are more qualified than workers, and even consider the latter to be more capable of sharing their concerns.

But if underrepresentation of the working classes among our elected representatives does not reflect the actual political preferences of citizens, what exactly does it reflect? Now that we have reached the final chapter of this book, you must know that, in my view, at least part of the answer lies in the capture of the electoral process by the weight of money.[44] In a country like the United States, it costs a huge amount to finance an election campaign, and even more to win one. Of course, candidates do not pay for everything out of their own pockets, but you can imagine that it is much easier for a middle-class candidate than for a working-class candidate to raise the funds from his or her circle of friends—or, if necessary, to obtain a bank loan. Even in France, where there is a ceiling on permitted expenditure, the availability of ready cash creates a dividing line between those who can and those who cannot run for office. Apart from anything else, a campaign commitment entails a serious financial risk when you know that you have to obtain 5 percent of the vote in the first round to stand a chance of being reimbursed.

The solutions would seem to be obvious. The first is to limit the weight of private money in election campaigns; I showed in previous chapters the urgent need for a genuine system of public funding and for a ban on private contributions above a certain ceiling (or of any size). This first stage—preferably together with a "democracy bank" that allows candidates to be on an equal footing for the reimbursement of expenses[45]—would clearly provide a partial solution to the problem.

But again, this is not enough. What needs to be done to ensure that our representatives are more like ourselves? How can it be guaranteed that, if workers represent 20 percent of the active population, they do not represent less than 2 percent of our parliamentarians? The answer is simple. If we want the system to change, well, it is necessary to force it open for the representation of all categories of workers and the new groups without secure employment. And the means to achieve that is the introduction of social seats in national parliaments.[46] This is the second part of the democratic revolution that I propose in this book.

For a Democratic Revolution: Making Parliament Socially Diverse

Today, the French National Assembly has 577 deputies, the UK House of Commons 650 members, the German Bundestag 598 seats, the US House of Representatives 435 members, and so on. What I propose is that tomorrow, in each of these assemblies, a significant proportion of seats—let us say a third, but it could be a half or more—should be reserved for members elected by proportional representation on lists that are genuinely *representative* of the social-occupational reality of the population. In France, for example, this could mean that at least 50 percent of the lists would have to be made up of blue-collar workers, employees, and workers in new forms of insecure employment.

One Person, Two Votes: Political Representatives and Social Representatives

To be more specific, two elections might take place simultaneously for the National Assembly (or the Bundestag, the House of Commons, or the House of Representatives). For the two-thirds of constituency-based seats, the electoral rules would be unchanged;[47] it would simply be necessary to reduce by a third the number of such seats, bringing it down to 385 in France or 433 in the United Kingdom.

For the remaining third of seats, there would be a PR system with national lists based on social-occupational parity. Thus, a *minimum* of half of the candidates on each list would have to have a working-class occupation at the time of the election. In France today, working-class citizens represent a little more than 48 percent of people in employment, and this is why I propose a provisional threshold of 50 percent that may rise or fall as that proportion changes. Social categories more in line with the histories of other countries, or with the terminology in use there ("manual workers," "blue-collar workers," and the like), might also be applied. But I understand the working-class category in a very broad sense that includes all the insecure workers, such as Uber drivers, Deliveroo deliverers, and so on, who labor under the control of the new micro-entrepreneurs.

In the case of France, these national lists would consist of 192 candidates, and the ones actually elected would be chosen in the order in which they appear on the lists and in accordance with the election results. But ninety-six candidates on each list would have to be in the working-class category (or potentially more, since 50 percent is the minimum threshold). Since the candidates are chosen from the top of the list down, so that the spirit of the reform is not distorted, at least every second candidate will have to be a worker; this will be a sine qua non for a list to be valid. We know only too well that, if financial or other penalties are applied after the event, political groups and movements often prefer to pay them rather than comply with representativity requirements. My proposal is simply that the principle of gender-parity lists, in place since the regional elections of 2000 in France and introduced recently in countries such as Argentina, Japan, and Tunisia for local and / or national elections, should apply to the election of social representatives to the Parliament, with the important difference that the principle of every second candidate being a worker is a minimum threshold rather than a fixed requirement that cannot be exceeded.[48]

Will it be difficult to constitute such lists? Clearly not—as we can see at once if we glance at the socio-occupational origins of union representatives. Thomas Breda, who has thoroughly studied this question, estimates that 34.6 percent of staff representatives are blue-collar workers (*ouvriers*) in France and 25.9 percent are employees (*employés*), while the corresponding percentages for union delegates are 32.8 percent and 19.1 percent. In other words, these delegates are just like the set of people they represent (33.1 percent blue-collar workers and 26.6 percent employees in the sample that he studies).[49] If there is a representativity deficit, it is at the level of political democracy as it functions today, not at the level of social democracy. Bringing social democracy into Parliament or the House of Representatives will make it possible to reduce some of this deficit.

This raises one last question: Who will be able to present lists for the election of the social representatives? In the model I propose, not only the existing political parties and movements will qualify, but also any recognized representative trade association or any organization that commits itself to presenting candidates in the next trade elections. I say "any organization" and not "any union organization," because the lists do not have to be constituted only by existing unions that represent workers at the time of the parliamentary elections. The logic here is the same as for political movements and parties: it is urgently necessary that our democracy acquire a new dynamism. Hence, success cannot be required in advance before an organization is authorized to present candidates.

Is there not a danger that such a system will end up multiplying the number of lists and making representation more fragmented? It is right to ask the question, and I will try to answer it. On the first point, let us note that in today's elections of constituency representatives, no particular conditions are required for a citizen to stand; he or she has only to be on the electoral register, which is why there are so many candidates in the first round (in two-round systems) or in the primaries (in first-past-the-post systems) in every constituency. So why would one want to restrict the candidates who can run in the election of social representatives? Once an organization is capable of presenting a national list of 192 candidates, at least 50 percent of whom are working-class citizens, it will be legally entitled to stand if, not being a political party in the terms of the law, it has either stood in the preceding trade elections or undertaken to present candidates in the forthcoming trade elections.

On the second, more important point, an election under proportional representation requires the setting of a threshold,[50] which I suggest should be 1 percent (although that can obviously be discussed). In other words, only lists that receive 1 percent or more of the national vote will qualify to have social seats in Parliament. This threshold may appear low, especially to anyone thinking of the present rules for labor union representativity; after all, in order to have the "representative" status to negotiate a collective agreement, an employees' union must have obtained at least 8 percent of the votes cast in the first round of the last trade elections nowadays in France.[51]

My own view is that this 1 percent threshold is not too low. First, what makes sense for collective bargaining does not necessarily make sense for electoral democracy, where a threshold of 8 or 10 percent seems much too high and—contrary to the aim of injecting new dynamism—would directly favor the most established parties and organizations. Even in Germany, the lower limit for a list to be represented in the Bundestag is only 5 percent. Second, we need to keep in mind the special situation of the newly precarious groups of workers, who suffer even more acutely than others from both the political and the social representation deficit. In the developed countries, union organizations were built historically around the model of wage labor, and their prime role is to stand together with the workforce in negotiations with the shareholders. However, work has less and less the character of wage labor, partly because of the development of micro-entrepreneurship in the shape of Uber or Deliveroo, but also because media outlets often pay journalists in royalties or require them to submit bills for their work. And where workers have to endure micro-entrepreneurship, it is necessary to think of microrepresentation: that is, political movements or labor unions representing a few (at least 1) percent of the vote should be present in Parliament to defend the interests of this new category of economically dependent workers.

Two Representatives for One College: A More Representative and United Assembly

So, this is the second revolution I propose: a revamped Parliament where a third of representatives are elected by PR on lists containing at least 50 percent working-class citizens. All the representatives, both political and social, would meet in the same assembly and have the same prerogatives. This is the fundamental difference from previous proposals to reform the representation of economic and social interests. Dominique Rousseau, for instance, proposes the creation of a social assembly.[52] But in his schema, this would be a third assembly, alongside the existing National Assembly and Senate in France, both of which would have the same prerogatives as before.[53] In my view, it is not by adding new layers that we will solve the problem of today's democratic deficit, but rather by profoundly changing the existing layers and, in particular, the functioning of the National Assembly / House of Commons / House of Representatives / and so on and the representativeness of those elected to sit on their benches.

You are probably asking yourselves how parliamentary groups will fit into the picture. In France today, it is necessary to have at least fifteen elected deputies to constitute a group—which is not a minor detail, since parliamentary groups play an extremely important role. In particular, they determine how sessions are organized and how committees are constituted. Should the minimum threshold of fifteen be lowered to take account of the arrival of new assembly members, some of whom may have been chosen from lists that do not feature in today's assembly? That is not what I am advocating here. The point of a socially mixed national assembly is not to multiply the forces present within it, through the creation of new parliamentary groups representing the interests of such and such a social group, but rather to introduce greater social representativity and social dialogue.

What is necessary, however, is a definitive ban on the holding of multiple offices by any elected representative—a ban, that is, not only on more than one simultaneous function but also on serving more than two terms in the assembly, even if they are not consecutive. New representatives—who, thanks to social parity, will no longer come only from the liberal professions or from positions allowing a quick return to employment—will have to be guaranteed a return to the job they held before, without suffering any kind of discrimination.[54] Furthermore, the firm for which they work should take into account the experience and skills they have gained from their time as assembly members. A ban on repeated terms in the assembly is also the best way to prevent the "bourgeoisification" of elected working-class representatives and the extreme professionalization of our political personnel.

Let Us Start Discussing!

Of course, the thresholds I propose here are not set in stone. I think that, to ensure real representativity, we need a daring and truly revolutionary reform—which is why I propose that a third of our representatives should be elected under a PR system, on lists including at least 50 percent working-class candidates. But the key thing is to get the reform started, and it may well be that the initial basis will be a little less ambitious, with, for example, only a quarter of representatives elected by PR. On the other hand, it might be possible to be more ambitious, so that, in countries where elections already take place under PR, the social parity requirement will apply to all lists.

Please also note that it is a dynamic reform, a reform "on the move." What I propose is that working-class citizens should make up at least 50 percent of the electoral lists for social representatives. But civil society is constantly evolving, and this will always have to be taken into account. Not only is the 50 percent threshold not fixed once and for all; it is meant to be adapted to each country's peculiarities.

Is there not a danger that, as various reactionaries will unfailingly suggest, the reform will leave us with a Parliament of incompetents? I do not think so. I have already partly responded to a similar point that is often made against random selection. First of all, the intelligence of the Parliament is not the sum of its members' competences; it is the intelligence of its representatives as a group (which increases with their diversity). Furthermore, the professionals most represented historically in France's National Assembly have included not only lawyers but also surgeons, pharmacists, and dentists. And does anyone really think that dentists are more capable of voting on laws than workers? Is it that they are more used to making people suffer? More seriously, it is clear that the argument does not hold water. Every new member arrives in the assembly with his or her experience, knowledge, and aptitudes, but no one is an expert in everything from the start. Although representatives can be induced to express themselves on the whole range of issues, collective deliberation is what enables them to make the best decisions collectively.

It is important to remind ourselves that, in the case of new deputies elected in the spring of 2017 from the pro-Macron République en Marche (LREM), everyone applauded the LREM for sitting them down on school benches and giving them a fortnight's training. Why was this necessary? Obviously because they were novices on the benches of the assembly. So why could not the same be done with working-class deputies? Why would a few years of financial speculation have made them more capable than factory workers of voting on a reform to labor law?

One key point in conclusion. The proposed mixed assembly, with its much greater proportion of employees and manual workers, will ensure that our elected deputies are more representative. But we are not talking of random selection, of representative citizens pulled out of a hat. They will be qualified individuals who, in choosing to present themselves on electoral lists to champion their ideas, have shown their capacity to win over voters through listening and debate. In terms of their mentality, this makes them more akin to union representatives than to randomly selected officials. And having had many opportunities to discuss and debate with politicians as well as union representatives, I can say that the former are by no means always more qualified or better informed for the task of scrutinizing a proposed reform.

Advantages of the Mixed Assembly: Its Members Are More Like Ordinary Citizens and Will Make Better Decisions

Today, in countries like France, working-class citizens make up approximately 50 percent of the active population. With the reform I am proposing, they will not constitute 50 percent of the Parliament, but they will make up *at least* 50 percent of the "social representatives," that is, of the third of parliamentarians elected by PR on social parity lists. That will already be close to a revolution in comparison with the present situation. And it might radically change the economic and social policies pursued by the government.

Another probable effect of this reform will be to strengthen the labor unions, and therefore working-class political representation. Nicholas Carnes has shown that the collapse of the workers' already weak presence in American legislatures was linked to the decline of the unions.[55] For when unions are closely linked to political parties, the position of union representative is one possible path to political office for working-class citizens. It is a narrow path, but at least it has the merit of existing;

when union membership is very low, all the paths to political representation seem to be closed.[56]

It may still be asked—and here we come back to the question of dual representation that I mentioned before—why politicians must absolutely be people in our own likeness. Why insist on ethnic, gender, social, or other kinds of diversity in politics, if they do not ultimately affect the decisions that are taken?

The fact is that they greatly affect the decisions taken, as Nicholas Carnes and others have documented in the case of the United States.[57] What he shows—and is it so surprising?—is that elected representatives vote in keeping with their occupational (and social) origins. A moment ago, we asked why policymaking reflects only the preferences of the most advantaged groups in society, and we saw that part of the reason is that these contribute most of the finances for election campaigns. But another part of the answer is that our representatives belong to the social class of the most advantaged. They therefore vote simply in accordance with their own preferences.

Let me return for a moment to what I called the hypocrisy of Silicon Valley philanthropists, our friends in Chapter 4 who grind their teeth at the idea of paying taxes but would like to be congratulated for their spontaneous generosity. They claim to be serving the public interest, but what of their actual preferences? They tell us that, even if the high-tech magnates contribute mostly to Democratic election campaigns, they are strongly opposed to any form of regulation, particularly of the labor market, and are eager to undermine the influence of unions.[58]

To make the workers' voice heard and give their preferences some representation, there must be people who were workers when they entered Parliament and will be workers again when they leave it.[59] As Carnes shows, if the share of workers in the US Congress had reflected their share in the population, the support in Congress for George W. Bush's tax cuts would have been reduced from 62 percent to 28 percent; a huge gift to the rich would not have been made. Thus, the best way to ensure that the preferences of the majority are finally considered is to introduce a greater mix in the occupational origins of the men and women who represent us. And that is the point of my proposal to build a social dimension into the national assembly.

These considerations on the social origin of parliamentarians are also applicable to gender. If it is so important to have male-female parity in politics, it is not only because of the principle of gender equality, but also because it has an impact on policymaking and the ways in which policy decisions are implemented.[60] In the US Congress, for instance, draft legislation introduced by women gains on average more co-sponsors than legislation introduced by men, and Republican congresswomen also have a greater chance of obtaining bipartisan support for the legislation they advocate.[61] In the case of India, Raghabendra Chattopadhyay and Esther Duflo have shown that when women—rather than men—headed municipal councils, there was more investment particularly in the provision of drinking water.[62] Interestingly, their study is based on the existence of reserved seats for women in India since the mid-1990s; all citizens (men and women) vote to choose their representatives, but only women do so for these seats.

India, the world's largest democracy, has also gone the farthest in introducing genuine social parity in its legislative bodies. Since independence, it has established quotas for social groups that have historically suffered discrimination (the "scheduled castes," also called "untouchables" or "Dalits").[63] This takes the form of constituencies (16 percent of the total) in which only candidates from those groups can run in legislative elections. There is nothing to stop them from being elected in non-reserved constituencies, but in practice that never seems to happen (and usually they do not even stand there as candidates). The official prop is therefore necessary: if the reserved constituencies did not exist, it is likely that no ex-untouchables would ever make it to the assembly. Similarly, we have seen that a prop is necessary in France, the United Kingdom, and the United States, since in effect the working classes are absent from Parliament there.

Of course, India has obvious peculiarities associated with forms of discrimination toward certain groups, and the mixed assembly that I propose for Western democracies differs in various ways from the Indian system of reserved constituencies. In particular, I suggest the introduction of socially mixed electoral lists, rather than reserved constituencies for working-class candidates. Nevertheless, it would be quite wrong to imagine that social exclusion is absent from our rich countries or that we have nothing to learn from Indian democracy. For decades now, it has been trying to use the rule of law to tackle and dissipate the consequences of extreme social inequalities.

Let us not be afraid to innovate! Let us not be afraid to rethink how our legislative bodies function by introducing into them a larger social mix. The great majority of citizens have everything to gain from it. For an assembly with greater social parity means not only representatives more akin to the citizens they represent, but also representatives who take account of the average citizen's preferences. Whereas resentment is what most people feel today toward politics and politicians, the kind of social revitalization I envisage will also involve winning back voters. Being better represented, they will relate more to the political process and, instead of staying away from the polling stations, will turn out to vote in greater numbers; they will also, I hope, accept that public money (from their taxes) should fund the operations of electoral democracy.

This is why public funding is so important. Only this time it must be evenly distributed: Democratic Equality Vouchers worth seven euros a year for each citizen, whatever his or her resources. Seven euros of public money in the shape of Democratic Equality Vouchers, plus strict limits on private funding so that no one can buy more votes than the ordinary man or woman in the street. Seven euros of Democratic Equality Vouchers plus democracy redefined as "one person, one vote." Democracy regained, modernized, and renewed. Democracy attuned to the reality of a twenty-first century already well under way.

Conclusion: The Prerequisites of "Permanent" Democracy

IN 1944, French women finally obtained the right to vote, more than 150 years after the first attempt at universal manhood suffrage was introduced in 1792.

It was not until 1948 that the United Kingdom abolished "university seats," which had given the privilege of a double vote to graduates at the most prestigious universities.

Although in 1870, ratification of the Fifteenth Amendment to the US Constitution guaranteed on paper the right of Afro-Americans to vote, it is only since 1965 that all black voters in the United States have been able to exercise their democratic rights. But even today those rights are sometimes limited, since many states disenfranchise anyone who has had dealings with the judicial or penal system, and this hits the black community particularly hard.

The first constitution establishing genuinely universal suffrage in Brazil, with no restrictions for education or literacy, was finally adopted in 1988.

And in Saudi Arabia, suffrage became universal (inclusive of women) only in 2015.

The history of universal suffrage has been bumpy and recent, just like the modern history of representative democracy. As for attempts to regulate the relationship between money and politics, their ancestry is even shorter. France, for example, had to wait until the turn of the 1990s to see the first real law on the funding of election campaigns and political parties, and even that is only a rough outline that deserves to be almost entirely rewritten.

What we are promised is democratic equality: "one person, one vote." The reality is quite different, and popular dissatisfaction with all the muddling through is plain to see. But it is possible to do much better; precisely because the history is recent, we can act upon it, change its course, become players ourselves. We cannot be fatalistic. We can and must use this unfinished history to rethink democracy and to dream wide awake of a better world. Such is the message of this book.

In the previous chapters, I highlighted the dangers of an oligarchic distortion of democracy in these early decades of the twenty-first century. And I proposed some solutions. These take their inspiration from two centuries of hopes, experiments, and failures to regulate the dangerous liaisons between private money and political democracy all around the world. My aim has been to give some historical truth to the idea of "permanent democracy," not in its (numerous) philosophical foundations, but in its practical application. To take one example: a referendum resulting from a people's initiative is a fine idea only if it goes together with strict regulation of campaign expenses—otherwise, private donations will ultimately decide the fate of this new expression of the people's will.

So, in this book I have closely examined the quantitative aspects of political funding and the attempts to regulate it through legislation. Unfortunately, as things stand today, the health of democracy is sometimes measured by the thermometer of private funding, and it has to be said that the fever is rising. I could mention a few of the key findings that have punctuated these pages. I could repeat that in 2016 the French government spent as much money on support for the political preferences of the top 0.01 percent—through direct or indirect political funding, and particularly tax relief on donations—as it did for those of the least advantaged half of the population. I could tell you again that in the United States in 2016 more than 5.4 billion euros of private funding were spent on election campaigns; that the UK Labour Party now relies more heavily on donations from corporations and wealthy individuals than on membership contributions (even if there has recently been something of an improvement); or that in the United States and Italy, two pioneers in the public funding of democracy in the early 1970s, the victories of populist parties—Donald Trump in the presidential election of 2016, the Five Stars Movement and the League in the legislative elections of 2018—occurred simultaneously with the final blow to the public funding of campaign expenditure.

In my view, the key point of which the reader should be aware is that new tools of direct democracy or a marginal change in voting systems would not be sufficient for our democracies to become genuinely representative. Unless the core issue of the funding of democracy is resolved beforehand, such innovations will yield no more than an illusion of greater representativeness and a further increase in frustrations.

The main difficulty is that the funding question is ignored in most countries, and that where academics and politicians do give it some attention they have failed to place it at the center of public debate. In the United States, Lawrence Lessig and Bernie Sanders are exceptions in this respect, as their election campaigns have highlighted the need to limit private donations. In practice, however, when the funding question has forced its way into the media, it has mostly prompted calls for the elimination of any kind of public subsidies. This is a particularly dangerous demand. What we hear from some is that it is high time to end the squandering of public money on a discredited political class. Special mention should be made here of Italy's Five Stars Movement, whose populist criticisms have finally borne fruit and put an end even to any partial reimbursement of election spending.

Well, I hope to have convinced you by now that the public funding of democracy—so long as it gives equal weight to all citizens—is more necessary than ever. We should reclaim this profoundly political measure and decide together how much we wish to be allocated to it. I have proposed seven euros per citizen, in the shape of Democratic Equality Vouchers. A little more might be in order, of course, but much less would not be desirable. Democracy has a price: it does not have to be exorbitant, but in the end it must be paid. What I have tried to show in this book is that it is preferable—for the representation of all citizens' preferences—that the cost is borne by public subsidies, rather than by the checkbooks of a few wealthy private donors.

Public Democracy, Private Democracy

The point is not only to advocate the public funding of democracy—direct subsidies to parties in accordance with precise rules, which today usually link them to past election results, but which in my proposed model follow an annual choice by all citizens—and to contrast this with private funding. More fundamentally, the debate counterposes the idea of "public democracy" to a drive to privatize the key forces of democracy, particularly the allocation of the public good. This drive is apparent, for example, in the numerous attacks on public broadcasting services, with the same underlying intent that one finds in speeches supporting privatization of the public health and education systems, and so on. It is as if the state no longer had a full role to play in deducting contributions, organizing redistribution, and guaranteeing access to fundamental public goods such as education, health, and information—as if it no longer had a role to play as a welfare state protecting everyone against the hazards of life.

These attacks against the redistributive state go together with an explosion of economic inequalities. In the past few decades, the richest sections of society have greatly profited from policies of privatization and deregulation: the value of private assets has been continually rising, while in many countries net public assets have entered negative territory. Now the super-privileged, who have benefited from economic privatization, would like to privatize politics as well. How? Once restrictions are lifted, all citizens can donate as much as they want—which means a very high concentration of donations—and candidates can spend to their heart's content. The end result is that the traditional parties of the Left stop defending the interests of the working classes. Following the conservative parties—but hiding behind the supposed constraints of globalization—they promote a lowering of corporate and wealth taxes, in favor of higher consumption taxes that place an increasing share of the burden of public spending on the shoulders of the least advantaged.

So, political inequalities continuously fuel economic inequalities, which in their turn foster economic inequalities, and so on. What is a positive escape route from all this? I would like to end by repeating my message: do not be afraid to allocate a few euros a year in public money to the funding of democracy! You already do this without knowing it. Or rather, most countries have a system whereby fiscal expenditure and tax relief for private donations mobilize the taxes paid by the majority so that a tiny privileged minority can use their wallets to bolster their political preferences. The first prerequisite for the regaining of democracy is to put an end to this "fiscal capture." With my proposals, the sums of public money spent for democracy—and especially for political parties—would not be greater than what is spent today in countries such as France, Spain, or Germany. But the sums would be equally spread among citizens. Democratic Equality Vouchers mean "one person, one vote." In countries such as the United Kingdom or the United States, where public funding is virtually nonexistent today, new public money would be disbursed for the functioning of political democracy. But at the same time, there would be much smaller sums of private money. To put it succinctly, it seems preferable to tax high incomes and to use the proceeds for the equal public funding of democracy, instead of leaving a handful of multimillionaires to use the same sums in support of candidates who will defend their economic interests.

I also think there should be an end to all the tax relief associated with donations to political foundations, or at least, to begin with, that they should be replaced with tax credits or a system of matching contributions, which would make all citizens equal from this point of view. As we have seen, there is an inherent contradiction in the idea of philanthropy in a democracy. But what if it was just collectively decided to make the highest earners (or largest owners) pay the most, instead of naïvely assuming that they will themselves contribute to the collective effort through the mechanism of philanthropy? What if it was decided to embrace public funding of the public good, instead of private funding of a public good that has in effect become privatized?

Naturally I understand people's distrust of political parties, and much of the evidence presented in this book shows that it is not without foundation. But this should not lead to a rejection of parties as such. My aim has not been to fuel the growing disenchantment with democracy or to hammer the traditional parties, but rather to dissect the past in order to prepare for the future. Nor is it a solution to write off democracy or the party system by throwing ourselves into the arms of right-wing populism. The only way forward is to rebuild the public funding of democracy, while tightly restricting private funding so that it is unable to capture democracy. A 200-euro ceiling on political donations may appear rather extreme, but it is the only viable solution in the long run. This is what we have learned from the little tour of the world that we have just completed.

Giving a Voice Back to the Working Classes

With Democratic Equality Vouchers and a drastic curtailment of private funding, politicians who today heed only the preferences of the rich (that is, of their financial backers) will tomorrow respond to the preferences of the majority who elect them. But the crisis of democracy is such that we need to go beyond the question of funding alone. To solve the representation deficit, it will be necessary to ensure that elected deputies are more representative of the population. This is the thinking behind a mixed assembly: to ensure that there is a significant proportion of working-class people in Parliament, with some elected under a PR system on lists embracing social parity. This should lead in turn to the emergence of new political movements, more popular in their composition and more aware of the reality of people's daily lives. The proposal will strike some as radical, but the truth is that it addresses today's radical exclusion of the popular classes from the political process. To revolutionize political democracy is also to take inspiration from social democracy—for example, from the fact that roughly half of union representatives are themselves blue-collar workers or employees. Why not also introduce time off from work for political representatives, in line with the model of union representatives? For, apart from the funding issue, time is one of the major problems facing working-class people who want to become involved in politics.

What position will be taken on all this by the labor unions, the traditional government parties of the Left, the new horizontally connected political movements, and, more generally, all the social and civic organizations that have emerged in recent years? I dare to hope that they will choose the path of a democratic revolution. I remember the figure of Colin Smith in *The Loneliness of the Long-Distance Runner,* that young English delinquent oppressed by authority figures who try to dictate his life. They say they want to raise him in the image of Ruxton Towers, the juvenile detention center to which he has been sent, and the governor there offers him the chance to gain privileges by excelling at competitive running. But the governor is self-interested: his motivation is not that Smith should succeed in life, but that the reformatory should win a sports competition against Ranley, a nearby private school. Colin Smith is a fine runner and is capable of coming first; he proves this by reaching the finishing line well ahead of the rest. But then he stops a few meters short and makes a bow as he lets the Ranley runner cross the line. Why? By voluntarily losing the race, Smith asserts that he is a free agent. He has demonstrated his talent, but he refuses to bend to the will of the powerful people who demand his victory.

The reader is in two minds, tempted to applaud Smith's splendid, uniquely forceful gesture in thumbing his nose at the authorities, but also well aware that he misses his opportunity by asserting his freedom in this way. In the end, Smith's decision leaves power in the hands of those who already have it. Stripped of privileges and returned to the machine shop, he even loses any possibility to protest. It is his mistake. It should not be repeated today. The working classes need to reenter the terrain of politics and electoral democracy. And the unions, new political movements, and citizens' organizations should help them by supporting the idea of a mixed assembly that allows them to present their own candidates to sit on its benches.

A Worldwide Struggle

The refounding of democracy concerns the whole planet. Although we have made a few ultra-brief side trips to Brazil and India, this book has essentially referred only to Western Europe and North America; it is one of its major limitations. Yet the lessons I have drawn from Western failures have a worldwide bearing: the new democracies of Africa, Asia, and Latin America will play at least as great a role as those of the West in constructing tomorrow's democratic ideal. And in many cases, responding to crises of their own, they may well take inspiration from historical experiences elsewhere, which are like an open book providing material to imagine a better world.

The corrupting role of money has just burst into the light of day in Latin America, for example. Of course, it is not as if no one was previously unaware that corporations could offer kickbacks to politicians; we need only look a few years back at scandals in France and Italy. Today, politicians are crashing to the ground. But what reforms will follow? The greatest democratic promises have always been built on the ground of crises. The proof is that Brazil has just taken a first step toward the public funding of its democracy. Let us hope that this will open the way for others.

I would also have liked to speak more of Africa, a major absence in these pages but not in the debate on forms of representation. The "price of a vote": many are the books that seek to understand what links corruption, ethnicity, public goods, and election results in various countries, and I would have needed much wider knowledge to dare to address this question. But it seems to me that, in a number of imperfect democracies, there is already an urgent need to think ahead and envisage an ambitious system of funding democracy. I have given much thought to this question in the case of the media. Of course, in countries where the government itself puts journalists behind bars, how can anyone think that the solution is to create a variety of political foundations? And in a country where the government controls who is allowed to run in elections, how can anyone imagine that the future of democracy hinges on public subsidies to parties and state funding for election expenditure?

Yet public funding is, in my view, the only path that will lead to the recovery of democracy. It is a path strewn with pitfalls, on which it will be necessary to fight both against private lobbies eager to preserve their financial electoral privileges and against a Far Right that has abandoned all hope in electoral democracy. But it is a path leading toward democratic equality: to one person, one vote. At last—and, let us hope, for a long time to come.

Notes

Preface

An online appendix is available on the website of the book: http://thepriceofdemocracy
.com/#en. It provides detailed information on all the data sources used to construct the
book's figures, as well as additional empirical evidence.

1. Géraldine Woessner (2018), "INFO JDD. Ce que révèle la liste des donateurs de
Macron," *Le Journal du Dimanche,* December 1, https://www.lejdd.fr/Politique/info
-jdd-ce-que-dit-la-liste-des-donateurs-de-macron-3811772; Julie Guesdon and
Sylvain Tronchet (2019), "Comment quelques centaines de grands donateurs ont
financé l'essentiel de la campagne présidentielle d'Emmanuel Macron," FranceInfo,
April 4, https://www.francetvinfo.fr/politique/emmanuel-macron/comptes-de
-campagne-d-emmanuel-macron/campagne-d-emmanuel-macron-decryptage-du
-systeme-d-ons_3426943.html.

2. See the note published by the Institute of Public Policies (2019), "Budget 2019:
Quels effets pour les ménages?" *Note de l'IPP,* no. 37, January.

3. Sam Wolfson (2019), "Why Ocasio-Cortez's Lesson in Dark Money Is the
Most-Watched Political Video," *The Guardian,* February 14, https://www.theguardian
.com/us-news/2019/feb/14/campaign-finance-but-make-it-viral-alexandria-ocasio
-cortezs-unlikely-video-hit.

4. See, in particular, Carrie Levine and Chris Zubak-Skees (2018), "How ActBlue
Is Trying to Turn Small Donations into a Blue Wave," FiveThirtyEight, October 25,
https://fivethirtyeight.com/features/how-actblue-is-trying-to-turn-small-donations
-into-a-blue-wave/.

5. Jennifer Epstein (2019), "Biden Tells Elite Donors He Doesn't Want to 'Demonize' the Rich," June 19, Bloomberg, https://www.bloomberg.com/news /articles/2019-06-19/biden-tells-elite-donors-he-doesn-t-want-to-demonize-the-rich.

6. See, for example, Paul Overby (2019), "Small Donors Hold the Key to Campaign Buzz and the Democrats' Debate Stage," NPR, March 23, https://www.npr.org /2019/03/23/705628236/small-donors-hold-the-key-to-campaign-buzz-and-the -democrats-debate-stage?t=1563261367757.

7. See Alex Isenstadt (2019), "GOP to Launch New Fundraising Site as Dems Crush the Online Money Game," *Politico,* June 23, https://www.politico.com/story /2019/06/23/republicans-win-red-2020-1377058.

8. Ruby Cramer (2019), "Elizabeth Warren's Campaign Turned to a Big Donor to Pay for the DNC Voter Database, Despite Her Fundraising Pledge," BuzzFeed, July 15, https://www.buzzfeednews.com/article/rubycramer/elizabeth-warren -fundraising-dnc.

9. Michelle Le Hee Yee, "In Need of Cash, Democratic Presidential Hopefuls Turn to Wealthy Donors," *Washington Post,* June 2, https://www.washingtonpost .com/politics/in-need-of-cash-democratic-presidential-hopefuls-turn-to-wealthy -donors/2019/06/02/725b2adc-824f-11e9-95a9-e2c830afe24f_story.html?utm_term= .bd30a71baa48.

10. A blockchain makes it possible to store digital data in a secure, decentralized manner. The "vote registration" is therefore unfalsifiable, because it rests upon a user-operated encryption system for each transaction.

11. Thomas Piketty (2019), *Capital et idéologie,* Paris: Le Seuil; English translation forthcoming, Harvard University Press.

12. Walter Lippmann (1993 [1925]), *The Phantom Public,* New Brunswick, NJ: Transaction Publishers. See also Walter Lippmann (1922), *Public Opinion,* New York: Harcourt, Brace. See Barbara Stiegler's (2019) excellent analysis in *"Il faut s'adapter." Sur un nouvel impératif politique,* Paris: Gallimard, which covers the long debate between Lippmann and John Dewey, and on which I partly base these remarks.

13. Lippman (1993), pp. 117–18.

14. Lippman (1993), p. 118.

15. Stiegler (2019), p. 63.

16. John Dewey (1946), *The Public and Its Problems,* quoted in Stiegler (2019), p. 114.

17. Mark Lilla (2017), *The Once and Future Liberal: After Identity Politics,* New York: HarperCollins.

18. Yascha Mounk (2018), *The People vs. Democracy: Why Our Freedom Is in Danger and How to Save It,* Harvard University Press.

19. Lilla (2017), p. 17.

20. See, in particular, Piketty (2019).

Introduction

1. On France, see Yasmine Bekkouche and Julia Cagé (2018), "The Price of a Vote: Evidence from France, 1993–2014," Centre for Economic Policy Research Discussion Paper #12614 (https://ideas.repec.org/p/cpr/ceprdp/12614.html); and, on the United Kingdom, Julia Cagé and Edgard Dewitte (2018), "It Takes Money to Make MPs: New Evidence from 150 Years of British Campaign Spending," Sciences Po Paris Working Paper (https://sites.google.com/site/juliacagehomepage/research). In both cases, the estimated price of a vote draws on empirical analysis of each candidate's expenditure and vote score, using variations between constituencies and election years; the results are presented in detail in Chapter 8. The political and economic literature on the influence of campaign spending on voting behavior is plentiful in the case of the United States, the country on which research has so far largely focused. For a review of this literature, see Stephen Ansolabehere, John de Figueiredo, and James Snyder (2003), "Why Is There So Little Money in US Politics?" *Journal of Economic Perspectives,* 17(1), pp. 105–130.

2. I am considering here the direct public funding of political parties and groups: that is, a little more than 63 million euros in 2016.

3. In 2016, 291,000 households declared one or more donations or membership fees to political parties in France, amounting to a grand total of 80 million euros. They benefited from tax reductions worth approximately 48 million euros, of which 29 million went to the richest 10 percent and 7.2 million to the richest 1 percent. See Chapter 3.

4. Donations to candidates—or to political parties—entitle donors to tax reductions as high as 66 percent of the sum in question. We shall return to this subject.

5. The average donation to a political party by the 0.01 percent of top-income French people is today higher than 5,000 euros. Of this, 3,300 euros are ultimately paid by the state and only 1,700 euros by the taxpayer in question. The average party donation by the 10 percent of citizens with the lowest incomes is 121 euros—entirely at their own expense. See Chapter 3 for a more detailed analysis.

6. Martin Gilens (2012), *Affluence and Influence: Economic Inequality and Political Power in America,* Princeton University Press, has well documented how today's politicians in the United States tend to address the preferences of the wealthiest groups (to the detriment of the least well off)—a phenomenon that he explains by the growing importance of private money in electoral competition.

7. We shall return to this at greater length. But we should note here that for anyone to benefit from a tax reduction linked to political donations or membership fees, he or she must first be liable to pay income tax. Thus, more than a half of households in France—the least well off—are effectively excluded from the tax advantages associated with the private funding of democracy.

8. In the United States, not only is turnout very low, but the minority who actually cast their votes are not representative of the electoral body as a whole. The weak participation automatically leads to a representation deficit. Moreover, abstention works disproportionately in favor of the Republican Party. According to survey data since the early 2000s, Democrats are overrepresented among abstentionists by roughly 16 percent; see Benjamin I. Page and Martin Gilens (2017), *Democracy in America? What Has Gone Wrong and What We Can Do about It,* University of Chicago Press.

9. Since 2014, Italy has introduced a system of *indirect* public funding of political parties, whereby the state pays to them a sum *proportionate to the income* of each citizen who expresses a political preference. In other words, the richer a citizen is in Italy, the more the state offers the chance to fund—gratis, out of general tax revenue—the political party of his or her choice. A poor citizen, on the other hand, has in reality no say over which parties will receive funding. See Chapter 2.

10. This is Peter Harris, owner of *inter alia* the famous Butlin's holiday complexes, who dipped into Shakespeare for his publicity slogan: "Our true intent is all for your delight." By all accounts, Harris is fond of his delights—only a long way from the historical spirit of the famous holiday camps for the English working classes.

11. On the pro-Trump spending in the last weeks of the campaign, a particularly useful source is Thomas Ferguson, Paul Jorgensen, and Jie Chen (2018), "Industrial Structure and Party Competition in an Age of Hunger Games: Donald Trump and the 2016 Presidential Election," Institute for New Economic Thinking Working Paper No. 66 (https://www.ineteconomics.org/uploads/papers/Ferg-Jorg-Chen-INET -Working-Paper-Industrial-Structure-and-Party-Competition-in-an-Age-of-Hunger -Games-8-Jan-2018.pdf).

12. Law No. 2017-1339 of September 15, 2017, on confidence in political life simply provided for "a loan arbiter in relation to political candidates and parties." By "facilitating dialogue between election candidates or political parties and groups and

credit institutions," he or she would "contribute to the legal and transparent funding of political life, with a view to promote (in accordance with Articles 2 and 4 of the Constitution) equal suffrage for all, plural expression of opinions, and equitable participation of political parties and groups in the democratic life of the Nation."

13. Many have forgotten that the Rassemblement du Peuple Français, founded by Charles de Gaulle in 1947, presented itself not as a party but as a "rally" of "the good people of France" *against* the traditional parties. To be sure, we would not expect to hear from the mouth of Emmanuel Macron a positively inflected phrase such as "good people" (*les braves gens*). However, the wish to promote a "movement" created "against the traditional parties" is fundamentally the same.

14. Yves Poirmeur, in his history of political parties in France, speaks of "political entrepreneurs" and "political markets." See his *Les Partis politiques. Du XIXe au XXIe siècle en France,* Paris: Lgdj, 2014.

15. In 2005 *Time* magazine, for example, named the "Good Samaritans" Bill and Melinda Gates, along with Bono, as its magnificent "persons of the year." They were supposedly "giving back their money rather than their voice"—but for what purpose if it is only to make their voices heard?

16. The shares were worth $50 billion at the time. This elicited a highly uncritical comment in a world-famous French evening paper: "In an age when rich countries are looking inward and trying to combat the havoc of globalization and the seeds of populism that it sows, digital fortunes aspire to a universality much greater than their own businesses, with resources greater than those of most states. . . . In this way, they highlight the need to redefine the role of nation-states, in a world where these no longer have a monopoly of the general interest." Universality of philanthropy against populism and nation-state egotism? There is something maddening about the argument, when you think that digital fortunes grow a little bigger every day through tax avoidance. Besides, large-scale recourse to philanthropy is a fiscal optimization strategy for these high-tech giants that claim to lecture governments in morality.

17. In Iran they would speak of the "Council of Experts."

1. The Cost of Democracy

1. See the estimates provided on the OpenSecrets website: https//www .opensecrets.org/news/2016/11/the-price-of-winning-just-got-higher-especially-in -the-senate/. To be precise, the average spending of a victorious senator in 2016 was $10.4 million, or $1.8 million more than in 2014. To this should be added the

expenditure of "independent committees," so that in total the expenditure in favor of a winning candidate was $19.4 million. We shall return in Chapter 7 to the ins and outs of American democracy.

2. This was the average spending of candidates who received more than 1 percent of the vote in the first round. It conceals major disparities, however, since some candidates incurred no expenses, while others spent 71,000 euros or more. We shall see in Chapter 8 the extent to which campaign spending influences the result obtained by each candidate.

3. I am not including here the purely formal cost of "organizing" elections. That is unavoidable. According to an estimate made in 2015 by Hervé Marseille for the French Senate, the organization of the presidential and legislative elections in 2012 cost the state between 259 and 354 million euros in total recorded expenses (on top of the flat-rate reimbursement of campaign spending, to which we shall return later). These included, for example, the costs of proxy voting, staffing polling stations at town halls, and holding municipally sponsored election meetings. In the United Kingdom, the cost of organizing the parliamentary elections in 2010 has been estimated at £113mn, or roughly £3.65 per voter. Patrick Scott and Sam Dean (2017), "How Much Will the 2017 General Election Cost?," *The Telegraph,* June 7 (http://www. telegraph.co.uk/business/0/much-will-2017-general -election-cost/).

4. This followed the Corrupt Practices Prevention Act of 1854, which made it compulsory for candidates to give a detailed breakdown of their spending but did not set any overall limit.

5. The reader may find in the online appendix to this book a chart of the evolution of total expenditure per candidate, as well as the evolution of average spending per candidate and of the number of candidates per election. Note that, until 1918, the costs of running an election—which accounted for a little under a fifth of total spending—were charged to the candidates.

6. In the online appendix, the evolution of average spending per candidate is presented in relation to per capita national income since 1868.

7. For obvious reasons, this form of expenditure was prohibited in 1883. The interested reader may refer to the excellent work: William B. Gwyn (1962), *Democracy and the Cost of Politics in Britain,* University of London, Athlone Press.

8. Christophe Jaffrelot explains the systematic corruption of the political class in India by the high cost of elections. According to his estimates, a candidate must come up with 130 to 140 million rupees (roughly 1.7 million euros) to get elected to

the lower house of Parliament. How can such a sum be raised? By entering into business (and most often being caught up in it): "We face a complicated situation today. You can never tell whether a deputy is primarily a businessman or a politician" (interview in *La Vie des idées*, February 2018).

9. Law No. 90-55 of January 15, 1990, concerning limits on election spending and the clarification of funding of political activities.

10. Speaking time and airtime are also strictly regulated in France during an election period. One can only welcome the principle of such rules, but the form they take today is no longer fit for purpose, and we shall discuss in Chapter 10 the ways in which they should be revised. Regarding self-promotion in the United Kingdom, a similar restriction has applied since the passing of the "1990 Broadcasting Act." In the United States, where in principle candidates can enjoy unlimited airtime—so long as they pay for it—TV advertising accounts for the largest share of campaign costs. We shall return in Chapter 8 to the structure of election spending on both sides of the Atlantic.

11. This was reinforced in 2004 with the passing of the Federal Electoral Reform (Bill C-24). With regard to Canada, the reader may consult Harold J. Jansen and Lisa Young (eds.) (2011), *Money, Politics, and Democracy. Canada's Party Finance Reforms*, Vancouver: University of British Columbia Press.

12. The state does, however, grant various kinds of indirect aid, such as the free provision of billboard space by local councils during campaigning periods. See Marie Göransson and Jean Faniel, "Le financement et la comptabilité des partis politiques francophones," in the weekly paper of the Centre de Recherche et D'information Socio-Politiques, January 1, 2008, pp. 6–92.

13. The election period lasts three months in Belgium, or forty days in the event of an early dissolution of Parliament. For a candidate standing for the Chamber of Representatives, as well as for his or her first "alternate" (substitute), the ceiling on expenditure is 5,000 euros (2,500 euros for other alternates). Only the "first" candidates, those at the top of a list, are authorized to spend more, the ceiling in their case being 8,700 euros plus 0.035 euros per voter registered in the electoral arrondissement (a very low figure by international standards). The Belgian electoral system for the Chamber of Representatives is based on party-list voting by proportional representation; the Chamber consists of 150 deputies directly elected in a single round, in eleven electoral constituencies. The number of candidates at the top of each list is equal to the number of mandates obtained by that list in the last elections plus one.

14. Thus, an average of nine candidates stood for election in France in 1993, compared with fewer than five in the United Kingdom in the previous year.

15. Whereas in France today, candidates in legislative elections can spend as much as 38,000 euros plus 0.15 euros per resident of their constituency, in the United Kingdom the ceiling is set at £8,700 plus £0.06 per resident of (rural) "borough constituencies" and £0.08 per resident of (urban) "county constituencies."

16. Yasmine Bekkouche and Julia Cagé (2018), "The Price of a Vote: Evidence from France, 1993–2014," CEPR Discussion Paper #12614 (https://ideas.repec.org/p/cpr /ceprdp/12614.html).

17. For figures for European countries, see for example the OECD's *Government at a Glance* publications.

18. Maurice Duverger (1951), *Les partis politiques,* Armand Colin.

19. Peter Mair (2013), *Ruling the Void. The Hollowing of Western Democracy,* Verso.

20. Mair is certainly not right when he points to the public funding of parties as one reason behind their crisis and their weaker roots in society; private funding most often is such a factor, promoting as it does a lack of government responsiveness to citizens' preferences. We shall return to this issue in Chapter 7.

21. Alan S. Blinder (1997), "Is Government Too Political?" *Foreign Affairs,* 76(6), pp. 115–126.

22. John H. Aldrich and John D. Griffin (2018), *Why Parties Matter: Political Competition & Democracy in the American South,* University of Chicago Press.

23. "While Jim Crow laws had many consequences, one of particular relevance . . . is that they made possible the ascension of the Democratic Party to become essentially the only game in town for aspiring politicians and thus for the ability to shape politics and policy in the southern states for half a century. They were, in many ways, akin to the one party in a one-party authoritarian state" (Aldrich and Griffin [2018], p. 119).

24. Robert Michels (1961), *Political Parties: A Sociological Study of the Oligarchical Tendencies of Modern Democracy,* New Brunswick, NJ: Transaction Publishers, originally published in German in 1911.

25. In the case of Michels, the disappointment was reinforced by the fact that he failed to be selected as an SPD candidate for parliamentary elections.

26. See Lipset's interesting preface to the 1961 edition of Michels's *Political Parties.*

27. The accounts of the AfD, a noisy newcomer on the political scene, are available only for the years since its foundation in 2013. I shall therefore disregard them in calculating the average spending of German political parties for the whole period from 1984 to 2015. But the party's success, though less talked about than Brexit or Trump's election, is one of the most disturbing political developments of recent years in Europe, since it marks the return of the German Far Right to Parliament for the first time since the Second World War.

28. It is not surprising that the average annual spending of the French Socialist Party was higher than that of the Republicans during the 2012–2016 period. This followed automatically from the PS victory in the legislative elections of 2012 and did not mean that it had healthier finances. Indeed, even when it is in power, the PS is much less fortunate than the Republicans in terms of private funding. But in France public funding partly makes up for this unequal access to donations.

2. The Private Funding of Democracy

1. Most notably through the Civil Service Reform Act of 1883.

2. See especially Arthur B. Gunlicks (1993), *Campaign and Party Finance in North America and Western Europe,* Boulder, CO: Westview Press.

3. The Federal Election Commission (FEC) was created only in 1975, following the passage of the Federal Election Campaign Act (FECA) in 1971 (amended in 1974). Similarly, in Canada, while donations to parties and election campaigns were prohibited in 1908 (with the Dominion Election Act), this had virtually no effect because of the lack of any enforcement agency. Eventually, donations became legal again in 1930.

4. The precise legal definition of a PAC is a committee whose purpose is to raise and spend money for the election or the defeat of a candidate. PACs must register with the FEC within ten days of their formation.

5. Such accounts are known as "additional national party committee accounts." For more details about these, the reader may consult the FEC site: https://www.fec .gov/help-candidates-and-committees/candidate-taking-receipts/contribution-limits -candidates.

6. This does not even include party donations from the cigarette industry association, the Verband der Cigarettenindustrie E.V.

7. Daimler is active not only in the automobile sector but also in aerospace.

8. Laws No. 88-226 and 88-227 of March 11, 1988, on the financial transparency of political life.

9. The CNCCFP was created by Law No. 90-55 of January 15, 1990, on the limitation of election spending and the clarification of the funding of political activities. It began work on June 19, 1990.

10. It is difficult to speak of "political parties" in France before 1901, given the major restrictions imposed by Article 291 of the Penal Code of 1810 and further tightened by the law of April 10, 1834. With the law of March 21, 1884, this article no longer applied to trade unions and professional associations, whose purpose was defined as "the study and defense of industrial, commercial and agricultural economic interests." But it continued to apply to parties, which were deemed to defend political interests at a national level. In *1884, la fabrique du syndicalisme,* Lormont: Le Bord de l'eau, Stéphane Sirot (2014) has convincingly shown how the authorization of labor unions was designed to avoid the politicization of workers and destabilization of the Republic; we shall return to this in Chapter 11, when we discuss the complex relations between parties and unions. In the late nineteenth century, however, political parties enjoyed a certain tolerance on the part of the authorities (see, e.g., Yves Poirmeur and Dominique Rosemberg [2008], *Droit des partis politiques,* Paris: Ellipses; and Jean-Claude Bardout [2001], *L'Histoire étonnante de la loi 1901. Le droit des associations avant et après Pierre Waldeck-Rousseau,* Lyon: Juris).

11. The size of membership dues was tightly regulated: the law of 1901 set a ceiling of 500 francs.

12. André Campana (1976) *L'Argent secret,* Paris, Arthaud. Readers interested in the vagaries of legislation on the corporate funding of political life in France may also like to consult the excellent writings of Éric Phélippeau, particularly his (2013) "Le financement de la vie politique française par les entreprises 1970–2012," *L'Année sociologique,* 63(1), pp. 189–223.

13. The CNPF (National Council of French Employers), founded after the Liberation in 1945, survived through the postwar period until 1998, when it was superseded by the Mouvement des entreprises de France (MEDEF, Movement of the Enterprises of France).

14. In other words, as the website of the CNCCFP (the French Commission on Election Financing) makes clear, a natural person under private law that sets itself a political aim is considered a political party if (1) it has benefited from state aid or has regularly designated an agent, and (2) it has filed accounts certified by one or two CNCCFP auditors. Article 4 of the Constitution of 1958 already defined political parties, but only in terms of their aims, particularly the casting of votes, the

organization of political life and debate, and the selection of candidates ("Political parties and groups shall contribute to the exercise of the popular vote. They shall be formed and exercise their activities freely. They must respect the principles of national sovereignty and democracy").

15. In addition, donations and membership dues to political parties and groups are capped at 15,000 euros a year per taxable household. It is interesting to note that the legislation limiting an individual's *total donations* to 7,500 euros a year—rather than specifying a sum for *each* party—was intended to close a loophole whereby parties in the early 2000s had set up microparties to maximize their funding from private sources. The annual accounts filed by various parties at the CNCCFP mention a number of political groups with surprising names such as "The Pink Fish Current" or "Party for the Defense of Animals" (which, I imagine, include fish), as well as groups defending real, if highly local, interests, such as the "Information Association for Residents of the 16th Arrondissement." This proliferation reminds one of the reactions to Article 291 of the Penal Code of 1810, the main aim of which had been to hinder the formation of political parties by banning associations consisting of more than 20 persons. The subsequent period saw a multiplication of election organizations consisting of branches with 19 members each—until the Law of April 10, 1834, finally clamped down by specifying that "the provisions of Article 291 are applicable to associations of more than 20 persons, even when these are divided into branches with a lesser number." On Article 291 of the Penal Code of 1810, see Yves Poirmeur (2014), *Les Partis politiques. Du XIXᵉ au XXIᵉ siècle en France,* Paris: Lgdj.

16. Before 1989, Belgian legislation did not provide either for a cap on campaign spending or for the legal definition and monitoring of political parties. From 1971, however, following an administrative decision by the Chamber of Deputies, the Bureau of the Chamber granted operating subsidies to recognized political groups. On Belgium, see especially Karolien Weekers (2009), "Explaining the Evolution of the Party Finance Regime in Belgium," *Journal of Elections, Public Opinion and Parties.*

17. The median wage in France is 1,772 euros a month; see http://www.insee.fr/fr/statistiques/1370897.

18. I say "apparently" because these were the figures released in dribs and drabs during the presidential campaign, although Macron's party, with a certain hypocrisy, took refuge behind the law by refusing to publish a detailed breakdown of the various kinds of donations or a list of its largest benefactors. It is interesting

to note that, while France developed more restrictive legislation on the size of donations than Germany, the United States, or the United Kingdom, and while donations by corporate entities have been prohibited there since 1995, French law no longer requires the publication of lists of donors or information about the size of their donations. It is as if a cap on donations meant there was no longer any need for transparency about the private funding of the democratic process (and vice versa).

19. Since the ceiling on donations was 7,500 euros, these sponsors could not together have contributed more than 4.5 million euros.

20. Figures obtained from the French Finance Ministry in October 2017 by the chairman of the Senate finance committee, concerning the one hundred taxpayers who received the largest tax reductions following President Macron's first round of measures. This has resulted from the conversion of the French wealth tax (ISF) into a property wealth tax (IFI) and from the introduction of a flat 30 percent tax on income from capital. See "Budget: les 100 plus riches gagneront 1,5 million d'euros par an chacun," *Libération,* October 26, 2017, http://www.liberation.fr/france/2017/10/26/ budget-les-100-plus-riches-gagneront-15-million-d-euros-par-an-chacun_1605917.

21. On the United States, see especially the studies produced by the Tax Policy Center and the Joint Committee on Taxation.

22. The following payments benefit from a tax reduction: (1) donations to an approved election funding association or a fiscal agent for the funding of an election campaign, which are written to the campaign account of a candidate or list; (2) donations to an approved party funding association; (3) subscriptions to political parties and groups.

23. It is important to note that individuals pay taxes in France even if they are not liable to income tax. Low-paid workers are in fact heavily taxed, at effective rates as high as 45 to 50 percent, because of their payment of consumption taxes and social contributions, whereas the comparable rates for the richest sections of the population are 30 to 35 percent. This is well documented in Camille Landais, Thomas Piketty, and Emmanuel Saez (2011), *Pour une révolution fiscale. Un impôt sur le revenu pour le XXIe siècle,* Paris: Le Seuil.

24. This is not the case in all countries. In Italy, for instance, while donations to parties entitle donors to a tax rebate, membership dues do not qualify for the same benefit.

25. Julia Cagé (2016), *Saving the Media: Capitalism, Crowdfunding, and Democracy,* Harvard University Press.

26. In the framework of the Federal Election Reform.

27. In Italy—where tax rebates associated with gifts to political parties were introduced in 1997—all donations between thirty and 30,000 euros per annum are tax deductible to the tune of 26 percent. In Germany, although companies may contribute without limit to political life, only the donations of physical persons entitle the donors to tax reductions. A full 50 percent of donations, up to 1,650 euros per person, may be directly offset against income tax. Donations between 1,650 and 3,300 euros are also deductible, under the rubric of exceptional expenditure.

28. In effect, the law does not treat members' contributions as donations, on the grounds that they entitle those who pay them to such perks as invitations to media events on election night.

29. The Revenue Act of 1971 did introduce tax incentives for political donations, but this system of rebates was ended in 1986 as part of a reform of the federal income tax code.

30. In Spain, individuals may donate as much as 50,000 euros per year and per party, as well as 10,000 euros per campaign. Since 2015, companies have no longer been permitted to make donations.

31. This scandal also led to upper limits on the amount that candidates in local elections were allowed to spend. See, for example, Eric Avis, Claudio Ferraz, Frederico Finan, and Carlos Varjao (2017), "Money and Politics: The Effects of Campaign Spending Limits on Political Entry and Competition," National Bureau of Economic Research Working Paper #23508 (http://www.nber.org/papers/w23508).

32. On the inequalities in Brazil, see Marc Morgan (2017), "Extreme and Persistent Inequality: New Evidence from Brazil Combining National Accounts, Surveys and Fiscal Data, 2001–2015," working paper, World Inequality Database.

33. The "8 per thousand" was introduced in 1985, the "5 per thousand" in 2005, and the "2 per thousand" in 2014.

34. I shall return to this in Chapter 9, but let us note here that the "2 per thousand" for the funding of political parties—or the "8 per thousand" for the funding of religions—differs from the German "church tax." In Germany, the state levies a tax for organized religions, and each religion returns a small part of this to the state to offset its additional administrative costs. The amount of the tax is a fixed proportion of the income tax raised by the particular region or *Land*: in general, 9 percent. It is not a public subsidy for the funding of religions, but a private payment made by members of the religion in question and merely administered by the tax authorities. By contrast, Italy's "2 per thousand," like the "8 per thousand," is a public subsidy: it

costs the individual taxpayer nothing (it does not affect their tax bill whether they put a cross in the box or not) and is entirely covered by the state.

35. The "2 per thousand" system was introduced in 2014 for income received in 2013, but the tax authorities and the government admit that its application in the first year was to say the least complicated. To do it full justice, I shall therefore focus only on the 2015–2017 period (that is, on income received in 2014–2016).

36. It was not the "tax democracy" system as such that taxpayers were rejecting, since the "5 per thousand" and "8 per thousand" have been considerable successes. More than a half of Italians today choose to use the "5 per thousand" system—more than 15 times more than use the "2 per thousand." And since 2007 the sums they have allocated under it have exceeded the legal ceiling on annual expenditure (400 million euros until 2014 and 500 million since 2015).

37. It should be added that this referendum result has never really been respected, since public funding, in more or less disguised forms, has been reintroduced in the years since 1997. We shall return to this in Chapter 6, where we discuss the challenges to the public funding of democracy in a number of countries.

38. The limit was 7.7 million euros in 2014, 9.6 million in 2015, and 25.1 million since 2017 (Paragraph 4 of Article 12 of Decree-Law No. 149 / 2013). The progressive raising of this ceiling is explained by the fact that the system has gradually replaced other, discarded forms of public funding.

3. The Realities of Private Funding

1. I shall use here fiscal declarations relating to income tax, which are accessible to researchers in anonymous form under the auspices of the Centre d'accès Sécurisé aux Données Administratives (CASD). Donations and membership dues to political parties should be entered in box 7UH of the tax return. All further details are given in the online appendix to this book, including figures on donations to Italian political parties by income level.

2. The annual average in the 2013–2016 period was 356,392. In the online appendix, I present the percentage evolution since 2013 of tax households that donated money or paid membership fees to political parties in France. The percentage fell from 1.12 percent to 0.79 percent over the period.

3. I should stress here one of the limitations of fiscal data: the fact that small donors not liable to income tax have no (financial) interest in declaring their donations may lead to an underestimation of their number. Still, Gabrielle Fack and

Camille Landais have shown that even this group do tend to declare their donations. Gabrielle Fack and Camille Landais (2010), "Are Tax Incentives for Charitable Giving Efficient? Evidence from France," *American Economic Journal: Economic Policy,* 2(2), pp. 117–141; Gabrielle Fack and Camille Landais (2016), "The Effect of Tax Enforcement on Tax Elasticities: Evidence from Charitable Contributions in France," *Journal of Public Economics,* 133, pp. 23–40. As we shall see, the data actually point to an over-declaration of donations, for evident fiscal reasons.

4. In the online appendix, I present the evolution of membership in the various political parties in France since the beginning of the new millennium, and I discuss the problems associated with the estimation of this figure.

5. The average was 282 euros over the period.

6. I have done this as part of a larger current research project with Malka Guillot on the evolution of political donations in France. In the online appendix, I also present results on the level of donations by age.

7. Membership fees do, however, vary considerably from party to party: some operate with a fixed sum, others have opted for a sliding scale, and still others—such as the Socialist Party—leave it up to local federations to decide.

8. In 2016, for example, they contributed 44.5 million euros out of total donations worth 79.9 million euros.

9. According to the figures of the World Wealth & Income Database.

10. By comparison, they get 10.8 percent of total income.

11. See, for example, "The Tax Bill That Inequality Created," December 16, 2017, https://www.nytimes.com/2017/12/16/opinion/sunday/tax-bill-inequality-created .html.

12. See the online appendix for further details and figures.

13. This figure of 56 million euros comes from estimates that I made with Malka Guillot on the basis of fiscal data. Regrettably, the French government publishes no estimates of its own regarding tax expenditure associated with donations to political parties. All that is available, in an appendix to the finance bill entitled "Evaluation of Ways and Means; Fiscal Expenditure," is an estimate of tax expenditure associated with all donations (that is, donations to political parties, as well as to all recognized public-interest foundations or charities).

14. For reasons of statistical secrecy (I am using sample income tax files and, to preserve their anonymity, each "checkbox" of interest has to contain a sufficient number of points), I have here aggregated the lower end of the distribution (between the first and fourth income deciles).

15. Moreover, since the beginning of the millennium, donations above 50,000 euros appear monthly on the website of the federal parliament, the Bundestag.

16. This is the grand total of donations above 10,000 euros received by Die Linke, the SPD, Die Grünen, the CDU, the CSU, and the FDP. Historically, the threshold in place was 20,000 deutschmarks, which became 10,000 euros when Germany switched to the single EU currency.

17. The increasing number is partly a mechanical effect. The threshold of 20,000 deutschmarks / 10,000 euros has not been revised since the 1980s, despite inflation and the rise in per capita national income.

18. These figures comprise donations by the professional organizations of the different *Länder:* Bavaria, North Rhine-Westphalia, Baden-Württemberg, and so on.

19. Ben Knight and Gianna-Carina Grün (2017), "DW Exclusive: How German Companies Donate Secret Money to Political Parties," September 22, http://www.dw .com/en/dw-exclusive-how-german-companies-donate-secret-money-to-political -parties/a-40610200.

20. For donations below 1,650 euros, 50 percent of the amount may be directly deducted from the tax liability; and for donations below 3,300 euros, the part above 1,650 euros may be deducted from total income as "special expenditure" (on the understanding that this sum cannot amount to more than 20 percent of total income).

21. The 104 million figure is based on a figure of 208.6 million euros for the average annual total of donations below 3,300 euros.

22. Until Decree-Law No. 149 / 2013 (converted, after amendment, into Law No. 13 / 2014), there had been no upper limit on donations.

23. In its accounts, the Communist Party (the Partito della Rifondazione Comunista—Sinistra Europea) makes public the size and origin of donations below as well as above 5,000 euros. But for reasons of consistency between parties, I do not consider these small donations here.

24. In 2013, according to OpenPolis (http://minidossier.openpolis.it/2016/06 /Partiti_in_crisi.pdf), Silvio Berlusconi contributed the great bulk of the 15 million euros that Forza Italia received in individual donations and in contributions from members elected to public office.

25. The fall in the number of donations in 2010 is therefore not surprising, since part of it was due to the change in reporting rules.

26. I might also have mentioned donations by the United & Cecil Club, probably the best-known of the associations thwarting the drive for transparency.

27. Multiple donations by the same donor to the same party in a given year are here counted as a single donation.

28. I am here using data from party accounts. According to the fiscal data, this amount was 128 million euros in 2013, 110 million in 2014, 95 million in 2015, and 84 million in 2016. The reader may refer to the online appendix for a discussion of the different sources of data. There, I itemize the data sources I used in this chapter to calculate the total amounts donated to political parties in France. Tax records and party accounts do not always match up—a phenomenon that sometimes reflects the use of donations to avoid paying taxes, which can be traced only in sections of tax returns that carry an entitlement to rebates. In 2013, as in 2014, the discrepancy between donations received by parties and sums declared to the tax authorities came to a total of more than 25 million euros, and that understates the scale of tax evasion when we bear in mind that a number of citizens do not declare their donations.

29. Article 26: "Dues payable by members holding elective office or performing a government function."

30. This subtle technical point explains why the percentage for the Communist Party is not 100 percent. However, the estimate of 53.5 percent corresponds better to the real situation, since elected Communist representatives receive a remuneration from their party.

31. It was by no means evident which parties should be chosen for this comparison, and I have to recognize a certain bias on my part. I considered that in Italy the party nearest to the French Socialist Party was not the Partito Socialista Italiano but the Partito Democratico, and that Forza Italia, the party of Silvio Berlusconi, probably came closest to the French Républicains, even if this raised a number of questions. There is also a "heroic" side to this comparative exercise, since the definitions of the variables included in party accounts differ strongly from country to country. To take just one example, donations by private persons in Italy include the contributions of elected representatives for certain years and certain parties— which requires us to make some hypotheses to isolate these two components, so as not to overestimate the donations received by Italian parties compared with those in other countries.

32. Since contributions from members in elected public positions are not included here, the information as to donations from private persons received by the Partito Democratico is incomplete.

33. See the figure in the online appendix. In the case of the United Kingdom, contributions from elected representatives are included in the total sum received in

donations (it is not possible to separate them from donations proper in party accounts, which is why they do not feature in Figure 33 either). The same is not the case for the other countries. Still, contributions from elected representatives account for only a small share of total donations.

34. Maurice Duverger (1954), *Political Parties: Their Organization and Activity in the Modern State,* London: Methuen.

35. It is therefore impossible to study how the size of these donations varies with the income of taxpayers.

36. In January 2017, the satirical paper *Le Canard enchaîné* published damaging allegations that over a period of eight years Fillon's wife, Penelope, had been paid a sum of 500,000 euros for largely bogus employment as his "personal assistant."

37. These donations are, by definition, given mainly in election years. But as the number and nature of the elections taking place each year vary from country to country, it is preferable to consider the average total donated per year over a given electoral cycle.

4. Beyond Politics

1. The reader will forgive a slight misuse of language in my running of these two terms together. This is partly due to the fact that "think tank," though in widespread use, has no basis in law. People sometimes also speak of "party institutes." The reader interested in this question may refer to Helmut K. Anheier and Siobhan Daly (2006), *The Politics of Foundations: A Comparative Analysis,* London: Routledge.

2. As with donations to political parties, this means 66 percent of sums donated up to a limit of 20 percent of taxable income. The consequences are similarly inegalitarian: the state covers a part of donations only for the richest sections of society.

3. In case the generous donors are incapable of cross-multiplication.

4. The reader will, I hope, forgive me for getting a little ahead of myself here, as the public funding of democracy will be the subject of Chapter 5. But it is difficult—as we shall see in the case of Germany—to treat political foundations separately from public subsidies.

5. They are available in the appendix to the draft budget setting out "the state's financial efforts in favor of associations." They appear with a delay of two years, however, so that the sums allocated in 2016 feature only in the draft budget for 2018.

6. Averaging 153,000 euros per senator and 135,000 euros per deputy, the parliamentary reserve cost a total of just over 138 million euros in 2016. The amounts began to be made public in 2014.

7. To what extent was this due to the fact that the Socialist Party was in power during this period? One can easily imagine that some cause-and-effect relationship was involved, but the lack of data for Sarkozy's five-year presidential term makes it difficult to demonstrate.

8. Terra Nova does not have the legal status of a foundation but is recognized as a "public utility foundation"; this gives it the same fiscal benefits with regard to donations by physical and legal persons, and to subsidies allocated by the prime minister or parliamentary deputies and senators. It is true that Terra Nova has been around for a much shorter time than the Jean Jaurès Foundation, but is this enough to justify the huge differences in the size of their public subsidies? Some will maintain that their needs are different, that the Jean Jaurès Foundation, with its much larger staff, evidently "needs" more money. But it is a false argument, which comes down to a systematic privileging of the past. So, which should receive more in public subsidies: the Jean Jaurès Foundation or Terra Nova? I do not have a pat answer to the question, any more than I have preconceived ideas about how much should be allocated to the Montaigne Foundation or the Gabriel Péri Foundation. What I do know is that precise and transparent rules of allocation are always preferable to discretion, especially when public money is at stake.

9. Public funding was introduced at the time of the law of July 24, 1967, on the internal organization of political parties, with the idea of getting around the Constitutional Court ruling of July 19, 1966, which limited the public funding of parties to reimbursement of their campaign expenses. In Chapter 5, I shall return in greater detail to the public funding of parties in Germany.

10. The Jean Jaurès Foundation is an exception in this respect, having been created in 1992 and immediately recognized as a "public utility" foundation.

11. As long ago as the early 1960s, these think tanks were receiving small subsidies for specific projects from the federal and regional (*Länder*) governments. In 1962, the Bundestag voted in favor of allocating funds to them for projects related to political education in developing countries. See Karl-Heinz Nassmacher (2009), *The Funding of Party Competition: Political Finance in 25 Democracies,* Baden-Baden: Nomos.

12. Banned by the Nazis in 1933 and reconstituted in 1947.

13. Foundations on the German model, heavily reliant on public funding, are also to be found in Austria, the Netherlands, and Switzerland. But they do not compare in terms of the funds available to them. Helmut K. Anheier and Siobhan Daly (2006) speak in this context of a "corporatist model" of think tanks, characterized by a kind of subsidiary relationship to the state.

14. In Spain, unlike in Germany, more than one foundation may be associated with the same party.

15. The annual average was lower than in previous years because of the economic crisis affecting the country. The reader will find in the online appendix the annual totals received by political foundations in Spain since 1995, as well as a breakdown of these sums by activity and by political party. In the 2007–2011 period, public subsidies to political foundations averaged 9 million euros per year.

16. Very few political foundations in the United States receive direct subsidies from the state. Some of them, however, such as the Brookings Institution, benefit from federal government contracts.

17. "Tax-exempt foundations," "public charities," or "501(c)(3) non-profit organizations," to use the terms employed by the Internal Revenue Service (IRS). It is important to underline this façade of political neutrality constructed by highly political conservative as well as liberal think tanks, and particularly that the IRS turns a blind eye to their actual commitment. We can see the double standards at work here, when we know that the need for nonpartisanship is one of the main arguments used in the United States by those who reject any idea that media outlets should be able to take the form of nonprofit foundations and therefore qualify for 501(c)(3) tax status. On this question, see Julia Cagé (2016), *Saving the Media: Capitalism, Crowdfunding, and Democracy,* trans. Arthur Goldhammer, Cambridge, MA: Belknap Press.

18. The *fonds de dotation,* or "endowment fund," is a new entity that was created in France by a 2008 "economic modernization law." This entity is much simpler to set up than a foundation yet offers a tax break to donors.

19. The characterization comes from the Sakura website: https://www.sakura -artangel.org/la-maison-laurentine. I wouldn't have allowed myself the liberty.

20. This deposit appears in the accounts of the Fonds Sakura, which are available online (a sound legal obligation linked to its endowment fund status), and which record founders' payments of 430,000 euros in 2013, followed by 150,000 euros in 2014, 40,000 euros in 2015, and 50,000 euros in 2016. To be continued! The reader may like to consult the excellent portrait of Muriel Pénicaud in the daily *Libération* for August 30, 2017: http://www.liberation.fr/france/2017/08/30/la-premiere-drh-de -france_1593136.

21. In France, endowment funds benefit from the fiscal regime applicable to nonprofit bodies. On the one hand, they are exempt from business taxes (corporate taxation, professional taxes, and value-added tax) on their economic activities so

long as these are for nonprofit purposes. On the other hand, since their statutes do not provide for the capital endowment to be used up, they are exempt from corporate taxes on all their income from property. Furthermore, payments into endowment funds entitle the donors to benefit from the sponsorship scheme (*régime du mécénat*), whereby enterprises liable to income tax or corporate taxes receive relief equivalent to 60 percent of their payments, up to a maximum of 0.5 percent of their turnover; private individuals may benefit from relief equivalent to 66 percent of their payments, up to a maximum of 20 percent of their taxable income.

22. David Yermack (2009), "Deductio ad Absurdum: CEOs Donating Their Own Stock to Their Own Family Foundations," *Journal of Financial Economics,* 94, pp. 107–123. There are several different types of foundation in the United States: independent foundations, family foundations, corporate foundations, community foundations, and "operating foundations." Yermack's article covers only family foundations, which, according to the most recent figures available on the Foundation Center website, numbered 42,000 in 2014.

23. Nonprofit organizations are also exempt from tax on their investment income, and private foundations pay only an indirect "excise tax" of 2 percent on their net investment income. These organizations are further exempt from local and state property taxes. See, e.g., Rob Reich (2006), "Philanthropy and Its Uneasy Relation to Equality," in William Damon and Susan Verducci (eds.), *Taking Philanthropy Seriously: Beyond Noble Intentions to Responsible Giving,* Bloomington: Indiana University Press, pp. 33–49. To be considered a "public charity," a US foundation must fulfill one of two conditions: either it must be engaged in a particular type of activity (schools, hospitals, and educational institutions, for example); or it must receive at least one-third of its financial support from the public at large, which is defined as individuals contributing at least 2 percent to its finances.

24. Jane Mayer (2016), *Dark Money: The Hidden History of the Billionaires behind the Rise of the Radical Right,* New York: Doubleday. While Mayer's focus is on the funding of the Far Right, it is important to note that, as we will see in Chapter 7, there are also quite a few billionaires on the left, beginning with George Soros, who may spend millions on the Democratic Party and candidates. This is not without dangers, for the Democrats as well as the Republicans. Research for this book was partly funded by the Institute for New Economic Thinking (INET), a think tank founded by George Soros, and this did not have any influence on its content. I do think, however, that public funding of research is preferable to private funding, and my own research has always been funded mainly by public money and national

research agencies such as the French National Research Agency (ANR). A world that increasingly depends on wealthy patrons of intellectual and quasi-intellectual salons for its research is indeed not a world that optimally encourages the independent production of truth. Reader beware.

25. This is how the Koch brothers created the Association for American Innovation (AAI), now called Freedom Partners. Oh, freedom, how sweet the name . . .

26. See Rob Reich, *Just Giving: Why Philanthropy Is Failing Democracy and How It Can Do Better,* Princeton University Press, 2018.

27. Benjamin I. Page and Martin Gilens (2017), *Democracy in America? What Has Gone Wrong and What We Can Do about It,* University of Chicago Press.

28. Robert Reich, Chiara Cordelli, and Lucy Bernholz (2016), eds., *Philanthropy in Democratic Societies: History, Institutions, Values,* University of Chicago Press.

29. As highlighted in Reich (2018), we must "consider philanthropy as an act with political dimensions, in the sense that philanthropy can be an expression of political power, . . . and in the sense that philanthropy is shaped by political arrangements. . . . Wealthy elites can pose problems for democratic politics, even—and perhaps especially—when elites direct their wealth toward the public sphere."

30. The ultimate in the reproduction of economic and political inequalities is the recent development of "money camps" in the United States. The purpose of these is to train in fortune management the children of billionaires, who, as soon as they arrive on earth, are given a mission by the Money God to improve the lot of "poor people"—that is, of all who have inherited nothing and are condemned to work to survive, and who, with the explosion of philanthropy and other forms of private conquest of the public good, are being deprived of the reality of one of their most basic rights: the right to vote.

31. Thomas Piketty has clearly demonstrated this in the case of American university endowments. Over the period from 1980 to 2010, their average rate of return was 8.2 percent, but this figure conceals enormous disparities: an average of 10.2 percent for Harvard, Yale, and Princeton, against "only" 6.2 percent for universities with an endowment lower than $100 million. See Thomas Piketty (2014), *Capital in the Twenty-First Century,* Harvard University Press.

32. Naomi Oreskes and Erik M. Conway (2010), *Merchants of Doubt: How a Handful of Scientists Obscured the Truth on Issues from Tobacco Smoke to Global Warming,* New York: Bloomsbury Press.

33. Justin Farrell (2016), "Corporate Funding and Ideological Polarization about Climate Change," *Proceedings of the National Academy of Sciences of the United*

States of America, 113(1), pp. 92–97. It has been shown that, between 1975 and 2002, 92 percent of "climate skeptic" books published in the United States were linked to conservative think tanks such as the Cato Institute, the Competitive Enterprise Institute, and the Hudson Institute; see Peter J. Jacques, Riley E. Dunlap, and Mark Freeman (2008), "The Organization of Denial: Conservative Think Tanks and Environmental Skepticism," *Environmental Politics,* 17(3), pp. 349–385.

34. The reader may find on the OpenSecrets (Center for Responsive Politics) website the annual total expenditure of ExxonMobil on lobbying activity, which came to more than $11 million in 2017 alone: https://www.opensecrets.org/lobby/clientsum.php?id=d000000129. See also the "exxonsecrets" site: https://exxonsecrets.org/html/index.php.

35. I mean public research, of course. In France, private research is stimulated by a research tax credit (CIR), but would these funds not be better used in the universities? Besides, for many companies, CIR is nothing other than an extra tax loophole.

36. I shall not dwell here on the key economic features of this media crisis—from the collapse of advertising revenue to the growth of internet competition that makes it very difficult to "monetize" information that is costly to produce; or from the quest for profit at any price to the stock market listing of various media that has sometimes created a vicious circle of disinvestment to guarantee sufficient profitability. I have already discussed these phenomena in *Saving the Media* and with Nicolas Hervé and Marie-Lucie Viaud (2017), *L'Information à tout prix,* Paris: INA Éditions, and they have been the object of numerous studies. We should note here, however, that the threats to media independence are themselves one of the reasons for the crisis, since the collapse of confidence often results in a reduced willingness to purchase.

37. Memories of a French song of my childhood, "Le Géant de papier," make me inclined to think of him as a "paper giant," his empire being built on accumulated debt that even someone completely new to these matters could hardly consider sustainable in the long term.

38. See the group's annual governance report at https://www. prisa.com/uploads/2017/02/igc-240217-completo.pdf. Roberto Rojas Alcantara appears among the owners of the group through the "GHO Networks, S.A. DE CV" company.

39. The ownership of Italy's main newspapers has been shaken up in recent years. We cannot go into the details here, but in brief, 2016 saw a rapprochement between *La Repubblica* (owned by the businessman, and politician, Carlo De Benedetti through the Compagnie Industriali Riunite) and *La Stampa* (then owned by Fiat Chrysler), as well as the withdrawal of Fiat, and therefore the Agnelli family, from

Corriere della Sera. The latter withdrawal may be seen as good news in the largely "industrialized" landscape of the press, since it marked the arrival of a media entrepreneur, Urbano Cairo (Cairo Communication S.p.A), at the head of RCS Media.

40. The purchase of *Time* was announced at the end of November 2017 and finally concluded in 2018. The Koch brothers had already given signs of their media ambitions in 2015, when they tried, unsuccessfully, to buy up outlets including the *Los Angeles Times* and the *Chicago Tribune.*

41. Bernard Arnault may be the owner of *Le Parisien,* but he is also an important French advertiser, who does not think twice before depriving *Le Monde* of publicity revenue. He has his reasons: in particular, he was unhappy that *Le Monde* published the *Paradise Papers,* which, among other things, highlighted the tax optimization strategies of this enlightened boss.

42. The so-called Bloche Law (Law No. 2016-1524, November 14, 2016), intended "to strengthen the freedom, independence, and pluralism of the media," has brought some important advances in France, but it remains woefully inadequate. For although it is good to see the introduction of enterprise-level ethical charters and committees "regarding the honesty, independence, and pluralism of information and programmes," such measures will not suffice in practice to guarantee editorial independence—partly because the composition of the committees is left up to the owners, and partly because the law does not specify how they should intervene in the event of actual conflicts between editorial staff and the owners.

43. I assume here, of course, that newspaper readers actually know the owners' identity and, above all, the sector from which they derive most of their income. In 2016–2017, working with Olivier Godechot in partnership with the Interdisciplinary Laboratory for the Evaluation of Public Policies (LIEPP) and Reporters Without Borders, I conducted a study of the political and general news media in France and Spain. One of the most striking conclusions was the lack of transparency surrounding media ownership. Here too, the law designed "to strengthen the freedom, independence, and pluralism of the media" is well short of its target. Paragraph 19 does stipulate that "each year, the publishing company shall bring to the knowledge of readers of the publication or online press service all information regarding the composition of its capital, in the event that 5 percent or more of the same is held by any physical or legal person." However, disclosure of the identity of physical or legal persons is in no way sufficient to inform readers about the precise nature of potential conflicts of interest. In any case, although this law came into force two years ago, it is

still not respected by a large number of publishers. Perhaps this is not so surprising, if we bear in mind that the paragraph in question did not provide for any clear sanctions in the event of noncompliance.

44. According to the *New York Times,* Thiel spent $1.25 million in support of Trump, donating both to super PACs and directly to his campaign.

45. See Carol Cadwalladr (2017), "The Great Brexit Robbery: How Our Democracy Was Hijacked," *The Guardian,* May 7, https://www.theguardian.com/technology/2017/may/07/the-great-british-brexit-robbery-hijacked-democracy.

46. Adelson has also entered the Israeli political process via the media, with the creation of the free daily paper *Israel Hayom,* which is a major backer of Benjamin Netanyahu.

47. See, for example, the excellent article by Anuj Srivas, "Subhash Chandra Joins List of MPs on Parliamentary Panels Handling Issues Linked to Their Businesses," *The Wire,* October 26, 2017, https://thewire.in/191131/subhash-chandra-joins-panels-linked-to-their-businesses.

48. An editorial in *Le Monde,* dated December 25, 2002, wrote of the opposition to Chávez from "a ruling class with oligarchic traditions that happily considers the state as its property."

49. Sylvain Laurens (2015), *Les Courtiers du capitalisme. Milieux d'affaires et bureaucrates à Bruxelles,* Marseille: Agone.

50. The *New York Times* article in question, which is cited by Aaron Horvath and Walter W. Powell in chapter 4 of Reich, Cordelli, and Bernholz, *Philanthropy in Democratic Societies,* is available online at http://www.nytimes.com/2013/12/30/nyregion/cost-of-being-mayor-650-million-if-hes-rich.html?pagewanted=all&_r = 2&. Horvath and Powell describe Bloomberg as a "mayoranthropist."

5. A Hope?

1. Despite the many debates that took place, the reader will forgive this long jump over the period between Roosevelt's address and the eventual legislative reforms. For a more detailed discussion of the question, see A. B. Gunlicks (1993), *Campaign and Party Finance in North America and Western Europe,* Boulder, CO: Westview Press.

2. To be absolutely precise, such funding dates back to the Presidential Election Campaign Fund Act of 1966 (Title III of Public Law 89-809). On November 10, 1966, Russell B. Long, the Democratic chairman of the Senate Finance Committee, made

this acute observation: "To obtain funds in very small amounts from a very large body of citizens is the best way of ensuring that no financial group can have undue influence." It is also interesting to note that, back in 1966, Long considered this law insufficient and thought that other regulations—especially on limits to campaign contributions—would need to be introduced. In the end, the Presidential Election Campaign Fund Act was revoked in 1967—or rather, it was rendered inoperative in expectation of a congressional decision on the allocation of funds.

3. It should also be noted that partial public funding of political parties was introduced in Costa Rica in 1954, in Argentina in 1955, and in Sweden in 1965.

4. The increase from $1 to $3 ($2 to $6 for couples making a joint return and ticking both boxes) took effect with the Omnibus Budget Reconciliation Act of 1993.

5. To facilitate comparison between years and between countries, all amounts are expressed in constant 2016 euros. Thus, 85 million euros corresponds to an actual total of $27.6 million in 1974.

6. Ronald Reagan, then governor of California, failed to secure the Republican nomination for the presidential election of 1976 (having also failed a previous time in 1968). He had to wait until 1980 to win both the nomination and the presidential election.

7. Only until 2014—we shall return to this later.

8. The fund doubles individual donations, not those made by PACs or party contributions. An individual may contribute more than $250, but the government will still pay only $250 to the candidate in question.

9. Moreover, in the calculation of these $5,000, each donor cannot count for more than $250. The simplest requirement is therefore to have twenty donors giving at least $250 each in twenty different states.

10. The law refers not to the Republican and Democratic parties but to each "major party," defining this as a party whose candidate obtained at least 25 percent of the votes in the previous election. To this day, however, these funds have never benefited anyone other than a Republican or Democratic candidate.

11. You should bear in mind, however, that this applies only to the main presidential campaign—that is, to the final stage between the nomination of candidates and the final vote in November. Before then, the candidates will have campaigned—and spent—for the primaries. And the national conventions of the two parties, with their high media profile, are also a once-in-four-years opportunity for candidates to make themselves better known to the public at large.

12. The spending cap for the first round of the 2017 presidential election was 16.851 million euros. For candidates who qualified for the second round, this rose to 22.509 million euros—or 0.43 euros per adult.

13. There are a number of other subtle differences to which we shall return at the end of this chapter.

14. "New" here signifies parties or candidates that did not stand or received less than 5 percent of the vote in the previous election.

15. Funding of the national conventions, like the expenditure ceiling, is fixed and index-linked.

16. The bold reader unafraid of sinking into pessimism in the face of a Kafkaesque legal process may profitably consult the Congressional Research Service (2008) Report for Congress: "Public Financing of Congressional Campaigns: Overview and Analysis." On the local and state funding of democracy, I heartily recommend Donald A. Gross and Robert K. Goidel (2003), *The States of Campaign Finance Reform,* Ohio State University Press, and David A. Schultz (2002), *Money, Politics, and Campaign Finance Reform Law in the States,* Carolina Academic Press. Much information is also available on the National Conference of State Legislatures website, especially the latest data on state laws concerning public funding; see http://www.ncsl.org/research/elections-and-campaigns/public-financing-of -campaigns-overview.aspx.

17. This is why, regrettably, I do not share the enthusiasm of Benjamin Page and Martin Gilens, who seem to think that these "clean election programs" will be enough to curb the capture of the democratic process. In my view, this can happen only if such programs are the only option open to all candidates—in other words, if it is no longer possible for a candidate to decide not to use public funding. In 2011, following the introduction in 2008 of a public funding system in Connecticut, the election for state governor ended in victory for Dannel Malloy (whose campaign had been financed with public money) against the millionaire businessman Ned Lamont. But there is every reason to fear that in the next election Ned Lamont—or a wealthy successor—will be more resourceful in his campaign plans and spend enough for public funding to be ultimately of no avail. Nothing in the law actually prevents it—that is the whole problem.

18. Arizona, Connecticut, Florida, Hawaii, Maine, Maryland, Massachusetts, Michigan, Minnesota, Rhode Island, and Vermont.

19. The states are Alabama, Arizona, Iowa, Minnesota, New Mexico, North Carolina, Ohio, Rhode Island, and Utah.

20. In particular, the amendments to the FECA in 1974 created the Federal Election Commission (FEC), a crucial institution for any effective regulation of campaign spending. The Watergate scandal began on June 17, 1972, with the break-in at Democratic Party headquarters, and ended in 1974 with the resignation of Richard Nixon.

21. The interested reader may refer to Lia Young and Harold J. Jansen (2011), *Money, Politics, and Democracy: Canada's Party Finance Reforms,* Vancouver: University of British Columbia Press.

22. Still, the Quebec law of 1963 did not provide for direct subsidies to political parties; that would come only in 1977.

23. In particular, parties can claim the reimbursement of a half of their expenditure on radio and television ads.

24. This scandal, which first broke in the press in 2002 and led the auditor general of Canada to order an official enquiry the following year, contributed to the fall of the government in November 2005.

25. See the graph in the online appendix.

26. On these proposals, see Éric Phélippeau (2010), "Genèse d'une codification. L'apprentissage parlementaire et la réforme du financement de la vie politique, 1970–1987," *Revue française de science politique,* 3.

27. For each deputy or senator associated with it, a political party receives an annual sum of 32,280 euros. In addition, parties receive 1.42 euros per vote won in the first round of the legislative elections (but only if they obtain more than 1 percent of the total number of votes cast). Various penalties may be deducted if they fail to comply with parity rules. For further details, the reader may refer to the website of the French National Commission on Campaign Accounts and Political Funding (CNCCFP): http://www.cnccfp.fr/index.php?r=4.

28. The creation of Macron's En Marche! does prove that new parties can emerge, provided that they can raise sufficient private money. This gives an advantage to new conservative forces, mostly sidelining movements on the left fighting for causes such as income redistribution.

29. In the online appendix, the reader will find the debt trends of the main French parties since 1990.

30. The reader will find details of these figures in the online appendix.

31. To be absolutely precise, public funding of political parties did exist in Belgium before 1989, in the form of a parliamentary allocation dating from the 1970s that parties could use to support their candidates. This system was not a shining

example of transparency, however, since the parties themselves decided behind closed doors on the sums to be allocated.

32. The law concerns the limitation and control of electoral spending and the finances and open accounting of political parties. The provision of Paragraph 5 was modified in 2003, so that today it is sufficient to have at least one elected member in one of the two chambers to be eligible for public funding. Paragraph 16 of this law determines the annual sums paid to the parties. I present here the sums in force today, the law of January 6, 2014, having modified the previous rules.

33. Here I am considering only the PSB (Parti Socialiste Belge, present exclusively in French-speaking Belgium) and not the Flemish-speaking SP.a (Socialistische Partij Anders), whereas I divide the amount of public funding by the population of Belgium as a whole. As a result, I actually understate, in comparative international terms, the size of public funding per Belgian adult. It is difficult to take parties in "couples," because their political alignments are susceptible to change. For example, it is not obvious that the French-speaking Mouvement Réformateur (MR) should be treated as parallel to the Open Vld (Open Vlaamse Liberalen en Democraten) in Flemish-speaking Belgium.

34. The Samusocial scandal, which led to the resignation of the mayor of Brussels in June 2017, involved excessive remuneration paid to public officials. The Publifin affair also broke out when the exorbitant payment of various leading politicians (mostly Socialists but also others) came to light; the politicians, who had been directors of the cross-community cooperative society Publifin, were involved mainly in electricity and telecoms distribution but also active in other sectors.

35. In the online appendix, the reader will find the shares represented by direct public subsidies in the total funding for major parties in Germany, Belgium, Spain, France, Italy, and the United Kingdom.

36. This position seems thoroughly justified in view of the huge inequalities involved in private donations, which we have reviewed in previous chapters. See, for example, Gunlicks (1993).

37. In 1966, a Constitutional Court ruling declared it unconstitutional for parties to use public funds for the purposes of political or general civic education. As we saw in Chapter 4, this eventually led to the extremely generous funding of German think tanks.

38. Unlike in France, this is based not only on national parliamentary elections (to the Bundestag in Germany) but also on elections to the European Parliament and regional elections. The funding is allocated at a rate of 0.83 euros per vote up to a ceiling of 4 million votes obtained, and one euro per vote for any beyond that limit.

39. Figure 49 shows the total public assistance paid to all German political parties since 2002. The interested reader will find in the online appendix the total amount received each year by all *parties represented in the Bundestag*. In 2015, for example, the parties present in the Bundestag received 155 million euros in direct public subsidies, or 96 percent of the total public assistance given to German political parties.

40. The reimbursement threshold is 3 percent of the votes cast for the European elections (as of today in France, European elections are one-round elections with a single national constituency and proportional representation with a 5 percent threshold for representation).

41. For the presidential election, all candidates also benefit from an advance of 153,000 euros. It should be stressed that candidates are entitled to a refund only of their "personal contribution"—and we can understand why. It would make no sense for the state to refund candidates' expenses that had been paid for out of donations from private individuals. This side of things sometimes seems to escape candidates or their campaign teams. Amazingly, in the 2017 presidential elections, François Fillon—perhaps on purpose, who knows?—kissed goodbye to 6 million euros of public money by funding his expenses above 10 million euros with contributions from his own party (not susceptible to reimbursement) rather than through his own personal contribution (as the other candidates quite logically did).

42. To the great displeasure also of French citizens in general. Not much was said about it at the time, but French taxpayers—including the least Sarkozyist among them—largely funded the Sarkozy campaign by virtue of the tax rebates accorded to donors. Thus, out of the 11 million euros reimbursed for his campaign expenses, the cost to the taxpayer may have been as high as 7 million euros; the exact figure is unfortunately not known.

43. From 2015 on, elections at the departmental level replaced cantonal elections in France. But to make Figure 50 easier to read, I have used the same term, "cantonal elections," for the whole period. Since Law No. 2013-403 of May 17, 2013, on the election of departmental councillors, the system of half-replacement every three years has ceased to exist, and new elections for all positions now take place every six years. This explains why the reimbursement of campaign expenses for cantonal / departmental elections was nearly twice as high in 2015 as in previous years.

44. The figure for the previous cycle was 268.8 million euros, or approximately 53.8 million euros a year.

45. The fact that provincial and local elections in Canada are regulated in their respective areas gives rise to large variations. For example, Ontario and Quebec still pay a tri-monthly allocation to their political parties.

46. Interestingly, Canadian electoral law ensures that, if the campaign lasts longer than the statutory minimum of 36 days, the ceiling on expenses rises proportionally. Thus, in the seventy-eight-day campaign of 2015, each party was entitled to spend C$675,000 (approximately 435,000 euros) a day, and each candidate C$2,700 (1,740 euros) a day.

47. In Germany today, campaign expenses are no longer reimbursed, and all public funding of parties is direct.

48. The annual public funding of the Socialist Party will fall from 24.9 million euros in 2016 to 7.8 million in 2018, and that of the Républicains from 18.5 million euros to 14.4 million. The big winner is Macron's La République en Marche, which will receive 20.6 million euros a year in direct public funding.

49. See the excellent Mediapart article on possible gifts to the campaign of Emmanuel Macron, which, if confirmed, should be treated under the law as disguised private funding: Antton Rouget (2018), "Campagne de Macron, les cadeaux du 'roi de l'événementiel,'" Mediapart, April 27.

6. The Public Funding of Democracy

1. This led in 1925 to the passing of the Honours (Prevention of Abuses) Act, which prohibited the sale of peerages or other official honors.

2. Although no party won an absolute majority, the Five Stars Movement—the main scourge of public funding—finished well ahead with 32.6 percent of the vote, and the League (the former Lega Nord), under the leadership of Matteo Salvini, came in third with 17.4 percent.

3. The relevant law, No. 195/1974, was proposed by the Christian Democrats and quickly approved by all the other parties, with the exception of the Italian Liberal Party. Before 1974, the funding of political parties in Italy had not been subject to any regulation.

4. The details of this system were a little complex, since, formally speaking, the public funds were not paid directly to political parties but to parliamentary groups. Still, the groups in the Senate and the Assembly were supposed to forward at least 95 percent of their funding to their respective parties.

5. See, for example, Martin Rhodes (1997), "Financing Party Politics in Italy: A Case of Systemic Corruption," *West European Politics,* 20(1), pp. 54–80; and Chiara Maria Pacini and Daniela Romee Piccio (2012), "Party Regulation in Italy and Its Effects," Working Paper Series on the Legal Regulation of Political Parties, No. 26, Leiden University, http://www.partylaw.leidenuniv.nl/uploads/wp2612.pdf.

6. The lucky winners of public tenders had to pay the parties in place a "compulsory tax" (or bribe) that could be as high as 10 percent of the bid. On the *Mani pulite* operation, see Sondra Z. Koff and Stephen P. Koff (2000), *Italy, from the First to the Second Republic,* London: Routledge.

7. On the passage from the "First" to the "Second" Republic, see Sergio Fabbrini (2009), "The Transformation of Italian Democracy," *Bulletin of Italian Politics,* 1(1), pp. 29–47; and Koff and Koff (2000). The reader with a knowledge of Italian may also consult Sergio Fabbrini (2011), *Addommesticare il principe. Perché i leader contano e come controllarli,* Venice: Marsilio.

8. Referenda are common occurrences in Italy. An "abrogative referendum"—the purpose of which is to "abrogate" or repeal a law—may take place at the request of 500,000 electors (or five regional councils); but more often, one or more parties are behind the popular initiative. In 1974, the Italian Liberal Party—which opposed the public funding of parties—supported an abrogative referendum to end the system, but without obtaining the required number of signatures. A first referendum on the issue nevertheless took place in 1978, supported by the Radical Party, just four years after public funding had been introduced. The vote against a change narrowly carried the day. In 1993, the force behind the referendum was the Transnational Radical Party, a successor to the Radical Party (dissolved in 1989), but interestingly it was more of a nonparty, since it had decided not to take part directly in electoral contests.

9. Subsidies to political parties were abolished after the referendum in 1993. But—and it is a big but—the reimbursement of candidates' election expenses was maintained, in the knowledge that the system of reimbursement introduced at the time was not based on any link with the real amount of campaign spending! A fund was established for each election and divided proportionately among the parties that obtained a sufficient number of votes, regardless of their actual spending during the campaign. Nor was this all: the maximum refund of election expenses was tripled (Paragraphs 9 and 16 of Law No. 515 / 1993)! In 1997–1998 (under Law No. 2 / 1997), the reintroduction of direct funding allowed taxpayers to allocate 0.4 percent (or "4 per thousand") of their income tax to political parties. The repeal of this law in 1999 ended such contributions, but in the interval the government used the "4 per thousand" to spend more than 11 million euros in 1998 and 77.5 million euros in 1999 for the funding of parties. In fact, although the "4 per thousand" was a real failure among the population, the government decided to allocate sums much higher than those chosen by citizens on their tax returns. This helps to explain why the popular

rejection in 2014 succeeded the popular rejection in 1993. For want of clear rules, public funding was widely seen as the cash cow that parties milked to their advantage.

10. Gian Antonio Stella and Sergio Rizzo (2007), *La Casta. Cosi i politici italiani sono diventati intoccabili,* Milan: Rizzoli.

11. In 2013, the Five Stars Movement waived any claim to a refund of the 42.8 million euros incurred in campaign expenses during the legislative elections.

12. In 2000, George W. Bush did not use public funding for the primaries, but he still chose it for the general election.

13. In the end, this super PAC spent more than $65 million during the general election of 2012. In 2016, it was the main super PAC backing Hillary Clinton.

14. He had himself benefited from them—as had the Republican candidate in 2008 and 2012, to the tune of $16.8 and $18.2 million respectively.

15. The case had been brought by a businessman, Shaun McCutcheon, against the Federal Election Commission (FEC). Shaun McCutcheon, in whose favor the Supreme Court ruled, wanted to be able to contribute more than the cumulative total then permitted for a single donor to several candidates: that is, $123,000 in two years. It is true that the ceiling on an individual's donation to a single candidate remained the same as before, but an individual could now contribute to the campaigns of as many candidates as he or she wished.

16. For the sake of readability, I consider here only contributors in the first and last deciles of income distribution. But if we take all ten deciles together, we find exactly the same phenomenon: the percentage of citizens who check the Presidential Fund box increases with the income decile (lower for the first than the second decile, for the second than the third, and so on). These results are available in the online appendix.

17. The only two candidates to have drawn on these funds in 2016 were Martin O'Malley and Jill Stein.

18. See the Open Secrets website: https://www.opensecrets.org/pres16/candidate?id= n00000528, and the FEC website: https://www.fec.gov/data/candidate/P60007168/.

19. A reform submitted by Senator Richard Durbin.

20. Aaron Wherry (2015), "Stephen Harper's Long Campaign," *Macleans,* August 2, https://www.macleans.ca/politics/stephen-harpers-long-campaign/.

21. See Richard Kelly (2016), "Short Money," House of Commons Library Briefing Paper Number 01663.

22. And Lord President of the Council from 1974 to 1976.

23. Some MPs went so far as to claim reimbursement for such things as dog food or a floating duck shelter. More seriously, many obtained refunds for nonexistent mortgage payments or rental payments on accommodation that they owned or did not occupy.

24. According to the general budget appropriations presented in the draft budget for 2018. My estimates are on the conservative side, since I present the figures corresponding to payment appropriations (the maximum permissible spending may be scheduled or paid in the course of the year to cover commitments made in the framework of commitment authorizations) rather than to commitment authorizations (the upper limit on spending commitments).

25. According to the yellow appendix "Personnel Assigned to Ministerial Cabinets," in the draft budget for 2018.

7. Are America's Aberrations a Danger for Europe?

1. In addition to the establishment of public funding for presidential elections, we should recall the restrictions on election expenses and private contributions that were introduced in 1971–1974: (1) a strict limit on private donations to candidates and parties, including a cap on what candidates may spend out of their own pockets on their campaign; (2) a ceiling on the sums that candidates and parties may spend in the course of elections; and (3) a $1,000 limit on what any individual may spend in favor of a clearly identified candidate.

2. Named after the Republican senator James L. Buckley, who had attacked the secretary of state and ex officio member of the Federal Election Commission, Francis R. Valeo.

3. On the French case, see, e.g., Elsa Forey (2016), "Une association proche d'un parti politique peut-elle contribuer au financement d'une campagne électorale?" *Actualité juridique, droit administratif* (AJDA).

4. On the successive decisions of the Supreme Court, and their consequences, I particularly recommend the excellent book by Timothy Kuhner (2014), *Capitalism vs. Democracy: Money in Politics and the Free Market Constitution,* Stanford University Press. A fine analysis of these judgments may also be found in Robert C. Post (2014), *Citizens Divided: Campaign Finance Reform and the Constitution,* Harvard University Press (2014); and Richard L. Hasen (2016), *Plutocrats United: Campaign Money, the Supreme Court, and the Distortion of American Elections,* Yale University Press.

Although I have closely read the various Supreme Court rulings, I must confess that I have also relied on these works for a better understanding of the legal arguments.

5. Hasen (2016) points out that, among the arguments in its *Buckley v. Valeo* decision, the Supreme Court highlighted the fact that a full page of publicity in a daily newspaper cost nearly $7,000 (in 1975), which was seven times more than the $1,000 ceiling on any individual's independent spending related to a candidate.

6. As Richard Hasen acutely observes, the conservative Citizens United association should be regarded here as essentially a Trojan horse. The issue as such was not so important to it, as it could have used its own political action committee; its real aim was to overturn—in the Supreme Court—an area of electoral regulation that Republican conservatives had been targeting for decades. A ship to be hit and sunk . . .

7. To be precise—although I cannot here review all the Supreme Court rulings since the mid-1970s—it was the *First National Bank of Boston v. Bellotti* decision in 1978 that first defined the right of corporations to free speech. It forbade states to limit corporate campaign donations in the context of legislative referendums.

8. In a long battle that began in 1882, Roscoe Conkling, a Republican politician and former senator, demanded for his client (the Southern Pacific Railroad Company) equal rights under the Fourteenth Amendment to the Constitution. This amendment, ratified in 1868, stated that "the equal protection of the laws" must be guaranteed to any person living on the territory of the United States; it was intended to protect the rights of former slaves. See Adam Winkler (2018), *We The Corporations. How American Businesses Won their Civil Rights,* New York: Liveright Publishing.

9. The corporate money must be invested in specific causes, not in favor of a particular party.

10. The relatively lower level of spending in 2012 is partly explained by the fact that, with Barack Obama standing for a second term, there were no real Democratic Party primaries.

11. I cannot discuss here the ins and outs of the global political and financial crisis that shook the markets early in this century. Suffice it to say that the US energy group went bankrupt in 2001 after it had doctored its accounts for a number of years, but that its soaring debt in the late 1990s had already troubled some financial analysts. Why raise doubts, though, about a corporation whose CEO (Kenneth Lay) was an adviser to the government on energy policy—especially as it had contributed generously to George W. Bush's campaign in 2000?

12. In recent years, many researchers have taken a strong stand on this issue: Lawrence Lessig, Larry Bartels, Benjamin Page, Martin Gilens, and Timothy Kuhner, to name but a few. Their proposals will be considered in Chapter 9.

13. I hope legal experts will excuse my treating these two instances together; I know that, although their roles may overlap, their attributions are different.

14. Campaign regulation is a clear instance of this. In the early 2000s, when a liberal judge was replaced with a conservative judge, this was enough for one ruling after another to lose currency; certain Supreme Court decisions were the exact opposite of others that preceded them. But the Constitution had not changed in between!

15. A ruling overturned in 1999.

16. Dominique Rousseau (2015), *Radicaliser la démocratie. Propositions pour une refondation,* Paris, Le Seuil.

17. As things stand, the nine members of the Constitutional Council (each of whom serves for a nonrenewable nine-year term) are appointed by equally weighted votes of the president, the speaker of the National Assembly, and the speaker of the Senate.

18. Gilens's (2012) *Affluence and Influence: Economic Inequality and Political Power in America,* Princeton University Press, study covers the period from 1964 to 2006 and such diverse questions as tax levels, the size of government, the war in Iraq, and abortion and gay marriage. See also Benjamin Page and Martin Gilens (2017), *Democracy in America? What Has Gone Wrong and What We Can Do about It,* University of Chicago Press. Here I am drawing simultaneously on findings in both these works.

19. Thomas Frank (2007), *What's the Matter with Kansas? How Conservatives Won the Heart of America,* Henry Holt and Company.

20. More than two-thirds of counties in Kansas lost part of their population, sometimes as much as 25 percent, between 1980 and 2000.

21. The data on local inequalities in the United States come from Estelle Sommeiller, Mark Price, and Ellis Wazeter (2016), "Income Inequality in the U.S. by State, Metropolitan Area, and County," Economic Policy Institute Report. Aggregate figures for other countries are available on the World Inequality Database website.

22. The only billionaires that Kansas people really know are "their" billionaires, the famous Koch brothers, whose corporate headquarters are in Wichita, but who, like every self-respecting American billionaire, also have an apartment in New York—in their case, at 740 Park Avenue.

23. I could also have taken the example of French cheese.

24. Or what Todd Tiahrt, the former Republican congressman from Kansas quoted by Frank, called a "crisis of the soul."

25. This "authenticity" can also be found in the speeches of Donald Trump, who can hardly be said to have won the 2016 election by virtue of his "morality."

26. See especially Raj Chetty, David Grusky, Maximilian Hell, Nathaniel Hendren, Robert Manduca, and Jimmy Narang (2017), "The Fading American Dream: Trends in Absolute Income Mobility since 1940," *Science,* 356(6336), pp. 398–406. This collapse in mobility was largely due to the strong correlation in contemporary America between parental income and children's higher education—a link established by Raj Cherry and Emmanuel Saez. See Raj Chetty, John Friedman, Emmanuel Saez, Nicholas Turner, and Danny Yagan (2017), "Mobility Report Cards: The Role of Colleges in Intergenerational Mobility," National Bureau of Economic Research Working Paper No. 23618 (https://www.nber.org/papers/w23618).

27. Richard Rorty (1998), *Achieving Our Country: Leftist Thought in Twentieth-Century America,* Harvard University Press.

28. See Facundo Alvaredo, Lucas Chancel, Thomas Piketty, Emmanuel Saez, and Gabriel Zucman (2017), "Global Inequality Dynamics: New Findings from WID. World," *American Economic Review,* 107(5), pp. 404–409. See also *World Inequality Report 2018* at wir.2018.wid.world.

29. Katherine J. Cramer (2016), *The Politics of Resentment: Rural Consciousness in Wisconsin and the Rise of Scott Walker,* University of Chicago Press.

30. Cramer uses the term "rural" in a broad sense, to characterize all areas of Wisconsin outside the two main urban agglomerations.

31. And there is some reality in the derision they face from the city dwellers who sometimes look down on them. But this feeling of disrespect is also fueled by media such as Fox News, which never stops telling viewers that "snooty liberals" snub Republican voters and label them "rednecks."

32. Arlie R. Hochschild (2016), *Strangers in Their Own Land,* University of Chicago Press.

33. Moreover, in a country like France (not the United States, where political contributions do not entitle the donor to tax deductions), the least well-off pay in the end to satisfy the political preferences of the most affluent.

34. I do not want to discuss here the pros and cons of particular works, but I think that Katherine Cramer is mistaken when she claims that Thomas Frank, in reducing everything to the ground of values, completely ignores the economic reality of the

ultraconservative vote. Frank does not ignore economics—on the contrary. But what he clearly grasps is that the Democrats have—wrongly—abandoned this terrain.

35. Larry M. Bartels (2016), *Unequal Democracy: The Political Economy of the New Gilded Age,* 2nd ed., Princeton University Press. Let me be clear that in my view it is an extremely important book, which is essential to the debate on today's representation deficit in the United States.

36. Thomas Piketty puts his finger on this political dimension of economic inequalities. If globalization, for example, were solely responsible for the explosion of inequalities, why would there be such differences in this respect between Japan, France, and the United States, three countries equally open to international trade? In the United States, in real terms, the minimum wage has continually declined since the 1960s, whereas in France it has regularly increased. This partly explains the growth of inequalities, and it is the consequence of political decisions. Similarly, the dramatic climb in US top incomes is the direct result of policy choices, such as the lowering of marginal tax rates. See Thomas Piketty (2014), *Capital in the Twenty-First Century,* Harvard University Press.

37. I can only advise the interested reader to consult the Database on Ideology, Money in Politics, and Elections at https://data.stanford.edu/dime, where Adam Bonica has made available a wealth of data on campaign contributions in the United States between 1979 and 2014. Also to be found there are links to numerous works published by Bonica and his coauthors, which shed light on the donors' motives.

38. According to the World Inequality Database (Wid.world).

39. Adam Bonica and Howard Rosenthal (2015), "The Wealth Elasticity of Political Contributions by the Forbes 400," working paper (https://papers.ssrn.com/sol3 /papers.cfm?abstract_id=2668780).

40. According to the data available at the OpenSecrets.org website.

41. Small contributions accounted for 32 percent. During the same election, the percentages for Mitt Romney were 50 percent and 18 percent respectively.

42. Maurice Duverger (1954), *Political Parties: Their Organization and Activity in the Modern State,* London: Methuen.

43. Jane Mayer (2016) illustrates this very well in *Dark Money: The Hidden History of the Billionaires behind the Rise of the Radical Right,* New York: Doubleday.

44. Larry M. Bartels (2013), "The Class War Gets Personal: Inequality as a Political Issue in the 2012 Election," for the annual meeting of the Midwest Political Science Association, Chicago, April 2013, https://my.vanderbilt.edu/larrybartels/working -papers.

45. "There are 47 percent of the people who will vote for the president [Obama] no matter what.[. . .], who are dependent upon government, who believe that they are victims, who believe the government has a responsibility to care for them, who believe that they are entitled to health care, to food, to housing, to you-name-it— that that's an entitlement. And the government should give it to them. And they will vote for this president no matter what. . . . These are people who pay no income tax. . . . [M]y job is not to worry about those people" (quoted from https://www.politifact.com/truth-o-meter/statements/2012/sep/18/mitt-romney/romney-says-47-percent-americans-pay-no-income-tax). This declaration, made at a fundraising event, was obviously not intended for the ears of the public at large. But in politics, you always have to be on your guard against discreet recordings.

46. According to *Politico,* the i360 company even refused to sell its data to Trump in 2015; see Kenneth P. Vogel and Cate Martel (2015), "Koch Brothers Freeze Out Trump," *Politico,* August 7, https://www.politico.com/story/2015/07/kochs-freeze-out-trump-120752.

47. "I turned down a meeting with Charles and David Koch. Much better for them to meet with the puppets of politics, they will do much better!" (tweet from @realDonaldTrump, July 30, 2016).

48. What did he gain by this? It was good for his big ego, of course, but such flattery did not come cheap. His presidential salary is by no means insignificant— $400,000 a year plus expenses of $50,000, a tax-free $100,000 travel account and $19,000 just for leisure—but it is hardly sufficient to make up for the initial outlay. Finally, there are the companies, *his* companies, which he did not stop pampering as president, in defiance of all the rules on conflicts of interest. As many observers have remarked, Donald Trump has succeeded in monetizing his presidency.

49. "Obama Extends Long-Term Trend of Fund-Raising Presidents," *Washington Post,* July 26, 2014.

50. But, as we saw, ultimately inactive.

51. The weight of money in election campaigns is one factor to bear in mind when seeking to explain the sea-change in political conflict observable today in the United States, but also in France, Germany, and the United Kingdom. This is well documented in Thomas Piketty (2018), "Brahmin Left vs Merchant Right: Rising Inequality and the Changing Structure of Political Conflict. Evidence from France, Britain and the United States, 1948–2018," WID.world Working Paper No. 2081/7. In the last few decades, we have gone from a left vote that came mainly from the

relatively uneducated popular classes to a system characterized by multiple elites: the educated elites vote on the left, while the high-income and high-wealth elites vote on the right. See also Thomas Piketty (2020), *Capital and Ideology,* Harvard University Press.

52. It is true that donations of $200 or more have to be published on the FEC website, but more and more individuals and corporations shelter behind super PACs to preserve their anonymity.

53. There are, however, regular expressions of concern about the uneven distribution of donations across Germany's political parties. See, for example, an article from August 1, 2017, in the *Süddeutsche Zeitung:* "Achtmal mehr Großspenden für FDP als für SDP und Grüne." This unequal distribution of private money—and of public funding associated with tax relief—is certainly not peculiar to Germany (as a study of the French data will remind us); nor are the suspicions concerning fake jobs in election campaigns, such as those that hit the CDU in 2017. See "SPD will Merkels Wahlkampffinanzierung prüfen lassen," *Frankfurter Allgemeine Zeitung,* August 21, 2017.

54. That page can be found at https://www.bundestag.de/parlament/praesidium/parteienfinanzierung/fundstellen50000.

55. In fact, these data essentially cover the years 1993–1994, because after January 23, 1995, companies were no longer permitted to contribute to the finances of political parties.

56. At the time of writing, the dispute had not yet been settled, but serious British media outlets such as the BBC and the *Guardian* were making this claim, and it is currently under investigation by the Electoral Commission.

57. The "selling" of visas to oligarchs has unfortunately become a common practice in many countries, including France. We should be aware that it is tantamount to the selling of votes, all the more reprehensible in the present context, where European governments refuse to welcome destitute refugees who ask no more than to be shown a little humanity.

58. He has also directly funded a number of MPs, including Nigel Adams, a member of the Conservative Party and fervent Brexit supporter.

59. The amounts were £125,000 in 2001, £2 million in 2005, £2 million in 2007, and £1 million in 2010.

60. As highlighted by Geoffrey Evans and James Tilley (2017), *The New Politics of Class. The Political Exclusion of the British Working Class,* Oxford University Press. They write: "Labour decided in the 1990s that it could no longer base its electoral

success primarily on working-class support. This led to the party attempting both to change perceptions of itself as a working-class party, and also to move its policy stance rightwards towards the Conservatives."

61. See in particular Evans and Tilley (2017).

62. Facundo Alvaredo, Anthony B. Atkinson, and Salvatore Morelli, "Top Wealth Shares in the UK over more than a Century," WID.world Working Paper No. 2017/2.

63. Office for National Statistics (2019), "Average Household Income, UK: Financial Year Ending 2018."

64. Another explanation for this move to the right has been offered recently by Stephanie Mudge. According to the sociologist, the conversion of the parties of the left to laissez-faire economics and neoliberalism is due to changes in the economics profession—economists have shifted from Keynesianism to the defense of free markets, privatization, and financialization—and to the gradual annexation of the parties by experts. See Stephanie L. Mudge (2018), *Leftism Reinvented: Western Parties from Socialism to Neoliberalism,* Harvard University Press.

65. The researchers estimate the increase in the value of government contracts at between $73,000 and $185,000 dollars, or 14 to 39 times the value of the average donation. See Taylor Boas, Daniel Hidalgo, and Neal Richardson (2014), "The Spoils of Victory: Campaign Donations and Government Contracts in Brazil," *Journal of Politics,* 76(2).

66. See, for example, "Rs 30,000 Crore to be Spent on Lok Sabha Polls: Study," NDTV.com, March 16, 2014, https://www.ndtv.com/elections-news/rs-30-000-crore-to-be-spent-on-lok-sabha-polls-study-554110. India is also the victim of significant "buying" and "selling" of votes—a phenomenon well documented on the independent Indian news site Scroll.in ("Why Selling Their Vote Is a Rational Choice for a Large Segment of Voters in India," May 11, 2018). On the other hand, one can only deplore the fatalism that makes the author of the article say that, for numbers of voters, the money they get from selling their votes is the only tangible benefit of democracy.

8. The Price of a Vote

1. Candidates who make it to the second round of legislative elections do not benefit from an additional entitlement. In this respect, you can only laugh at some of the dialogues in Season Two of the *Baron Noir* TV series: for example, when the Socialist baron Philippe Rickwaert (played by Kad Merad) explains to his former

assistant Cyril Balsan (now running for Parliament) that he can spend more than 38,000 euros, because the law states that it is permissible to exceed this limit by the number of residents in the locality multiplied by 0.15 euros. It's a pity he forgets to add that the spending cap is also increased "in line with the INSEE consumer price index minus the price of tobacco." Not a very telegenic detail? Anyway, it is no surprise that Balsan is elected, with or without this supplement.

2. Constituency populations based on legal residence are available on the website of the Institut National de la Statistique et des Études Économique (INSEE): https://www.insee.fr/fr/statistiques/2508230.

3. Surprisingly, the spending regulations do not apply to elections in municipalities with fewer than 9,000 residents. It would be interesting to study whether this leads to much higher per capita spending, but unfortunately the lack of limits in these smaller localities goes together with a lack of monitoring: candidates do not have to report their spending to the National Commission on Election Financing (CNCCFP), with the result that researchers—and citizens in general—are left in the dark. Nor does this absence of regulation apply only to election spending; mayors in localities with fewer than 9,000 inhabitants—which make up 97 percent of the total number in France—have been exempted from the ban on three identical and consecutive terms of office. In other words, there has been a big song and dance about reforms, while it is discreetly ensured that they do not clash with the interests of good old friends.

4. In the case of municipal elections—as well as the presidential election—the cap on spending is higher for candidates who make it through to the second round.

5. The size of localities varies enormously for municipal elections in France. In Bordeaux, for instance, the spending cap in 2014 was 239,771 euros.

6. See Yasmine Bekkouche and Julia Cagé (2018), "The Price of a Vote: Evidence from France, 1993–2014," CEPR Discussion Paper #12614 (https://ideas.repec.org/p /cpr/ceprdp/12614.html), and Julia Cagé and Edgard Dewitte (2018), "It Takes Money to Make MPs: New Evidence from 150 Years of British Campaign Spending," Sciences Po Working Paper (https://sites.google.com/site/juliacagehomepage /research).

7. Fortunately, there are a few exceptions. Eric Avis, Claudio Ferraz, Federico Finan, and Carlos Varjão (2017), "Money and Politics: The Effects of Campaign Spending Limits on Political Competition and Incumbency Advantage," National Bureau of Economic Research Working Paper No. 23508, have studied the effect of spending limits on electoral competition in Brazil. Also in a Brazilian context,

Bernardo S. Da Silveira and João M. P. de Mello (2011), "Campaign Advertising and Election Outcomes: Quasi-natural Experiment from Gubernatorial Elections in Brazil," *Review of Economic Studies,* 78(2), pp. 590–612, have examined the effectiveness of TV election publicity.

8. The legislative elections of 2017 are an unfortunate exception, since the data were not yet available at the time this book was written. One can only regret the long delay in publishing the campaign accounts of the different candidates, since analysis of these is an important dimension in the smooth operation of the democratic election process. With regard to our choice of polls, we concentrated on municipal and legislative rather than presidential elections, since, in order to identify the effects of election spending, it is necessary to study variations at the level of local polling districts; some candidates, even from the same party, raise and spend more money than others, depending on the locality and the year in question. In this way, we were able to crosscheck the electoral context and the popularity of parties against the specificities of the various constituencies and polling districts, whereas only rather crude correlations could have been identified in the case of presidential elections.

9. In the campaign accounts, "revenues" designates the total resources at the disposal of candidates allowing them to engage in election spending. The French electoral commission reports these revenues by their origin: donations; party contributions; candidates' personal contributions; and benefits or support in kind.

10. Of course, conservative mythology combines this with denunciations of social solidarity and "handouts."

11. See an interactive version of these graphs at thepriceofdemocracy.com. The reader may see there what has happened in each electoral district and look up individual candidates.

12. A number of forces might, however, pull in the opposite direction; one need only think of the last few weeks of Nicolas Sarkozy's campaign in 2012. Faced with inexorable defeat, some candidates may decide to go for broke and spend as if there were no tomorrow.

13. In technical terms, our regression analysis involves "fixed effects" by electoral district and election year.

14. In the neighboring district, his friend Nicolas Sarkozy would pale in significance with just 386,000 francs (a little under 80,000 euros) in donations.

15. In 1996, having been found guilty of collusion, Patrick Balkany received a suspended fifteen-month prison sentence, a fine of 200,000 francs, and a two-year disqualification from public office.

16. David Koch's candidacy allowed him to circumvent electoral laws, since candidates were not subject to the $1,000 ceiling imposed on other donors. He could therefore contribute as much as he wished to the campaign. Note that, with its 1.06 percent of the total (a little over 921,000 votes), the Libertarian Party achieved the best score in its history—that is, until 2012 and Gary Johnson.

17. Unfortunately, systematic information about the size of these transfers is not available to researchers.

18. André Campana (1976), *L'Argent secret,* Paris, Arthaud; Éric Phélippeau (2013), "Le financement de la vie politique française par les entreprises 1970–2012," *L'Année sociologique,* 63(1), pp. 189–223.

19. On the adverse effects of negative publicity—particularly for voter turnout—I heartily recommend the excellent book: Shanto Iyengar and Stephen Ansolabehere (1995), *Going Negative: How Political Advertisements Shrink and Polarize the Electorate,* New York: Free Press.

20. With his usual moderation, one of Trump's TV ads asserted that "staggering amounts of cash poured into the Clinton Foundation from criminals, dictators, countries that hate America." But we would have expected nothing less. See the ad at https://www.c-span.org/video/?416919-1/presidential-campaign-ads.

21. The first US regulatory measures in this field date from the Radio Act of 1927, which was later incorporated into the Communications Act of 1934. The idea was that candidates could not be discriminated against in their access to audiovisual media.

22. Since an amendment to Section 315 passed in 1959, this "equality" does not apply to newscasts, to bona fide news interviews with candidates, to "on the spot coverage" of news events, or to documentary programs. This gives a real advantage to outgoing candidates for office. On Section 315 of the Communications Act, see, for example, Eric Barnow (1990), *Tube of Plenty: The Evolution of American Television,* New York University Press.

23. In both cases, we are focusing only on the spending of the candidates' committees, leaving out of account the (also huge) spending by super PACs.

24. In Canada, although TV and radio broadcasters are required to make airtime available for candidates, that time is made available "for purchase." A tiny amount of it is free of charge, but in effect it is an American-style system.

25. See the excellent report "The Follower Factory," *New York Times,* January 27, 2018, https://www.nytimes.com/interactive/2018/01/27/technology/social-media-bots .html. It is by no means only politicians who buy followers; many celebrities and

athletes engage in the same practice. Season 6 of the excellent *Homeland* series dissects the operations of a secret, politically motivated bot factory, whose truculent boss, Brett O'Keefe, is evidently inspired by the conspiracy theorist and libertarian Alex Jones (the *Alex Jones Show* has a weekly radio audience in the hundreds of thousands, and he is also behind the fake news website Infowars.com). In July 2016, at the time of the Republican Party convention, Alex Jones took part in the America First Unity Rally organized by supporters of Donald Trump. If we think that the *Homeland* scriptwriters wrote more than a half of Season 6 before Trump was elected, we can only conclude that reality often goes beyond fiction.

26. Law No. 77-808 of July 19, 1977, on the publication and diffusion of certain opinion polls has been updated by Law No. 2016-508 of April 25, 2016, on the rules applicable to elections. The purpose of these laws is to prevent the publication of election surveys from interfering with free decisions by the electorate.

27. Particularly in the United States, candidates also use social media to assist fundraising among groups that were previously out of reach. Twitter is a widespread and effective tool for politicians running for office for the first time, who lack both political capital and sufficient media exposure. It does not help them to raise millions of dollars, but it can bring them many small donations and thus make them more competitive in an electoral landscape inundated with large contributions. See especially Maria Petrova, Ananya Sen, and Pina Yildirim (2017), "Social Media and Political Donations: New Technology and Incumbency Advantage in the United States," Centre for Economic Policy Research Discussion Paper 11808 (https://ideas .repec.org/p/cpr/ceprdp/11808.html).

28. Eitan D. Hersh (2015), *Hacking the Electorate: How Campaigns Perceive Voters,* Cambridge University Press.

29. In contrast to other authors such as D. Sunshine Hillygus and Todd G. Shields (whose 2008 *The Persuadable Voter,* Princeton University Press, had a large echo in North America), Eitan Hersh thinks that the use of commercial data by campaigns is not only uncommon but ineffective, in comparison with the simple use of public data such as localized census databases. He also tends to downplay the use made *up to now* of data from social media, though not its future potential. But the use of Facebook, for example, has so far been limited (fortunately, one might say) by the fact that the company does not sell some of its users' confidential information.

30. According to the company website, https://www.catalist.us (consulted in March 2018), the Catalist database contains information about more than 240 million citizens of voting age. This consists of a national list of 185 million registered

voters, collected from publicly available data at the level of individual states, plus additional information from commercial data concerning 55 million unregistered electors.

31. This figure was calculated in March 2018, on the basis of online data of the Federal Electoral Commission. The interested reader may find in the online appendix the annual evolution of this spending between 2007 and March 2018. The year 2008 was particularly lucrative for Catalist, since the campaigns of Barack Obama and Hillary Clinton spent hundreds of thousands of dollars each for access to information on its database.

32. NGP VAN came into being in 2010 through a merger between NGP (a technological fundraising corporation attached to the Democratic Party) and VAN (Voter Activation Network).

33. According to the figures in Jane Mayer (2016), *Dark Money: The Hidden History of the Billionaires behind the Rise of the Radical Right,* New York: Doubleday.

34. To be precise: 371,000 in late March 2018.

35. Figure provided by the organizers.

36. Although I cannot discuss it in this book, the vote of blacks and other minorities is another key issue in the functioning of democracy in the United States. The main problem has to do with the fact that it is very "easy" to lose your right to vote, often for life, particularly after a criminal conviction. In 2016, at the last elections, the right to vote was denied to 6 million Americans, more than one-third of whom were black. See, for example, Christopher Uggen, Ryan Larson, and Sarah Shannon (2016), "6 Million Lost Voters: State Level Estimates Felony Disenfranchisement," The Sentencing Project, October 6, http://www.sentencingproject.org/publications /6-million-lost-voters-state-level-estimates-felony-disenfranchisement-2016/.

37. The expression "hidden poll tax" or "hidden property qualification" was popularized in France in the late 1970s by Daniel Gaxie, who chiefly had in mind educational inequalities. Daniel Gaxie (1978), *Le Cens caché. Inégalités culturelles et ségrégation politique,* Paris: Le Seuil.

38. This law was canceled in 1830 in France. But for a long time, the "double vote" remained in force in other countries such as the United Kingdom, where graduates of the most prestigious universities, beginning with Oxford and Cambridge, could vote for parliamentary representatives both in their "university constituency" and in their home area. This system was abolished only in 1948.

39. See Thomas Piketty (2014), *Capital in the Twenty-First Century,* Harvard University Press.

9. Has the Last Word Been Said?

1. This point needs to be stressed, for too many conservatives justify the unlimited private funding of election campaigns by arguing that the rich contribute with their wallets, while the poor contribute with their time. In other words, everyone acts in accordance with their comparative advantage, and if the rich were banned from donating, the poor would have to be banned from grassroots campaigning. This argument is usually based on the notion of "scarcity," popularized in economics by Sendhil Mullainathan and Eldar Shafir: that is, if the poor lack economic resources, the rich, for their part, suffer from a lack of time. See Sendhil Mullainathan and Eldar Shafir (2013), *Scarcity: Why Having Too Little Means So Much,* New York: Henry Holt. The problem is that this does not correspond at all to reality. If politicians valued the time of the poor as much as the money of the rich, they would coddle their activists as much as their donors, instead of giving most of their attention to the latter.

2. Pierre Rosanvallon (2018), *Good Government: Democracy beyond Elections,* Harvard University Press, p. 1.

3. I would advise the reader to consult the four parts of Rosanvallon's investigation: *Counter-Democracy: Politics in an Age of Distrust,* Cambridge University Press, 2008; *Democratic Legitimacy: Impartiality, Reflexivity, Proximity,* Princeton University Press, 2011; *The Society of Equals,* Harvard University Press, 2013; and *Good Government: Democracy beyond Elections,* Harvard University Press, 2018.

4. I would add that, in a country like the United States, even this function has partly gone by the board, since it is the capacity of candidates to raise private funds that enables them to run even in primaries. Bernard Manin actually speaks of the end of "party democracy," seeing it as no more than an intermediate stage between nineteenth-century parliamentarianism and the current form of representation that he describes as "audience democracy." This form is defined by the "personal character" of "the link between the representative and his electors"; Bernard Manin (1997), *Principles of Representative Government,* Cambridge University Press, p. 220.

5. Rosanvallon (2018) also formulates this idea in the language of a "democracy of appropriation" (*démocratie d'exercice*). What is required, in his view, is to move from a mere "democracy of authorization" (with political parties as the pivot) to a "democracy of appropriation," through the creation, for example, of new bodies with the power to supervise and evaluate governments (pp. 9–11).

6. Dominique Rousseau (2015), *Radicaliser la démocratie—Propositions pour une refondation,* Paris: Seuil.

7. Rousseau also proposes fifteen-member citizens' conventions, established through random selection, whose task it would be to produce a normative proposal on a matter of public interest. We shall return at the end of this chapter to the question of random selection.

8. Unfortunately, Rousseau does not specify in his book the exact ways in which they would be elected.

9. The 545-member National Constituent Assembly (ANC) is endowed with unlimited powers for an indefinite period. Its task is to draft a new constitution, but it has not been recognized by the international community.

10. Parliament had been dominated by the opposition since the elections of December 2015.

11. This law requires political parties to alternate the members of the candidate lists between men and women, and to have half of their lists headed by a woman. In Argentina, a law on gender parity in political representation was passed in 2017: in the 2019 legislative elections, all the lists of candidates for Congress will have to alternate male and female candidates. In Japan, a Gender Parity Law was enacted in 2018. In the United States, by contrast, there is no law that affirmatively guarantees women's representation in politics. As a consequence, women currently hold only 23.4 percent of seats in the House of Representatives and 25 percent in the Senate, as detailed by the Rutgers Center for American Women and Politics: https://www.cawp.rutgers.edu/women-us-congress-2019.

12. However, Italians had to wait twenty-two years for the law of May 25, 1970, stipulating the circumstances under which a referendum was permitted and the forms in which it should take place.

13. The disallowed exceptions are fiscal and budgetary legislation, amnesty and pardon laws, and the ratification of international treaties.

14. The proposal may also come from five regional electoral colleges. On the people's referenda in Italy, see, for example, Johan Ryngaert (1982), "Le referendum d'initiative populaire en Italie: une longue traversée du desert," *Revue française de science politique,* 32(6), pp. 1024–1040.

15. In today's Switzerland, 50,000 citizens = 0.75 percent of the adult population.

16. At cantonal and local levels, citizens also have a right to propose new legislation (popular legislative initiative). See especially Antoine Bevort (2011), "Démocratie, le laboratoire suisse," *Revue du MAUSS,* 37(1). I am using here his data on the number of referenda.

17. On the "general people's initiative," see Michel Hottelier (2003), "Suisse: réforme des droits populaires de rang fédéral," *Revue française de droit constitutionnel,* 55(3).

18. Historically, France was the first modern Western democracy to admit the practice of direct democracy into its constitution. Thus, the Constitution of 1793 established not only universal manhood suffrage (a property qualification was reintroduced soon afterward) but also the possibility for at least one-tenth of electors, from a half of departments plus one, to submit any law adopted by the legislature for a people's vote.

19. In May 2019, a group of opposition parliamentarians won the right to launch such a referendum procedure to block the sale of the state's majority stake in Aéroports de Paris, the operator of Charles de Gaulle and Orly airports. However, while the organizers won the backing of a fifth of deputies and got the green light from the Constitutional Council, they still have to obtain the signatures of 4.7 million voters (which they may not succeed in doing).

20. "A referendum . . . may be held upon the initiative of one fifth of the Members of Parliament, supported by one tenth of the voters enrolled on the electoral register. This initiative shall take the form of a Private Member's Bill and shall not be applied to the repeal of a statutory provision promulgated for less than one year." Article 11 of the French Constitution: http://www2.assemblee-nationale.fr/langues/welcome-to -the-english-website-of-the-french-national-assembly.

21. Some US states, including California (as early as 1911) and Oregon, also allow for the holding of referenda on a popular initiative. See, e.g., Vincent Michelot (2010), "Le processus référendaire en Californie: un traves-tissement démocratique?" *Pouvoirs,* 133(2), pp. 57–68.

22. It is probably not by chance that Ayn Rand, in *Atlas Shrugged,* tells the story of a dynasty that made its fortune on the railroads.

23. Recall procedures have been introduced in fifteen US states, but until 2003 the only successful petition had been the one launched in 1921 against the governor of North Dakota.

24. On October 7, 2003, the electors of California were asked to reply to two questions at the same time: "Do you want to recall Gray Davis?" and, if they did (but without yet knowing the overall result), "Who do you want to replace him?" They had to choose among no fewer than 135 candidates—which may seem a huge number, but all that anyone needed to run was a sum of $3,500 plus sixty-five

supporting signatures. In the end, 55 percent of those who voted chose recall, and Schwarzenegger became governor with more than 3.7 million votes.

25. On the practice of recall votes, I would particularly recommend Thomas E. Cronin, *Direct Democracy. The Politics of Initiative, Referendum, and Recall,* Harvard University Press, 1980.

26. On a 53.4 percent turnout, the "yes" vote won with 57.5 percent of the total on November 29, 2009.

27. Medi-Cal, or the California Medical Assistance Program, is the state version of Medicaid.

28. According to the figures in Bevort (2011).

29. This example is given in Bernard Voutat (2005), "À propos de la démocratie directe. L'expérience helvétique," in Marie-Hélène Bacqué et al. (eds.), *Gestion de proximité et démocratie participative,* Paris: La Découverte.

30. We have been speaking of "popular initiative" referenda, but we should note that in most cases the initiative actually comes from a political party. This is particularly visible in Italy, where the task of collecting hundreds of thousands of signatures is extremely costly and requires great logistical organization. None of that is within the reach of ordinary citizens. It is true that nowadays there are online petition platforms, such as Change.org, which greatly facilitate the collection of signatures.

31. A little under 900,000 signatures were required for the vote to be held, and the recall campaign eventually collected 1.3 million.

32. And conversely, spending to oppose an initiative reduces this probability. John M. de Figueiredo, Chang Ho Ji, and Thad Jousser (2011), "Financing Direct Democracy: Revisiting the Research on Campaign Spending and Citizen Initiatives," *Journal of Law, Economics, & Organization,* 27(3).

33. The interested reader may wish to consult the numerous works of Karine Van der Straeten, particularly the collection of articles she edited in 2016 with André Blais and Jean-François Laslier: *Voting Experiments,* Springer International Publishing.

34. See Hélène Landemore (2017), "Inclusive Constitution Making and Religious Rights: Lessons from the Icelandic Experiment," *Journal of Politics,* 79(3).

35. See, in particular, Hélène E. Landemore (2012), "Why the Many Are Smarter than the Few and Why It Matters," *Journal of Public Deliberation,* 8(1).

36. James Fishkin (2009), *When the People Speak. Deliberative Democracy and Public Consultation,* Oxford University Press. In the Chinese experiment, conducted

in the town of Zeguo (Zhejiang province), Fishkin and his colleagues effectively helped the local authorities to identify the people's preferences with regard to development projects.

37. See Émile Servan-Schreiber (2018), *Supercollectif,* Paris: Fayard.

38. Myriam Revault d'Allonnes reviews, in particular, the works of Thomas Hobbes, Jean-Jacques Rousseau, and Hanna Pitkin. See Myriam Revault d'Allonnes (2016), *Le Miroir et la Scène. Ce que peut la représentation politique,* Paris: Le Seuil.

39. Manin (1997).

40. Manin (1997) writes: "The sources would suggest that courts heard an average of one such case a month."

41. On the corporate funding of German election campaigns, see Martin Höpner (2009), "Parteigänger und Landschaftspfleger: Eine Analyse der Parteispenden großer deutscher Unternehmen, 1984–2005," Working Paper 09 / 6 of the Max Planck Institute.

42. Benjamin Page and Martin Gilens (2017), *Democracy in America? What Has Gone Wrong and What We Can Do about It,* University of Chicago Press.

43. Although I concentrate here on Lawrence Lessig's proposal, it should be noted that he is not the only one to have championed this idea of a "democratic voucher." In *Plutocrats United* (Yale University Press, 2016), Richard Hasen both proposes that each US citizen should be given vouchers to fund election campaigns—or, to be more precise, a $100 voucher every two years, coinciding with an electoral cycle—and argues for a cap to be imposed on election spending and contributions. Hasen's suggested limits are rather high, though: no individual would be able to contribute or spend a total of more than $25,000 for a given federal election, or more than $500,000 for all federal elections in the course of a two-year electoral cycle. In December 2018, Representative Ro Khanna introduced a public financing bill, the "Democracy Dollars Act," whose goal is to "empower the average American by providing every registered voter with $50 'Democracy Dollars' to spend in federal elections: $25 for presidential, $15 for Senate, and $10 for House campaigns"; for particulars, see http://dearcolleague.us/2018/05/be-an-original-cosponsor-of-the-democracy-dollars-act/.

44. Lawrence Lessig (2015), *Republic, Lost. The Corruption of Equality and the Steps to End It,* New York: Grand Central Publishing.

45. In Chapter 6, I referred to what it seems proper to call Barack Obama's "hypocrisy" over private funding. Though so strident in his attacks, he did nothing to regulate private funding and ended up benefiting handsomely from it. It is moving

to read Lessig's account and to realize that in a way he felt betrayed by Obama on this issue. For a long time he believed, like many others, that Obama saw how the solution to every other problem depended on ending the corruption of American political life. But perhaps Obama did not understand this so well; or perhaps he simply chose, with eyes wide open, to continue the old style of politics. It was certainly an unfortunate choice—not so much for his two presidential terms as for the present state of the American political landscape, which he did not help to reform.

46. Lessig strangely excludes presidential candidates from this system. In my view, it would be more consistent to include them, even if it meant increasing the value of each democracy voucher.

47. Lessig does not specify how many.

48. The system was introduced under the "Honest Elections Seattle" law of November 2015, the result of a citizens' initiative. Candidates in the 2017 election could register for the program from January 1, 2016. Citizens not on the electoral register must apply to receive the vouchers. All details of the procedure are accessible online at http://www.seattle.gov/democracyvoucher.

49. For the mayoral election, the spending limit is $400,000 in the primaries and $800,000 dollars for the primary and general elections combined. All the limits are accessible at http://www.seattle.gov/democracyvoucher/i-am-a-candidate/campaign -limits-and-laws. However, candidates may ask to be exempt from these limits if one of their rivals who is not participating in the program spends a larger sum.

50. More vouchers have been issued, in fact, but two candidates—Jon Grant and Teresa Monqueda—were unable to accept this additional funding because of the spending cap of $300,000.

51. Of course, there is no clearly causal connection; Peter Holmes would probably have won without the democracy vouchers. But it should be noted that candidates who have chosen this innovative system, rather than purely private funding, have scored rather well on election day.

52. This contest was for Position 8 on the city council. The two victorious candidates for Position 9, Lorena Gonzalez and Pat Murakami, were also the only ones out of the total of seven who used democracy vouchers.

53. These figures come from Jennifer Heerwig and Brian J. McCabe (2017), "High-Dollar Donors and Donor-Rich Neighborhoods: Representational Distortion in Financing a Municipal Election in Seattle," *Urban Affairs Review,* 42(2), pp. 1–30.

54. The results of this study are summarized in Gene Balk (2017), "Do Seattle's Democracy Vouchers Work? New Analysis Says Yes," *Seattle Times,* October 13, https://www.seattletimes.com/seattle-news/data/ do-seattles-democracy-vouchers-work-new-analysis-says-yes/.

55. The libertarian "Pacific Legal Foundation," which had filed the initial complaint, appealed to the Washington State Supreme Court against this decision in December 2017. But in July 2019, the Washington State Supreme Court upheld the decision. In a unanimous opinion, Justice Steven Gonzalez wrote that "the Democracy Voucher Program does not alter, abridge, restrict, censor, or burden speech." See Daniel Beekman (2019), "Washington State Supreme Court Unanimously Upholds Seattle's Pioneering 'Democracy Vouchers,'" *Seattle Times,* July 11, https://www .seattletimes.com/seattle-news/politics/ washington-state-supreme-court-unanimously-upholds-seattles-pioneering-democracy-vouchers-program/.

56. A similar program is under discussion in Austin, Texas, and may soon be given the green light.

10. Toward a Democratization of the "Private" Funding of Democracy and a New Way of Publicly Funding Parties

1. Obviously, not any single political movement would be able to benefit from the public funding and some conditions need to be introduced. In my DEVs proposal, to benefit from the vouchers, a political movement needs to obtain at least 1 percent of them. This (rather limited) conditionality guarantees at the same time the vitality and dynamism of the democratic process and the "seriousness" of the political players.

2. The former benefits from a tax reduction of 396 euros (66 percent of the value of the donation), whereas the latter, not being liable to pay income tax, receives no fiscal benefit and has to pay the full cost alone.

3. Note, however, that there is no reason why this system, once in place, should apply only to political donations to parties or campaigns; in my view, it could and should be extended to all the currently tax-deductible donations to foundations. I have proposed a similar system for the popular funding of news media, which would include, for example, the creation of a new status of a "nonprofit media organization." See Julia Cagé (2016), *Saving the Media: Capitalism, Crowdfunding, and Democracy,* Cambridge, MA: Belknap Press.

4. For more on the UK Gift Aid system, see Kimberley Sharf and Sarah Smith (2016), "Charitable Donations and Tax Relief in the UK," in Gabrielle Fack and Camille Landais (eds.), *Charitable Giving and Tax Policy: A Historical and Comparative Perspective,* Oxford University Press.

5. All the details of how it works are accessible at https://www.gov.uk/donating-to-charity/gift-aid.

6. As we saw in Chapter 3, the level of fraud is not insignificant, at least in France, where personal tax returns may include donations to political parties that do not appear in those parties' accounts.

7. Scharf and Smith (2016).

8. The reason for this is that the public funding paid to the citizen's chosen political party is equivalent to a percentage of his or her tax bill.

9. It averaged less than 2 million euros a year during the 2012–2016 period, particularly because of the low level of donations to political parties.

10. That is, of expenditure in the 2015–2016 electoral cycle. The only spending at issue here is that of individuals and PACs, and I am using the Opensecrets data accessible at https://www.opensecrets.org/overview/index.php?display=T&type = A&cycle = 2016.

11. The amount of $1.5 billion is also six times less than the total that US households spend each year on Halloween celebrations: see Jean Zaid (2017), "Année record en vue pour Halloween," Franceinfo, October 30, https://www.francetvinfo.fr/replay-radio/vous-le-partagerez-aujourd-hui/annee-record-en-vue-pour-halloween_2421195.html.

12. The requirement that a movement should receive a minimum number of donations is also in the spirit of the "democracy vouchers" introduced for the Seattle local elections in 2017. See Chapter 9.

13. I could have considered other alternatives, using shorthand formulas such as "American-style" or "Italian-style." In the first of these, if citizens choose not to take up their Democratic Equality Vouchers, the public funding is in a sense "lost": the money in question is used for another purpose. This does not seem to me the right solution. To end the omnipotence of private interests in the democratic process, it is necessary to have a high level of public funding. The other ("Italian") solution would be to allocate any "leftover" funding in accordance with the preferences of those citizens who did express themselves—that is how the "8 per thousand" operates in Italy for the funding of religions. My system seems preferable, however. It is true that citizens who do not express themselves lose the right to decide how "their" funding should be allocated, but a rule pegging the allocation of "leftover" funding to

previous election results ensures greater stability in the system. After all, it is not unreasonable to assume that those who do not express themselves are, in their way, satisfied with the existing balance of things.

14. An apprenticeship period seems necessary, however, as does a period for regaining what has been lost. Citizens will not change overnight into enthusiastic supporters of the funding of political parties in which they no longer have any faith (or even, most often, of newly emerging political forces, which they sometimes rightly see as involving a change in form without any radical shake-up). Citizens must be given time, but it is my firm belief that each year more and more will grasp the opportunity offered by Democratic Equality Vouchers.

15. On the public funding of religions, the reader may like to consult Francis Messner (2015), *Public Funding of Religions in Europe,* Farnham, UK: Ashgate Publishing, especially the chapters on Germany and Italy.

16. See especially Shanto Iyengar and Stephen Ansolabehere (1995), *Going Negative: How Political Advertisements Shrink and Polarize the Electorate,* New York: Free Press.

17. The official campaign begins on the second Monday preceding the first round of voting and comes to a halt at midnight on the eve of the ballot. It then resumes on the day when the two frontrunners are announced and comes to a final halt at midnight on the eve of the second round.

18. The organic law of April 25, 2016, updated the rules governing presidential elections, including the allocation of speaking time. Previously, strict equality had been stipulated for candidates and their supporters throughout the "intermediate" period, which was naturally advantageous to the "smallest" campaigns. (Note, however, that this strict equality related only to speaking time, not to total airtime, and that the latter included TV and radio editorial material on candidates and their supporters.) On the rules governing pluralism during and outside election periods, see the information available on the CSA website, https://www.csa.fr.

19. See the CSA recommendation no. 2016-2 of September 7, 2016, to the radio and television services for the presidential election: https://www.legifrance.gouv.fr/affichTexte.do?cidTexte=JORFTEXT000033104095&categorieLien=id.

20. To be precise, seven minutes in the first round and five in the second, or a total of twelve minutes, against two hours for the Socialist Party and one hour and forty-four minutes for the Républicains.

21. See http://www.conseil-constitutionnel. fr/conseil-constitutionnel/francais/les -decisions/acces-par-date/decisions-depuis-1959/2017/2017-651-qpc/decision-n-2017 -651-qpc-du-31-mai-2017.149036.html.

11. Toward a Mixed Assembly

1. See the January 2018 "barometer of political confidence" published by CEVIPOF (the Center for Political Research at Sciences Po): http://www.cevipof.com/fr/le -barometre-de-la-confiance-politique-du-cevipof/ resultats-1/vague9 /. According to CEVIPOF figures, 27 percent is also higher than the level of confidence expressed in the media.

2. In 2018, 26 percent of the citizens surveyed by Gallup had "quite a lot" or a "great deal" of confidence in labor unions (28 percent in 2017 but only 19 percent in 2009).

3. In the online appendix, I have calculated from French post-election surveys and US Gallup data since the late 1970s that public trust has remained fairly stable in the case of the unions but sharply declined in the case of parties.

4. According to the 2017 edition of the *Tableaux de l'économie française* published by the National Institute of Statistics and Economic Studies: https://www .insee.fr/fr/statistiques/2569336?sommaire=2587886#titre-bloc-3.

5. Daniel Schlozman (2015), *When Movements Anchor Parties: Electoral Alignments in American History,* Princeton University Press.

6. Article 1 of the law of March 21, 1884, stated that Articles 291 to 294 of the Penal Code ceased to apply to trade unions. In other words, it opened the way for unions and professional associations to constitute themselves legally, without authorization from the government of the day.

7. Stéphane Sirot (2014), *1884, des syndicats pour la République,* Lormont: Le Bord de l'eau.

8. See, in particular, Yves Poirmeur (2014), *Les Partis politiques. Du XIXe au XXIe siècle en France,* Paris: LGDJ. The hostility to parties was by no means peculiar to France, as pointed out by Bernard Manin (1997), *Principles of Representative Government,* Cambridge University Press. In Britain and the United States, most of the inventors of representative government considered party divisions to be a threat to the system they wanted to establish.

9. The Charter was adopted in October 1906 at the ninth congress of the CGT, the General Confederation of Labor.

10. In Sweden, the Confederation of Swedish Unions (commonly known as LO) was founded in 1898 on the initiative of the Social Democratic Workers' Party and has remained tied to it ever since.

11. Historically, many secretaries of the CGT were also members of the Communist Party. It was not until the late 1990s that the union movement really went its separate way.

12. Florence Haegel (2007), *Les Partis politiques. Du XIXe au XXIe siècle en France,* Paris: LGDJ.

13. Originally constituted as the Labour Representation Committee in 1900, it became the Labour Party in 1906. On members' contributions, see Keith Ewing, Sheila Rowbottom, and Joo-Cheong Tham, eds. (2011), *The Funding of Political Parties: Where Now?,* London: Routledge.

14. It was not the first time that the Conservatives had struck at the financial basis of working-class representation. In 1927, following the defeat of the General Strike in 1926, the punitive Trade Disputes and Trade Unions Act led to a sharp decline in the income of the Labour Party. See Julia Cagé and Edgard Dewitte (2018), "It Takes Money to Make MPs: New Evidence from 150 Years of British Campaign Spending," Sciences Po Working Paper (https://sites.google.com/site/juliacagehomepage/research).

15. One of the party's aims, in Britain as in Germany, was to close the gap between representatives and their working-class base. Political parties "permitted the nomination of candidates who were close to the membership in their social position, living conditions, and concerns" (Manin, 1997).

16. See the figures in the online appendix.

17. See especially Taylor E. Dark (1999), *The Unions and the Democrats: An Enduring Alliance,* Ithaca, NY: ILR Press.

18. Similarly, in the United Kingdom, the Industrial Relations Act of 1971 provided that workers affected by the "agency shop" clause could refuse on grounds of conscience to join a union, so long as they paid to a registered charity a sum equal to the union dues.

19. James Feigenbaum, Alexander Hertel-Fernandez, and Vanessa Williamson (2018), "From the Bargaining Table to the Ballot Box: Political Effects of Right to Work Laws," National Bureau of Economic Research Working Paper No. 24259 (https://jamesfeigenbaum.github.io/research/rtw/elections/).

20. I proposed as much in *Saving the Media* for "nonprofit media organizations," arguing that their management should include shareholders, journalists, and readers; see Julia Cagé (2016), *Saving the Media: Capitalism, Crowdfunding, and Democracy,* Cambridge, MA: Belknap Press. But co-determination should also become a legal requirement in all companies (and in France, it is necessary to go beyond the

important, though much too timid, advance of the "Rebsamen Law" of 2015 on social dialogue and employment). Of the many studies published on this issue, I would particularly recommend Isabelle Ferras (2017), *Firms as Political Entities: Saving Democracy through Economic Bicameralism,* New York: Cambridge University Press.

21. Benjamin Radcliff and Martin Saiz (1998), "Labor Organization and Public Policy in the American States," *Journal of Politics,* 60(1), pp. 113–125.

22. Of course, I am not suggesting that everything would be perfect in a union wonderland. In Chapter 2, I referred to the hidden funding of various political parties, and I might similarly mention the secret union funds, especially as it is sometimes the same actors at work. In Germany, donations from employers' federations in the metal and engineering industries have played an important role for political parties, and in France it is the all-powerful metallurgical federation, the UIMM, that has contributed millions of euros in cash to the finances of the unions. See Roger Lenglet, Jean-Luc Touly, and Christophe Mongermont (2008*), L'Argent noir des syndicats,* Paris: Fayard. But there is no point in being nihilistic. It is true that neither social democracy nor political democracy has been without its scandals. However, unions have many advantages over parties, not the least of which is that the working classes are better represented in them. This is why it is necessary to take inspiration from the labor movement.

23. See the reference work: Richard B. Freeman and James Medoff (1984), *What Do Unions Do?,* New York: Basic Books. Five years earlier, the two researchers had used a fine formulation in describing what they called "the two faces of unionism": "Much union political muscle has been devoted to progressive social policy which provides no obvious material gains to unionized workers, save as members of the overall working population"; Richard B. Freeman and James L. Medoff (1979), "The Two Faces of Unionism," *The Public Interest,* 57, pp. 69–93.

24. The new precarious workers benefit very little from social representation. In a report from 2008 to the French labor ministry ("Le travailleur économiquement dépendant: quelle protection?"), Paul-Henri Antonmattei and Jean-Christophe Sciberras underlined the need to consider the conditions under which collective bargaining could operate for offshore workers without secure employment. In Spain, which in this respect is ahead of other European countries, the law permits self-employed workers not only to join the union organization of their choice, but also to create and join special professional associations, which, if recognized as representatives, may be consulted by the public authorities when actions affecting those self-employed workers are under consideration. See Olivier Leclerc and Fernando

Valdès Dal-Ré (2008), "Les nouvelles frontières du travail indépendant. À propos du Statut du travail autonome espagnol," *Revue de droit du travail,* 5, pp. 296–303. A report published in 2012 by Adalberto Perulli ("Travail économiquement dépendant / parasubordination: les aspects juridiques, sociaux et économiques," European Commission, 2003) also contains much interesting information: http://www.social -law.net/IMG/pdf/parasubordination_report_fr.pdf.

25. In the US context, a particularly interesting study is the one by Joshua L. Kalla and Ethan Porter (2019), "Correcting Bias in Perceptions of Public Opinion among American Elected Officials: Results from Two Field Experiments," https://osf.io /c2sp6.

26. See Katherine J. Cramer (2016), *The Politics of Resentment: Rural Conscious-ness in Wisconsin and the Rise of Scott Walker,* University of Chicago Press.

27. It was a "volatile" cabinet, as some of its members left it in the time it took him to post a tweet. Fortunately for him, though, he does not seem to have had much difficulty in finding another multimillionaire as rich as, or richer than, the one before. Also of note is that, for reasons not unrelated to the theme of this book, one-half of citizens in the United States own precisely nothing. In 2014, according to the World Inequality Database, the combined net wealth of the least well-off 50 percent of Americans was even slightly negative (–0.1 percent of total net wealth). See https://wid.world / country / usa / .

28. Michaela Tindera (2019), "The Definitive Net Worth of Donald Trump's Cabinet," *Forbes,* July 25, https://www.forbes.com/sites/chasewithorn/2017/07/05/ the-4-3-billion-cabinet-see-what-each-top-trump-advisor-is-worth/#4659d1615dfc. Estimates published by Quartz in December 2016 point to an even greater level of inequality, with the 17 cabinet members owning combined wealth of $9.5 billion (as much as 109 million Americans); see https://qz.com/862412/trumps-16- cabinet-level-picks-have-more-money-than-a-third-of-american-households -combined/.

29. Jennifer Calfas (2017), "Donald Trump Says He Does Not Want a 'Poor Person' in a Cabinet Role," *Time,* June 22, https://time.com/4828157/donald-trump-cabinet -iowa-rally-poor-person/.

30. Since 2014, parliamentarians in France must also make a declaration of interests. Alas, the process is not dazzlingly transparent and provides us with almost unusable data, since the documents available on the HATVP website are in an illegible scrawl. The French authorities have, however, mastered the use of spread-sheets—or at least I think they have. The "Regards citoyens" organization deserves

our praise for the efforts it has made to encourage the participative digitization of these data.

31. Nicholas Carnes (2013), *White-Collar Government: The Hidden Role of Class in Economic Policy Making,* University of Chicago Press. The use of sartorial aspects to describe social-occupational categories may seem an incidental detail, but a recent debate in the French National Assembly on how deputies should dress (after François Ruffin from La France insoumise turned up one day in a football vest) shows that it is far from trivial. I also cannot help thinking of an episode in the *Baron noir* TV series, where Philippe Rickwaert attends a session of the assembly wearing blue overalls and a red necktie to argue vehemently in support of pupils at vocational colleges.

32. We shall see at the end of this chapter that this is not without consequences, since members of Congress who were workers before entering politics vote on many issues, particularly economic ones, differently from people such as lawyers or company directors.

33. The figures for the United Kingdom come from the House of Commons Library and are available online at http://researchbriefings.parliament.uk /ResearchBriefing/Summary/CBP-7529.

34. The newspaper *Le Monde* has done a tremendous job in providing detailed computer graphics with reference to deputies in the National Assembly; see https://www.lemonde.fr/politique/article/2017/06/28/qui-est-mon-depute-notre-moteur-de-recherche-pour-mieux-connaitre-votre-representant-a-l-assemblee-nationale_5152291_823448.html.

35. In the United Kingdom, 23 percent of MPs elected in 2017 studied at Oxford or Cambridge, and 29 percent went to private schools (compared with 7 percent of the population). Data from Sutton Trust, "Parliamentary Privilege—The MPs 2017," https://www.suttontrust.com/wp-content/uploads/2017/06/ Parliamentary-privilege-2017_FINAL_V2.pdf.

36. It is true that Jean Lassalle claims on the National Assembly website to be an agricultural worker (http://www2.assemblee-nationale.fr/deputes/liste/cat-sociopro), but his real profession is as a political full-timer. Caroline Fiat, who is classified as a "skilled worker," is an assistant nurse on the payroll of the medical sector.

37. The data for the 1958–2012 period come from the works of Luc Rouban, one of the foremost researchers on the French political elites; see especially Luc Rouban (2017), "Le renouvellement du personnel politique," *Cahiers français* 297 (March–April), pp. 32–38. I have added the data for 2017 from information available on the National Assembly website.

38. Julien Boelaert, Sébastien Michon, and Étienne Ollion (2017), *Métier: député. Enquête sur la professionnalisation de la politique en France,* Paris: Raisons d'agir.

39. Or 431 deputies out of 577.

40. The particularly low figure for the United States is largely due to the fact that many elections are simply not contested.

41. Debate about the representation deficit goes back a long time. As early as 1911, in his famous *Political Parties. A Sociological Study of the Oligarchical Tendencies of Modern Democracy,* Robert Michels wrote of the oligarchic tendencies in modern democracies. Of course, the Social Democratic Party of Germany (SPD) had workers among its elected representatives, but this did not mean that they represented the working classes; Michels highlighted their tendency to become "petty bourgeois" once they assumed positions of power. To what extent is this true? It is by no means easy to give a definitive answer, and Nicholas Carnes (2013), for one, shows that at least in the United States workers continue to vote "like workers" for a long time after they are elected.

42. The FTSE NAREIT All Equity REITS Index.

43. Nicholas Carnes and Noam Lupu (2016), "Do Voters Dislike Working-Class Candidates? Voter Biases and the Descriptive Underrepresentation of the Working Class," *American Political Science Review,* 110(4).

44. Nicholas Carnes says as much in his new book, where he speaks of a "cash ceiling"; only the rich stand in US elections, because the campaigns cost a lot of money. However, he adds a second explanation: namely, that workers have fewer chances of being recruited and encouraged by the political elites (party leaders, professional politicians, or interest groups). In other words, since no one helps them to get a foot on the ladder, workers do not win elections and do not even run as candidates. Nicholas Carnes (2018), *The Cash Ceiling: Why Only the Rich Run for Office—And What We Can Do About It,* Princeton University Press.

45. In the Introduction, I mentioned the idea of a "democracy bank" that the short-lived justice minister François Bayrou floated at the beginning of Macron's five-year term. In my view, the failure of that idea was François Bayrou's failure, and it should not be given up so easily. For it meets a real need that candidates without independent means—and therefore without financial guarantees they can give to their banks—must address in order to take part in an electoral competition.

46. The thinking here is the same as that behind gender parity. If things had been left to take their course, instead of being subject to legal regulation, the glaring underrepresentation of women in Parliament would be even greater than

it is today. Moreover, it is a problem not only for our political democracy but also at the company level.

47. This is not the place to discuss the peculiarities of national voting systems, although in my view countries that allow for little or no proportional representation would do well to reflect on the extent to which it might be introduced. The key point is that the reform I am proposing could proceed without affecting the election of representatives for geographical areas. For example, Germany could retain its present "two votes" system for the election of political representatives, whereby one half of parliamentary mandates are attributed directly and the other half through party lists drawn up in each *Land*.

48. The male-female parity system established by Law No. 2000-493 of June 6, 2000, in France does not seem appropriate here, because my proposal is not for parity but for a minimum representation of certain socio-occupational categories. Not only can a list have more than the required minimum of ninety-six working-class candidates out of 192; it can also be compiled in such a way that the first five candidates on the list are workers. The point is not to end up with workers overrepresented in relation to other socio-occupational categories—that is a very remote risk—but rather to improve their representation in Parliament, in the knowledge that, compared with their place in the active population, workers form a small minority of representatives from geographical constituencies.

49. With a slight overrepresentation of intermediate professions and managerial staff among the union delegates. Thomas Breda (2016), *Les Représentants du personnel*, Paris: Presses de Sciences Po.

50. In some countries, it is true, elections under a PR system are held without the requirement of a threshold.

51. At the national trade level. The threshold is also 8 percent at the sectoral level, but the representativity threshold is 10 percent at the level of the firm or works. The rules for union representativeness vary from one country to another, and representativeness thresholds for the purpose of collective bargaining change over time.

52. Dominique Rousseau (2015), *Radicaliser la démocratie—Propositions pour une refondation*, Paris: Seuil.

53. To be absolutely fair, what Dominique Rousseau proposes is not so much to add a new layer as to replace today's Economic, Social, and Environmental Council (CESE) with this new assembly. Many will agree that the CESE needs to be reformed or simply abolished; no one seems satisfied with how this unrepresentative institution functions or with its anachronistic composition. In 2009, Dominique-Jean

Chertier's report "Pour une réforme du Conseil économique, social et environnemental" proposed various scenarios for a reform of its composition (periodic adjustment, a team of experts from civil society, and an assembly of intermediate bodies). In 2015, Proposal 10 in the "Rénover le bicamérisme" report by Claude Bartolone and Michel Winock (*Refaire la démocratie*) advocated a fusion of the CESE and the Senate. Emmanuel Macron, for his part, talked in his presidential election program of a "chamber of the future"—a chamber that the future still awaits. But this revolution has finally turned into a proposal to halve the membership of the chamber, which is a way of doing nothing while talking a lot of hot air. In the online appendix, I describe in detail the current functioning of the CESE.

54. This would be in the same spirit as the present guarantees for union representatives.

55. Nicholas Carnes (2013). See also Aaron J. Sojourner (2013), "Do Unions Promote Members' Electoral Office Holding? Evidence from Correlates of State Legislatures' Occupational Shares," *Industrial and Labor Relations Review,* 66, pp. 467–486.

56. Carnes and Hansen have also documented a positive correlation in individual US states between rates of unionization and the percentage of employees and blue-collar workers among elected representatives. Nicholas Carnes and Eric Hansen (2016), "Does Paying Politicians More Promote Economic Diversity in Legislatures?" *American Political Science Review,* 110(4), pp. 699–716.

57. Nicholas Carnes (2013).

58. See, in particular, the survey conducted by David Broockman, Greg F. Ferenstein, and Neil Malhotra (2017), "The Political Behavior of Wealthy Americans: Evidence from Technology Entrepreneurs," Stanford Graduate School of Business Working Paper No. 3581 (https://www.gsb.stanford.edu/faculty-research/working-papers/political-behavior-wealthy-americans-evidence-technology).

59. This is an extremely important point, because another corrupting influence on the political system, particularly in the United States, is the widespread "revolving door" between the world of politics and positions of power in society at large, obtained as a "reward" for services rendered in the legislature. In this connection, what counts is not so much social origins as future expectations. There is a vast literature on the subject in the political and economic sciences, which often links it to the weight of lobbies. I shall mention just one example for the interested reader: Marianne Bertrand, Matilde Bombardini, and Francesco Trebbi (2014), "Is It Whom You Know or What You Know? An Empirical Assessment of the Lobbying Process," *American Economic Review,* 104(12), pp. 3885–3920.

60. Beyond the gender of lawmakers, the gender of their children can also be a factor. Ebonya Washington has shown that the more these are girls, the more the legislator tends to vote along liberal lines on reproductive issues such as the right to abortion or contraception. Ebonya Washington (2008), "Female Socialization: How Daughters Affect Their Legislator Fathers' Voting on Women's Issues," *American Economic Review*, 98(1), pp. 311–332.

61. According to the results presented in Stefano Gagliarducci and Daniele M. Paserman (2016), "Gender Differences in Cooperative Environments? Evidence from the U.S. Congress," National Bureau of Economic Research Working Paper No. 22488 (https://www.nber.org/papers/w22488).

62. Raghabendra Chattopadhyay and Esther Duflo (2004), "Women as Policy Makers: Evidence from a Randomized Experiment in India," *Econometrica*, 72(5), pp. 1405–1443.

63. On the creation of quotas in India, I would recommend the excellent book by Francesca Jensenius (2017), *Social Justice through Inclusion: The Consequences of Electoral Quotas in India*, Oxford University Press.

Contents in Detail

Figures

Index